The Third Force in China

The Thir

CARSUN CHANG

Force in China

BOOKMAN ASSOCIATES

New York

MANUFACTURED IN THE UNITED STATES OF AMERICA
PRINTED BY RECORD PRESS, NEW YORK

Foreword

"Are we winning the cold war? This cannot be decided by looking at Europe alone. We must also look at Asia. The worst disaster since our victory has been the collapse of China under Communist attack and intrigue."

That statement was made by Winston Churchill on April 1, 1949. The fall of China to Communism is indeed an event of epic importance not only for the present but for generations to come. How did it happen? Who was responsible for it? What part did Soviet Russia play? What was the United States doing in China during this critical period? These are some of the questions which will be studied and investigated in the course of the coming years, for the turn of events in China since the end of World War II has already led to some major international crises and will continue to shape the course of world affairs.

I myself have had unusual opportunities of witnessing the long and bitter conflict between the Kuomintang and the Communists from its early beginnings up to the post-war period. I took part in the negotiations initiated upon the arrival in China of General George C. Marshall shortly after V-J Day. In the pages that follow I shall attempt to give as faithful an account as I can of my personal experiences, of what I saw, heard, felt, and tried to do during those critical years. The important role played by the United States in the development of major events in China is something that no one can deny. But unfortunately the subject has become so integral a part of American domestic politics—especially since the dismissal of General Douglas C. MacArthur from his post as Commander-in-Chief in the Pacific—and has aroused such bitter political emotions that it has become all but impossible for Americans to maintain an objective attitude to Chinese politics. As a Chinese, I hope that I can at least maintain a relatively objective attitude, and study the events as they appear to me to have really happened.

It is best for me to say at once that I am against Communism in China. But things which have already happened cannot be completely undone. It is my belief that it is much more profitable at the present juncture to be thinking about the future than to be engaged in sifting the ashes of the past. That does not mean, of course, that I do not have much to say about American policy towards China. Just as I was on the point of finishing this book, I read the important testimony of Secretary of State Dean Acheson before the Joint Session of the American Senate Foreign Relations Committee and the Armed Services Committee inquiring into the dismissal of General MacArthur, in which Mr. Acheson gave a clear and comprehensive statement of America's China policy.

It seems to me that American Far Eastern Policy during and after the war can be divided into three phases: (1) The Yalta Conference, (2) General Marshall's mission of mediation, and (3) the "hands-off-China" policy. With regard to all three phases Mr. Acheson gave an able defense. As a responsible statesman, he was obliged to justify what Roosevelt, Byrnes, General Marshall, and he himself had done, and he explained at length why the American policy, in its successive phases, had been adopted.

But if the question of why China was lost to the free world and fell into the Communist bloc is raised, I think that, in spite of all attempts at justification, we must admit the plain fact that the United States has suffered a major diplomatic defeat in the Far East. Accordingly, I shall express my views as a Chinese on some aspects of the points covered by Mr. Acheson, with no intention of assigning praise or blame, but with a view to presenting a more adequate picture of the significance of recent events in China.

(1) *The Yalta Conference and the Sino-Soviet Treaty of Friendship and Alliance.* In answer to Senator Alexander Smith's question about the secret deal made with Soviet Russia and about whether Chiang Kai-shek lost prestige by signing the Sino-Soviet Treaty of 1945, Mr. Acheson said: "No, I don't [think so] at all, and I don't think he thought he did. I think, as I told you this morning, he thought that the making of the Treaty of August 1945, between China and the Soviet Union was of great assistance to him."

Now, though the Yalta Agreement was a great wrong done to China both morally and politically, there was no other alternative for Chiang Kai-shek than to accept it and submit gracefully to American wishes. Not to have done so would have meant a serious rupture in Chinese-American relations and Chinese isolation—a thing which China could ill afford in those days. China had to bear the injury done her, but no Chinese in his proper senses would agree that the acceptance of so serious an infringement of his country's political and territorial integrity was anything to rejoice over.

As an aftermath of the Yalta Agreement, the Sino-Soviet Treaty of Friendship and Alliance was signed on August 14, 1945. It confirmed the concessions which the United States had made to Soviet Russia at China's expense at Yalta.

Attempting to make the most of a bad situation, China hoped that Soviet Russia would be contented with what she obtained both from the Yalta Agreement and the Treaty. The security of the U. S. S. R. beyond her own boundaries was assured. During General Marshall's mission of mediation, it was also agreed that the Chinese Communist Party could have its own army, and that it could have seats in the Chinese Government. That was another protection provided for Soviet interests. As a result of all these concessions, everybody expected that China and the Soviet Union would be able to maintain friendly relations for a substantial period.

It did not take long for China, at least, to be disillusioned. On her part, she faithfully observed the treaty, but after the Japanese surrender the Soviet Union refused to allow the landing of the Chinese army at Dairen, brought in the Chinese Communists from the Russian border, encouraged the infiltration of the Yenan Communists, and equipped them with the arms which they had taken away from the Kwantung army. Finally, at the time of the withdrawal of the Soviet army, Russia arranged matters so that the Chinese Communist army could occupy four-fifths of Manchuria. Thus Manchuria was converted into a stronghold of the Chinese Communist army and became a starting-point for its march into North China. The occupation of Manchuria by the Communists upset the whole balance of power in the Far East and also paved the way for the Communist domination of the whole of China later on. The United States, in spite of the warnings given by Mr. George F. Kennan and Major-General Albert C. Wedemeyer, did nothing to check the growth of Communist influence in Manchuria. The United States Government, on the other hand, took the attitude that this was a matter concerning China and the Soviet Union, and that it was better for the United States to have nothing to do with it. This failure to take any active steps might at first sight appear sound and logical, but it was soon plain that there was no way in which the United States could avoid being involved in the struggle of the two power blocs. The loss of Manchuria was the first step in the spread of Communist influence in China, Korea, and the Far East.

(2) *General Marshall's mission of mediation.* General Marshall came to China as a special representative of President Truman in December, 1945. He had two problems to solve: First, he had to arrange for a cessation of hostilities between the Kuomintang and the Chinese Communists, and then he had to call a national conference of representatives of the major political elements in China in order to find a solution to China's internal strife. Under the second item, it was Marshall's task (a) to reorganize the Government into a coalition government, (b) to integrate the two armies, Communist and Nationalist, into a National Army, and (c) to help promulgate a democratic constitution as the basis of the new government.

While General Marshall was performing his work in Chungking and Nanking, the Chinese Communists, with the encouragement and connivance of the Soviet Union, pursued a policy of double-dealing, that of carrying on negotiations while at the same time completing their occupation of Manchuria. They carried on negotiations in the hope that they would extend their power in the coalition government. If they succeeded in accomplishing this, they might join the government and postpone the overthrow of Chiang Kai-shek until a later date. They eventually realized, however, that Chiang Kai-shek was not prepared to give in to their demands, so they decided to continue fighting him.

While the Communists were pursuing their policy of double-dealing, to General Marshall there appeared to be only one possible course—to attempt to conciliate the Communists by offering them a share in a coalition government, to draft a new constitution, and to prepare a scheme for integrating the two armies. Apparently, he believed that there was nothing else for him to do, even in the face of the danger that negotiations might break down.

In other words, the postwar period in China had come to be dominated by a race between two great powers. The United States favored a united China, in which the different parties would co-operate in a single government, while the Soviet Union worked for a disunited China with the occupation of Manchuria by the Communists as the opening wedge in the conquest of the entire country. The Russian policy was much the easier one to carry out, as the nunists were confined to one corner of China which was rela- secure against attack. The United States policy was more diffi-) realize because it covered the whole of China. The Russian ches were also more complicated, because they aimed at de- ; not only the United States Government and the Kuomintang, so the Chinese democratic parties. Eventually, after having time and power by making Manchuria into a stronghold, the e Communists suspended the negotiations and resorted to war so that the United States was faced with a situation which it) means of coping with. Though General Marshall, in the nt he made on leaving China, placed the responsibility on the ds within the two parties, the real cause of the failure of his was Russian duplicity and trickery.

this connection, I should like to say a few words about the of Mr. Dean Acheson with regard to Greece. Senator Know- ked Mr. Acheson why United States policy in China had not facilitated the Central Government's action against the rebellious military elements within Chinese territory. The senator also asked why United States policy in China was the direct opposite of its policy in Greece, where it not only supplied the government with arms and sent a military mission which went as far as battalion level, but also kept the mission there under General Van Fleet until the Communist movement in Greece had been crushed. To both these questions, Mr. Acheson merely replied that United States policy in China was different from the policy in effect in Greece.

I have also had occasion, in this book, to refer to the case of Greece. My observations are concerned with the earlier portion of 1945. At the Lebanon Conference, British policy in Greece revealed itself to be the same as General Marshall's policy in China, namely, to form a coalition government and to integrate the two opposing armies. On their return to Greece, the Greek Communist army began to make trouble, whereupon General Scobie was sent there to stop "any attempts at a coup d'état or act of violence which is unconstitutional." This warning of General Scobie was very effective in stopping the attempt at violence by the Greek Communists.

If the United States, just after the Japanese surrender, had given a similar warning to the two armies of China, the declaration would have received the unanimous support of the Chinese people. British policy in Greece, which was backed up by force, was different from General Marshall's attitude when he told the Chinese, "I will do my best in my attempt at good offices between the Kuomintang and the Communists. If it succeeds it will be good for both of you and also for the United States. If it does not succeed, that is your affair."

The discrepancy between these two policies has meant all the difference in the world. If the problem had been handled with the discretion and circumspection which the gravity of the situation demanded, General Marshall's mission would not have been so fruitless nor its aftermath so disastrous. The American government should have seen to it that an alternative was provided in case negotiations broke down, an alternative which would have prevented the Chinese Communists from extending their power and the Chinese government from being weakened, as was assured by General Scobie in the case of Greece. In other words, the American government, by exercising better judgment, could have made the Marshall mission a success and kept China for the free world.

(3) *The hands-off-China policy.* After General Marshall's departure, the State Department felt uneasy about developments in China, and so Major-General Albert C. Wedemeyer, Chief of Staff to Chiang Kai-shek during World War II, was asked to take a trip to find means of ameliorating the Chinese situation. There was an interval of some seven months between Marshall's departure and Wedemeyer's visit to China and Korea; it was a period of hesitation on the part of the United States. Wedemeyer's trip, which, according to the American White Paper, was called a fact-finding mission, was undertaken at a time when there was hardly another fact about the Chinese situation that was worth knowing. The personal character of the Generalissimo, the development of the civil war between the Kuomintang and the Communists, the collapse of the Chinese economy as a result of inflation during the postwar period, were all so well known to the State Department that there was certainly no need for another fact-finding trip. Perhaps it was meant to disguise a mood of profound hesitancy on the part of the United States, for at a period when civil war was furiously raging, and the Chinese government was on the verge of bankruptcy because of inflation, it was difficult for the United States to find a policy which would not in one way or another involve her in Chinese politics. But anyhow the instructions given General Wedemeyer were that "he should make clear to the Chinese officials that he is on a fact-finding mission and that the United States Government can consider assistance in a program of rehabilitation only if the Chinese Government presents satisfactory evidence of ef-

fective measures looking towards Chinese recovery." In other words, Wedemeyer's trip to China was not undertaken in order to find a plan of settlement of the Chinese question nationally and internationally, but to give assistance to a program of rehabilitation if conditions were favorable to such a program. It did not take long for Wedemeyer to find out that so long as civil war on a grand scale was going on, it was impossible for China to devote herself to a program of rehabilitation; accordingly, he recommended establishing an international trusteeship of Manchuria by the Big Five Powers and granting economic assistance and military aid for a period of five years. The scope of this report went too far beyond the limited objectives of the State Department, and it was shelved. In 1948 the United States Congress passed a bill of aid to the extent of $463,000,000 to give a breathing space to China, and there the matter stood.

From 1948 on, the situation in China became so critical that no program of rehabilitation could save her. What had to be decided was whether the United States was willing to consider Mao Tse-tung as a representative of world communism, and if so whether she was willing to combat him. But at that moment the American Government was engrossed in these questions: Why should the United States support one party as against another in a Chinese civil war? Would not American intervention be contrary to the traditional policy of treating all the people of Asia as friends? Could the government of Chiang Kai-shek possibly be saved by American assistance? It was in this mood that the United States Government finally decided on the "Hands-off-China" policy. This amounted to America's declaring its belief that Chiang Kai-shek, even with American military assistance, could not prevent China from falling into the hands of the Chinese Communists.

While the American government was thus hampered in its dealings with China by the principle of non-intervention, the Soviet Union, as the leader of the Communist bloc, had for many years been working for the disintegration of China. The objectives of the Soviet Union in China were to overthrow the existing government, prevent the nation from developing along democratic lines and maintaining friendly relations with the free world, and finally to make her a part of the Communist empire. With this aim in view, the Soviet Union had recourse to every means at its disposal. It attempted to wreck the Chinese government by giving advice to the Communists, and by furnishing them with arms it helped them extend their control over Chinese territory. While the United States followed a policy of non-intervention and non-interference with the domestic problems of China, the Soviet Union had no such scruples and either covertly or openly supported the Chinese Communists. This difference of attitude explains why the United States lost and the Soviet Union won the diplomatic battle during the postwar period in China.

But after all is said and done, we, the Chinese people, must bear the major portion of the blame. There is no way in which we can disclaim our own responsibility for China's falling into the hands of the Communists. Why had we failed to put our republican form of government on a solid foundation before the war? Why did China fail to curb the growth of radical ideas? Why did China allow the Communist Party to grow to such proportions that it could no longer be controlled after the war? Why did the Kuomintang allow their party to deteriorate to such an extent that it could no longer function as it should? What was responsible for the spread of Communist influence? These and other questions are what all responsible Chinese will do well to think over. Over 2,000 years ago, Mencius, the illustrious follower of Confucius, recounted the following incident: There was a boy who sang:

> When the water of Tsang-lang is clear
> It serves to wash the strings of my cap;
> When the water of Tsang-lang is muddy,
> It serves to wash my feet.

Whereupon Confucius remarked: "Do you hear what he sings, my children? When the water is clear he washes his cap-strings in it, when it is muddy he washes his feet in it. The difference in use is brought upon the water by itself! A man must first despise himself before others can despise him. A family must first destroy itself before others can destroy it. A kingdom must first smite itself before others can smite it. . . ."

China has had a long history of 4,000 years. She has evolved her own way of life. She has created a marvelous civilization of her own. She has suffered much as a nation, having fallen successively into the hands of barbarian invaders like the Huns, the Mongols, and the Manchus. But she has always succeeded in liberating herself from their oppression. I am firmly convinced that China has enough vitality still to free herself from Communist imperialism. It is not for nothing that we Chinese have survived the vicissitudes of the ages. Our faith in human integrity, our love of freedom and democracy, our strong sense of individual worth, and above all our belief that the universe rests on a moral basis and that moral values will ultimately triumph—all this has become an integral part of our cultural heritage, and as long as it persists in the heart of the people, Communist materialism offers no permanent threat to Chinese culture.

I should like to treat one more matter of great importance in this foreword. The following pages will, I hope, make it abundantly clear that when I speak about democracy I do not mean that brand under which the fellow-travellers cooperate with the communists. The kind of so-called democracy which thrives under the protection of the Communist regime in China is a mockery and travesty of a free society, and of the rule of constitutionalism and individual liberty, by which democracy has been known from its very inception. The distinction is a basic and important one, and I hope that forward-looking Americans will join in the task of creating the proper atmosphere in which real democracy may flourish in China.

For this, the initial measure, bitter as it may be, will have to be withdrawal of support for a regime which has been consistently a denial and negation of constitutional rule. No one who has viewed the development of Chinese society within the last quarter of a century steadily and objectively can deny that the Chiang Kai-shek government, from the early Nanking days in 1927 to the present, has been such a regime. China would not be where she is if that singular person, with all the wonderful opportunities for creative statesmanship at his command, had established his government on the basis of law. As it was, he chose to be guided by personal whims and prejudices, likes and dislikes, with all the unhappy consequences which we all know so well.

The objectives which we, the Chinese, and our American friends must struggle for are in a sense identical, though perhaps our motives may differ. There can be no progress in Chinese society nor can China make any contribution to the free world until she succeeds in establishing a reign of law under which individual liberty and the sense of human dignity and integrity may be protected. Our American friends must make use of their tremendous resources, both material and spiritual, for the same end. If they should compromise, or if, for reasons of expediency, they should lend their support to a regime merely because it is anti-communist, in the full knowledge that it does not render more than lip-service to democracy, then they would be serving purposes which in the last analysis are inimical to the real interests of China and the free world alike. There is no question of choosing the lesser of two evils. With evil there is no compromise. Neither is there any question of the end's justifying the means. Such a dictum is valid only in terms of the Communist lexicon. In the world of free choice a moral act is a unit in which end and means both contribute to the total effect. It would be ridiculous for us to subscribe to Communist concepts in order to establish a non-Communist world order. It seems to me, therefore, that there is only one alternative for the thinking American. If he feels that the Chinese issue is sufficiently important for the future of the world to deserve his active interest and support, then he must align himself with those Chinese forces and leaders who seek only to establish a truly constitutional regime. I cannot believe that any other course is open to him.

I can assure him that we in China are not only working wholeheartedly for the new political and social movement—the Third Force—but that we are fully confident of its ultimate success. This new force is more widely spread and has more support than is ordinarily realised. The sponsors are now scattered, and some are even within the sphere of Communist control. But the time has arrived when they will be glad to be brought into a new unity of purpose. Their experiences have taught them that neither the conservative type of totalitarianism, enforced by the Kuomintang rule for the last quarter-century, nor the radical type of totalitarianism of the last three years so ruthlessly imposed by the Communist regime, can ever solve the problem of China. Their aim is the creation of a new China, based upon the principles of democratic constitutionalism, which can be brought into consonance with the traditional spirit of Chinese culture.

The Third Force is therefore something which grows out of the needs and context of Chinese politics and society. It has nothing to do with any policy of neutralism or aloofness from the Western democracies and the U. S. S. R. Rather it is sympathetic towards a rational study of Western political and social ideals so that a proper evaluation and a judicial selection can be made for the progressive development of Chinese society. This effort has been made for some time in the past by the Democratic League which was formed in 1937. Its program was the peaceful solution of the civil war in China, the establishment of a democratic regime, the adoption of a constitution accepted by all the people and a coalition government consisting of all the parties. This program was proposed before the arrival of General Marshall in China for his work of mediation, and agreed substantially with the Truman statement of 1945. Subsequent events have not given a chance to the implementation of the program, but our effort to establish a reign of law, to uphold social justice and the sovereignty of China, and to champion human rights and the free and unhampered development of the individual, remains as strong as ever.

This book was written during my voluntary exile in India. It might never have been brought to completion but for the encouragement of my hosts and good friends, Mr. and Mrs. Muir. They persuaded me to present a written record of much material that is either not normally available to the general reader or else so scattered in different books and periodicals that finding it would entail the expense of a great deal of time and labor. I shall be well satisfied if these pages serve to dispel some of the confusion which seems still to linger in the minds of many who are concerned with the Chinese problem.

My acknowledgments are also due to the editor of *The Statesman* of India for permission to reprint the chapter on Manchuria, to my brother Chang Kia-ngau, to Professor George E. Taylor who gave me valuable assistance when I was lecturing at the University of Washington in Seattle, and to Professor Edward S. Corwin, Professor Emeritus of Princeton University, who gave me valuable suggestions with regard to the chapters dealing with the Chinese constitution. Finally, my thanks are due to Miss Doreen Chu for typing the entire manuscript.

CARSUN CHANG

September 1952

Contents

Introduction

It is important to remind ourselves that until Pearl Harbor, China was fighting against Japan, in World War II, singlehandedly and without any assistance from the outside. I think that all Chinese, no matter what their political loyalties, were united in their determination to oppose Japanese aggression. The desire to fight for the preservation of the land and for the maintenance of its independence and integrity, has had a long history in China, and there was no reason to believe that it had grown any weaker during the struggle with Japan. I can very well cite my own experience by way of example. When in those days I was going with the government from Nanking to Hankow and finally to Chungking, the example of Wen Tien-Hsiang was continuously in my mind. He was Prime Minister during the Sung Dynasty when China was invaded by the Mongols, and he died a martyr. So also, when the Ming Dynasty came to an end, there were patriots everywhere who were loyal to the Chinese throne, fought against the Manchus to the bitter end, and, refusing to collaborate with the enemy, went underground when their cause was all but lost.

This spirit among the Chinese, this willingness to fight for their country, was fully manifested during the war against Japan. They knew that Britain and France were fully occupied in Europe when Hitler started the war in 1937, so that any help from them was out of the question. The United States was then still uncertain of its policy, choosing to remain neutral at least for the time being. She gave a limited amount of moral and material support to China before 1941, but there was no reason to hope that she would come out openly on China's side.

From the time of Pearl Harbor the situation changed radically. It was then that the Sino-Japanese struggle became a part of World War II. Soon afterward there were conflicting opinions current in Great Britain and China as to whether the defeat of Germany or of Japan should have priority as a war aim. China had been fighting Japan for years, and she fully expected that the Japanese conflict would be attended to first. But Britain and Soviet Russia insisted on the policy of defeating Germany first, so that the Chinese theatre of the war became a matter of subsidiary importance. China had lost her case. A few months before Germany surrendered, on February 11, 1945, the Yalta Agreement was signed. It declared:

> The leaders of the Three Great Powers—the Soviet Union, the U. S. A., and Great Britain—have agreed that in two or three months after Germany has surrendered and the war in Europe has ended, the Soviet Union shall enter into the war against Japan. For its part the Soviet Union expresses its readiness to conclude with the National Government of China a Pact of Friendship and Alliance, in order to render assistance to China with its armed forces for the purpose of liberating China from the Japanese yoke.

With this agreement, the Sino-Japanese war became strategically and legally a part of World War II: it was no longer a Chinese affair but one which was of equal concern to the three Allied Powers. This decision to send Russia to China's aid was made at Yalta by the Three Powers without China's participation and at a terrific price. That price was decided on by the three Powers, and China was asked to pay it. The war which had been waged by China alone until 1941 was now to be terminated with the assistance of Soviet Russia. In other words, the United States was unwilling to sacrifice American lives needlessly, and persuaded Soviet Russia to share the responsibility. Russia on her part was naturally unwilling to sacrifice herself for China's sake without an adequate quid pro quo. The price of Russian cooperation in the war against Japan included the following stipulations: (a) The status quo in Outer Mongolia engineered by the Russians would be maintained; (b) The commercial port of Dairen would be internationalised, the preeminent interests of the Soviet Union in this port being safeguarded; (c) The lease of Port Arthur as a naval base of the U. S. S. R. would be put in force once more; (d) The Chinese Eastern Railway and the South Manchurian Railway, which terminated at Dairen, would be jointly operated by a new Soviet-Chinese company, it being understood that the preeminent interests of the Soviet Union were to be safeguarded, and (e) China would retain full sovereignty in Manchuria. It was not contemplated either by President Roosevelt or by Prime Minister Churchill that Manchuria should be occupied by Soviet Russia, and through her, by the Chinese Communist forces. But the fact remains that this development paved the way for the Communist conquest of North China and ultimately of all China. Such an outcome was directly antithetical to the aims of the Yalta Agreement, which had as its chief aim the preservation of China's independence and integrity.

A similar situation growing out of the Yalta agreement developed in Poland. At the Yalta Conference it was decided that the boundary line between Soviet Russia and Poland should be drawn along the Curzon Line and that the Lublin Government, which was then functioning, should be reorganised on a broader, more democratic basis, to include democratic leaders from within Poland itself as well as political figures then in exile. The new government was to be called the Polish Provisional Government of National Unity. The Yalta Declaration pledged the provisional government to hold free and fair elections.

But we know that the Polish leaders in exile were summoned to Moscow and kept there in virtual captivity, that the rising in Warsaw was given no encouragement by the Russians though they were near enough to afford assistance to the insurgents, that the elections were manipulated by Moscow, and that Mikolajczyk had to flee from Poland. Poland was subsequently governed on Communist lines, and with complete disregard for the principles of democratic government and for the principles laid down at Yalta.

China and Poland are both neighbors of the U. S. S. R., one in Asia and the other in Europe. What happened in Poland since the setting up of the Provisional Government of National Unity happened also in China after an interval of four years, and both situations are direct consequences of the Yalta Agreement. There is, to be sure, a difference in Stalin's approach to the problems of China and to those of Poland, but the results are the same. As regards Poland, Mr. Churchill used to say that Great Britain's interest in Poland was a matter of honor, but Stalin stated emphatically that for the Russian people the question of Poland was not only one of honor but of security as well. Indeed, Stalin declared, not abstract security merely but the life of the Soviet Union was at stake. Poland was a battleground where the Soviet army was fighting, and she must be brought directly under Russian military power. Stalin's strong language meant that the Polish Government was to be completely dominated by Soviet Russia, as has been explained by Mr. Byrnes, who participated in the Yalta Conference, in his book *Frankly Speaking*.

The situation in China was entirely different. Until the Yalta Conference no state of war existed or was contemplated between Soviet Russia and Japan, and there was no active Russian army on the Asian front. From 1942 to 1945, Stalin and Molotov many times expressed the view that the United States should assume leadership in the Far East. Though Stalin's real intention of dominating China had its genesis as far back as 1924, yet at Yalta the move to bring Russia into the war against Japan was first made by Roosevelt and Churchill, and the price to be paid Russia was then limited to control of Dairen, Port Arthur, and the Changchun Railway. The Russian demands were restricted to the restoration of the situation prevailing before the Russo-Japanese war of 1904. Though a Sino-Soviet Treaty of Friendship and Alliance was decided on at Yalta, the first public reference to it was made two months later by Molotov himself, when he said, on the occasion of a dinner in honor of the Chinese Delegation to the San Francisco Conference, that he hoped soon to have the pleasure of welcoming Mr. T. V. Soong in Moscow.

When the negotiations of the treaty had reached their final stages, T. V. Soong was reluctant to put his signature to the agreement and preferred to resign his post as Foreign Minister, in which he was succeeded by Wang Shih-chieh. What prompted Wang to sign the treaty is something which only he himself knows, for it is obvious that no Chinese diplomat can afford to sign lightly any treaty which impairs China's sovereignty, and it is equally obvious that the Sino-Soviet Treaty which grew out of the Yalta Agreement is precisely that kind of treaty. Whatever Russia might promise to do in assisting China in her war against Japan, the fact remains that China was pledged to give up vital national interests to Russia. That was why Dr. W. W. Yen, China's senior diplomat, used to say that the situation reminded him of an episode back in the 1870's, when Chung Hou signed away the Ili concessions to Imperial Russia, except that the Yalta concessions were still larger in scope and much more serious. Yet Wang boldly put his signature to the treaty!

With one stroke Stalin placed Russia in the same position she was in previous to 1904. But Stalin overlooked the fact that the U. S. S. R. herself had renounced Russian privileges in Manchuria as long ago as 1921, so that the restoration of the status quo of 1904 was illogical and contradictory to avowed Soviet policy. During the long years since September of 1931, China had fought against Japan in order that she might regain her national entity, and now she was compelled by the Yalta agreements to transfer the interests, which Japan had seized on the strength of her military power, to another country. Was there ever a greater example of international mockery? That is why the signature of the Sino-Soviet Treaty of Friendship literally shocked the rank and file of the Kuomintang. But having no other alternative, and hoping for the best—hoping in other words that she might yet live in peace with Soviet Russia—China at last signed the treaty. That hope has now been blasted.

The time of Communism's triumph came later for China than it did for Poland, but the result is identical: both countries are today under Communist rule. The effect of the Communist domination of China on the world situation is much more serious, however. When Poland came under Communism, it meant little more than the addition of a new member to the existing group of satellites. The conversion of China to Communism, on the other hand, opens the way for China's active cooperation with Soviet Russia in forming a base from which to threaten her neighbors—Korea, Indo-China, and all of Southeast Asia. Russian hegemony over the huge land mass of her own territory added to that of China also has important consequences for India, Pakistan, and the Near East. Hence, the danger represented by Communist domination of China is much greater than in the case of Poland.

The conquest of China by the Communists has come as a great surprise to the world, and has frequently raised questions like the following in the minds of foreign observers: Why has China become Communist? Will the Communist government maintain its power? Will Communism benefit the Chinese people? Will they supinely follow the orders of the Kremlin? Why was Chiang Kai-shek defeated in such short order? How far will Chinese civilization be affected by the social and political policies of the Chinese Communists? Will the Chinese Communist government work for peace or for war in the present world situation? By way of offering some tentative answers to these absorbing questions, in this book I shall tell the story of my experience in Chinese political life, with particular reference to what I saw during the period of struggle between the Kuomintang and the Communists.

But first a more purely personal note. As a boy I was interested in politics. During my high school days, I saw the pictures of Kang Yu-wei and Liang Chi-chao posted upon the school gates, with the notice that they were "wanted" as a result of the coup d'état of 1898. When I went to Japan, I studied law and political science at Waseda University. At the age of twenty-one, I joined Liang Chi-chao's Constitution Party, whose program was to demand political reform under the Manchu Monarchy. After the revolution of 1911, Liang changed his mind and declared himself faithful to the Republic, which pledge he kept until his death. As a believer in human rights, the dignity of man, parliamentary government, and the rule of law, it is impossible for me to sympathize with the left-wing totalitarianism typified by Soviet Communism. Nor can I identify myself with the right-wing totalitarianism of Hitler and Mussolini. I believe implicitly that any change in the structure of government in China should be effected in accordance with the due process of law and not by means of violence. Constitutional government on a two-party basis has always appeared to me to be the best way to insure progress without bloodshed.

After the First World War there was a wave of sympathy in China for the methods of the October Revolution in Russia, but Bolshevik atrocities soon convinced me that it would be dangerous for China to follow such an example. From 1919 to 1922 I happened to be in Germany, where I was able to make a detailed study of the German Social-Democratic Party and of Communist activities both in Russia and in Germany. Incidentally, I was the first to translate the Soviet Constitution of 1919 into Chinese. After witnessing the activities of the Spartacists and of the Bela Kun Government in Hungary, I advised my countrymen that the Anglo-Saxon traditions of government were after all the best and safest models for China. Accordingly, I stood apart from the Kuomintang even when it was in its ascendancy during the Northern Expedition. After the establishment of the Kuomintang Government in Nanking in 1927, I published a magazine called *New Way* which opposed the "political tutelage" of the Kuomintang, which I knew meant nothing less than totalitarianism. It is my firm conviction that if the Kuomintang had established the government of China on a democratic basis over twenty years ago, then a solid legal foundation for social progress would long have been available. There would have been a parliament to pass socially useful legislation and an efficient civil service. The other parties would have been glad to work with the Kuomintang in a spirit of friendly cooperation and to wage a common war against the intransigeant Communists. But all my arguments for this view of a proper democratic policy were turned down by the Kuomintang. The publication of my paper was regarded by the Kuomintang as a criminal act, and I was subsequently kidnapped by its followers and detained in a house near the office of the Shanghai Garrison Commander, where I used to hear the trumpet call of the Garrison Commander every morning. After a period of detention of about a month, I was released and compelled to leave China. I went to Germany to earn my living as a Professor of Chinese Philosophy at the University of Jena. But before the occupation of Manchuria by Japan in 1931, I returned to China, passing through Mukden just one day before its fall. Being well aware of the critical situation in China, my friends met me and urged that we should not remain idle. This meeting was the beginning of the National Social Party of China, which later changed its name to the Democratic-Socialist Party. The aim of our party program was to transform China into a country based on social justice. From 1932 on, I travelled between Hongkong and Peking incognito, undetected by the Kuomintang agents. After the incident of the Marco Polo Bridge in 1937, the Kuomintang government held a conference in Kuling with the object of forming a united front. I was the first to agree to such a united front. After the outbreak of war in Shanghai on August 13, 1937, I was invited by the government to become a member of the Advisory Council of National Defense in Nanking. When the People's Political Council was later formed in Hankow, my party sent seven members to the Council after an exchange of notes on the question of a united front signed by myself and Chiang Kai-shek. From 1938 till 1944, I was untiring in my attempts to bring about reconciliation between the Kuomintang and the Communists. The Communist Party broke away many times from the People's Political Council, and the members of the Democratic League in which I was playing an important part, attempted repeatedly to bring them in again. The Chinese Delegation to the first UN conference at San Francisco, of which I was a member, consisted of members of the Kuomintang, the Communist Party, and the democratic parties. It foreshadowed a trend toward a multi-party coalition in China. When the Consultative Conference was called in the beginning of 1946, I was on my way from the United States to Britain to continue my study of the latter country's constitutional government. But after having made my first call on the Clerk of the House of Commons, I hurried back to China to join the Conference, only to find myself a week late in arriving. I attended the Conference during the second half of the session, and it was adjourned after the plenary session. I was called upon to draft the new Constitution, which was later adopted by the National Assembly summoned in 1947. General Marshall had arrived in China in December, 1945, and had worked as a mediator between the Kuomintang and the Communists and had got along quite well with both sides. But after a little more than two months the situation deteriorated, and civil war broke out again in the spring of 1946. General Marshall asked me, as a member of the Democratic League, to cooperate with him in order to persuade Chou En-lai, then the Communist representative in Chungking, to moderate many of his demands. From May, 1946, when the Nationalist Government went back to the capital (Nanking), the third party continued the work of mediation until General Marshall's recall. After the final breakdown of negotiations between the Kuomintang and the Communists, I found, as a man standing for peace and order, that there was no way of working with the Chinese Communists, so I supported the government on condition that the constitutional draft should be adopted and a government on democratic lines organized. The agreement, which Chiang Kai-shek signed, was that after the Constitution was adopted and a government formed on a democratic basis, a policy of truce with the Communists should be continued and negotiations for a coalition government renewed. But the Communist demand that the adopted Constitution be denounced was too much for the government to accept. The civil war was prolonged and extended until the Nationalist army was defeated and the government went to Formosa. That, in brief, was the history of Chinese politics between 1937 and 1948. What I heard, observed, and did during that period may be of interest to students of contemporary history.

The fight between the Communists and the Kuomintang has been an old problem since 1924. It took on a new aspect after Pearl Harbor because the United States Commander-in-Chief found that the Communist soldiers constituted a real fighting force and accordingly began to think of equipping them. During the war, the Communists pretended to be agrarian reformers, and so they were believed to be by some of the officials in the State Department. The U. S. Government advised the Nationalist Government to pursue a policy of moderation in dealing with the Communists in the hope that the latter would fight Japan and so put an early end to the war in the Far East. But real military collaboration between the Communist and the Nationalist armies was not translated into reality even before the war against Japan came to an end with the use of the atom bomb on Hiroshima and Nagasaki. Still, the United States favored peace and compromise in China, because so long as civil war continued between the Kuomintang and the Communists, there could be no united China. The United States wanted to stop the civil war and make China a united, strong, and independent democracy.

President Truman, making a statement of U. S. policy towards China in those days, declared:

It is the firm belief of the Government that a strong, united, and democratic China is of the utmost importance to the success of the U. N. organisation and for world peace. A China disorganised and divided either by foreign aggression such as that undertaken by Japan or by violent internal strife, is an undermining influence to world stability and peace, now and in the future.

The way to carry out this policy would have been to arrange an armistice between the armies of the National Government and the Chinese Communists and to call a National Conference of representatives of major political elements with a view to finding an early solution to China's internal strife. Concretely, the following objectives should have been achieved:

(1) Cessation of hostilities between the Nationalist army and the Communist army.

(2) Transformation of the Nationalist Government of Tutelage into a coalition government consisting of the leaders of the different parties.

(3) Transformation of the autonomous armies under party control into a national army under a united command.

(4) Adoption of a new constitution to which all parties could subscribe as a legal basis for the working of a coalition government.

(5) Summoning of a National Assembly for the purpose of adopting a new Constitution—an assembly in which all parties would be represented.

(6) Drafting of a common platform for a coalition government.

Each of these six points had been all but realised at the Political Consultative Conference. The cease-fire order was issued on January 10, 1946, twenty days after General Marshall arrived in China. The army reorganisation plan was agreed to in principle on the basis of a ratio of military force between the Kuomintang and the Communists of five to one, although the actual locations of the armies had not yet been worked out in detail. The ratio of members of the various parties in the coalition government and the Common Platform was also agreed upon. The National Assembly was called in May, 1946. The constitutional draft was first presented by me and every article was fully discussed. After two months of discussion the entire draft was passed. It was brought by air to Yenan by the Communist representative Ching Pang-hsien. Unfortunately the plane crashed, and Ching lost his life. Another Communist representative, Li Wei-han, the present Secretary-General of the State Council in Peking, then came to Chungking. He announced at the Committee meeting that this draft could only be considered part of the minutes, and that the Communists were not bound by it. His intention was that if in the future the National Assembly were called without the participation of the Communists, the Constitution could be denounced as illegal by the Communists. Unfortunately, Li's threat became real as a result of subsequent developments in the following year. But if the civil war had not broken out in Manchuria in April of 1946, this middle-of-the-road policy would have been a solution to the problem of disunity in China. A coalition government would have been formed with the Communists, even though that would appear to be asking for the impossible. But it was an experiment worth trying, and at that particular moment was certainly preferable to the continued existence of a state of civil war in China. A new constitution would then also have been agreed to by all the parties, and a national army organised. In other words, the unification of China would have been achieved in the way favored by the really democratic elements in the country. If the ideal of a democratic China had been realised, the war in Korea and Indo-China might have been avoided. Thus, the failure of the middle-of-the-road-policy in China was a loss not only to that country, but to the cause of world peace.

I would not go so far as to say that China, in those days, would have been able to resolve once and for all the conflicting interests of democracy and communism within the framework of a coalition government. Such a government would have been unique in any case in that, for the first time, a communist party would have been responsibly sharing power with democratic elements in the same state. But with skill, patience, and forbearance, something along those lines might have been worked out. Today, of course, this is no more than a pious reminiscence, and we are back to where we started, faced with the apparently implacable opposition of two political forces. But may it not be possible, after all, to eliminate or reduce this opposition?

One solution has been proposed by Mr. Bertrand Russell in his article "The Way to Avoid a Third World War." Mr. Russell said:

> The root of the problem is psychological. The Russians and the Americans are alike persuaded that the other side would start a war

if it felt confident of victory. Each side feels it must be truculent, for fear the other side would think it weak.

The situation is familiar and has almost always ended in war. But now the avoidance of war is more important than it used to be and it is more urgent than in the past to find a way out of the vicious circle.

The first step, and that is one which is eminently practicable, is a clear delimitation of spheres. The Russians should not give support to French or Italian Communists; we should make no official protest when Polish patriots or Hungarian cardinals suffer, whatever we may privately feel.

Africa would have to be alloted to the West; Asia would have to be divided. It should then be solemnly agreed that any interference of either in the other's domains, whether by armies or by propaganda, should be a legitimate "casus belli."

Mr. Russell calls his plan practicable. Is it really so? His idea, I am afraid, is based upon the concept of spheres of influence or balance of power which prevailed in Europe in the nineteenth Century. It is very doubtful that Soviet Russia will accept it. Soviet Russia may answer that the division into spheres of influence is a trick of capitalistic diplomacy which the Communists, the real representatives of the people, can never accept. From the point of view of the democratic forces, too, moreover, there are drawbacks to this scheme. The Russian Communist Party works horizontally with the people in all countries, in an underground way, so that disruption of the government in any country can not be traced to the Russian Government. Russian support of the Communists in other countries has always been denied by the Russian Government. Such support is clandestine and leaves no evidence. The revenue of the Russian Treasury is in the hands of the Communist Party and the budget is kept secret. We know, for instance, that the Russians gave financial support to the Chinese Communists out of the proceeds from the sale of Russian petroleum in China, but it is difficult to prove it, and still more difficult to protest effectively. Even should the democratic countries wish to follow Russia's example they are not in a position to do so, because their budget must first be approved by their respective parliaments.

Again, it might be relatively simple to mark out spheres of influence in backward areas, such as Africa or the South Seas, where no vocal popular will as yet exists and where the people can not foment rebellion against the government. But, if a country like Poland were to be given over to the Russians and incorporated in their sphere of influence, in accordance with Mr. Russell's proposal, would the leader of the peasant party, Stanislaw Mikolajczyk, agree to it? Would the leaders of the Liberal and Democratic Parties in Czechoslovakia, Rumania, and Bulgaria agree that their countries should remain permanently under Russian control? The status of Yugoslavia was not clearly defined by Mr. Russell in the course of his article. Would Russia tolerate a potentially powerful neighbor like Yugoslovia if the latter were incorporated in the West's sphere of influence?

Let us apply Bertrand Russell's concepts to the question of Korea. In Korea, we have a boundary established at the thirty-eighth parallel, the area north of which is under Russian influence while the southern part belongs to the free world. If there had been no invasion of South Korea by the North Koreans, whose army was trained by the Russians and whose arms were furnished by them, then there would have been no war in Korea. When, on June 27, 1950, the Northern Korean army swept down across the frontier, the United States and the United Nations felt obliged to come to the rescue of the South Korean Government, because that government had been created by a resolution of the United Nations. Thus war broke out between the North Koreans, supported by Russia, and the South Koreans, supported by the United Nations' army. When the United Nations' army reached the thirty-eighth parallel, the Indian Government warned that it should not cross it, because the Chinese Communists might intervene. Even without the United Nations' crossing of the thirty-eighth parallel the Chinese Communists could easily have found another excuse for intervention—such as protection of the hydro-electric power stations on the boundary between Korea and China. As it is, the Chinese Communists and the United Nations armies are facing each other on the Korean battlefront. Even supposing that they agree to a cease fire and agree to have Korea united under one government, I do not see how the new nation could avoid being swallowed up by her great neighbors, China and Soviet Russia, who are so near, while the United States has to send a protective expeditionary force across thousands of miles of ocean.

In China, the problem is just as complicated as in Korea. Will Bertrand Russell propose that China come under Russian influence? If this were accomplished, then 450 million people would come under Communist slavery. I can assure him that ninety per cent of the Chinese are anti-Communist and do not wish the Communist rule to continue. Such a division of spoils would also allow Communist China to carry on its policy of infiltration or fight openly in Southeast

Asia. If Mr. Russell proposes that South China come under the influence of the free world, will the present Communist Government give away the territory which they have conquered? The Chinese Communists today are even demanding possession of Formosa: how will they be persuaded to give up the meat which is already in their mouth? Even if they agree to such a partition, I do not see how that state of affairs can last long. The Chinese Communist army is now represented in Korea and to a lesser extent in Indo-China, and they are determined to "liberate" these countries, which they regard as victims of feudalism and colonialism. The conquest of China now paves the way for that of India, Pakistan, Southeast Asia, and the Near East. It is difficult to believe that the Chinese Communists and the Soviet Union will agree to any permanent partition of the world which does not fully satisfy their program of territorial expansion.

Bertrand Russell's proposal, I am afraid, is not practical or practicable. It might have worked among the imperial powers of the nineteenth century, but it certainly will not work today. A better way to solve the conflict between Communism and the free world can be found, it seems to me, if we examine the history of great movements which first caused a split in the social fabric and later brought a new synthesis and a new way of life. I am referring to such phenomena as the Reformation and the French Revolution. The Reformation was one of the great movements in European history expressive of a break in Christendom's outlook, but after many years of war, Protestantism and the Roman Catholic Church came to live together in peace. For twelve centuries the Christian faith had been accepted without question and the Church had looked after the religious needs of the people. In the course of this long period, the Church became corrupted by its temporal possessions and political power. Luther in Germany, Huss in Czechoslovakia, Zwingli in Zurich, and Calvin in Geneva started powerful reform movements. The open warfare provoked by these movements ceased temporarily when a religious peace was concluded at Augsburg in 1555, a peace which established the principles of freedom of worship and freedom of conscience. Later came the Thirty Years' War, waged from 1618 to 1648. The Treaty of Westphalia signed in 1648 stipulated, among other things, that the peace of Augsburg should be approved and extended to include the Calvinists. The fight between the Protestant and the Roman Catholic Church was thus concluded on the basis of toleration and freedom of conscience.

If the Reformation was the result of the corruption of the Church, the French Revolution grew out of the corruption of the aristocracy and the monarchy. At that time the French peasantry was still living under the most servile conditions. The burden of taxation bore heavily upon them, while the nobles and clergy were untaxed. The government was in the power of an absolute monarch, and no parliament had been called for a long time. When the États-Généraux were summoned in 1789, there was disagreement between the nobles, the clergy, and the commoners as to procedure in debating and voting. The representatives of the third estate, the commoners, organised themselves into a National Assembly and invited others to join them. A rumor arose that the king had gathered the army in order to dissolve the Assembly, whereupon the Bastille was stormed, a provisional government was formed, and a Declaration of the Rights of Man was issued. This was the beginning of the French Revolution that changed the map of Europe. The French Revolution drew attention to two competing principles of government, the revolutionary principle and the principle of legitimacy. The countries which belonged to the Holy Alliance stood for the principle of legitimacy and strove to preserve the status quo, or restore the status quo ante and to guard against the recurrence of revolution. But revolutions broke out in Italy, Greece, Spain, and the Balkans and could not be stopped. Subsequently, a middle way was evolved. In England reform bills were passed which were designed to extend the franchise of the people. In Austria and Prussia constitutions were promulgated and parliaments were established, so that governments responsible to the people began to take the place of absolute monarchies. Germany and Italy were united on a national basis. Civil liberty and constitutionalism were accepted as the general pattern of government everywhere, and in this way a new foundation was laid for the peaceful development of Europe.

These two movements, I think, furnish interesting matter for reflection. Out of the struggle between the Roman Catholics and the Protestants arose the principle of toleration and freedom of conscience which allowed for the co-existence of the two churches. Out of the struggle between the Holy Alliance and the revolutionary regime, constitutional and democratic government evolved. There was, to be sure, a period of confusion, a period of war and strife: the pains of childbirth were unavoidable.

Both the Reformation and the Revolution, regarded as spiritual and social movements, had a beginning and an end. They began with a deep dissatisfaction with the old institutions. During the first stage the dissatisfaction amounted to hatred. It was not confined to any particular place or country but was widespread and affected practically all of Europe. The opposition against the Roman Catholic Church was not limited to Luther's Germany, but had many antecedents in European history and many contemporary reflections. What was demanded by the revolutionists in France—Liberty, Equality, and Fraternity—was essentially what was demanded by the American revolutionists in the Declaration of Independence. In the words of Thomas Paine, it was the demand of the Age of Reason. When the revolutionary hatred developed, it expressed itself in formulas like "Down with the Papists" and "Down with the King." But the antagonism exhausted itself after having accomplished its work of reform, and finally all but disappeared, although it took some forty years after Luther had published his Ninety-five Theses before the peace of Augsburg was established to offer a first solution of the dispute between the two churches. From the beginning of the French Revolution in 1789 till the Congress of Vienna in 1815 there was a peroid of about twenty-five years during which a compromise between conservative and liberal forces was sought. It is probably reasonable to say that no socio-political movement can go on indefinitely, but must sooner or later come to some form of compromise with the old order, so that in the end a *modus vivendi* is worked out between the old and the new.

It is my firm belief that some such arrangement will be the outcome of what appears today to be an absolutely irreconcilable opposition between communism and democracy. If social justice, equality, and political independence become realities for all people instead of being, as at present, the prerogative of the chosen few, if they become concrete facts of life instead of remaining what they are at present, a consummation devoutly to be wished, the free world has in truth nothing to be afraid of from Communism. In the fullness of time, in proportion as the political and social aims of all peoples are achieved, Communism will have nothing to stand upon and will perhaps "wither away" indeed.

Specifically, in China the Communist movement has had a history of some thirty years: it has succeeded largely because of the existing maladjustment in China which began when it was exposed to competition with aggressive demands of modern societies in the middle of the last century. In this book I begin, therefore, with a study of the historical background from the viewpoint of China's social, political, and cultural development. Next, I shall discuss the part which the Kuomintang played under Chiang Kai-shek in the period which preceded that of Communist domination. Finally, I shall examine American and Soviet diplomacy in China during the period of World War II—the policy of the United States in abandoning its support of Chiang and that of Soviet Russia in backing the Chinese Communists, with the result that Chiang was defeated and Mao Tse-tung triumphed.

CHAPTER I

Historical Background

The simplest answer to the question of why China fell so easily to the Communists and was lost to the free world is that the United States withdrew its support from Chiang Kai-shek, while the Soviet Union always backed the Chinese Communist Party to the hilt. But to regard so important an international development in the light of so simple a formula is to choose deliberately a dangerous superficiality. The answer given does not even consider the immediate reasons for Communism's triumph, and they are many. They will become clear in the course of our discussion, but for the present, I think it will be profitable to examine the historical background, in order that we may see present-day events in relation to the state of Chinese society in the recent past. It is domestic conditions in China rather than the policy of foreign powers which have been chiefly responsible for what is happening today.

The present state of affairs in China may well be considered the fourth stage in the history of Chinese contact with Western influences, which began, for all practical purposes, with the Opium War in 1842. These four stages are:

(1)	1862-1894	Period of gun-making and shipbuilding
(2)	1894-1898	Period of political and social reform
(3)	1898-1924	Period of revolution
(4)	1924-Today	Period of totalitarianism

It is best that we examine each of these periods in some detail.

(1) *Period of gun-making and shipbuilding.* It is a matter of common knowledge that for centuries all foreigners were regarded by the Chinese as they had been regarded by the ancient Greeks, that is, as uncultivated and barbarous. The Huns, the Mongols, and the Manchus living on China's borders were hereditary invaders, and there was no apparent reason why Europeans who forced their way

into China during the modern era should be considered any differently from earlier intruders. After suffering defeat in the Opium War and signing the Treaty of Nanking the Chinese began to feel the urgency of their situation. It became aggravated when, during the Taiping Revolution, Great Britain and France sent 17,000 troops to occupy Peking and burned the Summer Palace. It was then that the eyes of the Chinese were opened to the superiority of Western arms and ships: these were the most obvious forms of Western superiority. But there were men, though they were few, who even then knew that this superiority was not merely a matter of guns and ships. Tseng Kuo-fan, Li Hung-chang and Prince Kung were among the leaders who saw the necessity for modernizing China along political and cultural lines. A few of the reforms they introduced show the extent of the impact of Western influences. In 1861 the Tsungli Yamen was established in Peking. In 1862 Tseng Kuo-fan built an arsenal in Anking. In 1863 the Kiangnan arsenal was created by Li Hung-chang. In 1863 Li also established a school of foreign languages, and a bureau of translation was attached to the Kiangnan arsenal. In 1866 Shen Pao-cheng built a dockyard in Foochow, and in 1867 a school of foreign languages was opened in Peking.

The creation of the Tsungli Yamen was epoch-making, because this meant the acknowledgment of the need to have a special organisation to deal with foreign countries, all of which had previously been regarded as tributary states, to be dealt with by the Ministry of Colonies. The Tsungli Yamen established the principle of equality with the outside world, and with it was created a school of foreign languages, in which English, French, Russian, German, the natural sciences and international law were taught. Prince Kung, Tseng Kuo-fan, and Li Hung-chang were liberal-minded and far-sighted statesmen who might have carried through a reform movement like the one in the Meiji era in Japan. But Tseng and Li were too much occupied with the struggle against the Tai-ping Rebellion from 1850 to 1864. After the fighting came to an end, Tseng Kuo-fan was no longer young and vigorous enough to undertake this new enterprise of reforming China. He had with him, however, a number of young men who worked as his private secretaries. The three Chinese ministers sent to the Court of St. James', Kuo Sung-tao, his son the Marquis Tseng Chih-tse, and Hsueh Fu-cheng were selected from his staff to carry on Tseng's work. These men spoke very highly of British political institutions which they observed at first hand, though the Peking Government paid no attention to their numerous reports and recommendations for reform. They knew for instance that the manufacture of guns and the building of ships were not the only things which China could learn from the West. Guns and warships were the products of technique, behind which were the sciences and the modern art of government. The schools of foreign languages and the bureau of translation managed however to serve as channels through which the Chinese learnt something about the cultural and scientific background of the Western countries.

But Chinese appreciation of Western civilisation was very limited in scope even after the third quarter of the last century. Hsueh Fu-chang's pamphlet, written in 1880, gives perhaps the best description of the Chinese mentality at this time. I shall quote from it, because it provides material not usually familiar to Western readers. Starting from the concept of change, Hsueh showed that change is the fundamental principle of all natural and social phenomena. His examples were taken mostly from Chinese history rather than from that of Japan or Europe, though the examples of the Meiji reform in Japan, and that of Peter the Great, who studied the art of shipbuilding in Holland, were not forgotten. Hsueh began by saying that

From the Tsin dynasty until today another two thousand years have passed, and now it is the Western countries who, because of their superiority in technology as well as in machines, have become so powerful that we must take notice of them. These foreigners can travel thousands of miles as if they were travelling from one house to the other; they master storms and waves with the same ease as the shaking of hands; they have opened the whole of the world to commerce and trade, and even if Yao and Shun were alive today, they could not possibly close their doors and insist upon living in isolation. Today it has become obvious that China must become integrated with the rest of the world. Because of a changing world situation the need for deliberate change is great. That does not mean that what has been handed down to us by former dynasties will have to be overthrown, but it does mean that we should have a new civil service, and the various ministries should be conducted on a new basis; the old army system must be discarded, and the whole of our educational system and the ideas underlying it will have to be revised and shaped in accordance with a new spirit.

The Western countries are run on a competitive basis. In order to be able to cope with them, China must change and do as they do.

We shall have to develop commerce and mining, otherwise they stay rich and we remain poor. Industry and manufacturing must be encouraged, otherwise they remain skilled and we unskilled. Railway and steamboat communication must be developed, otherwise they are fast and we are slow. Diplomacy, administration, and national defense must be reformed, otherwise they are strong and we are weak; they are able to work together while we are isolated. China now finds herself surrounded by powerful nations; how can she forget the art of accumulating wealth or the strengthening of her military defenses? Some may suggest that in imitating the foreigners we may become foreigners ourselves, but this idea must be refuted. We can remain loyal to our language and customs and even to our manner of dress, but knowledge and the development of natural resources is common property of all the people in the world. While the West discovered the secret of the natural sciences, we must not believe that it can monopolize this knowledge forever. If we study these sciences, perhaps in a hundred years we might be able to make important contributions. If Yao, Shun, Chou Kung, and Confucius were alive today, I am sure that they would recommend the same idea. We may describe this as using the barbarian's methods to change China to the end that China will be strong enough to change the barbarians. The world of change is endless, and the ways to meet these changes are endless too. If, living today, we insist upon the old ways of the primitive period, it would be as if, living in the days of Shen-nung when agriculture had already been developed, we continued to clothe ourselves with skins and drink the blood of animals. It would be like fighting the Tze-yu tribe, who made use of bows and arrows, with our bare hands. To follow the ways of the old would surely bring China to the verge of bankruptcy. But while we change our mode of living, there is no reason why the basic ideas of the sages should not guide us in our conduct."

I have quoted these words from Hsueh Fu-chang to show that while the country was anxious to imitate the West in the matter of developing its military strength, even in those days there were men who were able to see below the surface of things.

(2) and (3) *Periods of Reform and Revolution.* The defeat of China by Japan in the War of 1894 was destined to have a profound effect on the Chinese mind. It was a much greater blow to China than any of her previous humiliations. Hitherto Japan had been considered not only a small country but one possessing a merely derivative culture, having borrowed its Buddhism and Confucianism from China since the days of the Tang dynasty. That Japan should have acquired in a few years enough strength to permit her to defeat the

colossal empire of China was, to put it mildly, something of a shock. China had to sign a peace treaty with Japan in which the independence of Korea was recognised; the island of Formosa, the Pescadores Islands and the Liaotung Peninsula were ceded to Japan; an indemnity of 200,000,000 taels was to be paid to Japan; and four more ports were to be opened to foreign commerce. With this treaty began the mad scramble for concessions on the part of the great European powers: Germany asked for a lease of Kiaochow Bay, Russia for a lease of Dairen and Port Arthur, with the right to build a railway from Harbin, France for a lease of Kwangchow Bay, and Britain for a lease of Kowloon and Weihaiwei. The possibility presented itself that China might even be partitioned. It was then that the thought dawned upon its leaders that the mere acquisition of guns and warships offered no solution to the country's immense problems: something drastic and practical had to be done.

At this moment the portentous figure of Kiang Yu-wei appeared. He and his followers agitated for immediate and radical reforms, and a reform movement was launched in earnest. Professor Kenneth S. Latourette in his book, *The Chinese: Their History and Culture,* describes the period in these words:

> One or two major efforts by Chinese to save the Empire from disintegration were made by those who wished to effect changes in China, largely after Western patterns. The reformers were numerous and of varying degrees of radicalism. After the war with Japan many Chinese became convinced that they must adopt some of the Western devices which had enabled their enemy, whom they had thought of as much less strong than they, so easily to defeat them; reform societies were organised, some with influential members. The great Viceroy Chang Chih-tung for a time sponsored one of them and in a book called "Learn" while stressing loyalty to Confucianism and the dynasty, advocated [borrowing] some of the methods of the West, lest the Empire lose its independence as India, Annam, Egypt, and other states had done. Over a million copies of the little volume are said to have been sold.

Professor Latourette mentions three names in the reform movement: Chang Chih-tung, Dr. Sun Yat-sen and Kang Yu-wei. Chang's name comes first, giving the impression that he was the most important man of the movement. Actually, the order should be reversed. The man who organised the "Make China Strong" society, paving the way for reform three years before 1898, was Kang Yu-wei. Chang himself did not sponsor any reform measures. Kang Yu-wei had visited him in Wuchang in 1895 and asked him to be one of the sponsors of the society. It appears that Chang Chih-tung, when Kang called on him, promised to sign his name. Later he sent Kang a telegram saying that he would give his financial support, but asked that his name be withdrawn, perhaps out of fear of court reprisals. Chang Chih-tung was also very much opposed to Kang Yu-wei's desire to glorify Confucius as a reformer, so that he did not like to be involved in Kang's activities. In 1898, when Kang Yu-wei was received sympathetically in audience by the Emperor Kuang Hsu, Chang Chih-tung, then Viceroy of Hupeh and Hunan, fearing that Kang's zeal for the prosecution of his program might bring about his own downfall, began to sever his connection with Kang Yu-wei. That was the reason why he wrote his book *Learn,* which stood for reform, but was completely at variance with Kang's views. The book was submitted to the Emperor Kuang Hsu, who ordered that it should be widely printed and distributed within the realm.

Chang Chih-tung was in favor of reform, but he had very little to do with the Reform Movement of 1895-1898, of which Kang Yu-wei was the leader. He was born in Nanhai in Kuangtung Province, where contact between the Chinese and the Europeans had begun very early. While still very young, Kang Yu-wei passed his literary examinations in his own province, which was the usual way for a Chinese scholar to start his career of government service. Kang's reputation as a scholar began when he championed the modern school of Han philology. Han philology was the essential equipment of all Chinese scholars in those days; but Kang had the temerity to advance the idea that the texts of the ancient school of Confucianism were actually forgeries. He agreed with what he called the modern school, and it was in that spirit that he wrote, in 1891, his book called *The Forged Classics of the Wang-Mang Dynasty,* to prove that the so-called Confucian classics of the old school which were defended by Liu Hsin, the Chief Librarian of the Wang-Mang Dynasty, were forgeries, while the books of the modern school already in existence at the beginning of the Han Dynasty were the really authentic texts. Four years later, Kang published a second book under the title *The Idea of Reform in Confucius.* These two books came as a thunderbolt to the traditional Confucian scholars. They were an attempt to recapture the original meaning of Confucius which, Kang maintained, had been distorted by later emendations and interpolations. Kang called into question the state of Confucian scholarship which had been accepted with implicit faith for some 2000 years. He demanded a re-appraisal of all the Confucian classics, and in doing so stamped himself as an uncompromising iconoclast. His great disciple Liang Chi-chao had this to say about Kang's second book:

> Though Kang pays the highest compliments to Confucius, yet he believes that Confucius aimed to build a system of thought like the other systems of thought, those of Laotze, Motze or the Legalist school. In this way, Kang considers the Confucian school to be merely one of the many schools of thought. When Confucianism is thus placed on an equal basis with other schools, then the predominant position which successive generations of scholars have claimed for it is undermined.

Having thus undermined the position of Confucianism, Kang began to inculcate a critical attitude toward the study of all the classics. It was not his intention to overthrow Confucianism; he was, in fact, its most ardent exponent. But it was his contention that the time had arrived for sweeping away all the intellectual cobwebs which had accumulated through the ages so that Confucianism might be viewed in its own light. To this task he brought a vast erudition; he was familiar not only with Chinese history but with that of foreign lands as well. Kang studied assiduously the translations published by the Bureau of Translation and also those of the Society for the Diffusion of Knowledge under the direction of Timothy Richard, who was a Welsh missionary in China. While books issued by the Bureau of Translation dealt with gun-making, navigation, astronomy, mathematics, physics, and chemistry, those published by Timothy Richard were about Christianity and Western history, the study of which served to bear out Kang's views. Kang, in fact, regarded himself much in the same light as Martin Luther and the leaders of the Reformation.

Let us now consider Kang Yu-wei's political views and activities. Between 1862 and 1894, China was given a breathing spell by the Western powers, and Kang Yu-wei steadily pursued his program of reform. In 1888 he went to Peking and presented a memorial to the Emperor on the question of reform. But he was merely a scholar and too low in his official position for his memorial to be read by the Emperor. He then went back to his native province where he later published his book *The Forged Classics*. It so shocked the government, attacking as it did the very foundations of Chinese belief, that the Emperor ordered it to be burnt and banned. That was in the year 1894, the same in which the Sino-Japanese War broke out. The next year he went to Peking to take part in the state examination. After the peace treaty with Japan had been signed, he collected the names of thousands of candidates who had sat at the examination for another memorial to be sent to the Emperor, in which he asked for three things: (1) that no peace treaty should be recognized; (2) that the capital should be moved; and (3) that the government should be drastically reformed. He also led a popular demonstration. In spite of all this unorthodoxy, Kang received the doctor's degree after passing the examination. Then, in Peking and Shanghai he organised the "Make China Strong" society to which influential men like Chang Chi-tung and Yuan Shih-kai gave support. This society was the beginning of the real awakening of the Chinese people, out of which grew modern schools, newspapers, and cultural associations, some academic and some social—as for example, the one opposed to the binding of women's feet—all of which clamored for radical reforms. From that time the initiative for change in Chinese society no longer rested with the Court; it had become the responsibility of the nation's intellectual leaders. After more than ten years of agitation for social and political reform, in 1898 Kang was received in audience by the Emperor, an event which was unprecedented because Kang was then only a scholar (even though the highest degree had been conferred on him) and not a high official for which such audiences were reserved. During the audience Kang made the following recommendation to the Emperor: "My understanding of the international situation is that only a nation which can adapt itself to changing conditions can maintain itself. If China can change completely, she can become strong; a limited change no longer serves any purpose. What China is suffering from is that she is enslaved by her old ways and refuses to see that change is necessary. A new thing looks healthy, but when old it appears worn; when new it looks fresh, when old it is rotten; it is alive when new, moribund when old; when new it is vital, when old it becomes a matter of routine. This is the law of the physical world. It is the same with laws and institutions in the social world. No law or institution should last longer than a hundred years."

Kang Yu-wei then suggested three practical steps to the Emperor: issuance of a proclamation in the form of an oath to be subscribed to by the principal ministers to show the main direction in which China should go; canvassing the opinion of the intelligent leaders of the people to learn their view of what should be done; establishment of a bureau of codification to draft a constitution. What Kang had in mind was political and constitutional reform, similar to the reforms of the Mejii era in Japan.

In June, 1898, Kang Yu-wei was actually appointed Chief Adviser for reform by the Emperor. He was specially charged to send memorials directly to the Emperor, which was a right enjoyed only by Cabinet Ministers. Seven men were also appointed as his co-workers. Accordingly, from June 11, 1898, the Emperor Kuang Hsu showered upon the people numerous decrees of reform, covering the following subjects: (1) abolition of the state examination in which only the antiquated eight-legged essay was required; (2) the establishment, in its place, of a modern university in Peking; (3) provision for sending members of the Imperial family abroad for study; (4) development of industry, commerce, agriculture, railways and mining; (5) the rebuilding of Buddhist monasteries as schools; (6) training of a new army; (7) establishment of a bureau of translation to translate books dealing with natural and social science into Chinese; and (8) the drawing up of a budget of revenue and expenditure. These decrees took the conservatives by surprise. The reactionaries were jealous of the reformers, who had the support of the Emperor Kuang Hsu, but they knew that the Empress Dowager Tzu Hsi was strongly opposed to these measures. Thus, two factions arose in the Court—one siding with the Emperor and the other with the Empress Dowager. But the Empress Dowager was by far the more forceful personality, and the decrees which were issued in such profusion, were largely unheeded. It was inevitable that the friction would reach a point of crisis. The Emperor, in order to ensure that his decrees were duly carried out, summoned Yuan Shih-kai and gave orders that the Summer Palace, where the Empress Dowager was residing, should be surrounded by his soldiers so that she could not be informed by her spies of what was going on in the outside world. Instead of carrying out these instructions, however, Yuan rode on his favorite steed from Peking to Tientsin where he disclosed the move to the Empress Dowager's loyal supporter Yung Lo, with the added falsehood that he had instructions to murder the Empress Dowager. Whereupon, the Empress Dowager returned to Peking and incarcerated the Emperor. The Hundred Days of Reform were over as a result of this coup d'état, and the reformers had to flee for their lives.

Kang managed to escape to Shanghai, where he was transferred to a British warship which took him to the south. Liang Chi-chao took asylum in the Japanese Legation in Peking and was taken to Japan by a Japanese warship. With the Empress Dowager now on the throne, precipitate changes took place. All the reform measures issued by the Emperor Kuang Hsu were countermanded, and anti-foreign feeling was fostered so vehemently that it led rapidly to the Boxer Uprising of 1900. It was a blind explosion of madness and ignorance, and brought the Manchu Dynasty nearer than ever to its ultimate downfall.

After Kang Yu-wei had left China to live abroad, he had still upheld the monarchical system, and had started a movement to maintain the Emperor Kuang Hsu on the throne. However, his famous disciple Liang Chi-chao was not so certain and wavered between constitutional monarchy and the republican form of government which was then already being sponsored by Dr. Sun Yat-sen. Dr. Sun was all for revolution, and started a revolutionary career by capturing the capital of Kuangtung as early as 1895. Ten years later, he organised the Tung-Men-Hui, or the Revolutionary Society, at Tokyo, where the number of Chinese students had reached the maximum number of 20,000. The Tung-Men-Hui had a regular platform of which the following were the principal items: the overthrow of the Manchu Dynasty, the establishment of a Chinese Republic, the maintenance of world peace, the nationalisation of land, cooperation with the Japanese, and an attempt to get other nations to support the Chinese Revolution.

It is interesting at this juncture to enquire into the attitude of Liang Chi-chao who, though sympathetic with Dr. Sun, had by now established a Constitutional Party. During Liang's period of asylum in Japan, he had learned much about the history of Europe, and the liberal ideas of the nineteenth century in the realm of philosophy, science, and modern political thought made so strong an appeal to him that he decided to introduce them to his own countrymen. There is perhaps no man in the history of modern China who exerted as great an influence through his pen as Liang. His scholarship was not profound, but his knowledge was so embracing, and the style of his writing so charming and effective that anybody who could read immediately came under the spell of his personality. He was also an entrancing conversationalist, radiating a personal warmth and graciousness such as few modern Chinese scholars had ever shown. He was a master of brilliant political pamphleteering, and his articles began to be read all over the country with unprecedented enthusiasm. For a time Liang was a collaborator of Dr. Sun. But after 1904 he came back to the fold of his teacher Kang, and maintained that a constitutional monarchy was all that was needed. He had an abhorrence of revolution and gave example after example in Chinese history to show that inter-dynastic revolutions were costly and protracted. Besides, revolutions were likely to be followed by periods of tyranny and terrorism, as, for instance, that of the French Directorate. What China needed, then, was a rational course of action which would ensure steady development along constitutional lines. That Liang was prophetic in more than one respect no one can deny. But Dr. Sun's party appealed to the younger men who were students in Japan, and his Tung-Men-Hui grew in strength until it was reorganised into the Kuomintang, leading finally to the overthrow of the Manchu Dynasty. What followed in 1911 is so generally known that it is unnecessary for me to recapitulate the facts. It is sufficient to say that the days of republicanism were uncertain. During its chequered career it ran into many obstacles, it had to make many compromises, and when Yuen Shih-kai and his cohorts seized the reins of government, it seemed as if republicanism was destined to end in failure and disappointment.

The work of founding the Chinese Republic, in a word, offered no resemblance to the French Revolution, marked by internal conflict and terrorism between the Girondists and Jacobins. While the revolution was going on, Liang Chi-chao continued to write extensively on constitutionalism, parliamentary and local government, human rights, and freedom. Many of his party members became speakers in the provincial assemblies during the republican regime. Although a republican form of government was not what he espoused, since it had become a reality, he vowed to serve it and did till the day of his untimely death. If Dr. Sun, on his part, had willingly co-operated with Liang, subsequent developments in China might have been different. For the two men knew more of the art of government than most people, and their collaboration, like that of Washington and Jefferson, would have provided a solid foundation for the Chinese Republic. But that was unfortunately not to be. Power fell into the hands of Yuan Shih-kai, who was a political opportunist, and then followed a period of utter confusion.

This is not the place to give a complete record of what took place between 1911 and 1924, but a few landmarks should be recalled:

1913 The outbreak of the Second Revolution in June, and its suppression by Yuan Shih-kai.

1915 Yuan Shih-kai's attempt to restore the monarchy. Rebellion in Yunnan Province under the leadership of Liang Chi-chao and General Tsai Ao against Yuan.

1916 Death of Yuan Shih-kai. Li Yuan-hung succeeds to the Presidency of the Republic.

1917 China breaks off diplomatic relations with Germany. Restoration of the Manchu Emperor by General Chang Hsun, which lasts only 12 days. Feng Kuo-chang becomes President of the Republic.

1918 The Northern Military Party orders a general election and summons a Senate according to the provisional constitution passed in Nanking in 1911. They disregard the law of the parliament passed in 1912 by the constituent assembly in Peking. Hsu Shih-chang is elected President of The Republic. Dr. Sun declares the step taken by the Peking Government to be illegal, and organises a military movement led by a directorate of seven members.

1922 Hsu Shih-chang is ousted by General Wu Pei-fu. Li Yuan-hung comes back to the Presidency, and the first parliament dissolved by Yuan is recalled.

1923 Tsao Kun, supported by Wu Pei-fu, is elected President. The so-called Tsao Kun constitution is passed by the Parliament.

1924 Reorganisation of the Kuomintang. Tuan Chi-jui becomes Chief Executive of the Peking regime.

1925 On March 12, Dr. Sun dies in Peking.

1926 Northern Expedition starts under the leadership of Chiang Kai-shek.

The record explains itself. It shows at once that the democratic form of government failed completely in China. Why was this so? The reason was that the basic essentials of democratic government were lacking. First, there was no enlightened public opinion powerful enough to check the government. Secondly, the widespread respect for law which lies at the basis of all democratic government did not exist in China during this period. Thirdly, the leaders had no understanding of familiar democratic conventions governing the dissolution of parliaments and changes in the composition of cabinets. These basic conditions were all completely ignored, and from 1911 till 1924 the republican regime was merely a series of coup d'états marked by the rise and fall of personalities. By about the time of the end of the First World War, however, there was a ferment working in the Chinese mind, similar to that which followed the Sino-Japanese war of 1894. The October Revolution in Russia had given the Chinese a new source of inspiration. The fourteen points of President Wilson's program brought hope of a new world order. These influences were at work in the international field. Domestically also the Chinese mind tried to find the cause of the failure to evolve a stable and democratic government, and the manifestations of uncertainty were much more radical than those of 1862, 1898, and 1911: reformers now sought to abandon completely the Confucian tradition. This change of attitude took three forms: the Literary Revolution, the Anti-Confucian Movement, and a new emphasis on science and democracy. For the moment we shall not discuss the third point. The Literary Revolution and the Anti-Confucian movement, sponsored respectively by Dr. Hu Shih and Chen Tu-hsiu, in essence became the forerunner of Communist totalitarianism in China.

The need for a literary revolution in China had been felt as early as the beginning of the century. Huang Yuan-yung, a well known writer of the day, said in a letter: "In order really to save the country I believe a beginning must be made in the promotion of a new literature. We must endeavor to bring Chinese thought into direct contact with the contemporary thought of the world, for only in this way can it be stimulated and awakened. Also, it is essential that the basic ideals of world-thought be related to the life of the average man by the use of simple and simplified language and literature for the wide dissemination of ideas. Have we not heard that the Renaissance laid the basis for the overthrow of mediaevalism in Europe?"

But more than a decade had to pass before the ideas of Huang received wide acceptance. In 1917 Dr. Hu Shih, inspired by the work of Chaucer in England and Dante in Italy, started the *pei-hua* movement, and urged the following five points in a manifesto which he published on January 1: (1) all writing must have, first of all, real substance. In China beautiful phrases have frequently been substituted for real meaning. (2) The imitation of ancient writers is not as important as the development of real ideas. (3) Grammatical rules must be observed. In the Chinese language a sentence often does not have a subject or a verb. (4) "Call a spade a spade," without using phrases that are only meant for embellishment. Do not say you are sad when you do not feel sad. Do not speak of a fire of soya bean cake, because a fire today is often generated by electricity; do not use classical language to express a modern thought. (5) Do not avoid the language used by the masses.

While Chaucer in England and Luther in Germany really established new languages, the so-called literary renaissance in China did no such thing, as the *pei-hua* or the vulgar language had been in existence in China for hundreds of years and was used extensively in philosophical discussions and more especially in the writing of fiction. But it is true that it had never been considered a dignified medium of expression. It is to the credit of Dr. Hu Shih and his colleagues that they saw the potentialities of the vulgar language, and, by espousing its wider use, helped to start a movement for the liberation of Chinese thought. It was a movement which received immense support from the younger intellectual elements who called for a re-examination of China's past cultural heritage, together with the introduction of scientific method and the scientific approach in the study of society and government. It was at this time also that translations from the works of eminent European, English, and American writers, such as Tolstoy, Ibsen, Maupassant, Byron, Shelley, Emerson, Kropotkin, Marx, and Engels, appeared in rapid succession—all of which helped to create a new mental atmosphere.

Chen-Tu-hsiu, the founder of the Chinese Communist Party, was a man of more revolutionary outlook than Dr. Hu Shih, popularly considered the leader of the Literary Revolution. In an article called "The Literary Revolution," he made some pregnant remarks:

What is the origin of the contemporary Europe which lies so brilliantly before us? It is the gift of revolution. A revolution in Europe constitutes a change from the old to the new, while in China we hear only of a change of dynasties. Since the Renaissance in Europe, there have been revolutions in political, religious, ethical, and literary fields, and because of these revolutions there has been rejuvenation and progress; and so the history of Europe is a history of revolutions.

In China we have undertaken three revolutions against the Manchu Dynasty, and yet darkness has not disappeared from the scene, because these revolutions are very much like "the head of the tiger but with the tail of the snake." They began well enough, but were never carried to their logical end. The old dirt has not been washed away by blood. In the field of ethics, literature, and art, debris has accumulated to such an extent that even a revolution has not been able to cleanse them. A political revolution cannot produce a new social organisation as long as we are afraid of radical changes. Today, happily, the validity of Confucius' teaching is being hotly debated. This is pioneering work in the field of a moral or ethical revolution. A literary revolution is also being generally espoused, and principally by my friend Hu Shih. In spite of hostility on the part of the old scholars, I shall willingly support my friend in raising the banner of the literary revolution. On this banner there shall be three inscriptions: (1) The overthrow of aristocratic literature and the creation of popular literature for the masses. (2) The overthrow of classical literature and the creation of a new literature based on realism. (3) The overthrow of "hermit" literature and the creation of a social literature.

After the literary revolution the reform movement took the next step in demolishing the Confucian tradition. Chen Tu-hsiu espoused a revolution in thinking which was to go beyond the literary revolution. In a manifesto appearing in his magazine *New Youth,* he stated six basic principles for a new outlook on life. First, one must show a spirit of independence and not be a slave; men should be freed from the excessive domination of their parents and the government. Chen was impressed by the way in which European countries had managed to overthrow the institution of monarchy in order to gain political liberation, overthrow the power of the Church in order to gain freedom of conscience, establish a socialist economy in order to gain economic freedom, and grant the right of voting to women in order to free them from masculine domination. The second principle enjoins youth to be progressive and not conservative. "When one is confined to what is old, there is danger of degeneration. When one strives for something new, then the people will rise and support him. A nation which cannot change is not fit to survive." Thirdly, one must strive actively for progress. The struggle for existence can only be successfully waged if it is accompanied by a struggle for progress. If a nation refuses to face its difficulties and insists upon living in an ivory tower, then it cannot survive. "While the Europeans fight for progress, we in Asia are satisfied with contentedness and leisure, and this is the reason why the West is strong and we are weak." Fourthly, "We must no longer think in terms of isolation and exclusiveness, but of world politics. To-day, the world has become an area in which many families live together; in such an area China can not live in isolation. If it had not been for China's military defeats in 1894 and 1900, we might still be writing our 'eight-legged essays' or be wearing pigtails. It is time that we joined the community of nations." In Chen's fifth principle, he pays high tribute to Bentham's theory of utilitarianism and to the positivist philosophy of Auguste Comte, in the belief that China must pay attention to practical things, such as industry and commerce, and not only to things which are merely traditional and decorative and good only for ceremonial purposes. In the sixth and last principle, Chen appeals for the use of scientific method, believing that, while religion and literature are useful and satisfy man's imagination, his attention should be increasingly turned toward the study of science and practical questions. Progress in Europe, Chen Tu-hsiu affirmed, was primarily the result of the application of scientific method to the affairs of everyday life.

The whole burden of this new program was the demolition of the Confucian system, held to be sacred for over 2000 years. To that end, Hu Shih made use of some homely illustrations. With the slogan, "Down with the house of Confucius," he compared this house of philosophy built by the great sage with the streets of Peking, full of dust and sand, which are cleaned by coolies who carry pails of water on their shoulders, while in the West machines are used for that purpose.

Precisely at that time, the parliament in Peking was considering the establishment of Confucianism as the state religion. Hu Shih lashed out and wrote: "In regard to the traditionally handed down teachings of our sages, we must enquire whether or not they are adequate for us now. It is necessary to ask whether we must accept the conventional beliefs merely because they have been accepted without question by the majority. Are we bound to accede to all that the majority favors? Are there not other methods which are better, more reasonable, and more beneficial than the old ones?"

Chen Tu-hsiu went even further in trying to show that the Confucian teachings were not adequate in our days. He compared Confucianism to despotism and autocracy. He arraigned it for teaching a double standard. He declared that if the teachings of Confucius are to be respected we must obey the commands of the monarch, the father, the husband, and the elder brother, however unreasonable they may be, and thus be enslaved by a conservative and reactionary attitude. The most important principle in modern social organisation, he affirmed, is individualism. In the West, the individual is considered an independent entity enjoying his rights and property, and able to defend his privileges as a citizen. Confucianism, Chen Tu-hsiu believed, suppresses the initiative of the individual, and makes individualism impossible. In family relations, according to Confucian principle, the right of inheritance is limited to male children. The Chinese classics prescribe that a woman be enslaved to her husband, father, parents-in-law, and even to her own sons, and her world does not reach beyond her household. Equality of the sexes, which is so important a factor in the political liberation in the West, can never become effective in China under the guidance of the Confucian teachings. Confucius, living in a feudalistic society, developed his ideas of morality, rituals, politics, and social life in a feudalistic setting, and the resulting synthesis makes it virtually impossible to promote the welfare of the people. The new philosophy must be based on the conception of individual rights and human freedom, as well as on that of equality before the law, an idea with which Confucius was unfortunately not familiar.

It is not difficult to see how such a revolutionary philosophy, striking at the very root of China's traditional way of life and thought, and providing at the same time a tool in the form of *pei hua* to enable the people to become familiar with such revolutionary thought, would spread quickly over the entire country. The literary revolution, not only embracing a political philosophy, but turning its attention also to questions of morality and art, may perhaps be considered the strongest force that is transforming China from an absolute monarchy based on a Confucian philosophy to a democratic society based on the new ideas of human rights and individualism.

The leadership of this movement was unfortunately in the hands of Chen Tu-hsiu and Hu Shih only for a short time. Dr. Hu Shih, though a man of scholarly attainments, became for a time embroiled in immediate political problems and lost some of his detachment and objectivity, while Chen Tu-hsiu directed his energy to the organisation of the Chinese Communist Party. Chen was later purged from the party because of his Trotskyist inclinations. He died in Chungking in 1939, a believer in democracy, as is amply shown in his writings published posthumously. In the failure of the movement to lay a firm foundation for democracy in China, we find the genesis of the political developments, shortly after the First World War, which were characterized by a gradual drift towards totalitarianism, and which we will discuss when we deal with the reorganisation of the Kuomintang and the founding of the Communist Party.

It is, of course, much too sanguine to expect modern democracy to take root in China in so short a time when it has taken hundreds of years to evolve in a country like Britain. But we must bear in mind that, in spite of the vigorous attacks made on China's traditional beliefs during the last quarter of a century, the fact remains that the democratic spirit is deeply ingrained in the Chinese consciousness. From Mencius, who was perhaps the most energetic exponent of democratic rule in the ancient world, to the scholars of the Ming Dynasty, there is in China an unbroken line of thinkers who have espoused the cause of the individual and of his inalienable rights. The problem for the present is how to harness that spirit to political institutions which have become an indispensable part of constitutional and parliamentary life, so that it may be given full and unhampered opportunity to grow and flourish instead of being overwhelmed by the whims and the autocratic behavior of a small minority—as has so frequently happened in the chequered history of contemporary China.

CHAPTER II

Sun Yat-sen and the Trend Towards Totalitarianism

In order to form a clear conception of Chinese political developments after the First World War, or during the period from 1924 to the present, it is necessary to review the life and work of Dr. Sun Yat-sen. His work can hardly be separated into formal periods. It is therefore better to try to give a brief account of his life as it unfolded. Emphasis will be placed in this account on his "Three Principles of the People," and especially on his conception of the machinery of government, because in these things he showed his relationship to Soviet Russia and his Communist leanings.

In contrast to Kang Yu-wei and Liang Chi-chao, Dr. Sun Yat-sen was not only a republican statesman, but also a dynamic political personality. Dr. Sun was a Chinese political leader who was not tied down to the tradition of the old scholars; he received his education primarily from Western sources. He worshipped the leaders of the Taiping Rebellion and substituted the study of Western sciences for the study of the six classics. Because of Dr. Sun's foreign education, which he had received in Hong Kong and Honolulu, and because of the fact that he was not bound to conventional Chinese scholarship, he was able to follow a relatively simple path in breaking away from Chinese traditions. But more than that, Dr. Sun Yat-sen's personal background was conducive to making him the active revolutionary that he became so early in life. Mrs. Sun Yat-sen writes in the following way about her husband:

Dr. Sun came from the people. He came from the peasantry. His father was a farmer, and the people of his district were farmers. Dr. Sun was poor. Not until he was fifteen years old did he have shoes for his feet, and he lived in a hilly region where it was not pleasant to be a barefooted boy. His family, until he and his brother were grown up, lived almost from hand to mouth, in a hut. As a child, he ate the cheapest food—not rice, for rice was too dear. His main nourishment was potatoes.

Many times [Mrs. Sun continues] Dr. Sun has told me, it was in these early days, as a poor son of a peasant family, that he became a revolutionary. He was determined that the lot of the Chinese peasant should not continue to be so wretched, that little boys in China should have shoes to wear and rice to eat. For this ideal he gave forty years of his life.

In 1879, at the age of thirteen, Sun Yat-sen joined his brother in Honolulu, where he stayed for the next four years, and was deeply impressed by the orderly conditions about him as well as by the prevailing respect for law and confidence in its protection. It was in Honolulu too that he got his first view of the political democracy of America, which was later to play such an important part in the formation of his own political philosophy. After the Indo-Chinese war, in which Indo-China was wrested from China by France, and his return to his native land, Sun Yat-sen started his active career of furthering revolution, in accordance with principles that went far beyond advocacy of a reform movement merely. He aimed at the overthrow of the Manchu dynasty, and with it the monarchy as an institution. During the Boxer Uprising in 1900, he sent some of his followers to take Weichow in Kuangtung Province, and this was the first time that Sun Yat-sen raised his flag, now the national flag of China, the white sun in the blue sky.

With the organisation of the Tung Men Hui or the Revolutionary Society in Japan in 1905, Sun Yat-sen translated his political philosophy into an organised political movement. The platform of the Tung Men Hui included six points. To popularize this platform, some catch-phrases were coined that were later to play an important part in the founding of the Republic. The expulsion of the Manchus and the restoration of China could well be called Nationalism; the establishment of a republic could come under the title of Democracy, and the equal distribution as well as the nationalisation of land could be described as Socialism. From now on the targets were clearly in sight—not only Kang Yu-wei's political and constitutional reform, but the overthrow of the Manchu Dynasty.

Despite many reverses, persecutions, and rebuffs, and despite the fact that revolutionary uprisings in Canton in 1902, in Hunan in 1904, and other military operations in 1907, 1908, and 1909 proved to be failures, the revolutionary movement continued to grow. When the Emperor drafted new armies to defend his throne, younger revolutionaries who had worked together with Dr. Sun in Japan, volunteered and secretly spread their propaganda among the soldiers. It was not long, therefore, before the new army became a solid body of revolutionaries. In October of 1911, the revolution broke out in earnest and spread beyond the control of the government forces. The fact that the revolution broke out over a relatively unimportant matter, centering around the building of the Peking-Hankow-Canton railway, and ended in the overthrow of the Manchu Dynasty, is an indication of the decadence and corruption of the Manchu house, and the desire of the people for democratic government.

Thus far, Dr. Sun's appeal to the Chinese had been very successful, and he was the most popular leader among the Chinese students abroad. After the establishment of the Republic he could have accomplished much that was constructive and would have helped to stabilize China if he had had a group of co-workers capable of helping him in the task, as Washington had had Hamilton, Jefferson, Franklin, and Adams. But other forces got the better of him. Political power very soon passed into the hands of Yuan Shih-kai, a thoroughgoing opportunist. In the reorganised government administered by Yuan, Dr. Sun was only offered the post of General-Superintendent of Railway Construction, which was an administrative office in name only. After a short time, a leading member of the Kuomintang, Sung Chiao-jen, whom the Kuomintang had proposed as the next Prime Minister, was assassinated by Yuan's agents. The Kuomintang was so incensed at Yuan's recourse to assassination as a means of getting rid of his opponents that they resolved to fight. Their rebellion, or the Second Revolution, was soon crushed, and those provincial governors who were members of the Kuomintang were dismissed. Dr. Sun had to flee to Tokyo, and there he started the work of reorganising his party. One of the things he required of new members was to put their fingerprints on the application form. This did not make Dr. Sun popular. His party remained powerless, and it could do nothing against Yuan. The revolt was finally successful in the province of Yunnan, where an army under the leadership of General Tsai Ao, Liang Chi-chao's disciple, raised the flag against Yuan's monarchy. In the meantime, Dr. Sun remained in Tokyo, coming back to China after Yuan's death in 1916. When the first Parliament was called under Li Yuan-hung's presidency and Tuan Chi-jui's premiership, the question of breaking diplomatic relations and declaring war against Germany was raised. Dr. Sun had no confidence in a policy sponsored by the Northern military clique, and so was opposed to the policy of declaring war against Germany; but Liang Chi-chao was on the side of the Tuan cabinet and carried on negotiations with the ministers of the Entente Powers, because he saw that it would give China a chance to have a seat at the Peace Conference at Versailles and to ask for a revision of the unequal treaties. When in 1922 Hsu Shih-chang was elected President of the Republic by the parliament in Peking, in accordance with the Law of the Senate in Nanking, Dr. Sun reappeared on the political stage and formed a secession government in Kuangtung to fight Hsu Shih-chang, who was under the patronage of the Northern military clique. But Sun's right-hand man, Chen Chiung-ming, revolted against him on June 16, 1922. These years, from 1912 to 1924, were years of failure for Dr. Sun. An accurate appreciation of the situation may well be gained from a passage in Chiang Kai-shek's book, *China's Destiny*:

Although the Chinese Republic was founded in 1912, there was a period of thirteen years, until the reorganisation of the Kuomintang, in which the Nationalist Revolution experienced innumerable difficulties and obstacles. The experience of those thirteen years may be divided into two periods.

The first period dates from the insurrection of 1911 to the death of Yuan Shih-kai in 1916. At the time of the 1911 revolution, Sun Yat-sen's purpose was to overthrow the three-thousand-year-old monarchy and establish a democratic state. He did not consider that democracy consisted merely of a President, a Parliament, a Provisional Constitution, and a Cabinet. Because of this, he turned the Presidency over to Yuan Shih-kai. He believed that the revolutionists should constitute a non-govermental party, devoting their energy to education and industry, and implanting the foundation of the Three People's Principles in the minds and lives of the people. There were very few men in the party that understood this idea. Attention was generally centered on the text of the Provisional Constitution, in the belief that, if only a system of responsible government could be enforced, Yuan Shih-kai could be prevented from abusing his authority as President. They also thought that if a powerful political party could be organized to control the parliament, a responsible cabinet could be maintained to carry out the task of restricting the authority of the president. . . .

What Yuan Shih-kai feared was not the Parliament, but the influence of the revolutionary party in the Yangtse Valley and the Southern Provinces. Therefore, after the failure of the Second Revolution in the province of Kiangsi, Kuangtung and Fukien and in Nanking in the second year of the Republic (1913), the Parliament was dissolved by the President it had elected and the decree of dissolution was countersigned by none other than the Prime Minister of a Cabinet responsible to the Parliament. Immediately, after the dissolution of the Parliament, the Cabinet collapsed. Thereafter, the so-called Cabinet, and the provisional constitution itself were all controlled by Yuan Shih-kai, and were maneuvered at his pleasure. (From P. Jaffe's translation.)

There is no doubt that the man who destroyed the foundation of the Republic of China in its early years was Yuan Shih-kai. It was treason on Yuan's part to turn the Republic into a monarchy to satisfy his own ambitions. This monarchical movement aroused the moral indignation of the liberal statesman Liang Chi-chao and General Tsai Ao, who left Yuan and started the rebellion in Yunnan. The period after the death of Yuan Shih-kai was the period of warlordism. Dr. Sun described this period in his book *The Three Principles of the People* as follows:

Why did everybody in the beginning support a democratic form of government and not oppose the Republic? This is the main reason: after the successful expulsion of the Manchus, the revolutionary comrades in the various provinces, the new military caste which developed out of the revolution, and the old Manchu militarists who joined the revolutionary party, all moved in a like direction—towards the formation of a military caste. Each one wanted to be a small king in his own place, and form his own little domain as a base to extend his power. The militarists who seized Yunnan and Hunan wanted to widen their territory. (F. W. Price's translation.)

The meaning of these last sentences may be difficult to grasp for those who are not familiar with Chinese politics. What Dr. Sun had in mind was the movement towards a federation of self-governing provinces, which was first started in Hunan. Since the republican form of government under a united China had failed, some of the provincial governors tried to put their own provinces on an autonomous basis, with provincial constitutions decided on by the people themselves. These provinces were situated on the main route of Dr. Sun's plan for a Northern Expedition, so he regarded them as obstacles. Chiang Kai-shek has also criticised this movement in *China's Destiny*, calling it a mask for feudalistic partition. Because these provinces intended to try a new method of government and did not follow Dr. Sun's plan of military conquest, they were suspect. The motive of the movement towards a federation of self-governing provinces was really not so bad as Dr. Sun has pictured it.

In spite of Dr. Sun's failure in these thirteen years, he did not lose courage. Rather it brought to the fore the resources of his character as a revolutionist. And after the October revolution in Soviet Russia, he thought he had found a political ally.

Mr. John K. Fairbank has correctly described the attitude of Dr. Sun at this time in his book *The United States and China*:

> On his part Sun Yat-sen by 1922 had reached a low point in his fortunes after almost thirty years of agitation. He had seen the Manchu Dynasty collapse and had been proclaimed President of the Chinese Republic only to see the country disintegrate into warlordism and become more than ever the prey of foreign powers. His effort to unify China through warlord means had led him into dealings with opportunist military leaders at Canton. In June, 1922, a Cantonese militarist (Chen Chiung-ming) whom he had attempted to outmaneuver had turned the tables upon him. Sun was forced to flee, and reached Shanghai in August. It was just at this moment, when Sun had demonstrated his pre-eminence as China's Nationalist leader but his incompetence to complete the revolution, that he joined forces with the Comintern. In 1923 he began the reorganization of the Kuomintang on Soviet lines.
>
> This was purely a marriage of convenience. The entente announced in a joint statement by Dr. Sun and Adolph Joffe in January 1923 was a strictly limited arrangement. It stated that Dr. Sun did not favor Communism for China since conditions were not appropriate to it, that Joffe agreed that China needed unity and independence, and that Russia was ready to aid the Chinese Nationalist revolution. As Sun Yat-sen wrote to Chiang Kai-shek at the time, he had to seek help where he could get it. In other words, Sun now sought and accepted Comintern aid, but communism, in his mind, did not supplant his own Three Principles of the People as the programme for the Chinese revolution.

From now on began the collaboration of the Kuomintang and the Communists, which lasted for a period of three years. The Kuomintang was reorganised during this period and became even more important as a factor in Chinese politics. Chiang Kai-shek, after he returned to China from his mission of study in Moscow, was appointed head of the Whampoa Military Academy. Dr. Sun recast his *Three Principles of the People,* and in the new version of the book, he showed a friendly attitude towards Soviet Russia. During his stay in Peking for the purpose of negotiating with Tuan Chi-jui on the question of calling a National Assembly, he died, on March 12, 1925. Upon his death his political doctrines became the Bible for party members, and later for all the schools in China.

I shall here give a summary of Dr. Sun's Three Principles of the People and then attempt to show how his political ideas were influenced by Soviet Communism.

The Three Principles of the People, *San Min Chu I,* are derived from European sources: they are Nationalism, Democracy, and Socialism. When cast in Chinese terminology, these words lose their usual connotations and take on a specifically Chinese flavor.

(1) *Nationalism.* When the principle of Nationalism was first announced, it was directed against the Manchus, who were aliens in the eyes of the Chinese. Dr. Sun demanded emancipation and self-determination for the Chinese people, as the Italians had made these demands under Hapsburg rule. Later the meaning of nationalism was extended to include opposition to all forms of foreign imperialism, and especially against foreign economic exploitation. Dr. Sun said himself:

Since 1911 the exclusive control of the Manchus has disappeared from the scene, but foreign imperialism has persisted. The alarming bugle blast of partition has changed to the milder note of international control; in other words, political and military aggrandizement has taken a turn to become pure economic exploitation. But what is the difference? The net result is one and the same—the slow but sure elimination of China as a free and independent nation. The foreigners are robbing China to the extent of $1,000,000,000 annually, and this amount is increasing. Ten years ago, the excess of imports over imports was valued at $200,000,000 annually. At present it is $500,-000,000. The nationalist movement aims at the development of China and the deliverance of all Chinese from exploitation by the imperialistic, militaristic and capitalistic forces.

Dr. Sun Yat-sen considered two things to be essential for the salvation of the Chinese people. The first was the realisation of the danger of their position, and the second was "consolidation of the deep-rooted sentiment prevailing in the family and clan into a powerful national spirit."

In the last of his series of lectures on nationalism, Sun Yat-sen returned to Chinese tradition, like a man who had travelled many years abroad and had finally come home to settle down. In this lecture he stressed the fact that while China was backward in terms of material civilization she did not lack a political philosophy, as exemplified by books like *The Great Learning*. He mentioned five important virtues—loyalty, a sense of duty, benevolence, honesty, love of peace—all of which are emphasized in the Confucian classics; he contended that if any two of these virtues were universally accepted by the people, the country would become strong and prosperous.

(2) *Democracy*. In his lectures on the second principle, Democracy, or the sovereignty of the people, he contended that the theory of natural rights had no place in this system, since such a theory, when carried to its extreme, upheld special interests detrimental to the revolution and to political democracy. Dr. Sun said:

> By democracy, we mean the right to vote, the rights of initiative, referendum, and recall. The formula for guaranteeing these rights ought to be definitely embodied in the constitution, which, in turn, should be based on five divisions of power: legislative, judicial, executive, examinatory, and controlling. The above principles will prove adequate, not only in meeting the deficiences of representative government, but also in correcting defects of suffrage. While in other modern countries, the so-called democratic machinery is frequently run for the exclusive interests of the propertied class to the detriment of the common people for whom the machinery was ostensibly intended, the kind of democracy which we champion shall be in the full possession of the majority of the citizenry and shall not be monopolised by the privileged few. A point is to be noted. Our democracy is quite different from the traditionally accepted one based upon the theory of natural rights; we rather seek to develop a democratic system to meet the special needs of a reconstruction period. It is only upon those groups that are loyal to the republic that the political rights mentioned above, are to be conferred; and, needless to say, from those who sell themselves to the service of the imperialists and militarists, such rights are to be withheld.

In regard to the actual form of government to be adopted, Dr. Sun Yat-sen did not believe in the Anglo-American theory of constitutional law, but advocated the Swiss form of government in which the direct popular rights of initiative, referendum, and recall rest with the people.

Dr. Sun believed that there must be a distinction made between political power and ability, believing that possession of power does not necessarily imply the knowledge of its proper use. Following the example of the man who owns a car but does not know how to drive it and so hires a driver, he believed that while the people own the government, they may not have the ability to run it, and therefore they must get men of ability to do it for them. Dr. Sun stressed the distinction between the sovereign power of the people and the ruling power of the government. Because the people must have the power but do not have the ability, they can only be given the sovereign powers of universal suffrage, initiative, referendum, and recall. Apart from these, they must sit quietly in the car and let the driver do the driving. Because the ruling power of the government is to be in the hands of those who are able, Dr. Sun believed that the power of the government should not be limited to executive, legislative, and judicial functions, but the powers of examination and control should be added as well, so as to make the government all-powerful.

Dr. Sun's distinction between the sovereign power of the people and the ruling power of the government is open to criticism. It is indeed difficult to follow him in his belief that the legislature should form part of the government in the same way as in the case of those Western constitutional systems in which the executive organ comes under the control of the legislative body. If the peoples' power is limited to suffrage, referendum, recall, and initiative, while the legislature has no power over the rise and fall of the cabinet and the selection of high officials, then the executive power of the government is out of reach of the influence of popular opinion and free from popular control. There are important tasks that legislatures must perform, such as declaring war and formulating the national budget, which can make or break a cabinet, so it is hard to justify Dr. Sun's dividing the sovereign power of the people from the ruling power of the government. Experience during the last twenty years has shown us that under such a division, the government has very often, through its executive organ and the dominant party (for example, the Central Executive Committee of the Kuomintang), dictated and imposed their policies upon an unwilling but powerless legislature, thereby making Dr. Sun's five-power theory of government meaningless, and militating against the creation of an actual working democracy.

Dr. Sun's five-power theory, placing the executive, the legislative, judicial, control, and examination powers and functions of the government on an equal basis, is a theory that is actually the heritage of absolute monarchy. Dr. Sun believed that while the executive, legislative, and judicial powers of the monarch were in the nature of prerogatives, the power of examination and impeachment were to a certain extent separated from these prerogatives. In other words, there was a certain amount of separation of powers under the system of absolute monarchy. The major shortcoming of this conception becomes evident, however, when these five powers all function as parts of the ruling power of the government, eliminating any popular basis for the five-power theory. As long as these five powers are subordinated to a higher instance of power, whether it be the President or the National Assembly, the position of the officials in question can only be compared to that of responsible cabinet members, and sovereignty, which normally resides in the legislature, cannot be said to rest in the legislative body. Dr. Sun succeeded in establishing a five-power government, but in the process he neglected the importance of popular, democratic control by the people over the government through their representatives in the legislature, and thus he managed to undermine the very democracy he wanted to see prevail.

(3) *Socialism.* The third policy Sun Yat-sen advocated is a variety of socialism adapted to Chinese conditions. The actual definition of this principle is rather vague; its essential ingredients, however, are the equal distribution of land and government control of capital. Being opposed to Marx and his more radical methods, Dr. Sun advocated measures designed to prevent the centralisation of capital in the hands of a few. A declaration issued by the First Congress of the Kuomintang party says in part:

We hold this principle in regard to the equalization of land to be essential because economic inequality is primarily traceable to the fact that land is usually monopolised by a few. It is, therefore, imperative that the state make land laws, regulating the use of land, the taxation of land produce, and the assessed value of land. The value of lands privately owned, after having been properly assessed by their owners, must be reported to the government, which will levy taxes on them proportionate to their value; and if necessary, the government will exercise the right of eminent domain. These, in fine, are the essentials of our conception with respect to equality of the right to land.

All enterprises, be they in the hands of Chinese citizens or of foreigners, which partake of the nature of the monopoly, or assume proportions incommensurate with the financial resources of the individual entrepreneurs, such as banking and shipping industries, will be undertaken by the state, so that the economic life of the nation shall not pass into the control of the capitalist few. This, in short, is our notion of the regulation of capital. With the attainment of these two principles, economic democracy may be said to have been put on a firm footing.

This economic policy leaves room for widely divergent interpretations, so that both the Kuomintang and the Communists have professed to support it. The Communists claim that Dr. Sun's position is identical with their own, and they have not failed to make much of it.

In reviewing Dr. Sun's Three Principles of the People, three points in particular should be discussed: his attitude towards Soviet Russia, his criticism of Marxism, and his conception of an all-powerful government.

Sun's lectures on the Three Principles of the People have been described by Professor Fairbank as the product of a marriage of convenience. I think we can understand the implications of the program better if we bear this description in mind. Dr. Sun spoke about the October Revolution of Soviet Russia in these terms:

Many years of fierce warfare had not been able to destroy imperialism because this war was a conflict of imperialism between states, not a struggle between savagery and civilisation, or between might and right. So the effect of the war was merely the overthrow of one imperialism by another imperialism. But from the war there was unconsciously born in the heart of mankind a great hope—the Russian Revolution. When the Russians awoke and saw that Imperialism was wrong, they started a revolution within their own country, first overthrowing their own imperialisms; at the same time, to avoid foreign embarrassment, they made peace with Germany. Before long the Entente also signed a peace with Germany, and then all those powers sent soldiers to fight Russia. Why? Because the Russian people had awakened to the fact that their sufferings were due to imperialism, and that, to get rid of their sufferings, they must eliminate imperialism and embrace self-determination. Every other nation opposed this policy and so mobilised to fight Russia, and yet Russia's proposal and Wilson's were undesignedly similar; both declared that the weaker, smaller nations had a right to self-determination and freedom. When Russia proclaimed this principle, the weaker, smaller nations of the world gave their eager support to it, and all together began to speak of self-determination. The calamitous war through which Europe had passed, brought, of course, no great imperialistic gain, but, because of the Russian Revolution, a great hope was born in the heart of mankind.

Speaking about Lenin, Dr. Sun said:

The Slavic race of one hundred and fifty million people suddenly rose up and struck at imperialism and capitalism, warring for mankind against inequality. In my last lecture I told of the Russian who said "The reason the powers have so defamed Lenin, is that he dared to assert that the twelve hundred and fifty million majority in the world were being oppressed by the two hundred and fifty million minority." Lenin not only said this, but he advocated self-determination for the oppressed peoples and launched a campaign for them against injustice. The powers attacked Lenin because they wanted to destroy a prophet and a seer of mankind and insure their own security. But the people of the world now have their eyes opened, and know that the rumors created by the powers are false; they will not let themselves be deceived again. The political thinking of the people of the world has been enlightened to this extent.

Dr. Sun went on to make a comparative study of the revolutions in England, the United States, France, and Soviet Russia, and he came to the conclusion that Russia has effected the most modern revolution and the most successful one; she has levelled down not only the political classes, but also the economic classes of society. I must say that the hope which Dr. Sun saw in the example given by Soviet Russia did not represent his personal view alone; it was the outlook of the Chinese intellectual class. Liang Chi-chao also sent a mission of study to Moscow to see how the work of revolution was being carried out in Soviet Russia. Some of the members of the study mission were converted into Communists, while others, dissatisfied with what they saw, left Moscow and went to Western Europe. The publication by Soviet Russia of the secret diplomatic documents and the abandonment by her of concessions in Manchuria aroused immense sympathy among the Chinese. That was only a generation ago, and today with all of China under Communist rule, do we have to go far to find a manifest denial of those seemingly friendly expressions? Is there no end to duplicity and international cynicism? If Dr. Sun were alive today and witnessed the expansion of Soviet imperialism, especially since the Second World War, what would he say of his early enthusiasm for Russia, which he considered almost a Messiah among the nations? Would he still regard Russia as the hope of mankind?

To be fair, however, Dr. Sun was never subservient to Marxism. He never advised his party members to follow Marxist doctrine; on the contrary, he was critical of it. Dr. Sun, in the first place, was opposed to the materialist conception of history, which is the fundamental hypothesis of Marxism. He raised the question as to whether material forces in a crude sense have really been the critical, determining factors in the making of history, and his answer cast doubt upon this view.

Dr. Sun was also against Marx's view of the class struggle. Far from considering the brutal class struggle a perennial feature of social relations, Dr. Sun found the very opposite, that there was a force in modern society which tended to improve the position of capitalist and laborer alike.

Dr. Sun also contested Marx's theory of profit as representing an unearned increment, surplus value created by labor and confiscated by the capitalist. He took the Shanghai cotton mills during the First World War as an example: the profits realized by the mills came to several hundred thousand dollars. According to Marx, this surplus value was the product of the labor employed at the spindles and looms. But, said Dr. Sun, if we talk about yarn, we must talk about cotton, its raw material. The growing of cotton implied a farmer, soil, and fertiliser. Fertiliser, in turn, came from the chemists. When the yarn was ready, it must be transported for sale. Therefore, profit derives from many factors, and it is not true to say that labor is the only source of surplus value.

Our conclusion must be that, taking everything into consideration, Dr. Sun would be acceptable to Wall Street, and condemned by a Peoples' Court under Mao Tse-tung's regime.

There were, however, numerous occasions when Dr. Sun was prepared to accept communism. But, perhaps because this acceptance was a matter of expediency, or, as Professor Fairbank says, a marriage of convenience, Dr. Sun was unable to reconcile many of the conflicting claims of the Marxist ideology. It was this failure that was responsible for the instability and lack of unity within the ranks of his own party. The practical consequences of this situation brought about the establishment of the government at Hankow on the heel of the Northern Expedition in 1926 and its subsequent split, which led to the establishment of another government at Nanking under the leadership of Chiang Kai-shek.

As we examine Dr. Sun's political views today, we cannot help concluding that he tried to draw inspiration from many quarters without being able to fuse his many borrowings into a consistent whole. The borrowings in question are chiefly four in number and seem to have four separate origins: (1) a republican form of government; (2) the Swiss conception of the rights of initiative and referendum; (3) the Soviet-Russian idea of depriving reactionaries of civil rights and imposing a measure of dictatorship; and (4) the Chinese idea of the Examination Yuan and the Control Yuan. All four of these ideas went to make up his conception of an all-powerful government. The result was that the government he advocated was to be neither of the British parliamentary type, nor of the American congressional type, nor yet of the Swiss type, nor of the Soviet type. It was a product all his own, a political pot-pourri.

Dr. Sun had not much confidence in the British parliamentary system. He said:

> Europeans and Americans once thought that if they could attain to representative government, they would be absolutely satisfied. After our revolution in 1911, did we not achieve a parliament of representatives of the people? What benefits in the way of democracy did the people obtain? . . . No nation which employs a representative system of government can avoid some of its abuses. . . . So the hope of foreigners that representative government will insure the stability and peace of the state is not to be trusted.

But surely this is a very naive and superficial way of looking at representative government. A representative government depends for its success upon enlightened public opinion—which China did not and still does not have—upon the law-abiding character of cabinet ministers, members of parliament, and the people at large—phenomena which have not hitherto been characteristic of China—and upon a number of other factors which require time and opportunity for their proper growth and development. If these basic conditions are there, then a representative government can work effectively. Any high school student can see that if China, in a few brief years, after being subjected to a despotic form of government for centuries, made no success of representative government, it is not the fault of that form of government, but rather because of the fact that the Chinese people were unprepared for it. Dr. Sun was after all a revolutionary, without the patience to wait for the working out of changes by progressive educational work, or by the Fabian method of "permeation." He was all for dramatic changes, for government by fiat. When he saw that the parliament did not work out as he had expected, he tried to substitute something else for it immediately. He introduced the system of initiative, referendum, and recall so popular in Switzerland and in some of the states of the U. S. A., and he expected them to be adopted at once in China. If we follow the debate about the referendum in Great Britain and understand how it came about that she rejected it, we will be in a better position to realise that this form of government, with its long historical background in Switzerland, cannot be easily transplanted. If we consider the working of the Swiss system of plebiscites, we can see why Dr. Sun, looking at them from China, could not help being impressed by them. But how can a country like China, where there is nothing equivalent to the tradition of the *Landgemeinde*, can be expected to take to government by plebiscite is more than I can see.

Dr. Sun finally combined the four features of his theory of government into what he called the quintuple-power constitution. He thought that the people as a whole should exercise the four powers of voting, initiative, referendum, and recall. They only, as a sovereign body, were to exercise these powers. The ruling power, which he further divided into executive, legislative, judicial, control, and examination, he thought should belong to the government proper. Dr. Sun did not understand that such functions of a legislature as the passing of bills on taxation or the budget, debating questions of foreign policy and national defense, and the institution of the vote of confidence, are means which the people have of checking the government and calling it to account. He did not seem to like the idea of applying many checks to the operations of government. Once the government was elected, he thought it could carry on smoothly all its proper functions within the bounds of the quintuple-power constitution. His concept of an all-powerful government he described in these words: "If we construct a low-powered, weak government, its activities will be limited, and its accomplishments will be meagre. But if we put in a high-powered, strong government, its activities will be broad in scope, and it will accomplish great things."

Does this not seem to imply that Dr. Sun disliked the governments of the Western democracies because they are "low-powered" and cannot do things quickly and efficiently? His political sympathies seem to lie with the Germany of Bismarck, and with Japan since the Meiji era. He says:

Foreign scholars, in studying the historical facts of democracy, have deduced many new theories. One of the newest has been proposed by a scholar who says that the greatest fear of modern democratic states is an all-powerful government, which the people have no way of checking, but yet the finest thing would be an all-powerful government in the employ of the people, and working for the welfare of all the people. This is a new theory. What is both feared and desired is an all-powerful government. First the theory declares that the people dread an all-powerful government which they cannot control, then it asks how an all-powerful government which will work for the welfare of the people can be secured, and how it can be made responsive to the will of the people. In many nations where democracy is developing, the governments are becoming powerless, while in the nations where democracy is weak, the governments are strong. As I said before, the strongest government in Europe within the past few decades was Bismarck's government in Germany. That was certainly an all-powerful government; it did not advocate democracy, for at first it opposed democracy, but yet it became all-powerful. Of the governments which have supported democracy, not one could be called all-powerful.

Dr. Sun worked out his ideal of an all-powerful government on two assumptions: first, the people are ignorant and must allow able men to run the government; secondly, the men who do run the government should have no limitations placed upon their power. Dr. Sun called his theory a distinction between sovereignty and ability. Sovereignty belongs to the people, but the running of the government is the function of the ablest citizens.

Dr. Sun's theory of the four powers, of the quintuple-power constitution, and of the distinction between sovereignty and ability, lay the foundation for the so-called May 5 Constitutional draft. This draft was made a subject of revision by the Constitutional Revision Committee of the Political Consultative Conference, which was called in 1946 after General Marshall's arrival. The function of the Committee was to draft a constitution to which all parties could agree, including a full parliament and a responsible cabinet under the system of Dr. Sun. This will be dealt with in a later chapter on the Communist-boycotted Constitution, in which the questions of plebiscite, parliament, and responsible cabinet, will again be discussed. What I want to say here is that Dr. Sun did not espouse dictatorship in his lectures, but that he did speak highly of the modern development of Germany and Japan. It is safe to say that Dr. Sun came perilously near to the idea of dictatorship. If he had lived long enough to see the achievement of the first Five-Year Plan he would have spoken of Russia in the same terms in which he spoke about Germany and Japan. It often happens to a revolutionary leader that as a young man he begins his career with the romanticism of a democrat; then, meeting difficulties and opposition, he comes to esteem discipline above other social virtues—as in the case of Lenin with his Bolsheviks. When he grows old and loses his patience and likes to get things done quickly, he becomes a dictator. This is what happened to Cromwell and Lenin: it would have been the same with Dr. Sun. The idea of an all-powerful government must have seemed attractive to him as early as 1922.

Dr. Sun's policy of collaboration between the Kuomintang and the Communists introduced the latter formally to the stage of Chinese politics. There was friction, however, from the very early days of that cooperation, and Dr. Sun gave timely warning on that score:

> If Communism is a good ally of the Min Sheng principle, why do members of the Kuomintang oppose the Communist party? The reason may be that the members of the Communist party themselves do not understand what Communism is, and have discoursed against the San Min Principles, thus arousing a reaction within the Kuomintang. But the blame for these ignorant and reckless Communists should not be charged to the whole Communist Party, or to the principles of the party.

The Communists began to play an important role in Chinese politics very largely as a result of Dr. Sun's support and encouragement. But he should have realised that as Communists they were dedicated Marxists, and would never give up their beliefs to work under the banner of the San Min principles. Dr. Sun hoped to infuse new blood into his own party by collaborating with the Communists, while they, on their part, willingly agreed, since from that time on, they were no longer outlawed, and their influence began to reach the people under the protection of the Kuomintang.

The political status thus granted the Communist party by Dr. Sun provided the foundation for their present success.

CHAPTER III

The Formation and Policies of the Chinese Communist Party

The conception of the Chinese Communist Party as a group of native agrarian reformers or Chinese nationalists is still fairly prevalent, and it is advisable to give an account of the growth of this party from the days of its inception until today. From the very beginning, the Chinese Communist Party was organised as a branch of the Third International, so that its policy was controlled by the latter's Executive Committee. Communist China and Soviet Russia also signed a Treaty of Friendship, Alliance, and Mutual Assistance in February, 1950, and pledged themselves to consult each other in regard to all important international problems affecting their common interests and their peace and security. These two facts show that, to say the least, the Chinese Communist Party can have little independence of Russian policy-makers. Nevertheless, it is best to attempt to trace its history in order to see how the Chinese Communist Party stands in relation to the Soviet Union.

This history can be divided into three periods: first, the period of revolt, from 1921 to 1935; second, the period of agitation for war and of growth in power during the Second World War; and third, the period of anti-American imperialism since the end of the Second World War.

(1) *The period of revolt from 1921 to 1935.* It was in 1921 that the Chinese Communist Party was organised. As the October Revolution had made a deep impression on the minds of many young Chinese, several missions were sent from China to Moscow to study the new Soviet system. Some of the reports brought back were favorable, while others held that the measures of the Bolsheviks were too radical.

A Marxist society was founded by Chen Tu-hsiu in the first instance to study the theories of Marx. In 1920, the Committee on Colonies, which was a part of the Third International, sent its emissary Voitinsky to China to contact the Chinese. Voitinsky proposed to

Chen Tu-hsiu that he organise a Chinese branch of the Comintern; as a result of this contact Chen Tu-hsiu went to Moscow. Chen thus became the first sponsor of the Chinese Communist Party. The first congress of the party took place at Shanghai in 1921 on July 1, and consisted of thirteen delegates, one of whom was Mao Tse-tung. This congress, under the direction of the Comintern representative Malin, passed three proposals which were brought to Dr. Sun Yat-sen: (a) That the Kuomintang be reorganised to take in more workmen and peasants; (b) that a cadet school be founded in order to train young men for armed revolution; and (c) that the Kuomintang should work together with the Communists. Dr. Sun Yat-sen agreed with these proposals in principle, but made no decision. In the meantime, some Chinese students studying in Paris had already formed a Communist group; among the members were Chou En-lai and Li Li-san. Upon the formation of the Chinese Communist Party, these students converted their group into a branch of the Chinese Communist Party in France.

At the second congress, which took place in July, 1922, at Hangchow, the subject discussed was the basic technical question of Chinese revolution. The significant resolution was that the proletariat should work together with the democratic forces in order that a democratic revolution could be achieved quickly. It was decided that members of the Communist Party should be allowed to join the Kuomintang as individuals. A manifesto also made the proposal that the Chinese Communist Party request earnestly that the revolutionary democratic groups, like the Kuomintang and other revolutionary socialist groups, hold a round-table conference with the object of forming a democratic front. About the same time, on January 12, 1923, the Comintern gave instructions that since the organized working class in China was still very weak, the Executive Committee should recognise the cooperation of the Communist Party with the Kuomintang as a necessity in the early period of the former's career; but it emphasised that the Communist Party should not merge with the Kuomintang.

After the joint statement of Dr. Sun and Adolph Joffe, made earlier in the year, and the agreement that the Chinese Communists could work openly in Canton, a third congress was called in June, 1923, in that city of South China, and passed three resolutions: That the Chinese Communist Party should take up the leadership of the Chinese revolution, but the superiority of the Kuomintang should be recognised because of its experience; that in accordance with the resolution passed at Hangchow the members of the Party could join the Kuomintang as individuals; and that, under the protection of the Kuomintang, it should carry on propaganda work among the workers and peasants. In December of the same year, the Central Committee of the Communist Party decided that the tactic of splitting the Kuomintang by cooperating with its left wing and isolating its right wing, should be resorted to.

In 1923, also, Michael Borodin came to Canton as head of a Soviet mission and acted as adviser to the Kuomintang. He insisted that there should be a definite body of party principles, unity of party organisation, and strict party discipline. From that time on began the reorganisation of the Kuomintang.

In 1924, the Chinese Communists received formal instructions to join the Kuomintang as individuals. When the members of the Executive Committee of the Kuomintang were voted for, one third of the votes went to the Communist members, Mao Tse-tung, Lin Tsu-han, Li Tai-chao, Chang Kuo-tao, Chu Chi-pai, Tan Ping-san, etc. This handful of Communists joined the Kuomintang, which had then had forty years of revolutionary experience. The Communists joined the government, and worked as commissars in the army and as leaders in the central and local party headquarters. They worked under the protection of the Kuomintang, and were recognized as a legitimate organization. Thus the Chinese Communists knew no such frustration in their attempts to build a powerful party as had been the experience of the German Communists or the Bolsheviks, both of which groups had undergone many trials and suffered many grave setbacks.

The fourth congress of the Communist Party was held at Shanghai in January, 1925, at which time it reported that the membership had been increased to 1500 and the number of delegates was more than seventy. The party carried on propaganda first among Chinese workers in the Japanese cotton mills, and a federation of the trade unions was formed.

On the Soviet side, in working out the plan for Kuomintang-Communist collaboration, a Communist University for the toilers of the Orient and the Sun Yat-sen University, with Karl Radek as its head, were founded; to both of these institutions thousands of Chinese young men were smuggled to receive training. The collected works of Marx, Engels, Lenin, and Stalin were translated into Chinese by the Chinese students, and millions of copies were printed and sent to China on the Siberian railway.

It was at this point that the Communists began to create incidents. When a Chinese workman was killed in a Japanese cotton mill, they ordered a student demonstration. The demonstration was dispersed by the gunfire of the Shanghai Settlement Police, and many were wounded and arrested. Li Li-san, the leader of the Trade Union in the present Chinese Communist government, called for a general strike of 200,000 workers. The shops in the Shanghai Settlement were closed as a protest against the Shanghai Municipality. The British, American, and Japanese Governments sent warships and marines to Shanghai to prevent demonstrations and strikes. The same happened in Canton and in Shaki, which was a British settlement. These incidents helped to make the Communists more popular in the eyes of young Chinese.

In January, 1926, the Second Congress of the Reorganised Kuomintang took place. One fourth of the places on the Executive Committee fell to the Communists. Tan-Ping-san was appointed Minister of the Department of Labor, Mao Tse-tung was Acting Minister of Propaganda, and Lin Tsu-han was Minister of the Department of Peasants. Up to this time, the Kuomintang and the Communists had been enjoying their honeymoon.

While the alliance between the Kuomintang and the Chinese Communists was still in force, in 1926, the Northern Expedition was undertaken in order to destroy the warlords and unify China; Chiang Kai-shek was named Commander-in-Chief. The expeditionary forces were so successful that they soon reached the Yangtse Valley, indicating that the Kuomintang had indeed been revitalised by its reorganisation.

When Chiang Kai-shek reached Shanghai, however, a rupture between the Kuomintang and the Communists occurred, because the fundamental difference in the political programs of the two parties, which had existed all along and even before their "marriage of convenience," now came to the fore. Chiang Kai-shek won the cooperation of the Chief of the Blue Gang, Tu Yueh-sen, in his project of disarming the Communists in Shanghai where they were just then making preparations to attack the Shanghai Settlement. Meanwhile, the left wing of the Kuomintang took possession of Wuchang and Hankow and declared itself independent of Chiang, who had decided to make a clean break with the Communists. In order to counteract this policy the Communists held their fifth congress on May 1, 1927, in Hankow, at which it was reported that the membership had been increased to 58,000. The question most widely discussed was how to settle accounts with the Kuomintang. It was then also that Chen Tu-hsiu, founder of the Communist Party, came in for vigorous criticism and attack. To counteract the purge of the Communists in Nanking, new slogans like those of land revolution and democratic dictatorship of the workers and peasants and the directives of the Comintern, were accepted. Among these directives were the following:

(1) Reorganisation of the Hankow government in order to strengthen the leadership of the Communists.

(2) Reorganisation of the headquarters of the Kuomintang and selection of active members of the Communist Party to work in it.

(3) Arming 20,000 members of the Communist Party.

(4) Selecting 50,000 active members among peasants and workers to work in the Kuomintang army in order to expel the reactionary officers and replace them by the Communist members of the left wing.

(5) Establishment of revolutionary courts to try the right wing and counter-revolutionary members. The revolutionary courts were to be under the control of the Chinese Communist Party.

(6) Enforcement of land revolution and confiscation of the property of the landlords and the gentry.

It is clear that the Chinese Communist Party did not want to withdraw from the Kuomintang and become a party in opposition. After the purge in Nanking, Wang Ching-wei came from Paris and issued a joint statement with Chen Tu-hsiu to the effect that cooperation between the Kuomintang and the Communists should be maintained, and that they were ready to send military forces to fight the Nanking counter-revolutionaries. However, owing to the leakage of the above mentioned Comintern instructions, Wang Ching-wei began to lose his confidence in the Chinese Communists. On July 15, the Wuhan Government carried out its purge, just as Nanking did. Borodin was expelled and sent to Soviet Russia, and the Chinese revolution was brought back to its nationalistic basis. Chen Tu-hsiu, having been denounced by Stalin as a right wing opportunist, was replaced by Lominadge, a friend of Stalin, who became Secretary General of the Chinese Communist Party. The Party did not stop its work after Borodin's expulsion. Then the Wuhan uprising followed, which has been described by Leon Trotsky in his book, *Problems of the Chinese Revolution.*

Something more may be said about the Stalin-Trotsky controversy with regard to their policy in China. Stalin and Bucharin at that time were on the same side, and their policy was based on the concept of the bloc of four classes, the scholars, farmers, artisans and traders, organized to accomplish a revolution in China. But Trotsky, joined by Zinoviev, warned the party that the Chinese Communists would be the victims of this policy. Stalin defended himself at the plenum of the Executive Committee of the Comintern on June 15, 1927:

> In Russia in 1905, if we had had a large revolutionary organisation of the type of the present left Kuomintang in China, it is possible that we would not have had Soviets. . . . What would have been the consequences of that? The consequences would have been that the left Kuomintang would play approximately the same role in the contemporaneous bourgeois democratic revolution in China that the Soviets played in the bourgeois democratic revolution of 1905.

The resolution adopted at the July, 1927 plenum of the Central Committee shows its uneasiness about the situation in China; yet, from the wording of the resolution, it is clear that the Chinese Communist Party was determined at that time to move in a more radical direction.

> While the Chinese Revolution, in spite of the correct tactics of the Comintern, has suffered a great defeat, this can be explained first and foremost by the correlation of the class forces within the country. . . . On the other hand, it is necessary to recognise that the leadership of the Chinese Communist Party, which systematically rejected the directives of the Communist International, bears its share of the responsibility.
>
> The present period of the Chinese Revolution is characterised by its severe defeats and simultaneously by a radical regrouping of forces, in which a block of workers, peasants, and urban poor, is being organised against all the ruling classes and against imperialism. In this sense the revolution is passing for a dictatorship of the working class and peasantry. The experience of the preceding development has clearly shown that the bourgeosie is incapable of carrying out the tasks of . . . the bourgeois democratic revolution.

A short time before this report, Stalin called Chiang Kai-shek a fine revolutionary fighter, and exchanged portraits with him. But after the Shanghai massacre of April, 1927, and the Changsha Uprising, the Kuomintang and the Communists definitely broke with each other.

After the break, the Chinese Communist Party showed more of its true character by going about the pursuit of power in a characteristic manner—by means of violence. The so-called uprising in Nanchang, supported by the military commanders, Ho Lung, Yeh Ting, and Chu Teh, the present Communist Commander-in-Chief, lasted only three days and was dispersed by the Nationalist Army. Simultaneously with the uprising, the Communist Central Committee, under the chairmanship of Lominadge, held its eighty-seventh meeting. Chen Tu-hsiu was attacked by Mao Tse-tung and Chu Chiu-pai as a right-wing opportunist, who did not have an independent policy for the Chinese Communist Party, but rather let it be a tail of the Kuomintang. From now on, the Chinese Communists announced their own program—land revolution, armed uprising, and the establishment of a soviet government. Chen Tu-hsiu was labelled a Trotskyist and expelled from the party.

After Nanchang, a series of uprisings occurred in Hunan, Haifung, Lukfung, and Canton. Many Communists lost their lives and the cities suffered looting. The Communist Party could not then hold its conference in China and, accordingly, they went to Moscow. Under the auspices of Bukharin, the mistakes inherent in a two-directional policy—the rightist tendencies of Chen Tu-hsui and the leftist tendencies inclination of Chu Chiu-pai—were hotly debated and exposed. Four resolutions were passed:

(1) Political resolution. It is agreed that the revolution of China is a bourgeois-democratic revolution; as the motive power of revolution belongs to the proletariat class and to the peasants, the mission of the party is to establish a soviet government by means of armed uprising and by overthrow of the Nationalist regime.

(2) Soviet Government. More propaganda work should be done to clarify the nature of soviet government. During the uprising, cells should be formed in order to be ready for the formation of a soviet government after victory.

(3) Land Question.

(a) Property and land of the landlords and the gentry should be confiscated without compensation and distributed by the peasants' soviet.

(b) Ancestor-temples, monasteries, churches, and public property should be disposed of by the peasants' soviet.
(c) Usury should be declared null and void.
(d) All contracts of tenancy and other forms of exploitation should be burnt.

(4) Peasants' Movement. During the period of opposition to the warlords and the landlords, all the farmers and peasants should come under a united front, but when the time arrives for distributing land, the poor peasants and tenants, coming with the middle-class peasants, should fight against the landlords and rich farmers.

These four resolutions are hailed by the historians of the Chinese Communist party as comprising a theoretically sound policy which overcame the mistakes of the right and left wings.

From 1928 to 1931, the Secretary-General of the Chinese Communist party was Hsiang Chung-fah, who was later executed by the Kuomintang. The real power, however, was in the hands of Li Lih-san, now a permanent member of the Political Bureau at Peking and concurrently Minister of Propaganda.

In 1920, when fighting between Chang Hsueh-liang and the Soviet Union was going on along the North Manchurian Railway, which was under Soviet management, Li Lih-san, forgetting his Chinese nationality, issued a proclamation announcing steps designed to "protect the Soviet Union" and calling upon the Chinese Communist Party to take the side of the U. S. S. R. This was the first example of the Chinese Communists supporting Russian interests in a conflict between the Soviet Union and China.

A year later, while Chang was fighting against dissident groups, Li Li-san again seized the opportunity to urge his party to stage a general strike with the aim of fomenting uprisings and forming a Soviet Government. This was the origin of the so-called Li Lih-san Route. The policy led to the closing of many factories and to widespread unemployment, without, however, achieving any political result commensurate with the dislocation and suffering it provoked.

Simultaneously, uprisings were started in Changsha and Nanchang, but these were crushed. Thus, it may be said that at this time the foundation which the Communists had built up during all the preceding years was practically destroyed. The Russian representative of the Comintern, Mif, who was in China at this time, expressed his dissatisfaction with the strategy of Li Lih-san. Li was ordered to go to Moscow, where he stayed for fifteen long years, returning to Manchuria only at the end of the Second World War. After Li had gone, Chen Shao-yu (alias Wang Ming) was appointed Secretary-General, and twenty-eight Chinese who had been educated in Moscow came back to work with him. Some of these are now occupying important positions in the government at Peking, as for example Wang Chia-chiang, the present Communist Ambassador in Moscow; Chang Wen-tien, designated delegate to the UN; Liu Shao-chi, the right-hand man of Mao Tse-tung; and Chen Yun, also a member of the government. They are often called quasi-Bolsheviks, because they are known to be especially well-versed in Marxist theory.

While the quasi-Bolsheviks gave orders for general strikes, Mao Tse-tung, after the failure of a peasants' revolt engineered by him, withdrew to the Tsin-Kan mountains to train his red army. With the cooperation of Chu Teh he organised his military force and called it the Fourth Red Army of Workers and Peasants.

Mao's principles of basic training were these:

When the enemy comes forward, I withdraw;
When the enemy withdraws, I go forward;
When the enemy settles down, I disturb him;
When the enemy is exhausted, I fight him.

These constitute the basic principles of his classic guerilla warfare. When the Tsin-Kan mountain stronghold was surrounded by the Nationalist army, the communist army tired to break through and carried mobile warfare along the boundary line of Kiangsi, Hupei, Fukien and Kuangtung. Finally they managed to hold the mountainous area of South Kiangsi as their base. In three campaigns of encirclement, the government failed to annihilate them. The first campaign was that of December, 1930, and the second and third campaigns, under the leadership of Ho Ying-ching, were carried out in February and July of 1931. As a result of the last campaign, Communist territory was much reduced, and the Reds withdrew to their capital, Jui-King, but the occupation of Mukden by the Japanese compelled the Nationalist Government to transfer part of its forces to North China. Another campaign followed between October, 1933, and January, 1934, and the tactic of ringing the Communist bases with fortresses and applying a blockade of food and salt was adopted by the government—a policy which caused untold hardship for the civilian population. The Communists decided to attempt a breakthrough under the leadership of Chu Teh, Mao Tse-tung, and Chou En-lai. Mrs. Chou En-lai later told me that her husband had suffered from typhus on the way, and was lucky in that the only remaining dose of serum saved his life.

During the Communist stay in South Kiangsi, they looked upon the policy of land reform as the most vital feature of their revolution, and they made it an indispensable part of their guerilla tactics. In 1930 and 1931, the Chinese Communists began in earnest to establish a new government in South Kiangsi. One of their first acts was the publication of land laws, which proved to be mutually contradictory. At any rate, land confiscation and land distribution to new owners went merrily on, while at the same time the manpower of the rural areas was drawn off for military service and a war levy imposed upon the population. The net result was the impoverishment and exhaustion of the rural areas to such an extent that no further mobilization was possible. This situation brought on the collapse of the Chinese Soviet Government.

(2) *The period of agitation for war and of growth in power during the Second World War.* With the rapid changes in the international situation and the threat offered by the Rome-Berlin-Tokyo Axis, the Communist International held its Seventh Congress in 1935. The congress was attended by delegates from all parts of the world, and it passed a resolution for the "Formation of an Anti-Fascist Popular Front" which aimed to give support to the isolated U.S.S.R., and a second one urging war against the Axis powers. Acting on the instructions of the Comintern, the Chinese Communist Party published its August declaration, which stated that the policy of class struggle should be revised and efforts directed towards a unification of all social forces in order to carry on a war against Japan. This implied a reconciliation with the landlords and the rich peasants, who were reckoned anti-Fascist forces for the purpose in hand.

The policy of forming an anti-Fascist popular front, and the denunciation of the Japanese attack on Manchuria from 1931 on and of the rapid extension of Japan's power in North China, enabled the Communists to win wide popular support for an anti-Japanese movement. But before this movement got under way, Chiang Kai-shek succeeded in dislodging the Communists from Kiangsi, though without managing to annihilate them. It was at this time (1934 and 1935) that the Communist armies carried out their "Long March" to

Northern China—an epic undertaking—and there they succeeded in entrenching themselves until they began their conquest of China.

The Communist anti-Japanese maneuver was meant to embarrass Chiang, who had been saying that his policy was to resist Japan, but that he was not willing to lead the country in a large-scale struggle until full military preparations had been made.

Meanwhile, the National Salvation Association was organised to promote a resistance movement against Japan. The members of this association were fellow travellers of the Communist party and its willing tools. Among the members of this association were Shen Chun-ju, who is now Chief Justice of the Supreme Court under the Mao Tse-tung regime, and Shih Liang, the Communist Portia, who is now Minister of Justice. The association made demands which were obviously meant to embarrass Chiang, and, as a kind of Communist-front organ, it enabled the Reds to enlarge their sphere of propaganda activities. Chiang's stubborn refusal to yield to the demands for war against Japan led to a strange and unique incident, his kidnapping in Sianfu in December 1936.

This act was the work of Chang Hsueh-liang, former overlord of Manchuria, who had been appointed Commander in the Northwest after Japan's invasion of his domain. In kidnapping Chiang Kai-shek, Chang Hsueh-liang was collaborating with the Communists, for they had convinced him of the futility of carrying on the anti-Communist campaign and of the need to start a full scale war against Japan in order to retrieve Manchuria. It appeared at first to be almost certain that Chiang's arrest would end in his execution.

At this point, Moscow interceded by sending agents to participate with the Communist Chou En-lai in negotiations which eventually led to Chiang's release, effected on the condition that Chiang would then lead China to war against Japan. Moscow's policy of saving Chiang's life was a brilliant move, for by sparing the leader around whom the Chinese people and government could rally, it enabled China to hold out, singlehandedly against Japanese armed forces for over four years, from 1937 to 1941. Thus, from the fact that Moscow had a hand in the release of Chiang, we may conclude that Russia was also behind the agitation for war against Japan. The defeat of Japan as a military power was the primary objective of Soviet foreign policy in the Far East, and all other Russian political moves in that area must be considered in that light. To attain that objective the Soviet Union was even prepared to save the life of Communism's worst enemy in China.

Although war against Japan was decided upon at the time of Chiang's release, six months elapsed before this policy was put into operation. The Marco Polo Bridge incident of July 7, 1937, inflamed all China against Japan, and at once the United Front against the foreign aggressor, consisting of the Kuomintang, the Communists, and the other parties, was formed. The Communist Party issued a proclamation, "United Front for the National Emergency," in which it pledged itself to suspend its policy of peasant revolt, and to stand as a patriotic party interested only in the defeat of the foreign invader and the recovery of Manchuria. The Communists promised also to abolish their land confiscation (or land revolution) policy, to cooperate under the banner of the Three Principles of Sun Yat-sen, and to incorporate the Communist forces into the national armies with Chiang Kai-shek as Commander-in-Chief. This United Front agreement, negotiations for which went on for a long time, masked deep divergencies of policy. According to Chiang Kai-shek, the Communist Party made four promises: to fight for the realisation of the Three Principles of the People; to discontinue the policy of violent insurrection and the forcible confiscation of land; to dissolve its Soviet pattern government in order to promote the unification of the country; and to discard the name and insignia of the Red Army and incorporate it into the National Revolutionary Army under the direction of the National Military Council. But the Communist side maintained that these four promises must be preceded by the recognition of three other points: the immediate establishment of a democratic form of government, the convocation of a National Assembly to draft and promulgate a constitution, and social and economic reforms aimed at insuring the people's welfare. The two points of view were never reconciled, even with the creation of the United Front, so that the interpretation of rights and duties on both sides became a matter for open controversy during the war period. War had broken out on August 13, 1937 but the announcement of the United Front was not made till September 22. When the meeting of the Advisory Council of National Defense was first held in Nanking, the Communist representatives, Mao Tse-tung and Chou En-lai, did not appear, though when the People's Political Council was convoked in Hankow the following year, the Communist Party did send members to attend. In the meantime, bargaining went on about the matter of incorporating the Communist army into Chiang's forces; negotiations centered on the question of the number of divisions affected and the provision of financial support. When incorporation was finally decided upon, the Communist army pursued an entirely independent course of action. It issued monthly communiqués with regard to the campaign against the Japanese in North China. It also formulated a plan for expanding its numbers and territory and for working with the peasants in North China in order to consolidate the Communist position against the threat of possible post-war attacks by Chiang Kai-shek. It is obvious that there was doubt and suspicion on both sides: as the Chinese proverb has it, "They lie in the same bed, but dream different dreams."

Concurrently with this uneasy decision of the Chinese Communists to fight on Chiang Kai-shek's side, Soviet Russia was making China gifts of munitions and rendering other services to her. During those dark years from 1937 to 1941, when China, though in retreat, was fighting desperately, alone and without benefit of adequate equipment, the assistance offered by the Soviet Union was greatly appreciated—though, as we look backward, it was merely intended to enable China to carry on a war of attrition against Japan in Russia's interests and to give the Chinese Communists a chance to develop their power. There is no denying that Moscow had clearly foreseen view of future developments. The Chinese Communists were gradually working themselves into an impregnable position. They had the advantage of being able to fight behind the Japanese lines and the immediate opportunity of capturing any territory evacuated by the Japanese army. From Northern China they could send their military forces into Manchuria and establish contact with Soviet Russia. The Long March from Kiangsi to Northern China, far from signifying the rout of the Red Army, actually gave it possession of more territory in Northern China than it had had in Kiangsi. Then came the years of war against Japan, which proved immensely profitable for the Chinese Communist Party. Before the war they had been considered outlaws and bandits. During the war their status was legalised; they were even regarded as patriots. In fact, they were so popular that many young men left Szechuan and Yunnan to join them. And they were no longer encircled, as they had been in Kiangsi. On the contrary, they had free access to large areas in Northern China. That they had grown tremendously in power was the gist of a report which Lin Tsu-han, a member of the People's Political Council, made on September 15, 1944.

The Long March left the Communists with only a few thousand men, but ten years later, in 1944, they already had an army of

475,000 men, with a people's militia of 2,200,000, and they had built some eighteen administrative units in Hopei, Shantung and Suiyuan.

Turning now to the question of the policy of the Chinese Communists towards the United States, this policy presented no real difficulty. Not long after Pearl Harbor, the United States and the Soviet Union became allies, as co-signatories of the Atlantic Charter. In order to dispel any unnecessary suspicion in the relations between these two countries, the Third International was dissolved in May of 1943. As the Soviet Union was working closely with the United States, there was no reason for the Chinese Communists to be unfriendly to the latter country. They conducted no propaganda against American imperialism and capitalism. They claimed to be democratic; and to some Americans their democracy appeared to be of the American variety. They accused Chiang of immobilising his army by setting it to watch the movements of the Communists instead of fighting against the Japanese. They complained of Chiang's dictatorship, which did not allow freedom of speech nor freedom of association. These charges against Chiang and his government were largely justified, and the Americans listened with sympathetic ears.

The United States was interested in seeing China remain united in order that she might carry on the war against the common enemy, and felt that by being sympathetic to complaints lodged by the Chinese Communists they would immeasurably enhance the fighting capacity of China. Towards this end, American representatives were sent to sound out the attitude of the Kremlin regarding the Communist question in China. The most important of these missions were those of Henry Wallace, then vice-President of the United States, and General Patrick Hurley, personal representative of President Roosevelt. At the time of these consultations, the Soviet Union was still engaged in a life and death struggle against Hitler. As her hands were already full, the Soviet Union was naturally glad to lay aside the China question for the time being. It was for this reason that Stalin made the momentous suggestion that the United States take over the leadership of the Far East. The Chinese Communists were "disowned" by Moscow, and it appeared that the United States was to have a free hand in solving the Kuomintang-Communist question. We know that both appearances were deceptive.

While the United States was still making a conservative estimate of the military strength of Japan early in 1945 and was expecting that greater sacrifice of life and materiel would be required to gain the final victory, the Soviet Union, although an ally of America, kept secret from her the peace overtures which Japan was then attempting to make through the Soviet Union. Unaware of this, the United States considered the Soviet Union the only nation which could help save possible American losses in the final drive on Japan. Therefore, at the Yalta Conference the United States conceded to the Soviet Union, at China's expense, rights no less important than those enjoyed by Tzarist Russia in Manchuria. A Sino-Soviet Treaty was to be signed legalising those concessions. This was the price that the United States asked China to pay for Russia's participation in the remaining phases of the war against Japan.

With the signing of the Yalta Agreement in February, 1945, and the Sino-Soviet Treaty in August of the same year, the Soviet Union at one stroke took back the leadership of the Far East which Stalin had all but surrendered to the United States. Russia also instantly took the place of Japan, to dislodge whom the United States had spent so much blood and treasure, and from whom China had tried to win back her lost territories in fourteen years of bitter war, sacrificing untold lives and spending an incalculable amount of money. The Soviet Government, it is true, promised its moral and economic support to the Nationalist Government, but what value was to be attached to a Soviet promise of this kind? The Soviet army prolonged its occupation of Manchuria and withdrew in the spring of 1946, only after having let the Chinese Communist forces occupy, within one month, no less than one hundred fifty districts in the country. This sizable bridgehead predetermined the course of later military events, as a result of which the whole of Manchuria was rid of Government forces.

With their rear protected and sustained by the Soviet Union, the Communist armies proceeded to stockpile the huge supplies of Japanese ammunition and equipment available in Manchuria, and, spurred on by the apparently ineluctable historical law that whoever controls Manchuria can control North China, began their systematic attacks on Government strongholds in the Northeast. Aside from the sea approaches, the Government army's line of communication was like a slender worm which could easily be cut into pieces and destroyed. The conquest of this area paved the way for the Communist domination all over China.

(3). *The period of anti-American imperialism.* This period will not be dealt with here, because the succeeding chapters will make clear how the Chinese Communist Party became hostile towards the United States.

Before closing this chapter, however, I should like to say a few words about the attitudes of outsiders to the Communist movement in China at this stage. The Chinese Communists, during the war period, gave the impression that they were fighting a patriotic war. There were many who seemed to be convinced that the new influence of nationalism was responsible for this change. This interpretation was not limited to the Chinese, but was also made by foreign observers. Mr. John P. Davies, Jr.* of the State Department, for instance, (*vide* the White Book) had this to say in his report of June 24, 1943:

> As the Chinese Communists moved away from the World Revolution to Nationalism, they also moved in the direction of more moderate internal political and economic policy. Whether these other moves were in compliance with Comintern dictates is less material than that they were historically and evolutionally sound.
>
> The trend towards Nationalism is believed to be strongest among the soldiers and guerillas who have been fighting the National enemy. Although we have no accurate information on the subject, it is suspected that the political leaders of their party retain their pro-Russian orientation, and that they are, notwithstanding the dissolution of the Comintern, likely to be susceptible to Moscow direction. This probable schism with the party may prove at some later date to be of major importance.

Another report from Mr. John Stewart Service,* also of the State Department, dated August 3, 1944, says:

> The Communists actively support the war because this gives them an opportunity to mobilise, organise and indoctrinate the people, and to create and train an efficient army.
>
> They operate by preference in the areas behind the Japanese lines, because there they are relatively free from Kuomintang interference.
>
> Such policies as the abandonment of Land Confiscation are used as temporary expedients to help them carry on the war and to win unified popular support in the areas of their operations. It also has strong propaganda appeal in other areas.
>
> Their espousal of democracy appeals to the great majority of the

---

* Though the loyalty of both Mr. Davies and Mr. Service has been reviewed by the United States government, their description of the general situation in China after Pearl Harbor remains substantially correct.

people of China and is a good club for beating the Kuomintang. They realise that popular support must be their principal weapon against the superior arms of the Kuomintang in any contest of strength.

Their democratic claims, their engagement in guerilla warfare behind the enemy lines, and their proclamation of liberal policies based on private property, are also used in appealing to foreign sympathy and in winning the foreign support which they realise will be necessary, at least for a time, in the economic rehabilitation and development of China following the war.

These observations seem to have been based on the policy statements and proclamations of the Chinese Communists, and they reflect much wishful thinking. The Communists are Marxists whose fundamental intellectual commitment is to the so-called materialist dialectic. Even if they change or dilute their policy for a time in order to adapt themselves to a changing situation, they will never abandon their long-range view of political and economic development in terms of Marxist ideology. In this connection, Mao Tse-tung's article, "New Democracy," which was published on January 15th, 1941, after the Japanese attack on Pearl Harbor, is a very frank and honest statement of his policy and belief.

Mao Tse-tung never moved away from the objective world revolution; he turned to nationalism only because of the war of resistance against Japan. Further, he fought this war in order to realise the aims of world revolution. In the fourth section of an article which he called "China's Revolution is a Part of the World Revolution," he said:

> The 1911 Revolution, in its social character, was a bourgeois-democratic revolution, and not a proletarian-socialist revolution. It is not yet consummated, and therefore needs our further effort, because the enemies of this revolution are still strong at present. The word "Revolution" in Dr. Sun's famous saying, "The revolution is not yet consummated, and our comrades must still exert their efforts," refers to the bourgeois-democratic revolution.
>
> A change took place in the Chinese bourgeois-democratic revolution after the outbreak of the first imperialist world war and the formation of the socialist state on one-sixth of the earth's surface through the success of the Russian October revolution in 1917.
>
> Before that, the Chinese bourgeois-democratic revolution belonged to the category of the old bourgeois-democratic revolution of the world, and was a part of it. Since then, the Chinese bourgeois-democratic revolution has changed its character and belongs to the

category of the new democratic revolution. As far as the revolutionary front is concerned it is a part of the world proletariat-socialist revolution. Why? Because the first imperialist world war and the victorious socialist October revolution changed the historical direction of the world and drew a sharp dividing line between two historical stages.

Mao went on to say:

The significance of China's revolution is greatly magnified today because it is happening at a time when the political and economic crises of capitalism have brought the world step by step towards the Second Imperialistic War; when the Soviet Union has reached the transitional period from Socialism to Communism and has the ability to lead and to assist the proletariat, the oppressed peoples and all the revolutionary peoples of the world; when the proletariat force of the various capitalist countries is growing stronger and stronger; and when the Communist party, the proletariat, the peasantry, the intelligentsia, and the petty bourgeoisie of China, under the leadership of the Chinese Communist party, have become a mighty independent political power. At such a time should we not estimate that the world significance of China's revolution has been greatly magnified? We should. China's revolution is a magnificent part of the World Revolution.

Before the signing of the Sino-Soviet Treaty of Friendship, Alliance, and Mutual Assistance, Mao Tse-tung stated clearly that China cannot be separated from the U. S. S. R., and he used the following words:

We cannot be separated from the Socialist state or from the aid of the International Proletariat, if we wish to seek for independence. That is to say, we cannot separate ourselves from the assistance of the Soviet Union or from the victory of the anti-capitalist struggles of the proletariat of Japan, Great Britain, the United States, France, and Germany. Their victories help us, although we cannot say that victory in China must be preceded by the success of the revolutions of the above countries, but at least with regard to one or two of the above countries, it is true that we can win our victories only with their assistance. This is especially true of the aid of the Soviet Union, an indispensable condition for the final victory of China's war of resistance. To refuse Soviet aid will surely bring about the failure of the revolution. Is this not clear in the lesson of China's anti-Soviet movement after 1927? Is it not a dream to expect that China can establish a bourgeois society, led by her own bourgeoisie in a period when the world is in the midst of war and revolution and when socialism is destined to prosper?

If anyone thinks that the Chinese Communist has changed his views during the war period to espouse the principles of democracy, Mao's utterances should undeceive him. They reveal so well the true character of the present Communist regime in China and have so important a bearing on the present world situation that I should like to quote them more extensively. Here is Mao's view of democracy in China:

No matter how we may regard it, the proletariat, the peasants, the intelligentsia and other petty bourgeoisie elements in China are the basic forces that determine the destiny of the country. . . . The Democratic Republic of China which we are aiming to construct now can only be ruled by an alliance of all anti-imperialist and anti-feudal forces. It is a Republic of New Democracy, or a republic of the genuine revolutionary San Min Chu I, that included Dr. Sun's three revolutionary policies.

Mao Tse-tung divides governments according to their social character, into three forms: (1) republics ruled by the bourgeoisie; (2) republics ruled by the proletariat; and (3) republics jointly ruled by several revolutionary classes. He believes that the second form is only realised in the Soviet Union, though it is the final aim toward which all capitalist countries must evolve. He believes that it is better for China not to adopt the Soviet pattern, but to follow the third form.

Accordingly he proposed the following organisation for the government of China, from the central government down to the villages:

As to the question of governmental policy, this denoted the form under which a governmental power is constituted, or the form which certain social classes adopt in organising their government for opposing the enemy and for self-defense. Without an adequate form of government a country cannot be represented. In China, we can adopt the system of people's congresses of various grades, from the National Congress down to the village Assembly, through which governments of various grades are elected, but a system of genuine universal election, disregarding differences in sex, beliefs, amount of property, and standard of education in the suffrage, must be practiced, so that it will be fit for the proper status of the various classes in the country, for the expressions of peoples' opinions, for the direction of revolutionary struggles, and for the spirit of the New Democracy. Such a system is the system of Democratic Centralisation. Only with a government based on such a system can we thoroughly develop the ideas and spirit of all the revolutionary people and oppose the enemy of revolution with great strength. The spirit of not permitting a minority to monopolize power must be shown in the army as well as in the government, and such an aim can never be realised without a genuine democratic system. Its absence can be called inconsistency between the national policy and the governmental policy. A national policy of the joint rule of several revolutionary classes plus a governmental policy of democratic centralisation–this is the politics of New Democracy, the Republic of New Democracy, the Republic of a United Front, the Republic of the new San Min Chu I that includes Dr. Sun's Three Revolutionary Policies, and the Chinese Republic true in name and reality.

Although Mao Tse-tung says that the Soviet pattern of rule by the proletariat cannot be applied to China, yet he wants to see China adopt the system of People's Congresses of various grades. Is not this the Soviet system? The most fundamental difference between the Soviet system and Western Democracy is that there is no responsible government and no separation of powers in the Soviet Union. This system of no accountability to parliament and no separation of powers is called, in the U. S. S. R., Democratic Centralism. But how can a government be called democratic if it centralises every kind of power in its own hands and need fear no organized opposition? The phrase, "not permitting a minority to monopolise power," sounds fine, but it means nothing else than the elimination of the capitalist class, the intelligentsia, and other possible sources of political opposition.

The Communist government now in existence in Peking is organised on the basis of Mao Tse-tung's frank statement. It is called a Democratic Dictatorship. It is supposed to stand for joint rule by different classes and different parties. How far is it democratic? How far is it a joint enterprise? Doubtless, the leaders of the different parties who are participating in the government can offer a better and more adequate answer than I can. I wish they were in a position to speak out.

CHAPTER IV

Chiang Kai-shek's Achievement and Failure

The part which Chiang Kai-shek has played in the history of modern China will be a subject of heated controversy for a long time. As successor to Sun Yat-sen he enjoyed the unique distinction of being able to bring China under his unified control. In twenty years he lost everything which he had won, as a result of corruption and incompetence in his government. What was the reason for his success? And what was the reason for his failure? These are two immensely interesting questions which I shall attempt to answer in this chapter.

His achievements as leader of the Northern Expedition and the War of Resistance against Japan have given him a significant position in the history of China; yet, in a few short years he was defeated by the Communists and withdrew to Formosa, where he survives on the strength of foreign assistance. It is not for me to review in detail his military campaigns. What I am interested in is his character and personality, which determined to so great a degree the course of events in his own life and in the life of China.

First, let us consider the major events of Chiang's career from 1924 to 1930:

1924 Chiang is appointed head of the Whampoa Academy by Sun Yat-sen.

1926 Leads the Northern Expedition in July.

1927 Occupies Nanking in March.
His army reaches Shanghai in April.
Chiang retires as Commander-in-Chief in August.
Marries Soong Mei-ling, sister of the wife of Sun Yat-sen, in December.

1928 In April Chiang is recalled from private life to continue the Northern campaign.
In May his troops came into conflict with Japanese forces which try to prevent him from marching northward.

In June, Chiang occupies Peking.

In November, after Chang Tso-lin's assassination by the Japanese, Chang Hsueh-liang succeeds him as Governor of the Northeastern Provinces. By recognising the authority of Nanking, China becomes completely unified under Chiang.

1929 Fighting takes place between Chiang and the Kuangsi faction, whose headquarters is in Hankow.

1930 Yen Hsi-shan and Fen Yu-hsiang fight against Chiang.

In each of these campaigns, Chiang was successful; it was perfectly just that Stalin should call him a fine fighter. I myself came to hear of a story which illustrates Chiang's personal courage. In 1926, when Chiang was attacking Nanchang, capital of Kiangsi, during the time of the Northern Expedition, it happened that I went to Hankow, which was then already in the hands of the Nationalist army. The purpose of my trip was to study the state of Kuomintang-Communist collaboration. On the first day of the establishment of the provincial party headquarters in Hankow, there was a rally at which the left-wing leaders and some Russians made speeches. Kuo Mo-jo, the present Communist spokesman for the World Peace Council Meetings in Paris, Prague, Korea, etc. was one of the speakers. The speeches were chiefly denunciations of the bourgeois attitude of the right-wing elements of the Kuomintang. I realised that a split among the Kuomintang was bound to come. On my way back, passing through Kiukiang, I stayed there for a few days and bought some Kiangsi porcelain. Sung Chuan-fang, then Governor of the five provinces of Kiangsu, Chekiang, Kiangsi, Fukien, and Anhwei, was on a boat anchored in the middle of the Yangtse river in order to direct the movements of his own personal army against Chiang. I went on board, and discussed the military situation with Sung Chuan-fang. He felt very optimistic because he had just received information that Chiang, the Commander-in-Chief of the Northern Expeditionary Force of the Nationalist Army, had been killed outside the wall of the city of Nanchang. The news, of course, was untrue. But it was soon learned that Chiang had actually been in the fighting himself and had led about a hundred men to scale the city wall. Many of his men were killed in the attempt, but Chiang survived. This is an example of Chiang's personal valor; he would risk his own life and be at the forefront of the fighting the better to lead his soldiers. It was the same in many other campaigns. In his fight against Yen Hsi-shan and

Feng Yu-hsiang, Chiang was nearly outflanked and captured. But his determined advance forced Yen's army to retreat and saved his own life.

Chiang is also an expert in bribing the subordinates of his opponents. By promising money or position to the right-hand men under Li Tsung-jen, Yen Hsi-shan, and Feng Yu-hsiang, he induced them to betray their own leaders and surrender to him. In dealing with Chang Hsueh-liang, Chiang traded on the fact that the warlord of the Northeastern provinces was fond of gambling; he provided each of his emissaries with a checkbook, and instructed them all to play mah-jong with Chang. After gambling with him for many months, they won Chang to the Nationalist side without sacrificing a single soldier.

And Chiang is a man who is sustained by a classical horror of humiliation. In the Tsinan incident of May 3, 1928, the advance of the Nationalist army to Peking was blocked by the Japanese army and it took many months before the obstacle was removed. One of the things which Chiang said to his officers and soldiers at the time was this:

> In order to avenge our country's humiliation, you must free China from Imperialist oppression and must obtain the objectives of independence and liberty. Today you can only endure insults and prepare yourself for vengeance. It will take ten years to train the population in the firm belief of our forefathers that the lost territories can and must be recovered, and the national humiliation avenged. If you can do this it will not be difficult to attain liberty, equality, and harmony throughout the land.

His spirit of revenge can best be illustrated by his gambling. People who knew him well have told me that Chiang, as a young man, when he lost at poker or mah-jong, would insist on continuing the game and refuse to leave the table till he had at least recovered what he had lost. There is no doubt that Chiang is a man of determination with regard to both great things and small.

In the matter of the split between the Kuomintang and the Communists, Chiang has been accused of double-dealing and treachery. But from the very beginning the collaboration between the two groups was, as Fairbank has said, a marriage of convenience. The Kuomintang worked with the Communists in order to get Russian assistance. The Communists promised loyalty to the Nationalists because they needed Kuomintang protection for their own schemes. Both sides must share equally in the blame for the final split. The Kuomintang never agreed to the Communist theory of class-struggle and social revolution, and the Shanghai massacre of April, 1927, was purely a maneuver for power on the part of Chiang. It is difficult to decide the question of honesty or dishonesty when the behavior of individuals is involved, but in the case of a split between two parties, it is just about impossible to say which side is honest and which dishonest. Personally, I do not see an iota of honesty in the Communist policy of infiltration in China by working together with the Kuomintang.

In the few years between 1926 and 1930, Chiang made a number of enemies within his own party and among the Chinese Communists, the Kuangsi faction, the Yen Hsi-shan and Feng Yu-shiang factions, and among the generals of Kuangtung. Once they were defeated, he merely pushed them aside. In many cases he later reappointed them to some government posts, though he would never allow them to have a hand in his own army. Li Tsung-jen fought against him twice, once in Hankow and once with Chen Chi-tang, the Governor of Kuangtung, because against Chiang's wishes both of them wanted a declaration of war against Japan in 1935. Yet later Chen was appointed Minister of Agriculture and Li commander of a war zone of considerable military importance.

It was at this time also that a good deal of controversy arose within the party on the question of political tutelage. As part of the plan made by Dr. Sun it sounded well enough, but it was difficult to put it into practice without danger of evolving toward totalitarianism. As generally understood, the purpose of tutelage was to train the people in the practice of running a democratic government. But how was this to be done? How long should tutelage last? Chiang himself threw some light on this matter in his book *China's Destiny*:

According to the steps outlined in "The Plans for National Reconstruction" the period of tutelage follows the military stage, and the chief task is to introduce self-government. The criterion for the practice of self-government is based on the Regulations for the Practice of Local Self-government drawn up by Sun Yat-sen. Constitutional government depends upon the result of the practice of local self-government. The steps in this program are clear and logical and provide no grounds for controversy.

But for years after the removal of the capital to Nanking circumstances hindered progress in the basic task of political tutelage, from both the practical and the theoretical side, the question of how to carry out the work of political tutelage became a controversial issue and the question of how long this period of political tutelage should be continued was also hotly debated. Such dissension not only provided the feudalists and counter-revolutionists with pretexts for opposing the government, but also gave comrades within the party the appearance of wavering, with the result that arguments became more numerous, and there was no unity of action. We all know that political tutelage is the path that must be followed to attain democracy, without which the people's rights cannot be protected, and that otherwise the constitution to be framed in the future can only be a worthless piece of paper.

Here is a question of life or death for the Kuomintang and Chiang Kai-shek. If the aim of the Kuomintang members was democracy, they should have had confidence in the people and ruled in accordance with the general principles of a constitutional government based upon the sovereignty of the people. After the end of the Northern Expedition, which was the end of the military stage, they should have started introducing the constitutional stage immediately, following the schedule laid down by Dr. Sun—military government, tutelage, constitutional government. But Chiang is a soldier; his view was that the intermediate stage should be prolonged as much as possible. The other Kuomintang leaders saw the situation differently; men like Wang Ching-wei and Hu Han-min had their own interpretation of Dr. Sun's plan. They had been just as close to Dr. Sun as Chiang Kai-shek, if not closer, and they thought that they knew Sun's mind better, a claim which was not in fact extravagant. Political tutelage implies the training of the people for constitutional government. If this is accepted, then the practice of parliamentary rule and its attendant privileges and responsibilities, should have been introduced forthwith. These institutions are as essential in the cultivation of democratic virtues as is the swimming pool for one who is to be trained as a swimmer. So long as there are merely lectures on swimming for the swimming class, and no swimming pool, how can the student learn to swim? The Kuomintang, in the first ten years of its existence under the direction of Chiang Kai-shek, never allowed or legalised the existence of opposition parties. For my part, I do not see how an opposition party can get its necessary training except under a constitutional government which granted it equal rights with the party in power.

The people of China waited for twenty long years before the first election of the legislative assembly finally took place in 1947. Since the people never had any experience of elections during all these years, how could they be expected to vote intelligently when the election actually took place? The result was that the Kuomintang, still under the name of tutelage, kept the political power for itself alone. They talked much about local self-government, because, under the cover of local government, they could increase the number of their party members, whom they expected to appoint to all the offices in the villages; it was their aim to accomplish this and then announce that the stage of constitutional government could begin. This was Chiang's interpretation of political tutelage, and here lay the roots of internal conflict later experienced by the Kuomintang. So long as there was no constitutional government, those who controlled Kuomintang policy with regard to military, financial, and diplomatic policy, would appear to the elements not in power, and even to Kuomintang members, as arbitrary and dictatorial. Chiang, as the leader of the ruling group, held the reins of the party and government and grew in personal power. Since Chiang's power grew in this manner, it is no wonder that provincial governors like Li Tsung-jen, Pai Chung-hsi, Feng Yu-hsiang, and Yen Hsi-shan, rebelled against him. Chiang was a dictator in the eyes of these men, and when they opposed him he called them feudal-minded counter-revolutionists who were trying to overthrow the established government.

So long as there was no constitutional government, there was no parliament, no responsible cabinet, no freedom of the press and no freedom of association. Naturally opposition to Chiang's regime grew, and the Chinese Communists contributed to it, even though their own government was organised on a completely dictatorial basis. The democratic parties which really fought for democracy were then willy-nilly maneuvered into a position in which they had to side with the Communists against the government, when they could have given all their support to the government. It is a pity that Chiang lost the sympathy of large sections of the Chinese people by stubbornly refusing to give up his authoritarian government. This situation inevitably bred corruption and incompetence in the government, and when it was charged with these vices by people both within the country and abroad, there was nothing to say in its defense.

Even as late as the time when Chiang wrote *China's Destiny,* where he said, "We know that tutelage is the path that must be followed," he still firmly believed in his authoritarian views. By that time a good deal of damage had already been done. But Chiang seemed to be indifferent to or unaware of the evils of tutelage. Truly, as Lord Acton said, "Power corrupts and absolute power corrupts absolutely."

Chiang Kai-shek may have thought that he was dealing cleverly with his internal enemies, but he should have realised that so long as the opposition had just grievances and the people refused to support him, he would find it difficult to tackle the two major international issues which came to a head between 1931 and 1937. One was the question of Japan, and the other that of the Soviet Union's active support of the Chinese Communists. Chiang was sandwiched between these two enemies. The Japanese continued to take Chinese territory. First they seized Mukden and the other cities in Manchuria after having expelled the Chinese forces. In the next year they established "Manchukuo," which declared its independence from China. In 1933, Japan invaded Jehol and created a demilitarised zone in Eastern Hopei. In 1935 Japan went further and tried to create an autonomous North China.

Chiang was then called a traitor because he did not declare war against Japan. In the meantime the Chinese Communists got ahead of him and launched an anti-Japanese campaign in 1935. If Chiang fought against Japan, as the Communists demanded, he was afraid that the Communists would fish in troubled waters and extend their influence at his expense—which in fact they did from 1937 till the Japanese surrender. Chiang declared many times that he was preparing for war, but still made no decisive move—a policy which was in a sense justified because he knew that he was not fully prepared for a full-scale struggle with Japan. In the eyes of the Chinese Communists, Stalin was justified in signing a Mutual Non-Aggression Pact with Nazi Germany, but when Chiang Kai-shek wanted to wait one or two years in order to insure military preparedness before taking on Japan, they called him a traitor. Stalin could sign an agreement for the partitioning of Poland, but Chiang Kai-shek was not granted more time to prepare for a war of self-preservation. Chiang became increasingly embarrassed by the Communist-launched anti-Japanese campaign. But he kept quiet and bore the humiliation stoically even during the period of his kidnapping in Sianfu. It was not until a year and a half later when the Marco Polo Bridge incident occurred, that he decided to declare war against Japan. Before making this momentous decision, Chiang had his bosom friend Huang Fu, then President of the Peiping Political Council, make overtures of appeasement to Japan. General Ho Ying-chin signed the Ho-Uemetsu agreement in order to gain time. With the Communists at home, Chiang negotiated on the conditions under which they would fight on his side, at the same time holding conferences with the representatives of the democratic parties and the non-party leaders in Kuling. Not until he was quite sure of the formation of a United Front was the war against Japan started on August 13, 1937. After the outbreak of war there was a period of quietness for Chiang, because the die was cast, and all that remained was the prosecution of the struggle. When Northern China, Shanghai, and Nanking were lost to the Japanese, nobody complained, because the defeat of the Chinese army had been expected by everyone. The flower of the Chinese armies, whether they belonged to Chiang or Kuangsi, Kuangtung or Szechuan, sacrificed themselves with a clear conscience for the defense of their country. From Shanghai, the Chinese Army retreated to Soochow and Nanking. The blockade of the Yangtse Valley was unable to keep the Japanese from coming up to Hankow, whither the Central Government had been moved at this time. The German Ambassador Trautmann worked as a mediator and transmitted three peace conditions from the Japanese Government. If Chiang were a genuine Fascist, and desired to play such a role on the international stage, he could have agreed to an anti-Communist pact with Japan and Germany. The fact that he had no hesitation in turning down the Japanese conditions showed that he had little in common with the mentality of the Axis powers. In pursuing this policy, Chiang showed that he had little in common too with an opportunist like Stalin, who did not hesitate to sign the Mutual Non-Aggression Pact with Ribbentrop or the Pact of Neutrality with Japan. Chiang simply kept on fighting the Japanese, without worrying much about the consequences to himself, and at that stage of his career the hearts of four hundred and fifty million people were solidly behind him. When Wang Ching-wei, after his escape from Chungking, set up a rival government in Nanking, Chiang remained unperturbed. He knew the episode, taken from Chinese history, of a man who fought bravely against an enemy and who later died through treachery. The martyr Yueh Fei was not only a national hero, but was also considered a saint. Chiang must have had the image of Yueh Fei in mind when he pitted himself against the Japanese, with all the disadvantages on his side. And how the nation rallied round him, as he fought singlehanded, without any foreign assistance! With his stern will and self-discipline to provide the example, the people willingly and joyfully bore enormous sacrifices without so much as a whimper. All this is to the eternal credit of Chiang Kai-shek, and no Chinese would deny that in those days he was at the pinnacle of his prestige as a leader and patriot.

But somehow, after the Pearl Harbor incident, morale began to sag, and the weakness of the Nationalist Government was mercilessly exposed. During the war years, the coast provinces came under the Japanese occupation, and the main sources of Chinese revenue were lost. The deficit in the budget was made good by issuing banknotes to an extent that produced inflation on an astronomical scale. Food supplies had to be requisitioned from the landlords and peasants of the southwestern area of China, comprising the provinces of Szechuan, Yunnan, and Kweichow, for the army of three million men, and the burden on the people became unbearably heavy. As the value of the *yuan* notes went down every day, everyone, and most especially the men in the civil service and the intellectual classes, had to bear untold suffering. The financial administration had been in the hands of H. H. Kung for many years, and it was forbidden to criticize him or his policies. Chiang himself believed that the Chinese economy could never collapse because it was a rural economy. When the People's Political Council asked for a discussion of the subject, the request was rejected. Instead, in order to stop the inflation, the government resorted to selling gold. But the measure did not do much good, because the exchange rate for gold was manipulated by H. H. Kung and his friends in the banking business to their own advantage. The situation was accurately and fairly summarized in the report of John Service to the State Department, dated June 29, 1944, which was reproduced in the White Book:

China faces economic collapse. This is causing disintegration of the army and the Government's administrative apparatus. It is one of the chief causes of growing political unrest. The Generalissimo is losing the support of China, which, by unity in the face of violent aggression, found a new and unexpected strength during the first two years of the war with Japan. Internal weaknesses are becoming accentuated, and there is taking place a reversal of the process of unification.

1. Morale is low and discouragement widespread. There is a general feeling of hopelessness.
2. The authority of the Central Government is weakening in the areas away from the larger cities. Government mandates and measures of control cannot be enforced, and remain ineffective. It is becoming difficult for the Government to collect enough food for its huge army and bureaucracy.

3. The Governmental and military structure is being permeated and demoralized from top to bottom by corruption, unprecedented in scale and openness.

4. The intellectual and salaried classes, who have suffered most heavily from the inflation, are in danger of liquidation. The academic group suffer not only the attrition and demoralization of economic stress; the eight years of political control and repression is robbing them of the intellectual vigor and leadership they once had.

5. Peasant resentment of the abuses of conscription, tax collection, and other arbitrary impositions has been widespread and is growing. The danger is ever increasing that sporadic outbreaks of banditry and agrarian unrest may increase in scale and find political motivation. The provincial groups are making common cause with one another and with other dissident groups, and are actively consolidating their positions. Their continuing strength in the face of growing weakness of the Central Government is forcing new measures of political appeasement in their favor.

6. Unrest within the Kuomintang armies is increasing, as shown in one important instance in the "Young General" conspiracy late in 1943. On a high plane, the War Zone Commanders are building up their own spheres of influence, and are thus creating a new warlordism.

8. The break between the Kuomintang and the Communists not only shows no sign of being closed, but grows more critical with the passage of time; the inevitability of civil war is now generally accepted.

9. The Kuomintang is losing the respect and support of the people by its selfish policies and its refusal to heed progressive criticism. It seems unable to revivify itself with fresh blood, and its unchanging leadership shows a growing ossification and loss of a sense of reality. To combat the dissensions and schisms within the party, which grows more rather than less acute, the leadership is turning towards the reactionary and unpopular Chen Brothers clique.

10. The Generalissimo shows a similar loss of realistic flexibility and a hardening of narrowly conservative views. His growing megalomania and his unfortunate attempts to be sage as well as leader—shown, for instance, by *China's Destiny* and his book on economics—have forfeited the respect of many intel-

> lectuals who enjoy in China a position of unique influence. Criticism of his dictatorship is becoming outspoken. In the face of the grave crisis with which it is confronted the Kuomintang is ceasing to be the unifying and progressive force in Chinese society, the role in which it made its greatest contribution to modern China.

I do not think that the most fervent supporters of Chiang Kai-shek can take exception to this able analysis of the pathological political condition of China during this period. Although Mr. Service's report was written in 1942, the beginning of this condition can be traced back to 1940 and it remained unchanged till the time of Chiang's total defeat in 1948 and 1949. The only difference was that the scale of corruption, disaffection, and popular discontent was much more extensive in the post-war period.

What was the reason for this deterioration and collapse? The question has often been asked, and will no doubt continue to be asked by future historians. My own answer can be summarized in one little word—"tutelage": it is as simple as that. Tutelage meant in practice the desire of the Kuomintang's followers to perpetuate the conditions which placed political power in their own hands. They merely gave lip-service to constitutionalism as a sop to Dr. Sun's followers and to show that his teaching was not forgotten. Since there was no constitution, no parliament, and no responsible cabinet, all questions of defense, finance, and diplomacy were decided by the party. The people had no right to question the party. While the war was going on, Chiang Kai-shek was elected Tsung-Tsai, or Director-General of the Party, and his power became unlimited. Any expenditure which was approved by him was legally valid. He issued orders by means of notes in his own handwriting. In Chungking, Chiang's government was openly called "the note-writing government," and the system naturally led the way to a whole crop of abuses. Any minister who was in Chiang's favor—and this was especially true of Chen Li-fu—could go to his office and get a large sum approved for expenditure. Those ministers who were not close to him had to suffer. Tutelage, in the end, was not even rule by the party as a whole but degenerated to rule by personal whim. Chiang is a man who has confidence only in his relatives, in his brothers-in-law H. H. Kung and T. V. Soong and their subordinates, in the Chen Brothers, and in Chen Cheng, the present Prime Minister of Formosa. Though there was a People's Political Council which was supposed to serve as an open forum for discussion, yet when there was any question raised about the military or financial condition of the country, it was shouted down by the Kuomintang members, who preserved their majority by unconstitutional means. The opinions of the liberals and the opposition parties never had a chance to be heard.

It is natural enough that the absolute power of the Kuomintang led to abuses and rampant corruption. The Kuomintang has never had a record of sponsoring efficient government. As early as 1927, one year after the establishment of the Nanking Government, when Chiang Kai-shek was forced to retire and Sun-Fo, the son of Dr. Sun Yat-sen, was appointed President of the Executive Yuan, Wang Han-liang was appointed Minister of Finance. On arriving at the Ministry to assume his functions, Wang found no documents left in it, all the archives having been removed by the staff of T. V. Soong in order to embarrass Wang. It is also known that when, on the recommendation of the British adviser Reith-Ross, China changed over from the silver standard to a managed currency, all the top-ranking men in the government made great fortunes out of it. It never occurred to them that using information derived from the performance of official duties in order to amass personal fortunes is criminal. All the important members of the Kuomintang indulged in this practice without any compunction whatever.

The case of the Shanghai Stock Exchange, in which Mrs. H. H. Kung was involved in the buying and selling of cotton yarn, was once brought to the notice of Chiang Kai-shek. Wu Ting-chang, then Minister of Industry, was sent to Shanghai by order of the Generalissimo to make an inquiry. Wu brought all the documents back showing how Mrs. Kung was involved in the stock-market operations. Everyone expected that the Generalissimo would bring the case before the courts, the only proper thing to do, and show thereby that he had some respect for the laws of the land. But what actually happened? Wu Ting-chang was dismissed from the Cabinet and then appointed Governor of the distant province of Kueichow. Again, the gold-selling policy gave the influential families connected with the government a chance to amass immense fortunes. There is absolute justice in the criticism of Mr. Service that the government and military structure was being permeated and demoralized from top to bottom by corruption, which was winked at and perhaps even deliberately encouraged by Chiang, who allowed his relatives and subordinates to carry on private business while serving as ministers or generals in the civil and military services.

Another case was that of Lin Shih-liang. Lin was operating the Southwest Transport Company, which was chartered to bring in Lend-Lease goods from Rangoon to Chungking. The Company was a part of the Central Trust, which was under the control of the Central Reserve Bank, headed by H. H. Kung. It was discovered by Chiang's special-service men that the trucks of the Southwest Transport Company were transporting a great number of carloads of consumer's goods. Lin Shih-liang was arrested in a club where the special-service men gambled with him. An inquiry was held by the Government to find out whether the malfeasance was Lin's personal crime or if the whole Kung family was involved. The case dragged on for many months, and sentence was delayed as a result of Kung's influence and pressure. Finally, in order to exonerate the Kung family, Lin was made the scapegoat and executed. These are just a few examples of the hundreds of cases of corruption that arose in connection with the administration of government. Because there was no parliament, no official media of publicity, no check, and no accountability on the part of ministers, nothing could be done to stop the abuses. If someone had the courage to write an article in the newspapers about these cases of corruption, he was regarded as one who wilfully tried to undermine public confidence in the government, and he courted great personal danger. Is it not obvious that in this species of political tutelage lie the roots of demoralization and corruption of the government and the army?

Let me now give a personal estimate of the character of Chiang Kai-shek. For three or four years during the war, luncheon parties took place every Friday in Chiang's residence in Chungking, parties which were arranged by Wang Shih-chieh, the present Secretary-General. At the luncheon, a number of reports on foreign affairs were made by the councillors of the President's office. Guests were also invited. After the reports were made, the Generalissmo would ask the guests to express their views. I was frequently present as one of the guests, and so I had excellent opportunity to observe Chiang's conduct at close quarters.

From what I noticed myself and from other information, I know that Chiang was an early riser, hard-working, and very punctual. The first thing he did every morning was to write his diary. Next he prayed, for he is a Christian. After prayers, he read all the important documents, some official and some handed in by his special-service men. Then he read two newspapers every morning, *The Central Daily News* and the *Ta Kung Pao*. About ten o'clock he went to the National Military Council to hear the reports on the military situation. At luncheon, some guests from the provinces, the war zones, or from some foreign countries would be invited. The luncheon consisted of only four or five dishes; he lived a life of frugality and austerity. In the afternoon he would have a nap, and at tea-time he made appointments again. During the war he was kept very busy with his corps-training, which he personally supervised. The governors and commissioners of the different provinces and the high-ranking officers of army divisions and regiments were ordered to come to Chungking for indoctrination. They lived in barracks and attended classes like students. Chiang Kai-shek went to the Headquarters of the Training Corps at least twice every week. It was his hope to train a group of faithful party-members. Who would have believed that many officers and civilians belonging to this corps would go over to the Chinese Communists later?

Chiang is an emotional man; he is not cool and level-headed. If a report came to him saying that someone had tried to organise opposition against him, he would become very irritated, without first ascertaining whether the report were true. My own experience will illustrate this point. When I left Talifu to attend the People's Political Council meeting at Chungking, I stayed with my brother Chang Kia-ngau, who was then Minister of Communications. During a Cabinet meeting one day, Chiang showed him a telegram saying that the student demonstration, then going on in Kunming, was taking place at my instigation. I told my brother that I knew nothing about it, but that I would write to my political friends in Kunming to make an inquiry. Next day, my brother went to Chiang to transmit to him what I had said, whereupon Chiang jumped to the conclusion that "it must have been started by his political friends." Since at that time Lo Lung-chi, now with the Communist Government, was supposed to be my agent in Kunming, a letter of inquiry was sent to him. Lo answered that ten days prior to the student demonstration he had had an attack of typhoid and had been confined in Room 214 of the Municipal Hospital, so that he knew nothing of the demonstration. Since my Institute of National Culture was established in Talifu, and since it is a two-day trip by bus from there to Kunming, I do not see how my thirteen students doing post-graduate work could have had anything to do with the student demonstration in Kunming. A week later I called on the Chairman of the Board of Trustees of my Institute, Chen Pu-lei, who showed me a note written by Chiang himself ordering that the Institute be closed down. I went to Wang Shih-chieh, then Secretary-General of the People's Political Council, asking him to book air passage for me in order that I might proceed to Talifu via Kunming, to close the Institute and disband the staff and students. Wang said, "All right, you can have your air passage." It was on a Friday that I got the ticket from him, but to be certain I asked him whether the permission to go was definitely granted. Wang said to me, "You have already got your ticket. How can you suspect that the permission is not definite?" On Saturday, when I was invited by Wang to have dinner with him, I asked him again whether I could really fly the next day. Wang was very annoyed that I should put the same question to him so often, and he said, "The ticket is in your hand—how can you be so suspicious?" On Sunday morning, when I was on the point of leaving my brother's home for the airfield, a telephone call came from Wang saying that the Generalissimo had asked for the return of the air ticket. From that time on I had to stay in Chungking, and even when I went to attend the Committee meetings of the People's Political Council, special-service men followed me. Imagine the leader of an opposition political party being treated in this manner in any democratic country! I gave this as an example of Chiang's impulsive and emotional approach to all problems, and of his failure to make adequate inquiry before deciding upon a course of action. When a leader's decision is made according to his good pleasure, not only is there no assurance of justice, but there is an open invitation given to all manner of abuses. Unscrupulous and wily officials study his moods and make use of him. Chiang is a man disposed to concentrate power in himself alone, and he will not trust men of ability. He is the leader of the Kuomintang, head of the National Military Council, and was for a time President of the Executive Yuan. He has unlimited powers, and he feels he must decide everything by himself, since he has confidence in nobody. It was a well-known fact that the commander of his forces at the front had to follow Chiang's instructions word for word and was never allowed to use his own discretion. Around him Chiang prefers to have inferior men who will follow him blindly rather than men of initiative and integrity. This side of his character has been also described in the pages of the White Book published by the State Department, in which the Secretary of State agreed with the report of the United States Ambassador.

You also say that the Generalissimo cannot be expected to provide that leadership, as he seems incapable of change and gives every evidence [of a disposition] to persist in personal rule, which has resulted in the present sad state of affairs.

Furthermore, in your report of June 14th, you described the Generalissimo's assurance of agreement with your recommendation regarding the conduct of military operations by General Ho Ying-chin with General Barr's close collaboration, and his subsequent instructions to the contrary that all operations were to be carried out under the Generalissimo's instructions, through his "incompetent" chief of staff.

Your report of June 22nd. states that it would appear that the Generalissimo's predisposition to appoint his old and personally trusted comrades, regardless of their proven corruption or lack of ability, to posts of responsibility, still outweighs his desire for good government.

To give a further example of this peculiar characteristic of Chiang Kai-shek, which is the evidence of the feudal mind par excellence and which certainly is not conducive to the intelligent conduct of any modern government, let alone a good government, I will cite the case of lend-lease. When goods came to China under that arrangement a bus service was organized between Rangoon and Kunming to take care of it. The military department complained of delays. Subsequently my brother gave up the work of supervising transportation on the Burma Road, and Yu Fei-peng, Chiang's trusted follower, succeeded him. Yu, however, brought the lend-lease goods from Rangoon only as far as Lashio in Northern Burma. One month later Yu made a report to the Generalissimo that all the goods had been moved away from Rangoon, but he did not state where they had been moved to. My brother had not felt that he could render any report until the goods were safe in Kunming. But Yu Fei-peng was satisfied with Lashio, which is still on the Burma side, and he let it go at that, meanwhile giving Chiang the false impression that everything was in order. When the Japanese Army captured Lashio, they of course captured all the arms, munitions, and spare parts warehoused in the town.

Chiang is not a man who abides by law or believes in the rule of law. How much he respects constitutional practice can be gathered from the following remarks which he made in the early years of the republic to the party members of the Kuomintang:

Attention was generally centered on the text of the provisional constitution in the belief that, if only a system of responsible government could be enforced, Yuan Shih-kai could be prevented from abusing his authority as President. They also thought that if a powerful political party could be organised to control the parliament, a responsible cabinet could be maintained to carry out the task of restricting the authority of the President. They also copied the form of British and American politics, believing that if two major parties existed side by side, the mould of democracy would have been set.

Chiang then concluded by saying that

What Yuan Shih-kai feared was not the parliament, but the influence of the revolutionary party in the Yangtse Valley and the Southern Provinces.

By "influence" Chiang meant the governors who commanded the army. Constitution and parliament in Chiang's mind are tools which can be manipulated. He does not believe in the inviolability of a constitution decided on and promulgated by the people. He does not understand why there should be so much fuss made over the constitution. To him all government is personal government: constitutions are luxuries which at most serve the purposes of the one who is in power. During the tutelage period, constitutional amendments were made with regard to the position of the Chairman of the Chinese Republic. When Chiang was himself the Chairman he gave himself real power in the constitution with regard to policy making. When later Lin Sen was Chairman of the Republic, he became a mere figurehead and the real power went into the hands of the President of the Executive Yuan—who was Chiang himself. The constitution was simply remade to fit the changed circumstances. Chiang regards all institutions with complete indifference, being certain that he can manipulate them in any way he chooses. Imagine having more than 3700 members of the National Assembly, which is the constitutional organ that elects the President and the Vice-President of the Chinese Republic! When the Communists were in Chungking, Chou En-lai and myself were both opposed to such an unwieldy number, but the Kuomintang insisted on having it or there was to be no agreement. When the National Assembly actually was in session in 1947, its operations proved to be most awkward and difficult, which was a foregone conclusion. And Chiang never appears to think that laws representing the popular will should be carefully observed; he changes them when they do not suit him. I remember well that, after the rules concerning the People's Political Council were published, when the number of candidates was found to exceed the number fixed, he just increased that number to suit his purposes. Laws are only putty, to be moulded into any shape and form according to the mood of the moment, and that is how China was governed in the most critical period of her modern history, threatened by a large-scale foreign invasion on the one hand and by the determined expansion of the Communists on the other.

Chiang has his own way of running modern administrative machinery. During the war years, a committee of supervision was set up to regulate the executive planning and supervisory functions of the government. Chiang made himself the chairman. This meant a further concentration of power in his hands. One day the Committee sent its members to inspect the work of the different ministries and to study the qualifications of their staffs. The committee sent some young men to the Ministry of Communications. Now, the secretaries of the Ministry knew that it was impossible for these young men to report on the qualifications of a railroad or radio engineer who had been many years in service, and accordingly they made the comical recommendation that they would do the investigating for the young men and furnish them with a report. To this the investigators agreed with alacrity. They found the resulting report good, accepted it, and submitted it to Chiang Kai-shek—to the satisfaction of everybody!

Chiang also set up a planning board of which he was again the Chairman, but actually the work of direction was done by the Secretary-General. This board, as everyone understood, was to collect economic data and make plans for the development of industries, commerce, etc. During and after the war, the scope and the difficulties of this kind of work were such that only the most painstaking and exacting efforts on the part of the best qualified technicians and scientific experts could make any appreciable contribution. But to Chiang it was just another organisation, one more over which he could preside, and he made use of it in speeches and propaganda. Naturally, the board did everything except planning.

Another peculiar trait of Chiang Kai-shek is his concern with minute details, unmindful of the fact that the limited resources of a single man, even though he may consider himself a superman, scarcely suffice for discharging the most basic and general functions of government. Chiang's preoccupation with petty and extraneous details intensifies the haphazard effect of his policies. Thus, he made China pay a high price in signing a treaty of friendship and alliance with Russia in 1945, and granting that he did this because he valued the friendship of the Soviet Union, it is incomprehensible that six months later he should allow student demonstrations to break out which proved to be hostile to Russia. Even if Chiang had had no previous knowledge of these disturbances, how could he allow his henchman Chen Li-fu to provoke the demonstrations without consulting him first, and then allow them to get out of hand so that Russia could only believe that China suddenly had changed her attitude. Chiang's government, for all practical purposes, had always been a government of his temperament, for his temperament, and by his temperament. It has not been the fortune of his countrymen to see a steady, cool, rational, and consistent development of any policy under Chiang's government. His mind is diffused and cannot concentrate on those matters which are fundamentally important. Chiang even plumes himself on being a literary artist. Dr. John C. H. Wu, former Chinese Minister to the Vatican, once showed me his Chinese translation of the Psalms, in which the Generalissimo had made some changes or comments. As a political leader, one would think that Chiang had enough political problems to occupy his attention. How is it possible for him to find time to read and correct Chinese translations of the Psalms?

Such is the balance sheet of Chiang's personal character, of his strength and weakness. It is possible that he is not this kind of person by nature, that he is the product of circumstances; these, however, are all of his own making. The fact remains that his self-established rule gives encouragement to the sycophants, flatterers, and toadies by whom he is surrounded, and that he spurns men of integrity, honor, and ability who, out of self-respect, cannot remain in the company of these shameless hangers-on—or, if they do, must sooner or later fall victim to their wiles and intrigues. This is not to deny that Chiang has his greatness. As a fighter on the battlefront, as a revolutionist executing the will of Dr. Sun, and as a leader in the war of resistance against Japan, he made a great contribution to China, and he will be remembered, accordingly, as a patriot. While the early attempt at collaboration with the Communists was one fraught with difficulties, Chiang managed to pull through; when his government ultimately collapsed in 1948-1949, its failure was due not so much to lack of American support, as it is still widely but erroneously believed in America, but to its inherent defects, deriving very largely from the peculiar characteristics of Chiang's personality and his methods of rule. As we look back now to the twenty-five years of his trusteeship, it is apparent that he had a unique opportunity of evolving a strong and powerful government that would be able to withstand the destructive tactics of the Communists. He had the support of all his countrymen; he had defeated, for the first time in the history of modern China, a powerful foreign foe, the Japanese; his treasury was full as a result of the seizure of enemy assets and because of American aid; he had millions of brave and seasoned soldiers; and his prestige at home and abroad at the conclusion of the war was higher than that of any single Chinese leader in modern times. Yet, with all these helpful factors which he could easily have used to good advantage, his government disintegrated so rapidly that it was a surprise even to the Chinese Communists that they succeeded in defeating him so ignominiously in so short a time, and that he had to find refuge ultimately on the lonely island of Formosa where he maintains a skeleton government on the strength of an abnormal international situation. There is indeed nothing to which we can compare so tragic a failure.

What, then, is the outlook for the future? What chances are there for the residue of the government under Chiang Kai-shek to stage a comeback and to regain control over the mainland? I am prepared to give him the benefit of the doubt and to say that he may bring about a dramatic turn of events. But if my analysis of his character, of his psychological and mental make-up, of his beliefs, and of his lack of faith in democratic methods, is at all trustworthy, is it too much to say that, for his own good and for the good of the hundreds of millions of his countrymen now under the Communist yoke, it is best for him to bask in his past glories, which are genuine, and to leave the work of salvation to those who are better qualified to cope with the situation? What is urgently needed to overcome the present crisis in China is not a "strong man" whose twenty-odd years of arbitrary rule has brought nothing but a deluge of corruption and a red inundation, but rather the cultivation of law-abiding habits, a willingness to submit the main issues of national life to open and intelligent discussion so as to reach a just and equitable solution, a consciousness at least among the leaders of the importance of constitutional and parliamentary processes, and a substitution of rational understanding for unstable, unreliable, and whimsical practices. This can come about only when the nation's intellectual resources are gathered together for maximum exploitation and unhampered expression and not smothered under the weight of an enlarged ego.

CHAPTER V

The Shadow of a United Front During Wartime

Let us continue to review the story of the political developments in China during the war. The most important of these was the formation of the United Front. We know that the Communists were working on the basis of a popular front as early as 1935, and that they began to negotiate for such an arrangement with the Kuomintang before the Marco Polo Bridge incident in 1937. This idea of a united front led ultimately to the formation of the People's Political Council.

Officially it appeared as if the People's Political Council were an organ created by the Kuomintang of its own volition; actually it arose out of the demands and pressure of the democratic parties.

After the Marco Polo Bridge incident, an Advisory Council of National Defense was formed, consisting of fifteen members, with Wang Ching-wei as the chairman. Mao Tse-tung and Chou En-lai did not attend the meetings, because their negotiations for the regrouping of the army and for assuring its financial support were not yet concluded. Dr. Hu Shih was also a member, but as he is a man of a cautious nature and was of the opinion that China could not fight Japan singlehandedly, he was sent abroad to do propaganda work for the government. Dr. Hu Shih left the Council only a few days after its establishment. The leader of the Youth Party also took part in the meeting. When the first meeting took place, I was in Kuling and knew nothing about it. On the day of the outbreak of war at Shanghai, I went to the travel bureau of the Shanghai Commercial Bank to book passage on the Yangtse River, and received my steamer ticket. A few minutes later, when passing the office again, I was asked to give back the ticket. The reason was that Kiang-ying, a strategic point on the Yangtse, had been blocked, and no boat could go down to Shanghai. The agent did not wish to tell me the news openly, and took me to his room. I booked another passage as far as Nanking. My arrival at Nanking on August 17 coincided with the Japanese bombing of that city. The steamer was anchored on the other side of the river, and when the bombing was over, I landed and went to see my brother, Chang Kia-ngau, then Minister of Railway Administration, and asked him to buy me a railway ticket to Shanghai. When the government authorities learned that I was in Nanking, they came to tell me about the establishment of the Advisory Council of National Defense and asked me whether I had received the wire of invitation to attend the meeting. But, frankly at that moment, I was more interested in seeing my family than in political discussions. I wanted to go to Shanghai by car, but the report of the Japanese bombing of the British Ambassador Sir Knatchbull-Huguesson's car came, and I was told that travelling by car or rail was not safe. Accordingly, my plan of seeing my family had to be given up. After the first days of panic were over, many party leaders who believed in democracy came to me to express their opinion that the fifteen-member Advisory Council of National Defense could not meet the needs for a united front, and they pressed for a reorganisation of the Council. In the meantime, the military defense of Shanghai was abandoned, and the government was so busy with the withdrawal from Nanking to Hankow that the question had to be postponed.

The question of a People's Political Council was revived when the government was transferred to Hankow. The number was now increased from fifteen to one hundred and eighty, and the council was to remain as an advisory body. According to its constitution, its members were nominated by the government, which saw to it that the majority belonged to the Kuomintang. Only about thirty members were representatives of the Chinese Communist Party and the democratic parties. The constitution also provided that a motion could be brought up for discussion with the signature of twenty members. The motion thus signed would be referred to a committee for amendment of its contents and wording. After the committee stage, it would come before the full session. If it were passed by a majority it would be sent to the government as a resolution. Since a resolution of the People's Political Council did not possess the force of a parliamentary bill, the government was free to decide whether it should be carried out or merely shelved. In the next session, the government would give an answer in tabular form with remarks indicating that the resolutions had been referred to the various ministries. The Council's report on the war situation was referred to a committee on military affairs, to which I belonged. Any criticism concerning the Minister of Defense was, however, always worded as mildly as possible, because matters of defense were in the hands of Generalissimo Chiang himself, and any criticism would in fact be lèse majesté. None of the ministers could be impeached, of course. When too many questions were raised concerning the work of H. H. Kung, the Minister of Finance, Chiang, as Speaker of the Council, would announce to the meeting that no answer was necessary. This cut short all questioning and saved H. H. Kung much embarrassment. Though the council put up a show of being a united front, I doubt that it introduced any reforms in the government service.

There was one thing, however, which the People's Political Council boldly attempted, and that was a reconciliation between the Kuomintang and the Communists. At the beginning of each session, the Kuomintang was anxious to know whether the Communist members were attending or not. The New Fourth Army incident was one of the clashes which nearly culminated in another split between the Nationalists and the Communists. During an early meeting, Chou Enlai proposed to the Government that the Communist forces, which were scattered in the provinces of Kiangsi, Fukien, Chekiang, and Hunan, should have a new formation to be called the New Fourth Army, consisting of four regiments and ten thousand men, and that the new corps be sent to the north of the Yangtse valley. When this army was formed, only a part of it was sent to the front. Its attempt to recruit the deserters from the Nationalist Army aroused the attention of the Government, and the commanding officers of the New Fourth Army were arrested. The Communists contended that the government's aim was to restrict the Communists' activities. By way of protest, the Communist representatives on the People's Political Council refused to attend the meeting. When the minority parties were asked by the government to serve as mediators, the Communists made two demands: adoption of rehabilitation measures and adoption of measures for provisional settlement, each of which contained twelve points. The Communists said that their members would attend future meetings if these conditions were accepted. An earlier resolution passed by the People's Political Council said, however, that the attendance of members could not be made conditional, and the Communist proposals were rejected.

One interesting development grew out of these meetings of the Council, and that was that a movement was started in earnest to strive for a democratic form of government and to end the civil war. Its program mentioned two vital issues—democratization of the government and nationalization of the army. The first objective implied the Kuomintang's giving up tutelage, and introducing constitutional government without delay. With this process of democratization accomplished, it was thought that the Communists would no longer be in the disadvantageous position of enjoying no freedom, or having no right of parliamentary and cabinet representation. The second objective meant that the army should belong to the country as a whole and not to the parties, and called for the merging of the Nationalist and Communist forces under one unified command. With these demands the members formed what later came to be known as the "Democratic League." It was the aim of the League to stop the recurrence of civil war by means of democratization. It was thought that since the Kuomintang and the Communists had separate armies as tools with which to realise their political aims, if democratization were not achieved, war would be the only means of solving China's political problems and no peaceful development would be possible. The Communists maintained that so long as there was tutelage, no party other than the Kuomintang could enjoy freedom of association, freedom of assembly, and freedom of the press, so they refused to hand over their army to the Government. Thus the cessation of the civil war depended on the nationalization of the army, and the nationalization of the army depended on the Kuomintang's guaranteeing that it would give up tutelage and adopt democracy. This was the point of controversy between the Kuomintang and the Communists. To take up this problem and solve it was the main task of the Democratic League. The League was formed in 1939, five years before the arrival of General Marshall, whose attempt at mediation in China was to be made along precisely the same lines on which the Democratic League had been working.

The Democratic League consisted of the minor parties and other groups outside of the Kuomintang and the Communists as, for instance, the China Youth Party (organised by the Chinese students in France to combat Communism at the time when Chou En-lai organised the Communist Youth in Paris), the Democratic-Socialist Party which believed in peaceful means of putting socialism into practice, and the Rural Reconstruction Group, of which Liang Shu-ming was the leader. Liang believed that life in the rural areas, which served as the basis of the country's economy, should be modernised. He knows Mao Tse-tung well, and had discussed with him the League's program, as he did also with Chiang before the work of negotiation started. Lastly, there was the Vocational Education Group, of which Huang Yen-pei, the present Minister of Light Industries in Peking, was the leader. These four groups knew each other well and had brisk exchanges of views in the People's Political Council and in its Standing Committee. One day in the summer of 1939 the leaders of the four groups gathered at my house, and after much discussion decided to publish a paper in Hongkong to be called *Light,* as an organ of the League, with Liang Shu-ming as chief editor. Another magazine, *The People's Constitution,* was later published in Chungking, and many articles were written on the subject of human rights in order to counteract the Communists in their policy of curtailment of evil rights. I must add that the League was the only organisation based on liberal and democratic principles of any importance in the last thirty years of totalitarian rule in China. Though it went out of existence when Communism swept over the country, it has now been revived as the vanguard of the Third Force.

The Kuomintang reaction towards the formation of the League was openly unsympathetic and unfriendly. After always having had its own way, it regarded with displeasure any challenge of its unrivalled authority, and it decided to dispatch Sun Fo and Wu Tieh-cheng to Hongkong to curtail the League's activities. The official newspaper of the Kuomintang in an editorial called the League's existence into question, as the announcement of its formation had not been accompanied by the names of any individuals, and it was therefore to be considered an anonymous organization. This question of anonymity was brought up by the Kuomintang before the Standing Committee of the People's Political Council, whereupon I stood up and said that I myself, together with Mr. Huang Yen-pei, Mr. Tso Shun-sen and Dr. Lo Lung-chi, would be responsible for anything concerning the League. The question was then dropped.

It is interesting to recall that the League tried every means to promote democratic measures before the People's Political Council, and through it into the government, but being in the majority, the members representing the Kuomintang had no difficulty in defeating the League on these issues. There was once a motion, for instance, which appeared on the agenda after having been signed by twenty members, calling for a discussion of the following subjects: (1) that the existence of the different parties should be legalised; (2) that personal freedom should be guaranteed; (3) that corrupt officials should be dismissed; and (4) that the special-service organization (the Intelligence Service) should be disbanded. Chiang's close followers, Wang Shih-chieh and Chang Chun, knew that there was going to be fireworks and tried to persuade Tso Shun-sen and myself to withdraw the motion. We answered that any motion bearing twenty signatures was entitled to come before the P. P. C. for discussion, even though the Kuomintang, as the majority party, might reject it. Tso and I were later invited by Chiang to have dinner with him. In the course of the conversation he too tried to convince us that if such a motion were put on the agenda it would only expose the incompetence of the Government and lower the morale of the army at the front. But nevertheless the motion was introduced, after having been somewhat diluted and modified. Eventually, the speaker of the Council tried to kill it, and succeeded in doing so with the concurrence of the Kuomintang's refusal to tolerate opposition of any sort.

Even so, the program of the League aroused general approval among the people, because every Chinese was firmly of the belief that the recurrence of civil war should be stopped and that a democratic form of coalition government should be adopted and established. Many professors and students, especially those in Chungking and Kunming, joined and worked for the League. The leadership of the League was in the hands of some half-dozen men, Liang Shu-ming, Huang Yen-pei, Tso Shun-sen, Li Huang, Lo Lung-chi, and myself. Later we asked the members of the National Salvation, Shen Chun-ju (now Chief Justice of the Supreme Court in Peking) and Chang Pai-chuen, leader of the Peasants and Workmen's Democratic Party (now Minister of Communications in Peking), to join us. Shen Chun-ju, as a fellow-traveller of the Communists, kept silent or expressed sympathy with them, but worked well with the League nevertheless. After Hongkong was lost to the Japanese, the newspaper *Light* had to close down, and its editor Liang Shu-ming came back to Chungking and worked in Southwest China. Though the Kuomintang was not pleased with us, the League continued its efforts for reconciliation between the Kuomintang and the Communists. When General Marshall arrived in China it was natural for him to ask the Democratic League to cooperate with him to bring about peace and democracy. The details of this program will be dealt with later.

In the meantime, the People's Political Council became from May to September of 1944 the scene of debate between the Kuomintang and the Communists on three vital issues: (1) problems connected with the legalisation of the Communist Party; (2) the size of the Communist army; (3) the relationship between the Communist-controlled regions and the Central Government. It is interesting to see where each party stood on these questions:

(1) Legalisation of the Communist Party

Government side	Communist side
Party affairs for the duration of the war should be conducted in accordance with the "Program of the War of Resistance and National Reconstruction," and, after the conclusion of the war, according to the National Government's decision. A People's Congress should be convened to adopt a constitutional government. The Chinese Communist Party was to obey the laws of the National Government and enjoy the same treatment as other parties.	1. The government was to adopt democracy and safeguard the freedoms of speech, press, assembly, association, and person. 2. The Government was to lift the ban on political parties, recognise the legal status of the Chinese Communist Party and the various anti-Japanese parties and groups, and set free all political offenders. 3. The Government was to permit the people to enforce local self-government in fact as well as in name.

(2) Size of the Communist Armies

Government side	Communist side
The 18th Group Army and its units in various localities should be reorganized into four armies, consisting of ten divisions, with their designations to be decided by order of the Government.	In consideration of the needs of resistance against Japan, the record of achievements in the war of resistance, and the present strength of the troops, the Government was to organise the Chinese Communists troops into sixteen armies, consisting of forty-seven divisions with 10,000 men per division. As a compromise the Government must approve the organization of at least five armies of sixteen divisions. The Government must give full material aid to the 18th Group Army and the new Fourth Army. With regard to the weapons, munitions, and medicines furnished to China by the Allied countries, the Government must apportion and distribute them equitably among

Government side	Communist side
	the various armies of China, and the 18th Group Army and the New Fourth Army should be given the share due them.
(3) The Communist-Controlled Regions	
1. The Shensi-Kansu-Ninghsia Border Area shall be renamed the North Shensi Administrative Area, and its administrative organ called the North Shensi Administrative Office.	1. The Government was to recognize the Shensi-Kansu-Ninghsia Border Government and the popularly elected anti-Japanese governments in the bases in North China as legally constituted local governments, and recognize all measures taken to meet war exigencies.
2. The said Administrative Office shall be under the direct control of the Executive Yuan.	2. During the period of the war of resistance the status quo was to be maintained in areas garrisoned by the Communist troops, and readjustments were to be considered after the conclusion of the war.
3. The area shall carry out the laws and orders of the National Government.	3. The Government was to order its military and political organs to lift the military and economic blockade of the Shensi-Kansu-Ninghsia Border Area and the various anti-Japanese bases.

It is clear that the two parties stood wide apart on these basic issues, and the so-called United Front was nothing more than a phantom which had no reality. A united front in a democracy is a political maneuver for the purpose of having all parties come together to form a coalition government, and to make it possible for each party to place the national interest above the party interest. Since the Kuomintang, during the entire period of the war, maintained its policy of tutelage, there was no alternative for the Communists but to expand their army and area of control under the pretexts afforded by the war.

The Communists thus set up their own administrative units behind the Japanese lines, making use of the so-called United Front as a façade. The gap between the two sides became wider every day, and no attempt at reconciliation on the part of the third parties could have any effect. Each side had reasons for its own stand. In a letter to the Communists, the Government spokesman, Chang Chi-chung, gave his version of the situation thus:

> It is absolutely true that the National Government's memorandum has accepted most of the opinions put forward by the divisional commander Lin Piao last year and those raised by you at Sian recently. Yet you still stated emphatically that the divergence of views is too great. But the real reason for the divergence is the steady increase in the requests of the Chinese Communist Party. What you asked for at Sian was more than what Lin Piao asked for last year. The twelve points raised by the Chinese Communist Party outnumber the requests you made at Sian. The present letter adds the eight so-called verbal requests to the twelve points. Since requests increase with time, the divergence of views naturally widens. Take for instance the question of the North Shensi Border Area and other anti-Japanese bases. Lin Piao requested that the North Shensi Border Area be turned into an administrative area within its original area, and that all the other areas be reorganized and obey the laws and orders of the National Government. The document you signed at Sian did not mention other anti-Japanese bases. The twelve-point proposal of the Chinese Communist Party asks for the recognition of the Shensi-Kansu-Ninghsia Border Area and for governments "elected by the people," governments to be anti-Japanese in character. Under such conditions of constant change and gradual expansion of requests, which side should be held responsible if the conversations cannot be brought to a successful conclusion?

The Communist stand was explained by Lin Tsu-han in the following words:

> In the face of grave national crisis, we should unite under the leadership of Generalissimo Chiang, and should exert all our efforts in the prosecution of the war of resistance. United, our strength can be increased. I believe that our country has strength. We have a population of 450,000,000, and that is strength. As to how we can bring about unification, the answer is, by the ushering in of a democratic government even during war. . . . It is not that China does not have strength. Our strength can be turned to account only by adopting the democratic form of government. Our war is fought for justice and against aggression. We must have a democratic government, because our war is an all-out people's war.

Thus matters stood till the time when General Marshall came, and for those of us who were in the know and who were all too familiar with the unwillingness of either side to come to an understanding, it was almost a foregone conclusion that the Marshall mission was to bear no fruit.

However, with all the real points of difference between the Kuomintang and the Communists, I make bold to say that if Generalissimo Chiang had changed his tactics and agreed to a real coalition government to include the Communists and the minority parties, the Communists would have accepted such a government. In 1939, Chou En-lai accepted the position of Deputy-Chief of a sub-division of the Military Council. If ministerial positions had been offered to the Communists, they would no doubt have been glad to accept them. The People's Political Council could then have been converted into a Parliament, to which the Government would have been accountable. The Kuomintang would still have been in the majority, and with the help of the non-Communist parties, as long as it was reasonable and stood for the best interest of the nation, it could have controlled the government. Let us take the case of Greece by way of comparison. After the Lebanon Charter of 1944, six E. A. M. ministers joined the anti-Communist Premier, Papandreou, and national unity between the Communists and Nationalists was established—even though later, because of the question of the demobilization of the resistance forces, the ministers resigned. The Greek coalition government was very short-lived, but still it shows that a coalition government which includes the Communists is not an impossibility.

As I see it, if a coalition government had been formed in China at the beginning of the war, it would have had the following advantages: (1) What the Communists did with regard to military and civil affairs in Northern China would have had to come before the cabinet, and what was objectionable could have been checked. (2) The advice of the Communists, which would have been most useful in matters of reform, might have been a remedy for the incompetence of the Government. (3) The Government would have had a broader and more popular basis.

Such a government could have provided a much better solution than the one proposed by Chiang, namely, that Northern China be assigned to the Communists and that the Communists could expand their army, train their militia, carry on their propaganda among the people, and do anything else they liked within their areas. In proposing this, the Government had its fears, and therefore maintained a military and economic blockade around the Yenan area. The American government was certainly not to be blamed if it thought that Chiang was more interested in fighting the Communists than the Japanese.

If a real coalition government with the Communists had been formed, a great number of domestic and international misunderstandings would have been avoided. With the Communists and other parties in the government, I am certain that the corruption of the Kuomintang officials could have been checked. Also the taking over of Japanese properties at the end of the war would have been better administered instead of being the occasion for open looting. If only the statesmanship of the Generalissimo had been more elastic, things might have turned out differently. If he had proved to be as able as the British showed themselves to be in dealing with the Greek Communists, the picture of China today might be a completely different one. The Greek Government in Cairo was a much weaker one than that of Chiang Kai-shek in Chungking, yet the Greek Government managed to solve the following difficulties: The return of King George, the Cabinet change from Metaxas to Papandreou, the mutiny in the Greek army and Navy, and the civil war in Athens in December, 1944. Although the Communist Party in Greece was unusually strong during the period of these crises, yet today the government of Greece is democratic, not communist.

The situation of China and Greece during World War II presented a number of similarities, but the results, after the surrender of Germany and Japan, were completely different. This was due, not to the cleverness of the Chinese Communists, but rather to the lack of wisdom of the anti-Communists, and more especially to the inflexibility and stubbornness of Chiang Kai-shek.

CHAPTER VI

Ambassador Hurley and Mao Tse-tung 1944-1945

The military situation on the Chinese front in 1944 was a most critical one. The Chinese army was showing signs of collapse. Many cities and many provinces had been lost. But the war of resistance was being waged courageously, and the forced evacution of one city after another aroused no discontent among the population. The enemy offensives in that year were carried on as if the Japanese were irresistible.

On May 18	Loyang was captured and Kaifeng was lost.
On June 6	Huan-Kiang was occupied.
On June 18	Changsha was captured.
On August 8	Hengyang fell.
On August 28	Lishui in Chekiang province was lost.
In September	Japanese forces crossed from Hunan to Kuangsi Province.
On November 12	Kweilin, the capital of Kuangsi, fell.

This is an impressive list of Chinese losses to the enemy. I remember that during one of the meetings of the People's Political Council when a debate on the loss of Loyang and Kaifeng took place, all the members from the province of Honan complained bitterly about Tang En-po, Commander-in-Chief on the Honan front and loyal supporter of Chiang Kai-shek. Voices were raised during the speeches and tears ran down the audience's cheeks when the speakers told how the Chinese army had scattered like a flock of frightened birds. Only the Generalissimo's promise that Tang En-po would be deprived of his command pacified the Honan members. That incidentally was the first occasion on which the Generalissimo openly admitted the incompetence of his personally selected officers.

By early July the situation had already become so bad that President Roosevelt sent a message to Chiang saying: "I feel that the case of China is so desperate that, if radical and promptly applied remedies are not immediately effected, our common cause will suffer a disastrous setback."

Following the fall of Kweilin, the capital of Kuangsi, there was talk of a fourth wartime capital, since Chungking had been the third after Hankow and Nanking. As Szechuan is the richest province of West China, which supplied food for millions of soldiers at the front, there was great concern over where the government could go if Chungking were lost. The province of Sikang, further west, would be the place where the government might seek shelter, but the terrain is mountainous and the fields do not produce rice. In addition to the question of a wartime capital there were other important questions demanding consideration: how to revitalize the army and the government machinery through a process of democratization; how to bring the Kuomintang and the Communists into harmonious collaboration; how to ascertain the probable future attitude of the Soviet Union, which was supporting the Chinese Communists. These three questions were so interwoven that it was impossible to find the answer for one without also finding answers for the others at the same time. With these difficulties it seemed that the Generalissimo had entered a maze from which he could not extricate himself. The revitalization of the army and the government machinery meant overhauling and reorganizing the government, whether it were a coalition government or a war cabinet, either of which would include the Communists and the democratic parties. But this democratization was impossible because the Generalissimo insisted that a coalition government could only be formed during the constitutional stage of China's political development. The Communists, on their part, were convinced that so long as Chiang did not try to democratize the Government and guarantee the fundamental freedoms, it meant that he wanted to keep a monopoly of power; accordingly, they were not prepared to hand over their army to the Government or concentrate their force for a speedy defeat of Japan. And again, the real nature of Chinese Communist policy, and the question of whether they were independent or merely tools of the Soviet Union, could be ascertained only when the policy of the Kremlin was clarified.

While these harassing problems were still unsolved, another disturbing factor appeared on the scene, and that was the conflict between Chiang Kai-shek and General Stilwell. President Roosevelt had asked that Chiang place Stilwell in command of all the Chinese and American forces, and that Chiang give him full responsibility and authority for the coordination and direction of the operations required to stem the tide of the enemy's forces. Had this course of action been followed, perhaps things might have turned out differently, because the United States Government would then have been more directly responsible for handling the situation in China. But Chiang and Stilwell openly split on the matter of supplying the Communists with American arms, and it was clear that sooner or later a showdown between the two could not be avoided. It was Stilwell's contention that the main objective of the war was the defeat of Japan and that all armies, regardless of whether or not they were Communist, should be trained and equipped for battle. The Generalissimo saw things differently: in his eyes there were two enemies, Japan and the Communists. If the Communist army were also equipped with American arms, then the Communists might become so powerful that he himself might be overthrown by them.

One day the Generalissimo invited the representatives of the democratic parties and the leaders of the non-partisans to his house for a talk. As I went in, I had no idea about what would be discussed. The conference began on the subject of the Honan campaign. Then, suddenly, the Generalissimo changed the subject to Stilwell, and told us of the difference of opinion between them on the question of the distribution of arms. He said: "I am the Commander-in-Chief and Stilwell is the Chief-of-Staff appointed by me. How can he propose giving arms to the Communists without my approval? He knows nothing about China and the Communist Party. What should be done with the Chinese Communists is my business. He has nothing to do with it." The speech was a shock to all of us. All we could say was that we should be cool and level-headed in dealing with the United States, but as we left the house, it was evident that the friction was coming to a head. As I showed in the last chapter, the Communists in Northern China had so grown in power that from the point of view of internal politics the Generalissimo could not afford to give them arms which he himself needed badly in order to insure his supremacy. General Stilwell was direct and straightforward by nature, and he had no conception of what was going on in the mind of the Generalissimo. The result of this clash was that Major-General Albert C. Wedemeyer was appointed to replace Stilwell.

At this pont, General Patrick Hurley came into the picture. The American White Book relates that after his appointment as Ambassador, General Hurley outlined his understanding of the purpose of his mission and of United States policy in China in the following terms: (1) to prevent the collapse of the Nationalist Government; (2) to sustain Chiang Kai-shek as President of the Republic and Generalissimo of the armies; (3) to harmonise relations between the Generalissimo and the American Commander; (4) to promote production of war supplies in China and prevent economic collapse; and (5) to unify all the military forces in China for the purpose of defeating Japan. Stilwell's removal made matters simpler for General Hurley because it meant the resolution of the conflict between Chiang and the United States Commander.

Hurley's task was now to ascertain the intentions of the Soviet Union and the precise nature of the relations of the Kuomintang and the Chinese Communists. I first met General Hurley at a dinner party given by the Chinese Ambassador Wei Tao-ming. He looked to me like a forthright and outspoken man, one who would call a spade a spade. He had been sent to China by President Roosevelt as a kind of political trouble-shooter, and he was the first high-ranking American official to go from Chungking to Yenan to mediate between the Nationalists and the Communists, as he was the first to break the ice by talking of a coalition government consisting of the representatives of the Kuomintang, the Communists, the democratic parties, and the non-partisans. In a talk between the American Ambassador Gauss and the Generalissimo which took place on August 31, 1944, the latter told Gauss: "China should receive the entire support and sympathy of the United States Government on the domestic problem of the Chinese Communists. Very serious consequences for China may result from the American attitude. In urging that China resolve differences with the Communists, the United States Government's attitude is serving only to intensify the recalcitrance of the Communists. The request that China meet Communist demands is equivalent to asking China's unconditional surrender to a party known to be under the influence of a foreign power. The Communists are growing arrogant and refuse to continue negotiations since the arrival of the group of American observers in Yenan. The United States should tell the Communists to reconcile their differences and submit to the Nationalist Government of China."

Three months later, however, in a report from Ambassador Hurley to the State Department, we read: "At the time I came here Chiang Kai-shek believed that the Communist Party in China was an instrument of the Soviet Government in Russia. . . . He now feels that he can reach a settlement with the Communist Party as a Chinese political party without foreign entanglements. When I first arrived, it was thought that civil war after the close of the present war, or perhaps before that time, was inevitable. Chiang Kai-shek is now convinced that by agreement with the Communist Party of China he can (1) unite the military forces of China and (2) avoid civil strife in China."

According to Hurley's account, it seems as if the Generalissimo's attitude toward the Soviet Union and the Chinese Communist Party had undergone a complete change within only a few months. But was that true? I would like to go back again to the three key aspects of the situation: (1) revitalization of the army and the government machinery through the process of democratization, (2) reconciliation between the Kuomintang and the Communist Party, and (3) ascertaining the real attitude of the Soviet Union towards China and the Communists.

As the first of these objectives depended largely on the realization of the second and third, I shall deal with them in reverse order. To begin with, as regards the Soviet Union's attitude towards the Communists and China: Before General Hurley flew to Chungking, he went to Moscow to find out the truth about Soviet policy towards China. According to the American White Book, this was what Molotov told Hurley:

Although he said that the Soviet Government had unjustifiably been held responsible for various happenings in China during recent years, Molotov stressed that it would bear no responsibility for internal affairs or developments in China. Molotov then spoke of the very impoverished condition of the people in parts of China, some of whom called themselves Communists but were related to Communism in no way at all. It was merely a way of expressing dissatisfaction with their economic condition and they would forget this political inclination when their economic condition improved. The Soviet Government should not be associated with these "Communist elements" nor could it be blamed in any way for this situation. The solution of the entire situation was to make the Chinese Government work in the common interest and cope with the tasks before it and to make life more normal in China. Molotov said in conclusion that the Soviets would be glad if the United States aided the Chinese in unifying their country, in improving their military and economic condition and in choosing for this task their best people. . . . He gave little new information but he confirmed statements made previously that his government would be glad to see the United States taking the lead economically, politically, and militarily in Chinese affairs. Molotov made it clear also that until Chiang Kai-shek tried by changes in his policies to improve Sino-Soviet relations, the Soviet Government did not intend to take any interest in Chinese governmental affairs.

The Molotov conversation was in fact a reaffirmation of what Stalin had said to Vice-President Wallace on June 21 of the same year. To quote the White Book again:

> Stalin had agreed with Ambassador Harriman in Moscow that support of the Generalissimo was desirable during the prosecution of the war and expressed keen interest in a settlement between the Kuomintang and the Communists, basing his interest on the practical matter of more effective fighting against Japan rather than upon any ideological considerations, and adding that he felt the United States should assume a position of leadership in the Far East.

From the Molotov talks, General Hurley drew the following four conclusions in his report to the State Department: (1) that the Russian Government does not recognise the Chinese Communist Party at all; (2) that Russia is not supporting the Communist Party in China; (3) that Russia does not want dissension or civil war in China; and (4) that Russia desires more harmonious relations with China. There was indeed a whiff of freshness in the naive and straightforward approach of the General towards a problem which the subtlest minds in China had found complicated for over twenty years. It was not without reason that Hurley was nicknamed the "Big Wind." However that may be, I do not believe that the State Department was convinced by Hurley's interpretation of the Soviet attitude —nor was the Generalissimo converted by him.

Chiang put no obstacle in Hurley's way when the latter desired to call on Mao Tse-tung, a démarche which his position as Special Representative of President Roosevelt entitled him to make. Chiang wanted him to find things out for himself in Yenan.

Hurley's previous talk with Molotov had also made him anxious to proceed to Yenan to initiate the work of reconciliation with the Chinese Communist Party. Accordingly, on November 7, 1944, Hurley flew to Yenan and held a two-day conference with Mao Tse-tung. As a result of this conference, he brought back a five-point draft entitled "Agreement between the National Government of China, the Kuomintang of China, and the Communist Party of China," which was signed by Mao Tse-tung as Chairman of the Central Executive

Committee of the Chinese Communist Party. This Agreement read as follows:

(1) The Government of China, the Kuomintang of China, and the Communist Party of China will work together for the unification of all military forces in China for the immediate defeat of Japan and the reconstruction of China.

(2) The present National Government is to be reorganized into a Coalition National Government embracing representatives of all anti-Japanese Parties and non-partisan political bodies. A new democratic policy providing for reform in military, political, economic, and cultural affairs shall be promulgated and made effective. At the same time the National Military Council is to be reorganized into the United National Military Council consisting of representatives of all anti-Japanese armies.

(3) The Coalition National Government will support the principles of Sun Yat-sen for the establishment in China of a government of the people, for the people, and by the people. The Coalition National Government will pursue policies designed to promote progress and democracy and to establish justice, freedom of conscience, freedom of press, freedom of speech, freedom of assembly and association, the right to petition the government for the redress of grievances, the right of writ of habeas corpus and the right of residence. The National Coalition Government will also pursue policies intended to make effective the two rights defined as freedom from fear and freedom from want.

(4) All anti-Japanese forces will observe and carry out the orders of the Coalition National Government and its United National Military Council and will be recognized by the Government and the Military Council. The supplies acquired from foreign powers will be equitably distributed.

(5) The Coalition National Government of China recognises the legality of the Kuomintang of China, the Chinese Communist Party, and all anti-Japanese Parties.

This agreement, according to Hurley's report, was drafted with his assistance. The National Government's answer, however, was that it was not acceptable. The Kuomintang objection was based on its stand on political tutelage, according to which the Kuomintang was, as it were, the headmaster and the people and other parties schoolboys. Among the schoolboys the Communists were the naughtiest and must be whipped. This was the attitude of the Kuomintang members.

They could not therefore agree to the Hurley-Mao Tse-tung draft, for such agreement would be equivalent to allowing the schoolboys to run the school on an equal footing with the headmaster.

The National Government then submitted a three-point counter-proposal.

(1) The National Government, desirous of securing effective unification and concentration of all military forces in China for the purpose of accomplishing the speedy defeat of Japan, and looking forward to the post-war reconstruction of China, agree to incorporate, after reorganization, the Chinese Communist forces in the National Army [which forces] will then receive equal treatment with the other units in respect of pay, allowance, munitions, and other supplies, and to give recognition to the Chinese Communist Party as a legal party.

(2) The Communist Party undertakes to give their full support to the National Government in the prosecution of the war of resistance and in the post-war reconstruction, and to give over control of all their troops to the National Government through the National Military Council. The National Government will designate some high-ranking officers from among the Communist forces to membership in the National Military Council.

(3) The aim of the National Government to which the Communist Party subscribes is to carry out the Three Principles of the People of Dr. Sun Yat-sen for the establishment in China of a government of the people, for the people, and by the people, and it will pursue policies designed to promote the progress and development of democratic processes in government.

In accordance with the provisions of the Program of Armed Resistance and National Reconstruction, freedom of speech, freedom of the press, freedom of assembly and association, and other civil liberties are hereby guaranteed, subject only to the specific needs of security in the effective prosecution of the war against Japan.

In this three-point proposal there was no provision for a Coalition Government, which was the principal demand of the Communist Party. What the Chinese Communist Party was to get from it was only a promise that they would be given recognition as a legal party. This meant that they would not be allowed to have any share in the government. The term "legal party" could also be interpreted to mean that the Communist Party, if they did something "illegal," could be placed under ban again.

In compensation for this single promise, the Communists were expected to incorporate their army as a part of the National Army.

The Communist high-ranking officials would also be appointed to membership of the National Military Council. With regard to civil liberties, they were promised the guarantees given in accordance with the provisions of the Program of the War of Resistance and National Reconstruction. The guarantee under this program meant, in fact, nothing at all. My own experience was that my institute in Talifu, established as a part of this program, had been closed down, and I myself was not even allowed to go to Chengtu to give a lecture when the West China University sent me an invitation to do so.

When this three-point program was handed to Chou En-lai on November 22, 1944, he left for Yenan and did not come back to Chungking until January 24 of the next year, after much persuasion from Ambassador Hurley. On February 3, 1945, Wang Shih-chieh, a devoted follower of the Generalissimo, presented the following draft to Ambassador Hurley:

> In order to intensify our war effort against the enemy and strengthen our national unity, it is agreed that the National Government should invite the representatives of the Kuomintang and other parties, and some non-partisan leaders, to a consultative meeting. This meeting is to be named the Political Consultative Conference, and its membership is not to exceed —— persons.[1]
>
> The function of this conference is to consider: (a) steps to be taken in ending the period of political tutelage and establishing constitutional government, (b) the common political program to be followed in the future and the unification of armed forces, and (c) the manner in which members of parties outside the Kuomintang will take part in the National Government.
>
> If the said Political Consultative Conference succeeds in reaching a unanimous conclusion, it will be submitted to the National Government for consideration and execution. During the Political Consultative Conference, all parties should refrain from recrimination of any kind.

The so-called Political Consultative Conference which took place during the next year was mentioned for the first time in Wang's draft and opened the door for negotiations upon which the Chinese people, the Communist Party, and the Democratic League had set their hopes for many years. When Chou En-lai received this message, he told Hurley that he felt that a basis for cooperation was being reached.

1 Number not specified.

That was something to the credit of Ambassador Hurley. Without his American "push," that basis would never have been found. Ambassador Hurley laid the foundation for General Marshall's work of mediation.

Hurley's observations on the real attitude of the Soviet Union were, however, much too optimistic.

In April, 1945, Ambassador Hurley left Washington for Chungking. He travelled by way of London and Moscow. He reported to the State Department on his conference with Stalin and Molotov. At this conference Hurley reiterated what Molotov had told him the year before, and went on to relate what he had done about accomplishing a reconciliation between the Communists and the Kuomintang. He made clear the American insistence that China supply her own leadership, arrive at her own decisions, and be responsible for her own policies. He also told Stalin that President Roosevelt had authorized him to discuss this subject with Prime Minister Churchill and that the concurrence of Churchill and Eden, who was then Foreign Secretary, had been obtained in the policy of endorsing China's aspirations to establish for herself a united, free, and democratic government, and to unify all the armed forces in the country in order to bring about the defeat of Japan. Stalin answered that the Soviet Government would support the policy. He added that he would be glad to cooperate with the United States and Britain in achieving unification of the military forces in China. The last sentence in Hurley's report read: "Stalin agreed unqualifiedly to America's policy in China as outlined to him during the conversation."

This word, "unqualifiedly," attracted the notice of the Chargé d'Affaires in Moscow, Mr. George F. Kennan, who commented on Hurley's report in a telegram to Mr. Averell Harriman. This comment was so prophetic that I shall quote it at length:

> I refer specifically to the statements which were attributed to Stalin to the effect (1) that he expressed unqualified agreement with our policy in China as Ambassador Hurley outlined it to him, (2) that this policy would be supported by the Soviet Government, and (3) that we would have his complete support, in particular, for immediate action directed towards the unification of the armed forces of China with full recognition of the Chinese National Government under the leadership of Generalissimo Chiang Kai-shek. . . .

There was, of course, nothing in Ambassador Hurley's account of what he told Stalin to which Stalin could not honestly subscribe, it being understood that to the Russians words mean different things than they do to us. Stalin is, of course, prepared to affirm the principle of unifying the armed forces of China. He knows that unification is feasible in a practical sense only on conditions which are acceptable to the Chinese Communist Party. . . .

Actually I am persuaded that in the future Soviet policy respecting China will continue to be what it has been in the recent past: a fluid, resilient policy directed at the achievement of maximum power with minimum responsibility on portions of the Asiatic continent lying beyond the Soviet border. This will involve the exertion of pressure in various areas in direct proportion to their strategic importance and their proximity to the Soviet frontier. I am sure that within the framework of this policy Moscow will aim specifically at (1) reacquiring in substance, if not in form, all the diplomatic and territorial assets previously possessed on the mainland of Asia by Russia under the Czar. (2) Domination of the province of China in Central Asia contiguous to the Soviet frontier. Such action is dictated by the strategic necessity of protecting in depth the industrial core of the U.S.S.R. (3) Acquiring sufficient control in all areas of North China now dominated by the Japanese to prevent other foreign powers from repeating the Japanese incursion. This means, to the Russian mind, the maximum possible exclusion of penetration in that area by outside powers including America and Britain. . . .

It would be tragic if our natural anxiety for the support of the Soviet Union at this juncture, coupled with Stalin's use of words which mean all things to all people and his cautious affability, were to lead us into an undue reliance on Soviet aid or even Soviet acquiescence in the achievement of our long-term objectives in China.

It seems marvellous that Kennan's analysis should coincide so nearly with what the Soviet Union did to China in the next few years. If he had come to China with General Marshall and given his advice with regard to the evacuation of the Russian army, to the advance of the Chinese Communist army into Manchuria, and to the Sino-Soviet Friendship Treaty, then a better settlement of the relations between Soviet Russia and China in regard to Manchuria might have been made, a settlement which would have had an effect on the solution of all the questions relating to the Chinese Communists. The situation in China might then have been very different.

After Ambassador Hurley's return to Chungking, he continued to exert himself in the interests of reconciliation. On August 22, 1945, he brought Mao Tse-tung from Yenan to Chungking, which was really a great accomplishment in terms of diplomacy. Then, three months later, he handed in his letter of resignation to President

Truman and ended his work in China. Hurley's achievements in formulating a basis for negotiation between the Kuomintang and the Communists and bringing the idea of a Political Consultative Conference to the point of realization, is all to his credit. Without his direct attitude, the frontier spirit so typical of the people of Texas and New Mexico, it was possible that no settlement and no negotiation could have been started and made. Whether the Political Consultative Conference was a failure or a success is beside the point: the fact remains that it was Hurley, with the pioneering spirit of the frontiersman, who brought about the convocation of the Political Consultative Conference in 1946.

The reason that I deal with Mao Tse-tung and General Hurley in the same chapter is that it was through them that the idea of a Coalition Government was put on the market. Mao Tse-tung's article on the Coalition Government in his political report to the seventh Congress of the Chinese Communist Party was very much inspired by Hurley's visit and by the five-point agreement which Hurley brought back. Without Hurley's visit and encouragement, Mao Tse-tung would probably not have kept the idea so firmly and so steadily in mind—even though, with such widely divergent backgrounds and preconceptions, the two men might have totally different ideas of what a coalition government should be. After all, Hurley is a democrat in the Western sense, while Mao is thoroughly trained as a Marxist and Stalinist.

Mao Tse-tung's report on the Coalition Government was made to the congress of the Chinese Communist Party, which had not held any meeting after the sixth Congress in July of 1928. This idea of a Coalition Government had been advocated by the Comintern when it was sponsoring a popular front with the bourgeois class. The project was also being upheld by the democratic parties in China as early as before the war. It seems strange that the Communist Party in China, which stands for dictatorship, should suddenly, in 1945, side with the political ideas of the bourgeois parties. It is interesting, therefore, to inquire precisely what was in Mao Tse-tung's mind.

"This seventh Congress will decide the destiny of 450 million people and spell defeat for the Japanese aggressor," Mao began. He also boasted that the Chinese Communist Party had now a roll-call of 1,210,000 party members, a population of 95,500,000 in the areas it controlled, an army of 910,000 men and a militia of 2,200,000. But the central theme of Mao Tse-tung's address was the Coalition Government. His political platform consisted of two parts—a general outline, and specific stipulations. First, his general outline, which is so important that it is worth quoting in full:

Starting from the premise of the defeat of the Japanese aggressor and of the reconstruction of a new China, we, the Chinese Communists, agree with the great mass of the Chinese people on the following points: (1) China should not be ruled by a kind of institution which in the hands of the bourgeois-landlord class is dictatorial, feudal, fascist, and anti-popular. This kind of institution has proved its bankruptcy through the ruling bloc of the Kuomintang during the past eighteen years. (2) It is impossible for China to have a democratic form of government which is run by the liberal and bourgeois class. The reason for the failure of [the attempt to rule] China . . . by a democracy of the old type is, on the one hand, that the liberal and bourgeois class, under the present circumstances, is politically and economically very weak, while, on the other hand, there is the Communist Party which is alert, strong, and can lead the great mass of peasants, petty bourgeoisie, intellectuals, and the proletariat class. (3) It is impossible for China at her present stage to build up a socialistic state; her mission rather lies in resistance to the anti-nationalistic and feudalistic oppression.

What is our program? This question will naturally be raised. Our program is that after the thoroughgoing annihilation of the Japanese aggressor, a democratic and allied government should be set up, which will have an absolute majority of the people as its foundation and be based on a united front. This is the institution of new democracy. This institution can meet the requirements of the great majority of the Chinese people. It can get the consent of many millions of workers in industry and also of millions of peasants and tenant farmers. It will and can get the support of 360,000,000 peasants. Also it can and will be supported by the petty bourgeoisie, the liberal bourgeois class, the enlightened gentry, and other patriots.

The demands of these different classes might be different, so that a conflict of interests could exist between them, such as the clash between management and labor. To ignore this kind of difference is false and hypocritical. These instances of conflict should not be allowed to develop to such an extent that they go beyond the requirements of the common interest. The different interests can be adjusted. Such an adjustment will facilitate the fulfilling of other important tasks during the period of the New Democracy. The political institution of the New Democracy will fight against national oppression from the outside, and abolish the internal feudalistic and fascist oppression; yet, what we want to set up is not a democratic government of the old type, but a political institution which is based upon a united front, an alliance of all democratic classes. This proposal quite agrees with the platform of Dr. Sun Yet-sen because, in the declaration of the first Congress of the Kuomintang, he said: "The modern institution of democracy is controlled by the capitalist class and becomes an instrument of oppression directed against the common people. Under the Kuomintang's principle of democracy, we understand that the democratic power is held by the common people, not monopolized by a few." This wise political advice should be observed by the Chinese people and the Chinese Communist Party and all other democratic groups, and they must be ready to fight against any person and any faction which opposes it. This is the way to realize the principle of New Democracy, the completely right course.

The structure of political power under the New Democracy should be democratic centralism. The people's congress . . . decides the general policy and elects the government, as in the Soviet system. It is democratic, and at the same time, centralized. In other words, it is based on a democratic foundation and also on centralized direction. Only this system shows its popular basis. The people's congress . . . exercises its highest power, yet the government . . . can manage the affairs which are delegated to it by the people's congress in a centralized manner and can also guarantee the democratic activities of the people.

After reading these words, it is very hard to say whether Mao Tse-tung is a believer in democracy or a believer in dictatorship. If we call him a believer in proletarian dictatorship, we are refuted by his claim that the Soviet type of socialism cannot be applied to China. If we call him a democrat in the Western sense, we are contradicted by his claim that he is opposed to the hegemony of the bourgeois class. Mao Tse-tung uses the word "Democracy" in so many senses that we can scarcely say whether he is a Marxist or an anti-Marxist, a believer in dictatorship or an opponent of dictatorship, a friend of popular sovereignty or an enemy of popular sovereignty.

Let us examine further Mao Tse-tung's attitude with regard to Marxism and socialism.

All the above is the conviction of the Chinese Communist Party, which at the present stage stands for a democratic revolution of the liberal and bourgeois class. This minimum program contrasts with our maximum program. Putting this minimum programme into practice will bring China a step forward, because China will make progress from her colonial and semi-colonial or semi-feudal status to a bourgeois-democratic form of government. After her defeat of the

Japanese aggressor, China will be built up as an independent, free, democratic, united, and prosperous country.

There are, then, according to Mao, two programs, minimum and maximum. For the present moment he is satisfied with putting into practice the minimum program, which he calls a democratic revolution, and under which the Chinese Communist Party is willing to form a coalition government with the other parties. Yet Mao Tse-tung shows himself a Marxist when he comes to the subject of Communism, the attainment of which is the maximum program. In the same report he says:

We Communists never conceal our political program. It is quite true that our future or maximum program is to make China a Socialist or Communist state. The name of our Party and our Marxist Weltanschauung gives us the highest, the most beautiful, the most brilliant ideal. When we Communists join our Party, we know that we are fighting for a democratic revolution for the present, and also for a socialistic, proletarian class-revolution for the future. In spite of the antagonism, slander, and denunciation of other groups, we are determined to oppose them. Those who are skeptical of us should not be attacked but convinced by us.

Here Mao appears to be a convinced Marxist. Yet he warned his Party members in the following way:

If a Communist or a sympathiser of Communism looks down upon this democratic revolution which will be carried out with the bourgeois class, and is not ready to sacrifice himself for this kind of work, but indulges in mere talk of Socialism or Communism, then he is one who is more or less a traitor to Socialism or Communism. It is a tenet of Marxism that the realization of Socialism must go through the stage of democracy. The time for realizing democracy in China must be a long one. It is completely Utopian to want to build up China as a Socialistic state without having brought about unity under the New Democracy, without having achieved economic development under private capitalism and cooperatives, without scientific development on a national and popular basis, and without a population of many millions of men who are individually liberated and developed. In simple words, it is impossible to build up Socialism in a state ruined by feudalism or semi-colonialism, without having a bourgeois-democratic revolution first.

On the strength of these words it appears that Mao does not hope to build China into a socialistic state at once. From the economic point of view, Mao knows well that a country which has not undergone a stage of economic development through private capitalism, cannot enter the socialistic stage. In this Mao is quite sincere. He uses this argument to convince his own party members that it is better to do the work of democratic revolution than to dream of a socialist society now. But it would be a mistake to take it for granted that, since Mao renounces socialism for the present moment, he will also give up the political methods—such as violence, and depriving "reactionaries" of civil rights—which are the favored ways of dealing with political opponents in the Soviet Union. Mao believes that his Communist Party is strong enough to take over the leadership of China permanently because he believes that the mass of peasants and workers will constitute the rank and file of the Communist Party.

From the date of drafting the five-point proposal in November, 1944, till the Soviet evacuation of Manchuria in March, 1946, the Chinese Communist Party, it appears to me, was sincere in its demand for a coalition government with the Kuomintang and other groups participating. But it was to be a coalition on its own terms, and unless these terms were met, it would not relinquish control of its army. On this Mao was quite specific:

> These people said to the Communists: "If you give up your army, we shall give you freedom." If these words were sincere, then the parties which had no army should have enjoyed freedom long ago. Between 1924 and 1927 the army of the Communist Party was so small that it did not count. Yet after the purge of the Kuomintang was started, the Communists had no freedom whatsoever. The Democratic League and the Democratic faction of the Kuomintang had no military force, yet neither of them enjoyed any freedom. During these eighteen years, the workers, peasants, and students, intellectuals and bourgeois have had no army, and, accordingly, no freedom. Did they organise an army for a feudalistic partition and oppose military or civil orders? No! Just because they had no army, they lost their freedom.

In other words, Mao had no confidence in the sincerity of Chiang Kai-shek when he said that the Communist Party would be legalized on condition that it hand over its army to the Government. On this matter it is generally agreed that Mao's point was well taken.

Mao goes on to argue:

> They say that the army should belong to the country. That is quite right because in every country the army is a national service.

The question is, what does the word "country" mean? Is it a country of landlords, bankers, compradores, which is feudalistic, fascist, and dictatorial? Or is it based upon popular will under the principle of New Democracy? When China is constituted on this basis and a democratic government is formed, all armies should be put under the control of such a government, in order to give protection to the fundamental freedoms of the people and to fight against the foreign aggressor effectively. Once such a Coalition Government and a united Commander-in-Chief are established, the army within the areas of liberation will be handed over [to the Government]. At the same time, the Kuomintang army should be handed over too.

Although Mao Tse-tung knew that there was little hope of reaching any satisfactory arrangement with the Government, he was prepared to be accommodating, since the path of negotiation was already opened. Accordingly, in August of 1945 he paid a visit to Chungking and had a series of talks with Chiang Kai-shek. Besides these personal talks on the highest level, there was also a conference at which the National Government was represented by Wang Shih-chieh, Chang Chun, Chang Chi-chung, and Shao Li-tse, and the Communist Party by Chou En-lai and Wang Jo-fei. That Conference issued a "Summary of the Conversations between the Chinese Government and the Representatives of the Chinese Communist Party," in which the results were divided into three categories: (a) what was agreed upon, (b) what was proposed, and (c) what was rejected.

(a) What was agreed upon:

1. It was agreed that China now is on the threshold of a new era of peaceful reconstruction, and that peace, democracy, solidarity, and unity should form the basis of the nation's concerted efforts. It was likewise agreed that under the leadership of President Chiang, cooperation should be perpetuated and resolute measures taken to avert internal strife, so that a new China, independent, free, and prosperous, may be rebuilt.

2. It was agreed that the period of political tutelage should be brought to an early conclusion, that a constitutional government should be inaugurated, and that necessary preliminary measures should be immediately adopted, such as the convocation by the National Government of a Political Consultative Council to which all parties and non-partisan leaders will be invited, to exchange views on national affairs and discuss questions relating to peaceful national reconstruction and the convocation of the National Assembly.

3. Both parties agreed that the question of the election of the delegates of the National Assembly and the revision of the constitutional draft of May 5 should be decided by the proposed Political Consultative Council.

4. It was agreed that fundamental freedoms will be guaranteed by the Government. The existing laws and decrees should either be abolished or revised. The Government stated that a common attribute of constitutional government is that all parties are equal before the law and that this fact will be given immediate recognition.

5. Both parties agreed that the Government should strictly prohibit all offices other than law courts and police to make arrests, conduct trials, and impose punishment.

6. The Government representatives stated that the Chinese Communist Party may submit a list of people who they think should be released as political prisoners.

7. Both sides agreed that local self-government should be vigorously promoted.

(b) What was proposed:

It was proposed by the Chinese Communists that the Government should effect an equitable and rational reorganization of the entire Chinese army, decide on the program and different stages of re-organization, re-demarcate the military zones, and inaugurate a conscription and replenishment system with a view to unifying the military command. The Chinese Communists expressed their readiness to reduce the troops under their command to twenty-four divisions or to a minimum of twenty divisions.

The Government representatives stated that the national troop reorganization program was being carried out and that the Government was willing to reorganize the Communist-led troops up to twenty divisions if the other issues coming up in the present talks could be satisfactorily settled.

The Government indicated that the question of having Communist personnel in the National Military Council and in the various departments under the Council, could be considered and discussed by the Government.

With regard to the question of militiamen in the liberated areas, the Government expressed the view that the matter would have to be determined in accordance with local conditions and needs.

(c) What was rejected:

1. When the Communist representatives proposed that the popularly elected governments in the liberated areas should be recognized,

the Government representative pointed out that after the surrender of Japan, the term "liberated areas" became obsolete and that the integrity of the administrative authority should be respected.

2. An initial formula advanced by the Communists was to demarcate the provincial and administrative areas according to the conditions that now exist in the eighteen liberated areas.

The Government replied that the demarcation of provincial boundaries would involve changes of unusual latitude and that the question should be considered carefully and could not be resolved in a short time.

3. A second formula was proposed by the Communists, asking the Government to appoint nominees from the Communist Party as Chairman and members of the provincial governments of the Shensi-Kansu-Ninghsia Border Region and the provinces of Jehol, Chahar, Hopei, Shantung and Shansi. They further asked that Communist nominees be appointed deputy-Chairman and members of the provincial governments of Suiyan, Honan, Kiangsu, Hupeh, and Kuangtung, and deputy Mayors of the special municipalities of Peiping, Tientsin, Tsingtao, and Shanghai. They also requested participation in the administration of the Northeastern Provinces.

After lengthy discussions the Communists modified their proposal by requesting the appointment of their nominees as Chairman and members of the provincial governments of Shansi and Suiyuan and as deputy-Mayors of the special municipalities of Peiping, Tientsin, and Tsingtao. The Government replied that the Communist Party might nominate some members who possess administrative ability for appointment. But if the Communist Party should insist upon nominating the Chairman, Deputy-Chairman or members of a provincial government for specific provinces, this would not be sincerely endeavoring to achieve military and administrative integrity.

4. The Communists proposed a third formula which suggested that general elections be held in the liberated areas under the existing popularly elected governments.

The Government replied that popular election of the provincial government functionaries could only be held after the status of the province had been definitely defined, following the promulgation of the Constitution.

5. The Communists put forward a fourth formula, that in all liberated areas the provincial governments retain their status until a constitutional provision for the popular election of provincial officials were put into effect. The Communists also suggested that this problem be submitted to the Political Consultative Council for settle-

ment. The Government indicated that they hoped an agreement could be worked out.

6. The Communists asked for the severe punishment of traitors and the disbanding of the puppet troops. The Government said "yes" to the first part, while as to the second part, the Government expressed the idea that the disbanding of the puppet troops would not be carried out if peace and order would be disturbed thereby.

7. When the Communist representative asked that Communist troops be allowed to participate in the task of accepting the surrender of Japanese troops the Government answered that the participation of the Communist Party in accepting the surrender of Japanese troops could be considered after the troops of the Communist Party accepted the orders of the National Government.

An accident that occurred towards the end of Mao Tse-tung's trip to Chungking should be mentioned here. One day Mao was invited by Chiang to see a play; during the performance, a message was brought in to the effect that Mao Tse-tung's car had been shot at, and one person in the car killed. Fortunately, Mao was not then in the car, and the attempt at assassination failed. When the news was spread in the hall, Chou En-lai's face became pale and he ran to talk to Chang Chun. After the play a dinner took place, and at the table Mao Tse-tung toasted Chiang, wishing him "Long life for ten thousand years." This meant a farewell to Chiang. Though bargaining for the number of seats of Governors and deputy-governors and members of the provincial government was still going on, the Communists put forward many questions during the negotiations so that Mao could go back immediately.

If one studies carefully the subjects which were brought up during the talks, it appears to be doubtful that the Communists were really sincere and earnest about democracy and coalition. If they were, why should they desire, besides the promised twenty divisions, a line of defense running from the Border Region eastward to Hopei and Shantung? This line could only mean that they planned an occupation of China north of the Yellow River. Although at this time they had not infiltrated into the Northeastern provinces, they had made, as it were, an advance subscription for Manchuria. It can be assumed that they must have known that the Soviet Union after the Yalta Conference would occupy Manchuria and make room for them. The demands for democracy and coalition put forward by Mao were merely a show to satisfy the United States, while the demands for governorships in North China were aimed at building a line of defense for themselves.

From this portion of the record, it should be clear that the Chinese Communist Party preached democracy and unity on the one hand while fortifying itself, on the other, in its geographical stronghold of North China and linking up with Soviet Russia in Manchuria.

CHAPTER VII

General Marshall's Mission and the Political Consultative Conference

General Marshall came to China in December, 1945. It was his mission to arrange for a cessation of hostilities between the armies of the National Government and the Chinese Communists and to find an early settlement of internal strife in China through a conference of representatives of major political elements, which would decide the questions of army integration, coalition government, and a new constitution. His aim was analogous to that of the Lebanon Conference to settle the Greek question which was called in May, 1944. I do not know whether the State Department had the Lebanon Conference in mind in sending Marshall to China. Though the aim of General Marshall in China and that of Great Britain in dealing with wartime Greece show striking similarities, yet the results in the two countries proved to be completely different; why reconciliation between the two rival parties was effected in Greece and not in China is a subject worthy of close examination and study.

The Chinese National Government in 1946 was in a much stronger position than the Greek Government in 1944, because Greece was at that time under the Axis occupation, and the Greek government was seeking shelter in Cairo. Secondly, the return of the King was opposed by the Greek Communists and the question of a regency had to be solved. The Greek Communists were on the point of forming a government at the headquarters of the E. A. M., whereas the government of Chiang Kai-shek was never shaken during the war. Because of E. A. M. propaganda, mutinies broke out in the Greek army and navy which were suppressed by the Greek Government in cooperation with the British commanders. Papandreou then came on the stage as Prime Minister. He was a more far-sighted statesman than Chiang Kai-shek, because he saw clearly that without a government on a broader basis, one that included the Communists, the situation could not be properly handled.

The Greek King in time issued the following statement: "We must have, outside Greece, a government as representative as possible, made up of all trends of patriotic opinion, to the exclusion only of those who have collaborated with the enemy." These words sound very much like the Chinese Communist demand for the "cooperation of all anti-Japanese parties."

Though the Communists all over the world have clamored for cooperation among all anti-Fascists, they have consistently tried to monopolize all power for themselves. Papandreou, in his opening speech at the all-party conference, made the following charges against the E. A. M., which Chiang Kai-shek with slight verbal modifications might very well have used against the Chinese Communists:

It is the responsibility of the E. A. M. that they did not look only towards the liberation of the country, but wished to prepare in advance for their domination after the war. Therefore, their first aim was to monopolize the national struggle. They did not allow anyone else to take to the mountains and fight the invader. They prevented Greeks from fulfilling their patriotic duty. They made themselves a state within the state and considered their opponents as enemies of the country.

These words of Papandreou could well be applied to the Chinese Communist Party, which tried to destroy all the Kuomintang guerilla bands and to keep North China exclusively for itself, a policy explicitly announced by Lin Tsu-han in his speech to the People's Political Council. They would be approved and heartily endorsed by Chiang Kai-shek because the Communist occupation of North China and the expansion of the Communist army to 450,000 and of the militia to 2,500,000 meant a Communist monopoly of the national struggle and preparation well in advance for domination after the war.

But Papandreou knew where to stand firm and where to stretch a point. He knew that it would be a better policy to have the Communists within the government than to leave them out. Accordingly he worked for the inclusion of six Communist ministers in his cabinet—they resigned of their own accord—because in that way they could be more effectively controlled. This "open-door" policy of Papandreou was much more statesmanlike than the "closed-door" policy of Chiang Kai-shek.

The results of the Lebanon Conference were embodied in a signed Charter which consisted of eight articles expressing the following aims:

(1) The reorganisation and establishment of discipline in the Greek armed forces in the Middle East under the Greek national flag.

(2) Unification and discipline of all guerilla bands in Free Greece under the orders of a single government, and also the setting in motion, when the moment arrives, of all fighting forces of the nation against the invader.

(3) Cessation of the reign of terror in the Greek countryside and firm re-establishment of personal security and political liberty of the people, when and where the invader has been driven out.

(4) Continual care for sending sufficient supplies of food and medicine to enslaved Greeks and also to the mountains of Greece.

(5) The securing, once the country has been liberated in common with the Allied forces, of order and liberty for the Greek people in such a way that, uninfluenced by material or moral pressure, they may sovereignly decide both on the constitution and social regime and on the government which they want.

(6) Imposition of severe sanctions against traitors to the country and against those who have exploited the misfortune of our people.

(7) Care in advance that the material needs of the Greek people shall be immediately satisfied after liberation.

(8) Full satisfaction of our national claims and the creation of a new, free, and great Greece.

Is not the creation of a new, free, and great Greece the same kind of ideal as the creation of "a strong, united, and democratic China"? Is not unification of all guerilla bands in Free Greece under the orders of a single government the same as the proposal of President Truman that autonomous armies should be eliminated as such and all forces integrated effectively into the Chinese National Army? The government of national unity of Greece answers accurately to the demand by the Chinese for a democratic coalition government. The goals of both countries were identical, yet the results were radically different. Let us try to find out the reasons for that difference through a study of the events which occurred before and after General Marshall's arrival.

According to the American White Book, General Wedemeyer sent a report to Washington on November 20, 1945, in which the following conclusions were expressed by him:

(1) The Generalissimo will be able to stabilize the situation in South China, provided he accepts the assistance of foreign administrators and technicians, and engages in political, economic, and social reforms, through honest and competent civilian officials.

(2) He will be unable to stabilize the situation in North China for months or perhaps even for years unless a satisfactory settlement with the Chinese Communists is achieved and followed up realistically by the action suggested in paragraph (1).

(3) He will be unable to occupy Manchuria for many years, unless satisfactory arrangements are reached with Russia and the Chinese Communists.

(4) Russia is, in effect, creating favorable conditions for the realization of the Chinese Communists' and their own plans in North China and Manchuria. These activities are violations of the recent Sino-Russian Treaty and related agreements.

(5) It appears a remote possibility that a satisfactory understanding will be reached between the Chinese Communists and the National Government.

These conclusions show that Wedemeyer had a real grasp of the international and domestic situation in China at that time. In simple language, there were three things which Wedemeyer clearly saw to be obstacles to the unification of China: the corruption of the Kuomintang Government, the Communist occupation of North China, and the Soviet plot in Manchuria. It was always the habit of Chiang Kai-shek to say that the objective of the war was to restore the sovereignty of Manchuria and that the duty of the National government was to restore Manchuria's lost territory. The stand was perfectly correct, but the question was how to attain the objectives set up. In this respect I quite agree with Wedemeyer that Chiang Kai-shek was quite unprepared to do so. A Chinese proverb says "A dyke which is built at a cost of millions of dollars can be wrecked by an anthill." Chiang did not realize that there was a loophole in China's situation which could completely wreck the project of unification. Manchuria was that loophole by which not only the unification of China under Chiang Kai-shek but also the mission of General Marshall came to nought.

In the early stages of Marshall's trip, the outlook appeared very promising because, through his mediation, the order for the cessation of hostilities was issued, the Political Consultative Conference took place, and the five items on the agenda were passed unanimously. General Marshall's mediation efforts were fruitful on three vital points: the cessation of hostilities, the convocation of the Political Consultative Conference, and the plan for the reorganization of the Chinese Army, both Nationalist and Communist.

(1) *Cessation of hostilities.* We know now that the Japanese surrender on August 10 was a surprise to the Chinese Communists, because no preparations had been made for it. From the day of Japan's surrender the headquarters of the Chinese Communist Party concentrated all its efforts on the deployment of the Communist army in different directions in order to grab more and more territory in North China. Chu Teh, the Commander-in-Chief, issued seven emergency orders in one day, commanding the different units of the Communist army to occupy the important cities and villages of North China. On August 13, the Communist organ *Daily Liberation* published an editorial entitled "The Urgent Task Before Us." Land reform, to which the Communists attached primary importance, was only slightly touched upon as one of the urgent tasks to be fulfilled, the rest of the editorial being devoted to the inspiring sentiment, "Bravery, more bravery for a great counter-attack," and advising party members to harvest the fruits of victory. The so-called "great counter-attack" meant no less than civil war. Mao Tse-tung's arrival in Chungking on August 28 was a move to slow down the advance of negotiation. There is reason to believe that the State Department in Washington had an inkling of that fact. In President Truman's instructions to General Marshall at the time of his departure Secretary Byrnes enclosed the replies to General Wedemeyer in which one finds the following directions:

(1) He may put into effect the arrangements to assist the Chinese Nationalist Government in transporting Chinese troops to Manchurian ports, including the logistical support of such troops.

(2) He may also proceed to put into effect the stepped-up arrangements for the evacuation of Japanese troops from the China theatre.

(3) Pending the outcome of General Marshall's discussions with Chinese leaders in Chungking for the purpose of arranging a national conference of representatives of the major political elements and for a cessation of hostilities, further transportation of Chinese troops to North China, except as North China ports may be necessary for the movement of troops and supplies into Manchuria, will be held in abeyance.

(4) Arrangements for transportation of Chinese troops into North China may be immediately perfected, but not communicated to the Chinese Government. Such arrangements will be executed when General Marshall determines either (a) that the movement of Chinese troops to North China can be carried out consistently with his nego-

tiations, or (b) that the negotiations between the Chinese groups have failed or show no prospect of success and that the circumstances are such as to make the movement necessary to effectuate the surrender terms and to secure the long-term interests of the United States in the maintenance of international peace.

This shows how carefully conceived was the United States' policy in order not to court involvement in a civil war between the Kuomintang and the Communists. While an agreement in regard to the cessation of hostilities was reached in the middle of December, fighting was still going on around Chihfung. The settlement of the problem of Chihfung throws an interesting sidelight upon the political situation. Chou En-lai was fond of repeating the story of Chihfung, which indicated, he thought, that the Soviet Army in the neighborhood of Chihfung wanted to hand over the city to the Kuomintang army. When General Marshall came into the picture he decided that Chihfung rightly belonged to the Communists and that this city should not be turned over to the Kuomintang but to the Communists. It was not till the eve of the Conference that, through the advice of General Marshall, the cessation of hostilities actually came into effect. General Marshall's arbitration in this case won the confidence of Chou En-lai and his colleagues and also showed that he was not partial to the Kuomintang.

(2) *Convocation of the Political Consultative Conference.* After the question of a cessation of hostilities had been settled, the P. C. C. was opened the next morning at ten o'clock. Leaders of all political parties, as well as prominent social and civic leaders, participated in the discussions. The conference was attended by thirty-eight people—eight from the Kuomintang, seven from the Communist Party, four from the Youth Party, two from the Democratic League, two from the Democratic-Socialist Party, two from the National Salvation Association, one each from the Vocational Education Society, the Rural Reconstruction Society, and the Third Party, and nine members with no party affiliations.

The scope of consultation of the conference was to work out a program for peaceful work toward national reconstruction in China. The work was divided up among the special committees dealing with (a) governmental organization, (b) development of an administrative program, or a program for peaceful national reconstruction, (c) military affairs, (d) preparing a draft constitution, (e) establishing a National Assembly. Let us discuss the achievements of the special committees with regard to these projects.

(a) The first committee worked out a plan for the reorganization of the government, in which the Kuomintang suggestion for broadening the basis of the government was adopted for discussion. While the Youth Party proposed a revival of the Central Political Council, the Kuomintang held that the existing project for a State Council should be left intact. Thereupon the discussion centered on the distribution of the membership in the State Council. The Kuomintang insisted on nominating 50 per cent of the members, while the Communists proposed the so-called 3-3-3-system, one-third to consist of Kuomintang members, one-third to consist of members of other parties, and one-third to consist of civic leaders without party affiliations. The committee decided that: there should be forty State Councillors; the State Council should be competent to decide on legislative principles, administrative policy, important military measures, financial and budgetary measures, and the appointment of ministers with or without portfolio; in case the President of the Government was of the opinion that the execution of any decision was difficult, he might submit it for reconsideration. If three-fifths of the State Councillors upheld the original decision, it would be carried out accordingly. If a resolution before the State Council involved changes in the administrative program, it must be passed by a two-thirds vote of the State Councillors present.

Such is a summary of the resolution on the organization of the government adopted by the P. P. C. After the end of the full session of the P. P. C., Chou En-lai took a trip to Yenan, and upon his return he requested Chang Tung-sun, a member of the present State Council in Peking, and myself to join the State Council. It appeared to me then that the Communists might not be insincere in their desire to form a coalition government. The finding of a satisfactory solution centered around the question of awarding fourteen seats to the Communists and the Democratic League. As mentioned above, it was stipulated that if a resolution before the State Council involved changes in the administrative program, it must be passed by a two-thirds vote of the State Councillors present. It was assumed that the Kuomintang government could easily command a majority vote, so that they could make any change in the administrative program if a majority vote were required. This stipulation of a two-thirds vote would make a change in the administrative program impossible, even though it had been decided on by the P. C. C., if a two-thirds voting power of the State Councillors were not in attendance. A two-thirds vote of the forty councillors meant a fraction more than twenty-six votes. The Communist Party demanded that they, in alliance with the Democratic League, be granted fourteen seats, so that, in case the Kuomintang got twenty-six votes, they would still fail to command the necessary fraction of a vote. In other words, this provision would effectively block the Kuomintang's making administrative changes to its own liking. Naturally enough, the question of fourteen seats became a bone of contention between the Kuomintang and the Communists. As late as October, 1946, we find in a letter from Chiang Kai-shek to General Marshall that he agreed that besides the twelve seats already promised, he would give one more seat to a non-partisan, who would be recommended by the Communists and agreed upon by the government. So, ten months after the P. C. C., this question of seats on the State Council had not yet been decided. This does not mean that the failure of the P. C. C. hinged wholly on this question, but it was a very essential factor in that failure.

(b) The functions of the committee working on an administrative program for peaceful reconstruction of the nation were of the utmost importance inasmuch as it was concerned with the problem of bringing the period of tutelage to an end and inaugurating a constitutional government. An administrative program was therefore formulated as the criterion of policy for the period prior to the actual inauguration of a constitutional government. The program was cast in ten paragraphs, headed respectively, general principles, the rights of the people, political problems, military affairs, foreign relations, finance and economics, education and culture, rehabilitation and relief, Chinese residents overseas, and annexe. It was agreed that the principles of "democratization of government," the "nationalization of armies," and the equal legal status of various parties should be recognized as the indispensable means of achieving the peaceful reconstruction of the nation. Recognising Dr. Sun Yat-sen's Three Principles of the People as the highest guiding principles for national reconstruction, the entire nation, under the leadership of Chiang Kai-shek, would be marshalled to work for the building of a united, free, and democratic China. The basis of a bill of rights was included, stipulating that the "people's freedom of person, thought, religion, faith, speech, publication, assembly, union, residence, travel, and communication should be safeguarded." Existing legislation that conflicted with the above principles would be revised or revoked. Any organ or person, other than the judicial or police authorities, would be strictly prohibited from acts of arrest, trial, and penalization of the people; and offenders against this principle would be punished. The law relating to arrest and the transfer of the accused for trial, as promulgated by the government, would be put into force immediately by express orders.

Under the paragraph "military affairs," we find the following principle: "The army belongs to the state. It is the duty of the soldier to protect the country and love the people and to ensure the unity both of the military organization and the military command. The army and the political parties should be separated from each other; military and civil authority should be vested in different hands; all troops of the country should be reorganized into a lesser number of units in accordance with the provision of the 'military reorganization plan.' "

In the paragraph headed "foreign relations," it was agreed that the provisions of the Atlantic Charter, the Cairo Declaration, the Moscow Four-Power Declaration, and the Charter of the United Nations, should be observed. All remnants of Japanese influence in China should be extirpated according to the provisions of the Potsdam Declaration.

It is interesting to note that in the paragraph on "economics and finance" the Chinese Communists made no demand for confiscation of land from the landlords or for nationalization of capitalist-owned industry, but were satisfied with the provision that "any enterprise which partakes of the nature of a monopoly or which cannot be undertaken by private initiative should be classified as a state enterprise." With regard to land reform, they were content with the provision that the land law must be put into operation so as to attain the objective of "he who tills the soil also owns it"—which was much more moderate than their policy in the liberated areas.

What the Chinese Communists considered really important at this time was not the question of confiscation of land or capital, but the preservation of their authority in the liberated areas under their control. There was therefore a provision in the annexe to the effect that "In the recovered areas, where the local government is under dispute, the status quo shall be maintained until a settlement is made according to Articles 6, 7, and 8 of Chapter III on political problems in the program of the National Government after its reorganization."

(c) The framing of a resolution on military problems involved the most difficult task of reconciling widely divergent points of view. In the end, these differences were overlaid with a number of fine-sounding phrases which have never been translated into reality: "the army belongs to the state"; "all political parties should be forbidden to carry on party activities openly or secretly within the army"; "no party or individual may make use of the army as an instrument of political rivalry"; "no soldier on active service may serve concurrently as a civil official"; and "the minister of defense shall not necessarily be a military man."

All the principles which are included in the last paragraph must seem to a Westerner, living under a democratic form of government, to be quite natural and normal. But in China, where warlordism has prevailed since the establishment of the Republic, these rules sound extraordinarily like the realization of an ideal, because the people have waited a long time for the government to be taken out of the hands of soldiers and put into the hands of civilians.

While there was agreement upon the separation of the army from any party affiliation and upon the segregation of civil and military administration, there was a stalemate over the question of army reorganization. According to previous decisions, the Central Government forces were to be reorganized into ninety divisions within six months and the Communist army reduced to twenty divisions. During the consultations on military affairs the Government put forward the proposal that the nation's entire armies be integrated and reduced to fifty or sixty divisions. However, the Communists, while agreeing in principle with this proposal, hoped that the proportionate strengths of the various forces would be maintained, and that the different units would not be merged. Both parties insisted on their respective points of view for a long time, until a decision was reached by altering the term "reorganization through the merging of the units" into "Reorganization by centralized action."

In the resolution on military affairs, a three-man commission was authorized to work out a plan for the reorganization of the Communist army. On February 25, an agreement on the basis for "Military Reorganization and Integration of Communist Forces into the National Army" was reached, and was signed by Chang Chih-chung as representative of the Government, Chou En-lai as representative of the Communist Party, and General Marshall as the Advisor. The agreement provided that at the end of twelve months the armies were to consist of 108 divisions, each not exceeding 14,000 men. Of these, eighteen were to be formed from Communist forces. The deployment of the armies at the end of the first twelve months was to be as follows:

Northeast China	5 armies of National Divisions 1 army of Communist Divisions
Northwest China	5 armies of National Divisions
North China	7 armies of National Divisions 3 armies of Communist Divisions
Central China	9 armies of National Divisions 1 army of Communist Divisions
South China (including Formosa)	4 armies of National Divisions

Of paramount importance was the article on demobilization, which stipulated that during the twelve months immediately following the promulgation of the agreement, the Government should demobilize all units in excess of eighteen divisions. It was also stipulated that the Communist Party should prepare, within three weeks of the promulgation of this agreement, a complete list of its military units, stating their character, strength, armament, and the names of brigade and higher formation commanders. This report should include a list of the eighteen divisions to be retained and the order of demobilization during the first two months. But the statement concerning the Communist military units was never handed in by Chou En-lai after the agreement was signed. This may be taken as an indication that the Communist Party never intended to give up civil warfare, but that their negotiating for military reorganization and their participating in the Political Consultative Conference were tactics adopted in order to allow the Soviet Union to make room for them in Manchuria. Though their intention of joining the Government may have been sincere, yet the failure to hand in the report on their military units is a significant indication that they were preparing for eventual civil war. So long as it suited them, the Communists would occupy North China and join the Coalition Government; when it no longer suited them, they would make Manchuria their base for fighting a civil war.

(d) The Resolution on the Draft Constitution presented the fundamental principles according to which the constitutional draft of 1936 should be revised and re-written. I shall give here only a summary of this document. The Political Consultative Council was to establish a Committee for reviewing the Draft Constitution, and draw up a comprehensive scheme for the revision of the 1936 Draft Constitution on the basis of the principles recommended by the Political Consultative Council.

A. Concerning the National Assembly:

(a) The entire electorate, when they exercise the rights of election (initiative, referendum, and recall), are called the National Assembly.

(b) Pending the election of the President by universal suffrage, he shall be elected by an electoral body, composed of the members of the district, provincial and national representative assemblies.

(c) The exercise of the rights of initiative and referendum will be defined by appropriate laws.

B. Concerning the Legislative Yuan:

The legislative Yuan will be the supreme lawmaking body of the State and will be elected by the electorate. Its functions correspond to those of a Parliament in a democratic country.

C. Concerning the Control Yuan:

The Control Yuan will be the Supreme organ of control of the State and will be elected by the provincial assemblies and the self-governing areas of minority peoples. It will exercise the functions of consent, impeachment, and control.

D. Concerning the Judicial Yuan:

The Judicial Yuan will be the Supreme Court of the State and will not be responsible for judicial administration.

E. Concerning the Examination Yuan:

The Examination Yuan will be in the form of a Committee whose members will be appointed on the nomination of the President of the National Government and with the consent of the Control Yuan. Its functions will be mainly to examine candidates for civil service and technical experts. Members of the Examination Yuan shall be without party affiliation.

F. Concerning the Executive Yuan:

The Executive Yuan is the supreme Executive organ of the State. The President of the Executive Yuan is to be appointed on the nomination of the President of the National Government and with the consent of the Legislative Yuan. The Executive Yuan is to be responsible to the Legislative Yuan. If the Legislative Yuan has no confidence in the Executive Yuan as a whole, the latter may resign or ask the President of the National Government to dissolve the former. But the same President of the Executive Yuan may not ask for the dissolution of the Legislative Yuan for a second time.

G. Concerning the Presidency of the National Government:

The President of the National Government may promulgate emergency decrees according to law, when the Executive Yuan has so decided. But the action must be reported to the Legislative Yuan within one month. The right of the President of the National Government to call the Presidents of the Executive, Legislative, Judicial, Examination, and Control Yuan into conference need not be written into the Constitution.

H. The Province is to be regarded as the highest unit of local self-government. The powers of the provinces and the Central Government will be divided according to the principle of "fair distribution of power." The Provincial Governor is to be elected by the people. The province may have a Provincial Constitution which, however, must not contravene the provisions of the National Constitution.

I. All freedoms and rights which are generally enjoyed by the peoples of democratic countries should be protected by the constitution.

J. A separate chapter on elections should be provided in the Constitution. Only those of twenty-three years of age and over have the right to be elected.

K. Concerning fundamental national policies:

A separate chapter in the Constitution should be devoted to fundamental national policies, including items on National Defense, Foreign Relations, National Economy, Culture and Education.

L. Concerning amendments to the Constitution:

The right to amend the Constitution shall be vested in a joint conference of the Legislative and Control Yuan. The proposed amendments should be passed by that body in which is vested the right to elect the President of the National Government.

Why were these principles adopted as a basis for revising the constitutional draft of 1936? What was the Communist attitude towards them? What was the Kuomintang attitude? These questions will be explained in the chapter on the Communist-boycotted Constitution.

What I wish to say here is that most of the principles were suggestions made by me in the name of the Democratic League. By means of my explanations to the Communists in order to secure their understanding and cooperation, and by means of similar conferences with the Kuomintang, these principles were passed. The details of the story will come later.

(e) I come now to the last resolution concerning the National Assembly. The Committee working on plans for the convocation of the National Assembly met with a great deal of difficulty, and it was only a few hours before the closing of the Conference that an agreement was reached. While all parties had recognised the 1,200 delegates who were elected to the National Assembly in 1937, which had to be called off because of the war, the Communists and the Democratic League had at first only accepted those delegates as representatives of the Kuomintang, and on this ground they demanded an increase of representation from other parties. However, in the end, all the members of the Committee agreed to look upon the delegates of 1937 as representatives of the electorate. The problem then centered around the creation of seats for new delegates. While the Kuomintang proposed an increase of 600 delegates, of whom 230 were to represent the Kuomintang, the Communists presented a formula demanding that the new delegates be increased to 800, and that the representatives of parties other than the Kuomintang and those without party affiliations total more than one-third of the entire delegation. It was finally agreed that 700 new delegates were to be elected, including 220 from the Kuomintang, 190 delegates from the Communist Party, and 70 without party affiliations. It was further agreed that the constitution could only be adopted with the concurrence of three-fourths of the delegates present, and non-Kuomintang delegates to the assembly could constitute more than one-fourth of the total representation. The Communists, hoping to gain from one to two hundred more seats through regional representation, felt confident that in this way the Communists and the Democratic League representatives would be able to hold more than one-fourth of the seats of the National Assembly.

The resolution concerning the National Assembly ran as follows:

(1) The National Assembly shall be convened on May 5, 1946.

(2) The National Assembly is empowered to adopt the Constitution.

(3) The Constitution shall be adopted by a vote of three-fourths of the delegates present.

(4) The 1,200 geographical and vocational delegates who have been or are going to be elected according to the electoral law of the National Assembly shall be retained.

(5) The geographical and vocational delegates for the Northeast provinces and Taiwan shall be increased by 150.

(6) Seven hundred seats shall be added to the National Assembly, and they shall be apportioned among the various parties and social leaders.

(7) The total number of delegates to the National Assembly shall be 2050.

The last act of the Political Consultative Conference was the apportionment of seats. Each party hoped to get as many as possible, so there was a good deal of horse-trading about the distribution of the seven hundred seats. It was settled as if it were a question of spoils to be won by the most vocal party. The Youth Party was particularly insistent on its demands for a bigger share. The closing of the Political Consultative Conference was fixed for the afternoon, so the division of spoils stopped before four o'clock on that day.

Looking back at the Political Consultative Conference, I may say that the five resolutions mentioned, had they been carried out, would have meant a secure future for China, because they represented assent achieved through negotiation, and not by violence and war. They also represented the mutual tolerance and moderation of the parties concerned. It was a great pity that after only one and a half months, civil war broke out again in Manchuria between the Kuomintang and the Communist army and nullified all the resolutions of the Political Consultative Conference.

It may be asked: How great was General Marshall's influence over the Political Consultative Conference? General Marshall's chief function was the issuing of the order for the cessation of hostilities and furthering the agreement on a basis for military reorganization. The rest of the resolutions of the Political Consultative Conference represented work accomplished by the Chinese members themselves. The foundation of the Political Consultative Conference was laid down in the two slogans, "the democratization of politics," and "the nationalisation of the army," which had been proclaimed by the Democratic League for many years.

At this time, the enlightened members of the Kuomintang, like Chang Chun, Sun Fo, Wang Shih-chieh, and Shao Lih-tse wished very much to see the end of political tutelage and the emergence of the stage of constitutionalism, because this was the last part of the revolutionary work of the Kuomintang. The achievement of the Political Consultative Conference was the expression of the consensus of the Chinese people as a whole. However, General Marshall's personality had much to do with its success. Chou En-lai told me many times that General Marshall never once attempted to deceive him during his mediation efforts. Chou En-lai very often cited the fact that when the five armies of the National Government were transported to Manchuria by the American fleet, General Marshall gave the exact number of divisions and troops in minute detail and not in merely general terms. Chou En-lai has always shown great confidence in General Marshall; even now, when he is more than ever in the opposite camp, I do not think that his appreciation of General Marshall has lessened in any degree.

During the period of my co-operation with General Marshall concerning the settlement of the question of the city of Changchun, I myself and some of my colleagues of the Democratic League worked as mediators between Chou En-lai and General Marshall, at the latter's request. When the fighting was going on in Changchun, General Marshall was afraid that it would spread and break the order of the cessation of hostilities, so he requested the members of the Democratic League to exert their influence upon Chou En-lai and ask him to be moderate.

My own impression of General Marshall is that he is neat, disciplined, well-informed, and deliberate. Other people might talk, but he choose to think things over himself. On one day he held three conferences, from nine to eleven in the morning, from two to four in the afternoon, and from eight to nine in the evening. He was a hard worker. He took notes himself of what we discussed. In the afternoon he would show these notes to us and say: "If there is anything wrong you can correct it." After his notes were corrected or confirmed, he brought them to the Generalissimo. His transmission of messages from the Generalissimo to the Communists or to the members of the Democratic League, or vice versa, was so accurate and painstaking that he won the confidence and respect of all sides in China.

Thus, what was requested in the statement of President Truman on United States policy towards China—the end of the Kuomintang's political tutelage, the convocation of a National Conference or representatives of major political elements, the elimination of autonomous armies and their integration into a National Army, and other arrangements for a democratic form of government—was apparently all settled by the Political Consultative Conference.

But while the Conference was passing the resolutions, a plot was being hatched in Manchuria which wrecked the mediation work of General Marshall. The Soviet Union did not like to see the development of a united, democratic, and prosperous China in the Far

East, as was contemplated by General Marshall and the State Department. The words of General Wedemeyer that Russia was, in effect, creating favorable conditions for the realization of the Chinese Communists' and possibly their own plans in North China and Manchuria, became a reality after February of 1946.

CHAPTER VIII

The Red Plot in Manchuria 1945-1946

Shortly after the Plenary Session of the Political Consultative Conference, I received an invitation from the Northeastern Citizens Club to deliver a lecture. As the Northeastern Provinces (commonly known abroad as Manchuria) constituted a danger spot in Asia, I took this opportunity to tell the people of these provinces about the possibilities for living in peace with their neighbor, Soviet Russia.

I began by giving them a résumé of the three wars which had been waged since 1894 for possession of the Provinces. The question first came into prominence in international politics in the wake of the Sino-Japanese war of that year. When negotiations were going on for a peace treaty, China had to cede the Liaotung peninsula to Japan. But following the protests of Russia, Germany, and France against Japan's acquisition of the peninsula, she renounced her claim.

During the hectic period of scrambling for concessions in China by the various European powers, Russia obtained a twenty-five year lease of Dairen and Port Arthur, together with the right to construct a Chinese railway to connect the territory with the main line across Manchuria. In this way Russia obtained a stranglehold on Manchuria. Japan, however, continued to nurse a sense of grievance against the three European powers which had taken the Liaotung peninsula from her grasp. In 1904 she went to war with Russia, and by a crushing defeat inflicted on the Muscovite forces, both military and naval, she was able to recoup all she had lost or failed to win in 1894, and in addition converted Korea into a Japanese colony. From that time until Pearl Harbor, Japan worked assiduously to consolidate her position as the dominating power in Far Eastern affairs. She converted Manchuria into a Japanese protectorate which she named "Manchukuo," and tried hard to set up a nominal self-government under her influence even in North China.

At the Yalta Conference, Roosevelt and Churchill backed Russia's claim that her rights as they existed before the Russo-Japanese War be restored to her, i.e., the rights in Manchuria, a share in the joint management of the Chinese Eastern Railway, and the use of Port Arthur and Dairen.

Having thus dealt briefly with these three wars, I went on to draw a parallel between the past history of Manchuria and that of Alsace-Lorraine and Poland. The cases are similar except that in Manchuria the population is virtually all Chinese. Alsace-Lorraine had changed hands three times—by the Treaty of Westphalia it was ceded to France; after the Franco-Prussian War of 1870 it was returned to Germany, only to come under French domination once more in 1919. Poland, after the partition undergone in 1772, 1773, and 1795, disappeared as a separate entity from the map of Europe, and regaining her independence in 1919, to be partitioned again in 1939, and once more lose her independence and become a Communist satellite.

The history of these European lands shows clearly how unsettled and how much at the mercy of powerful neighbors is the lot of provinces or smaller countries sandwiched between powerful and ambitious rivals. From these parallels, the peoples of the Northeastern Provinces of China can draw but cold comfort. However, I went on to argue that the relations between the two neighboring states need not be so bitter as those prevailing between France and Germany over Alsace-Lorraine, or those of Russia and Poland. One had only to look eastward across the Pacific to observe the continuously friendly relations maintained by the U.S.A. and Canada. To the observer thousands of miles away, it seemed obvious that the U.S.A. was so powerful that she could have swallowed up Canada as a 49th State. Why, then, had this not happened? The Canadians know how to combine their political Dominion status with a shrewd coordination of their economic life with that of the U.S.A. Under certain conditions American capitalists are encouraged to establish branch factories in Canada to produce for the Canadian market, thus giving work to Canadian labor and making it unnecessary for Canada to import the goods produced. The late Prime Minister, Mr. MacKenzie King, declined the offer of a title from the King-Emperor because he appreciated the political value of maintaining Canadian democracy on a basis similar to that of the United States. The matter was put to me succinctly by the first Canadian Ambassador to Chungking (General Odlum) when he said "Canada has to serve two masters, the Empire and the U.S.A., so she must behave herself." A study of Canada's attitude cannot but be valuable in solving this Chinese

Carson Chang standing (arrow) as China signs the United Nations Charter at San Francisco.

Carsun Chang on arrival at airport at Nanking on his return from Shanghai to resume talks with Nationalists and Communists.
From left to right: Wang Shih-chih, Wu Tih-cheng, Yang Chun-ming, Carsun Chang, Hsu Fu-lin, Lei Chen, Wu Ling, Huang Jen-chih, Tsing Yun-tien, Chen Chia-kang, Yu Chia-chu, Shen Chun-ju, Lo Lung-chi

problem of living at peace with an equally powerful neighbor, Soviet Russia.

At this point, I directed the attention of the audience to Sino-Soviet relations. All loyal citizens of China must admit that China will have to remain on friendly terms with Soviet Russia. The general approval of the signing of the Sino-Soviet Treaty of Friendship and Alliance shows that a desire for such peaceful relations exists on the Chinese side. If the same attitude of friendly cooperation existed on the Soviet side, there would be no real difficulty in arriving at an understanding. If the Soviet Union were capable of taking a long-term view, she would see that a stable and democratic China would be a better neighbor than a Communist China, which might well serve Communist purposes for a limited period, but whose subversive activities and calculated cruelty would alienate the sympathy—would indeed have earned the hatred—of millions of Chinese men and women towards anything Communist. The creation of a Communist China does not, to my way of thinking, represent the real and permanent interests of the Soviet Union. At the end of the recent war, most Chinese, Nationalists and Democrats included, were sincere in their desire to promote a policy of friendship towards the Soviet Union, but this aim was shattered by Russia's China policy. Exploiting the opportunity to occupy Manchuria, they formed a link with the Chinese Communists, supplied them with arms surrendered by the Japanese, and encouraged and aided them in developing Manchuria as a strong military base. How this was achieved is a long and tortuous story which may be divided into three phases: (a) Soviet obstructionism, (b) bargaining, and (c) delivery of Manchuria to the Chinese Communists.

While the negotiations were going on in Moscow in 1945 for the Treaty of Friendship and Alliance, the then Chinese Foreign Minister, Wang Shih-chieh, thought of tying the Soviet Union down by means of agreements so that all Russian aid would go to the Nationalist Government and not to the Chinese Communists. That was why, in addition to the Treaty, there was an exchange of notes in which the following articles may be found:

(1) In accordance with the spirit of the aforementioned Treaty and in order to put into effect its aims and purposes, the Government of the U.S.S.R. agrees to render to China moral support and aid to be given entirely to the National Government as the Central Government.

(2) In the course of conversation regarding Dairen and Port Arthur and regarding the joint operation of the Chinese Changchun railway, the Government of the U.S.S.R. regarded the three Eastern Provinces as part of China and reaffirmed its respect for China's full sovereignity over the three Eastern Provinces and recognized their territorial and administrative integrity.

(3) As for the recent developments in Sinkiang, the Soviet Government confirms that, as stated in Article V of the Treaty of Friendship and Alliance, it has no intention of interfering in the internal affairs of China.

These three points merely reaffirm the principles already laid down in Article V of the Treaty. Since Wang Shih-chieh suspected the sincerity and good faith of the Soviet Government, he asked that these points be recapitulated in the exchange of notes in order to pin Russia down more firmly, and to limit drastically her interference in Chinese politics. But Soviet Russia has never been tied down by "scraps of paper" or "agreements" or "articles" as the world knows now only too well. While Russia officially signed a treaty for the support of the National Government, she was secretly plotting the overthrow of that government. With one hand she signed the Treaty, while with the other she directed the preparations of her willing tools, the Chinese Communists, in Manchuria. Soviet duplicity enabled Russia to declare, even after Communist control of the three Eastern Provinces had been made possible by her aid, that they are after all a part of China, and that Russia has nothing to do with them. When the U.S.A. conceded privileges to Russia at Yalta and when the Chinese Government signed the Treaty in 1945, both were outwitted and outmaneuvered by Soviet Russia. It would be hard to find in history a more flagrant betrayal of international faith or a more flagrant violation of a solemn treaty than the actions of the U.S.S.R. in Manchuria between 1945 and 1946. This dishonesty can best be shown by a study of the three phases referred to earlier.

(a) *Soviet obstructionism.* What Russia had in mind at the time of the signing of the Treaty with China was that she would be able to do as she liked in Manchuria without any immediate danger of the armies of the Central Government being sent to Manchuria. It must have come as a surprise and a shock to the Russians when, after the surrender of the Japanese armies, the American authorities decided that, in order to control the repatriation of the Japanese armies, the American forces should organise by air-lift and fleet transport the movement of Chinese Nationalist armies to North China and Manchuria. This was a slap in the face to the Russians, because it made it easier for the Nationalists to recover their territories and nullify the advantage of the Communists. The Russians and the Chinese Communists dared not oppose openly the transportation of the Nationalist armies to Manchuria, because Manchuria was, after all, Chinese territory. But Soviet Russia did everything in her power to prevent the landing of a Chinese army in Manchuria.

After the Japanese surrender, Hsiung Shih-hui was appointed Director of the Headquarters of the Generalissimo in Manchuria, and my brother, Chang Kia-ngau, was appointed Chairman of the Economic Commission. At the same time that Manchuria was redivided into nine provinces, the appointment of governors of these provinces and mayors of the different cities was announced.

The Director, Hsiung Shih-hui, in his second talk with Marshal Malinovsky, the Soviet Commander-in-Chief, asked the latter to agree to the landing of the Chinese troops at Dairen. Malinovsky retorted that, according to the terms of the agreement, Dairen was to be a free port. This he interpreted as meaning that it was exclusively a commercial port, and that its use for landing troops of any nationality whatsoever would be a violation of the Sino-Soviet Treaty. Therefore, the Chinese proposal could not be accepted. As an alternative, the Chinese planned to land their army at Yingkow, but the Soviet riposte through the Commander-in-Chief was to the effect that the area was infested with brigands and bandits and that Soviet Russia could not assume any responsibility for any attacks that might be made by these bandits. These moves rendered impossible the landing of Nationalist troops, not only at Dairen, but also at other ports along the North coast—while the Chinese Communists proceeded to occupy them smoothly, with the connivance and cooperation of Soviet Russia.

At this time, Chang Kia-ngau, as Chairman of the Economic Commission, came back to Chungking and had talks with the Communist leader Tung Pih-wu. The Chinese Communists knew very well that the Nationalist expedition to Manchuria was by no means strong enough to put the three provinces completely under Central Government control, so Tung Pih-wu, who must have known of the exchange of views between the Kremlin and Yenan, agreed to the landing of the Nationalist army at Yingkow, and the agreement created an opening for the taking over of the three provinces.

In addition to the Soviet attempts to block the landing of the Nationalist army, the Soviet army intrigued with the Yenan Communists to allow them to garrison the route from Shanhaikwan to Mukden in order to close the door to the Central Army's advance into Manchuria. At the time of the Japanese surrender, the Yenan Communists were allowed by the Soviet army to penetrate into Manchuria via Inner Mongolia, Chahar, and Jehol before the arrival of the Central army. Moreover, in Heilungkiang, Kirin, Antung, and Harbin, and on the Korean border, Soviet Russia organized the Allied Democratic Army, consisting of natives of the three provinces under the supervision of the Soviet officers with the Chinese Communists.

In October, when American warships were patrolling off Dairen and some American sailors went ashore on a sight-seeing visit, the Russians made as much fuss as if a landing of the Chinese Nationalist army with the support of the American fleet was about to be forcibly attempted. Tension became so acute that Soviet Russia installed a Chinese Communist as Mayor of Changchun, and Chang Hsueh-shih, brother of Chang Hsueh-liang, one of the pioneers sent to Manchuria by Mao Tse-tung, was on the point of organizing an independent government of Manchuria.

In November, an order was issued from Chungking to the effect that the headquarters of the Generalissimo should withdraw from Manchuria. When the Soviet Commander-in-Chief heard of the impending withdrawal, he sent the following message to Chinese headquarters:

> The Soviet Army, according to plan, is scheduled to withdraw at the end of November. If the Soviet withdrawal is carried out before the arrival of the Central Army, Manchuria will come under the complete control of the Chinese Communists. Soviet Russia expects to see the power of the Chinese Government established in Manchuria.

This remarkable statement implies that any departure of the Chinese Government from Manchuria after the signature of the Sino-Soviet Treaty would create an international sensation and might provoke American intervention. Though Russia did not view with favor the arrival of the Central Army, the refusal of the Chinese Government to stay on in Manchuria would put Russia in a very awkward position. Hence the Russian Commander-in-Chief's advice to the headquarters of the Generalissimo to "stay put," with the obvious suggestion that Russia had no intention of setting up an independent government in Manchuria. Chang Hsueh-shih might have toyed with the idea of such an independent government, but he was dissuaded by Moscow. He had gone so far as to summon a mass-meeting at which he was to announce the launching of the new government and the establishment of a Bank of Manchuria empowered to issue bank notes. On the day of the meeting a plane arrived from Moscow with a special message; after a few minutes the rally broke up. The contents of the Russian message are unknown, but the fact remains that the idea of an independent government expired with its arrival. Obviously the Kremlin had made a change of policy and a crisis was averted.

(b) *Bargaining*. Though the Northeastern headquarters of the Generalissimo stayed on in Manchuria at the request of the Soviet authorities, China was nevertheless unable to exercise full control over the provinces. The Soviet policy was to restrict Chinese control to the Changchun Railway line and the strips of territory adjoining this line. In short, the function of the Central Army was to protect this railway. The complexity of Soviet policy is best understood in terms of these considerations:

Russia's attitude towards the Nationalists in Manchuria. The Chinese Nationalist Headquarters, now that it had decided to stay on, embarked on a policy of conciliation and cooperation with the Soviet authorities, and outlined its policy for Russia's benefit in a memorandum sent by the Director of the Headquarters to the Soviet Commander-in-Chief in January, 1946. The gist of the memorandum was that five Chinese armies would be sent to Manchuria, one to be stationed in Changchun, two in Mukden, and two in Harbin. In each of the nine provinces, there would be a "security task force" of 20,000 men. The Chinese Government announced that it had no intention of keeping a military force for national defense in Manchuria.

Marshal Malinovsky was very satisfied with this information, and agreed to the landing of the Chinese army at Yingkow, a point agreed upon earlier by Tung Pih-wu and Chang Kia-ngau but only now put into practice when Soviet consent had been obtained. Malinovsky also ordered the withdrawal of Communist troops from the section of Shanhaikwan to Sinminfu, and allowed the Central Army to occupy this area. From this point also, the city of Mukden came into Central Government hands, and the four cities, Harbin,

Changchun, Mukden, and Kirin, were administered by the mayors nominated by the Central Government.

With regard to the administration of the nine provincial governments, when the Director of the Headquarters requested the Soviet Commander-in-Chief to help in the work of withdrawal or disbanding of the so-called "Allied Democratic Army," the latter answered that it was difficult for Soviet Russia to render any service in this kind of work. Because of this refusal, most of the governors, high commissioners, and mayors, after being appointed by the Central Government, had to sit idly in Mukden. The intention of Soviet Russia was to postpone the administrative taking over of these provinces by the Central Government till the question of the location of the Nationalist and Communist armies had been settled by the Political Consultative Conference. At another time, when Chinese Headquarters requested the Soviet Commander-in-Chief to help in the work of taking over provincial administration, he answered that if the question of economic cooperation could be solved, that of the provincial administration would follow naturally. Soviet Russia adopted her obstructionist policy in order to preserve the status quo until the outcome of the Political Consultative Conference in Chungking was known. If the conference were successful, the Chinese Communists would know how to protect their own interests. If it were a failure, the Northeastern Provinces would be kept as a preserve for the Chinese Communists by Soviet Russia.

Consolidation of the Soviet economic position in the Northeastern Provinces. Militarily the aim of Soviet Russia was to maintain a balance of power between the Chinese Central Government (whose control was to be restricted to the railway trunk line and the cities along this line) and the Chinese Communists (who were allowed to occupy as much territory as possible outside the railway line). However, this allocation of spheres of influence between the Nationalists and the Communists did not satisfy Russia's ambitions. She wanted to play an important role in the economic life of the Northeastern Provinces. In the name of "preeminent interests," and in accordance with the Yalta agreement, Soviet Russia tried to control the key industries in Manchuria. She sought and still seeks to exercize economic influence not only along the main trunk line, but also in the different provinces, because the industrial enterprizes, the joint management of which Soviet Russia had asked for, were spread over all the Provinces. By such economic control, Soviet Russia would become the real master of these Northeastern Provinces, irrespective of whether the Nationalists or the Chinese Communists controlled the local government in Manchuria.

When the Central Government began to negotiate with Soviet Russia for the taking over of the mines, factories, and other enterprizes, Soviet Russia's answer was that all these factories and power plants had been managed by the Japanese for the purpose of carrying on the war, so that they were legitimate war-booty for Soviet Russia. Chang Kia-ngau protested, saying that booty is a term which can only be applied to military equipment, and that it is unreasonable to consider industrial and mining enterprizes as booty. In November, 1945, the economic adviser to Marshal Malinovsky, Slatkovsky, handed over to Chang Kia-ngau a list of 154 enterprises, including coal and iron mines, power plants, steel and iron works, chemical industries and cement works, which should be jointly managed by Soviet Russia and China. This list covered 80 per cent of all the industries in Manchuria. Chang Kia-ngau told Marshal Malinovsky that in order to avoid any suspicion of negotiating under duress, it would be better to start negotiations after the withdrawal of the Soviet army. In January, Chang Kia-ngau had another talk with Malinovsky and his economic adviser. Malinovsky said: "The suggestion of joint management of these industries is offered as a guarantee of the national security of Soviet Russia." He also said that his mission in Manchuria was to help in the restoration of Chinese sovereignty and to solve the problem of economic cooperation. Before the settlement of this problem he could not make a schedule of dates for the withdrawal of the Soviet Army from Manchuria.

While the negotiations were going on, some small factories and power plants were given back to China. As for the remaining industrial enterprizes, Soviet Russia held that they should come under the joint management of China and Soviet Russia. After three months of negotiation about twenty enterprizes were placed on the list for joint management by Soviet Russia. These were so scattered that there were one or two enterprizes in each province, insuring that Soviet economic control would be spread all over Manchuria.

In March, 1946, Chang Kia-ngau, after prolonged negotiations with the Russian economic adviser Slatkovsky, brought the list to Chungking. The object of his trip was to make a report to the Minister of Industry, Wong Wen-hao, the Minister of Foreign Affairs, Wang Shih-chieh and the Generalissimo. They had talk after talk because the situation in Manchuria between China, Soviet Russia, and the

Chinese Communists had so deteriorated by that time that Chiang could not make up his mind whether or not he would accept the list of enterprises to be jointly managed. The Generalissimo finally agreed to Chang Kia-ngau's returning to Mukden to sign an agreement with Soviet Russia, but the next day he ordered him not to go. This procedure of agreeing and then changing his mind was repeated many times. Then anti-Soviet student demonstrations instigated by Chen Li-fu broke out in Chungking, Nanking, and Shanghai, and Sino-Soviet friendship was admittedly at the lowest ebb. One day, Chang Kia-ngau was already waiting at the airfield to leave for Mukden when he was again stopped by a telephone message from the Generalissimo. This was the last attempt my brother made to return to Mukden. He had brought the list of ten to twenty jointly managed businesses to Chungking in the expectation that it would be approved by the Generalissimo and that economic cooperation between Soviet Russia and China could be established to serve as a foundation for friendly relations between the two countries, but with the deterioration of Sino-Soviet relations in the month of March, 1946, that expectation was never realised. In the latter part of March he received a telegram from the Russian side, saying that Marshal Malinovsky would still be in Harbin until the end of the month, and that if he could come by that time, Malinovsky would receive him. This meant that Soviet Russia was still expecting to win more economic concessions from the Central Government, although her essential plan was to allow the Chinese Communists to occupy Manchuria. Later Chang Kia-ngau went back to Manchuria to carry on routine work in the Economic Commission. He had no further contact with the Soviet authorities.

Russia's connection with the Chinese Communists. Russia's policy in Manchuria was to play a complicated game of double-dealing. As the Sino-Soviet Treaty had been signed, they could not disregard the position of the Central Government and never formally recognised the political position of the Chinese Communist Party there in the Northeastern Provinces. In their dealings with the Director of the Headquarters of the Generalissmo, they referred to the Chinese Communists sometimes as "local forces," sometimes as "bandits." They had no scruples about the language they used if their end—keeping Manchuria for the Chinese Communists—could be attained. The story of the presence of many Communists in Manchuria requires clarification. One group, the so-called "indigenous Communists," had previously belonged to the "anti-Japanese allied force." After the conquest of Manchuria by the Japanese they sought shelter on the Russian border. They depended for their very existence on Soviet Russia and were trained as Communists. Others who were expelled from Manchuria by the Japanese were also ordered to join them. When the Soviet army advanced into Manchuria in 1945, all of them were ordered to accompany it. They were appointed to the different localities to perform specific tasks. Another group, the Chinese "political workers," who received their education and training in Moscow, and Chinese military officers who were trained there, were also ordered to go with the Soviet army. They were appointed organizers of the local military forces and were labelled "Soviet-trained Communists."

The third group, the Yenan Communists, comprized the Communist army of Yenan, which collaborated with Soviet Russia and penetrated to the south of Mukden via Inner Mongolia and the north of Hopei Province. Soviet Russia combined these three kinds of Communists and supplied them with arms captured from the Kwantung army of Japan. Soviet Russia distributed these arms while claiming that bandits came and stole them from the munition dumps. Everybody knew, however, that the Soviet army left the doors of the munition depots open in order to equip the Communists. Altogether, after being properly armed, they made a formidable force in Manchuria, spreading all over North Manchuria and Antung.

At the Political Consultative Conference, the Chinese Communist Party mentioned that their local force in Manchuria should be maintained as it was. What they meant was the combined force of these three kinds of Communists. When the Director of the Headquarters asked the Soviet Commander-in-Chief to dissolve this force, the answer was that he might try to disband the "local force" which was organized in Manchuria, while with regard to the Yenan Communist army, which had penetrated into Manchuria by way of North China, Soviet Russia could not get rid of them, because they belonged to the Chinese Communist Party, which was recognised as a partner at the Conference table.

It is interesting to see how Soviet Russia and the Chinese Communist Party worked in coordination to further the expansion of the Communist force in Manchuria. To achieve this end the negotiations of the Soviet Army with the Headquarters of the Generalissimo in Manchuria and the negotiations of the Chinese Communist Party with the National Government in Chungking were carried on simultaneously.

Those who dealt with the Soviet Commander-in-Chief had the impression that the Russians at first intended to get hold of Manchuria for themselves. If the Chinese Government would give them all they demanded, the Soviet policy was to let the Communist force stay behind as a purely local force and not allow them to play any open part. The Chinese Communists were at first anxious to display themselves on the political stage of Manchuria, and that was why a movement for an independent government was contemplated by Chang Hsueh-shih—but the Kremlin made short work of it. Soviet Russia and the Chinese Communist Party, however, played their cards well. If Russia got all she wanted directly from the Central Government, Manchuria would be a bulwark for her security and a base for the growth of the Chinese Communist force. If the Chinese Communist Party at the P .C. C. meeting succeeded in winning a strong position in Manchuria, that would also be a gain for Russian interests. Soviet Russia pursued both objectives at the same time, just in case either of them should not give the desired result.

After protracted negotiation with the Headquarters of the Generalissimo, the Russians found that their demands would not be satisfied by the Central Government, and so they allowed the Chinese Communist force, which had been organized and equipped by them from the very beginning, to play their part openly. This was why the battle of Changchun was started by the Chinese Communists. During the battle, the Russian engineers attached to the Changchun Railway Administration withdrew on the pretext that they could not carry on their work under such conditions. It was sabotage on the Soviet side. After Changchun was recaptured by the Central Army, Russia believed that the Central Army would take all Manchuria by force and that the Central Government would have no intention, then, of negotiating with Moscow. She then adopted the alternative measure that the control of Manchuria must be carried out by the Chinese Communists themselves.

(c) *Delivery of Manchuria to the Chinese Communists.* After March, 1946, Russia found out that the Central Government had discontinued negotiations aiming at joint administration, and that the P. C. C. was in a state of deadlock. As the time for the withdrawal of the Soviet Army was near, the Russians changed their tactics and decided to hand over Manchuria to the Chinese Communists. The Chinese Government was kept ignorant of the withdrawal of the Russian army, while the Communists were informed of its movements two or three days in advance. The Communists occupied the cities evacuated by the Russians and defended them when the Nationalist army came to take them over. The city of Changchun, after being evacuated by the Russians on April 14, 1946, was first occupied by the Communists. Most of the other cities lay beyond the reach of the Central army and were left to the Chinese Communists on the spot by the Soviet Army. Furthermore, the Soviet Commander-in-Chief explicitly told the Headquarters of the Generalissimo that, with regard to the cities north of Changchun, he could not wait for the arrival of the Nationalist Army, and that the Soviet Army must therefore allow the local forces (the Communists) to occupy them. Here arose the question of delay in the withdrawal of the Soviet Army. The Soviet side maintained that the delay was in accordance with the request of the Chinese Government that the Soviet Army wait until the arrival of the Nationalist Army. Chiang Kai-shek's intention was to make Soviet Russia responsible for the occupation of any city by the Chinese Communists. But Russia paid no attention to this seemingly clever move on the part of Chiang. Concealing their movements from the Chinese authorities, they allowed the Communists to occupy as many as 105 cities in Manchuria in one month. This meant that 90 per cent of Manchuria fell into the hands of the Chinese Communists.

The manner in which the Chinese Communists were equipped by the Russians should also be made clear. According to a Chinese report, the booty which fell into Soviet hands from the Japanese Army consisted of the following:

Japanese War Prisoners	594,000
Aircraft	925
Tanks	369
Armored Cars	35
Field Artillery Pieces	1,226
Machine Guns	4,836
Rifles	300,000
Wireless Sets	130
Motor Cars	2,300
Towing Vehicles	125
Horses and Mules	17,497
Supply Vehicles	21,084

Most of the Japanese prisoners of war were sent to Siberia for indoctrination, but the gunners were ordered to join the Chinese Communist army. This military help was given to the Chinese Communists to counter-balance the American equipment which went to the thirty-six Nationalist divisions. The army of the Communist Commander-in-Chief, Lin Piao, comprising about 200,000 men who later fought on the Korean front, was unequipped at the time of its penetration from North China into Manchuria, but was shortly afterwards armed with seized Japanese weapons.

In addition to the war booty, other military equipment was given to the Chinese Communists by the Russians on a barter basis, in exchange for Chinese agricultural products. But the most important aid was given when the Nationalist authorities were not allowed to go north of Changchun. Here were schools for the training of Communist officers, pilots, and sailors under Soviet instructors. The Communists finally became such a formidable force that they were in a position to challenge the Nationalist army.

Provided with the proper background information, we should now be able to see clearly the consequences of the Yalta Agreement and the Sino-Soviet Treaty. It may be true that Russia would have taken Manchuria in any case, even if she had not been permitted to do so. But the consent given by the U. S. A., Britain, and later by China through treaty agreement made all the difference in that the Soviet seizure then became legalized and the signatory powers could only remain silent. On the pretext of fighting Japan, Soviet Russia came into Manchuria, worked with the Chinese Communists, equipped them with arms, and built up Manchuria as a military base for the expansion of international Communism. As a Chinese proverb says: "While a tiger is being driven away at the front door, a wolf enters by the back door." That was what happened in Manchuria.

Even had an efficient government existed in China, it would have been difficult to suppress the combined Moscow-Yenan power in the far north of China. It was impossible after eight years of exhausting war. After this new and grave situation had arisen, it became the subject of serious discussion between China and the United States until General Wedemeyer, as special representative to China, suggested establishing a trusteeship for Manchuria. That suggestion was shelved and not acted upon. General Marshall, too, at the beginning of 1946, was still hoping that the problem could be settled by a truce or by the formation of a coalition government.

It was, I think, an act of negligence on the part of the Nationalist Government that it did not take the initiative in bringing such a grave situation to the attention of a "fact-finding commission," or encouraging other discussions on an international level in order to find a remedy. Instead, it was confident and arrogant, and believed that the problem could be solved by its own military strength. But the reinforcements it sent to Manchuria were cut to pieces by the Communists, and the military expenditure involved aggravated the nation's inflationary situation and hastened its financial collapse.

Both China and the United States should have seen the threat represented by the Soviet advance into Manchuria. When matters came to such a point, the question was no longer one of Chinese domestic politics, but of international Communist aggression. General Marshall, in his role of mediator, suggested to China the remedy of a party truce. His idea was to put the Nationalist Government on a democratic basis. That was certainly the right thing to do: it was what all Chinese liberals and democrats had desired for many years. But to meet such a gigantic international plot, much more drastic action was needed. The Moscow-Yenan combined force in Manchuria was a more powerful enemy than Japan was at the height of her military power. If China could not rid herself of the Japanese menace during all the years between 1937 and 1945, how could she meet Soviet Russia's challenge in Manchuria in 1946, diplomatically—much less militarily—without external help? After many years of war she was financially exhausted. Though her army was equipped with American weapons, the morale among officers and men was very low, and in the matter of successful propaganda the Nationalists were far behind the Communists. A complete miscalculation on the part of China and her allies had permitted Soviet Russia, in alliance with the Chinese Communists, to drive in a wedge to split China, while the U. S. A., after making great sacrifices in fighting Japan, had lost a crucial diplomatic battle. General Marshall, in spite of everything, went on with his work of mediation. But notwithstanding the personal respect which he earned from the Chinese and the patient work he did till the end of 1946, his mission was wrecked from the moment that the Manchurian crisis became an ugly reality.

CHAPTER IX

Mediation Continues

The attempt at effecting a reconciliation between the Kuomintang and the Communists by means of a united front, a coalition government, and a united command, was begun much too late in China. When a foreign enemy is within a country, a united front has meaning, because it represents a first step in the process of getting rid of the enemy. In China, negotiations aimed at establishing a coalition government and nationalizing the army began when the Japanese had already surrendered and there was no longer any threat of invasion to act as a spur to reconciliation. That was the situation in the beginning of 1946. Though some progress was made in the Political Consultative Conference in January and February, the Communists were not interested in a respite from strife. After their infiltration into Manchuria, with their back protected from attack by the Soviet Union, they felt more secure, and they even started the battle of Changchun. Before the city fell into Communist hands, I sent a member of my Democratic-Socialist Party, who is at present Minister without portfolio in the National Government of Taiwan, to let Chou En-lai know that, as Changchun had been handed over to Chiang Kai-shek by the Soviet Union according to the newly signed treaty, the arbitrary capture of this city by the Communists indicated that they would take any city as and when they felt strong enough to do so. There would then be no meaning to all this talk about the cessation of hostilities and the end of civil war. I persuaded Chou En-lai to see that the Communist army, even if it could take the city, should stay outside the city walls, and seek a settlement of the question through negotiation. Chou En-lai's only reply was that the security of the Nationalist officials in the city would be guaranteed.

It was under such circumstances that General Marshall started his task of mediation in 1945 and 1946. After the close of the Political Consultative Conference, General Marshall's work dealt with two major subjects—the battle of Changchun and related issues (from May to June), and establishing the list of delegates to the National

Assembly (in October and November). In between these two periods there was the matter of the Committee of Five, which was proposed on August 1 by Dr. Leighton Stuart when he was appointed American Ambassador. Its task was to consider the question of the reorganization of the government. But Chou En-lai insisted that the cease-fire order should come first, and in consequence nothing much was ever done by the Committee.

General Marshall, after his return from Washington on April 18, sent me a telephone message through Lo Lung-chi and asked me to have a talk with him about the settlement of the Changchun battle in the hope that peace would prevail and the work of unifying China go forward. During our exchange of views General Marshall proposed the following conditions for a truce: (1) That a Nationalist token force should enter Changchun; (2) that the railway line should not be used for transporting the army; and (3) that a non-partisan—neither a Kuomintang nor a Communist figure—should be appointed Mayor of Changchun. The proposal was brought to Chou En-lai for his approval. All the members of the Democratic League pressed for reconciliation from the Communist side, but Chou's reply was that it was difficult for a Communist commander to give up a city once his forces had occupied it. It was the unanimous opinion, however, that he should agree to the proposal, and this, accordingly, he did. Next day we brought Chou's reply to General Marshall, who transmitted the information to the Generalissimo during a dinner party. But what General Marshall had proposed and Chou En-lai agreed to was rejected by Chiang!

It is interesting to recall that the Battle of Changchun was planned during General Marshall's absence from China, and the day of the capture of the city was the day of General Marshall's return to China. He was thus called upon to extinguish the fire the moment he arrived; but it was much harder now to stop the fighting than it was to have the cease-fire order issued in January. Chiang Kai-shek is a soldier, and he considered the loss of Changchun a blow to his prestige and was determined to recapture it. When the capital was moved back to Nanking from Chungking, he went to Manchuria to direct military operations himself. At that time the Communist army was not yet in a position to successfully oppose the Kuomintang army which was equipped with American weapons; the Communists kept Changchun for a month and then lost it. With this capture there was talk in Nanking and Shanghai that the Nationalist army might advance as far north as Harbin. General Marshall was waiting in Nanking for the Generalissimo's return, and he was probably worried that the further advance of the Nationalist army might prove offensive to the Soviet Government. Fortunately, the Nationalist army stopped at Changchun and Chiang returned on June 3.

It is important to relate that before Chiang started for Manchuria he conveyed a three-point message to Chou En-lai through General Marshall. He stipulated that the Chinese Communist party must make every effort to facilitate the restoration of communications, that in any agreement regarding the Manchurian issues provision must be made for carrying out the military demobilization and reorganization plan within specified dates, and that the Generalissimo would not commit himself to further agreement without an understanding that when field teams or high staff groups reached an impasse, the final decision would be left to the American member.

On June 6, it was agreed that there should be a truce of fifteen days. Later, at the suggestion of General Marshall, it was extended till noon of June 30, and during these twenty-four days we worked hard to find a solution.

With the first two points of the Generalissimo's demands, members of the Democratic League could have nothing to do, because they lay within the scope of the Committee of Three. With regard to the last point, when Chou En-lai got notice of it, he was furious. Chou said to me, "The question of a truce is a Chinese affair. It is already a disgrace that we have an American member among the field teams. I don't mind working with an American, but how can we leave the final decision to him? Even if a Soviet Communist worked in the field team, it would be better to have me beheaded than to agree that the final decision should be left in the hands of a Soviet member." I am convinced that these words came straight from Chou En-lai's heart, because Chou and Tung Pih-wu were *Chinese* Communists; both had as much as said that they would fulfill their duty to China first, and then to Communism. As Chou's objection to this point was so strong, we had to go to General Marshall to ask for an explanation —for the field team was his business. General Marshall explained that the Committee of Three was the highest organ appointed to deal with the order for a cessation of hostilities. The field team would go to the place where there was fighting and then investigate the causes of the fighting. The three members—the Nationalist, the Communist and the American—when they had accepted the on-the-spot report, would send it to the Executive Headquarters at Peiping. If agreement could not be reached, however, the fighting would drag on. What should

Representatives from all the parties as they assembled in Wu Tih-cheng's house: From left to right: *Front Row:* Carsun Chang, Chen Chi-tien, Shen Chun-ju, Shao Lih-chih, Chou En-lai, Tso Shun-shen, Ko Mo-jo, Li Wei-han, Tsen Chi, Wu Tih-cheng. *Middle Row:* Huang Jen-chih, unknown Communist member, Chang Po-chun, Lo Lung-chi, Wu Ling, Tsiang Yun-tien, Li Huang, unknown Nationalist member. *Back Row:* Yang Shu-min, Yu Chia-chu.

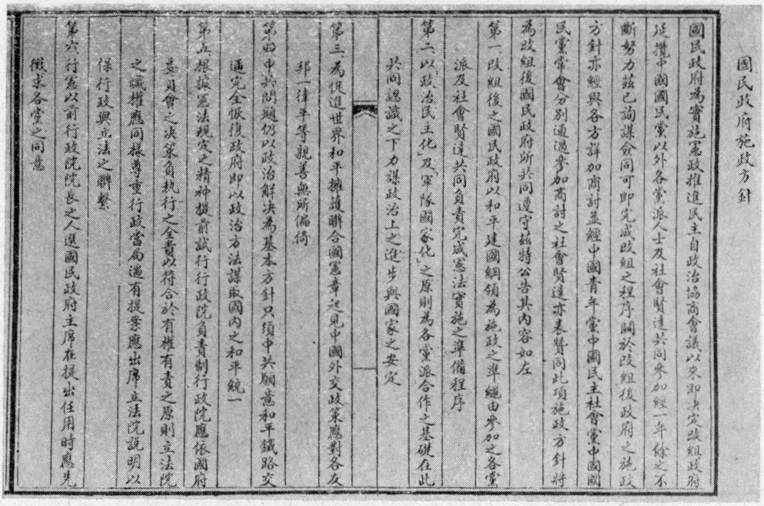

國民政府施政方針

國民政府為實施憲政推進民主自政治協商會議以來即決定改組政府延攬中國國民黨以外各黨派人士及社會賢達共同參加經一年餘之不斷努力茲已商談僉同可即完成改組之程序關於改組後政府之施政方針亦經與各方詳加商討並經中國青年黨中國民主社會黨中國國民黨常會分別通過參加商討之社會賢達亦表贊同此項施政方針將為改組後國民政府所共同遵守茲特公告其內容如左

第一 改組後之國民政府以和平建國綱領為施政之準繩由參加之各黨派及社會賢達共同負責完成憲法實施之準備程序

第二 以政治民主化及軍隊國家化之原則為各黨派合作之基礎在此共同認識之下力謀政治上之進步與國家之安定

第三 為促進世界和平擁護聯合國憲章之見中國外交政策應對各友邦一律平等親善無所偏倚

第四 中共問題仍以政治解決為基本方針只須中共願意和平鐵路交通完全恢復政府即以政治方法謀取國內之和平統一

第五 根據憲法規定之精神提前試行行政院負責制行政院應依國府委員會之決策負執行之全責以符合於有權有責之原則立法院之職權應同樣尊重行政當局遇有提案應出席立法院說明以保行政與立法之聯繫

第六 行憲以前行政院院長之人選國民政府主席在提出任用時應先徵求各黨之同意

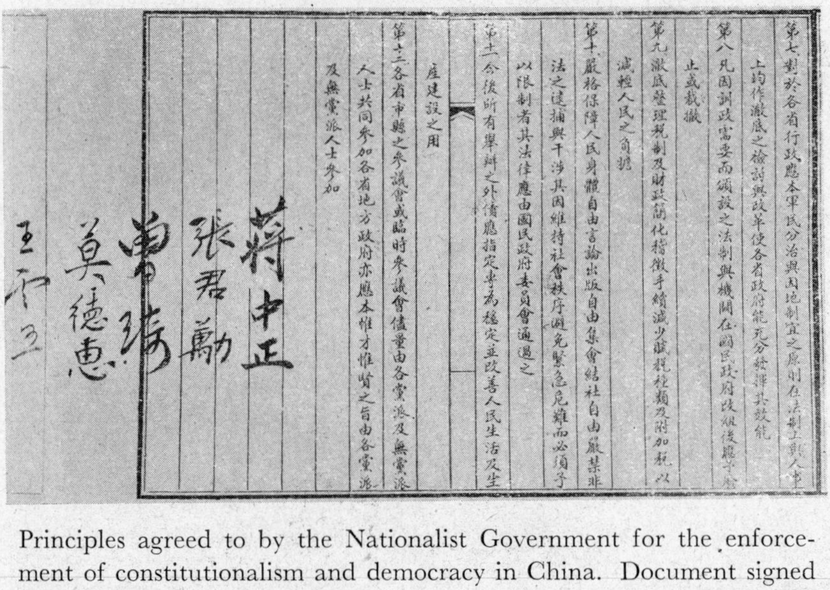

第七 對於各省行政應本軍民分治與因地制宜之原則在法制上與人事上均作澈底之檢討與改革使各省政府能充分發揮其效能

第八 凡因訓政需要而頒設之法制與機關在國民政府改組後應予廢止或裁撤

第九 澈底整理稅制及財政簡化稽徵手續減少苛稅雜稅及附加稅以減輕人民之負擔

第十 嚴格保障人民身體自由言論出版自由集會結社自由嚴禁非法之逮捕與干涉其因維持社會秩序避免緊急危難而必須予以限制者其法律應由國民政府委員會通過之

第十一 今後所有舉辦之外債應指定專為穩定並改善人民生活及生產建設之用

第十二 各省市縣之參議會或臨時參議會儘量由各黨派及無黨派人士共同參加各省地方政府亦應本惟才惟賢之旨由各黨派及無黨派人士參加

蔣中正
張君勱
曾琦
莫德惠
王雲五

Principles agreed to by the Nationalist Government for the enforcement of constitutionalism and democracy in China. Document signed by (right to left) Chiang Kai-shek, Carsun Chang, Tseng Chih, Mo Teh-hui and Wang Yun-wu be done, therefore, when there was disagreement? The American member had the right to render his own report. He was authorized to make investigations regarding military activities within his area. He could also issue orders in the name of the Executive Headquarters to stop the fighting at once and to separate the contending forces. This explanation, given by General Marshall, was conveyed to Chou, who promised to forward it to Yenan. Yenan's reply came back after many days, and General Marshall was glad to have it when Lo Lung-chi and I told him the news. This is how it was worded in the American White Book: "The Chinese Communists made concessions in granting the deciding vote to Americans on teams and in the Executive Headquarters regarding matters pertaining to cessation of hostilities procedures, interpretation of agreements, and their execution." On the highest level of the Committee of Three, General Marshall assured Chou En-lai that he did not want to exercise the deciding vote. This had a soothing effect upon Chou En-lai's objection.

During the truce days, besides the question of the deciding vote, an agreement for the resumption of communications was reached. It was also agreed that the order of cessation of hostilities would be applied to Manchuria. These two tentative agreements would become effective, however, only when the other questions were settled.

But the Generalissimo was more interested in the question of the location of the various military formations in North China, because the Communist army was giving him great concern. The demands which the Generalissimo asked General Marshall to convey to Chou En-lai on June 17 show in what direction his mind was working:

(1) The evacuation of Chinese Communist forces from Jehol and Chahar Provinces before September 1, 1946.

(2) The occupation by Government forces of Chefoo and Weihaiwei in Shantung Province.

(3) The reinforcement of Tsingtao with one Nationalist army.

(4) The evacuation by the Chinese Communists before July 1, 1946 of all localities in Shantung forcibly occupied by the Communist troops after noon of June 7, 1946.

(5) The immediate occupation of these localities by the Government army commencing September 1, 1946.

(6) The reinforcement of troops in the Tientsin region by one Government army commencing September 1, 1946.

(7) Government occupation of various points then held by Communist forces, such as Harbin, Antung, Tung-hwa, Mutankiang and Paicheng.

These demands were too much for Chou En-lai. General Marshall advised him to fly back to Yenan to consult the leaders of the Communist Party, but Chou frankly told Marshall that nothing justified such a trip. Chou En-lai preferred to have the political questions settled first before any talk of evacuation of North China began. The Generalissimo's position was that political adjustments at this time were difficult, if not impossible, unless military re-adjustments were first effected in order to avoid clashes. This talk took place on June 27, three days before the expiration of the terms of truce.

During the negotiations Chou En-lai was generally moderate and did his best to see that the work of peace and unity be carried forward. The Generalissimo, on his side, later reduced some of the June 17 demands. He asked that the Chinese Communist Party evacuate North Kiangsu Province and Harbin within ten days, adding that these would be occupied by Government troops within one month. As a compromise measure he agreed to Communist officials being appointed in Northern Manchuria. It seemed for a while that the two sides might come together after all.

In early October, General Marshall got the idea that he himself should go to Shanghai to bring Chou back. But he was afraid that if he failed it would cause a sensation not only in China, but also in the United States, so he told no one about his trip. One day, early in the morning, he went out in his own car and spent about two hours driving around the city till his plane was ready. He left Nanking about ten o'clock and arrived in Shanghai about noon. He telephoned to Chou En-lai at once and invited him to luncheon. When General Marshall asked Chou to go back to Nanking, his reply was still a flat no, in spite of all Marshall's persuasion. From the middle of September till Marshall's arrival in Shanghai, the Kuomintang-Communist negotiations were at a complete standstill.

Most of the members of the Democratic League were then living in Shanghai, and they maintained contact with Chou En-lai. When General Marshall failed to bring Chou back, the third group tried to find out under what conditions Chou would return to continue the negotiations. His first condition was the issuance of a cease-fire order, especially with regard to the fighting around Kalgan. But while everything was being done about securing this, the Government one day announced the capture of Kalgan and also its eight conditions for the cessation of hostilities. Whereupon Chou En-lai said to me: "If the Government is proud of the capture of Kalgan, what is the use of my going to Nanking?" The Government, however, sent Shao Lih-tse to Shanghai to offer an explanation of the new development to members of the Democratic League and to Chou En-lai. Shao impressed upon them that the eight conditions were not definitive, and that the main thing was to return to Nanking. After two days, two planes brought the members of the Democratic League back; Chou En-lai and his Communist colleagues flew in another plane.

From now on mediation was carried on through the good offices of the third group, and no longer through General Marshall. There was a free exchange of views between that group and Chou in the conference room of the Bank of Communications in Nanking. The first thing we studied was the Government's eight conditions, which were:

(1) The restoration of communications to be immediately effected in accordance with the agreement tentatively reached by the Committee of Three last June.

(2) The method for settling disagreements among the team members of the Executive Headquarters to be in accordance with the agreement tentatively reached by the Committee of Three last June.

(3) The tentative agreement reached last June by the Committee of Three for the redisposition of troops in Manchuria to be carried out according to a fixed schedule without delay.

(4) The Government troops and Communist troops in North China and Central China to continue in occupation of localities now under their control until agreement by the Committee of Three is reached for the redistribution, reorganization and demobilization of troops, Government and Communist alike, for the unification of the armed forces in China.

(5) Whatever understanding is reached by the Five-Man Committee headed by Dr. Leighton Stuart, it is to be confirmed by the Steering Committee of the P. C. C. without delay.

(6) Questions of local government, excluding Manchuria, to be settled by the newly organised State Council.

(7) The Constitutional Draft Committee to be convened immediately and the agreed draft to be submitted to the National Assembly, through the National Government, as the basis for its action.

(8) Concurrent with the proclamation of the cessation of hostilities, which is to be effected immediately following the agreement of the Communist Party to the foregoing procedure, that party is to announce its intention of participating

in the National Assembly by publishing its lists of delegates thereto.

These eight conditions were chiefly the continuation of the subjects discussed in May and June, though some additional subjects were also included. After our talk with the Government, we found that these conditions were so worded that the cessation of hostilities and the appointment of government officials were to be applied only to the provinces inside the Great Wall. Manchuria was not included in the scope of the eight-point program. This was because Chiang maintained that, after the Japanese surrender, the sovereignty of Manchuria must first be restored, before any talk could begin about the appointment of the officials who would run the local government in that region. Chiang was not definitely opposed to the appointment of Communist officials, but he insisted that Manchuria should first come under his control. In June, Chiang had promised that Communist officials might be accepted in North Manchuria—which could have been understood to imply that North Manchuria might be placed under Communist control, and when this was not mentioned in the eight-point program, it gave us some cause for surprise.

It was to be expected that Chou En-lai would refuse to accept the eight-point program for discussion as long as hostilities did not cease. I then advised the Generalissimo that he should make it possible for Chou to discuss any subject he liked and not confine him to the eight points. Chou En-lai accepted this suggestion and promised to come to the round-table conference.

One evening, during one of the conferences, somebody reported the news that an order for the cessation of hostilities had been issued by the Generalissimo, who had also requested that a list of the delegates of the National Assembly be handed in by the different parties. What the Generalissimo said concerning the meeting of the National Assembly was:

In the meeting of the National Assembly, the Government will reserve quotas of the delegates for the Communists as well as for the other parties in the hope that they will participate in the making of the constitution. The Government also hopes that the Communists will authorize their representatives to participate in the meetings of the Committees to discuss the immediate implementation of the measures for the cessation of hostilities, the disposition of troops, the restoration of communications and the reorganization and integration of armies as proposed in my statement of October 16.

This arbitrary move on the part of Chiang displeased everybody. All the members expressed the view that it was a breach of faith for the Government to issue such an order without the prior consent of the different parties. Many threatened to leave Nanking. Chou En-lai too was naturally unhappy about this information, but he secretly rejoiced that the third group and he were now on the same side.

On the same evening the Government also announced that, as of the next day, the meeting of the Steering Committee of the P. C. C. and the Committee of Three would be resumed. A luncheon party was arranged in Sun Fo's house to which Dr. Leighton Stuart was also invited. When the luncheon was over, Chou En-lai began to question Chiang's close follower Wu Tieh-cheng: "We live in the same city and there is not much distance between your house and mine: why then did you not consult me before such an order of cessation of hostilities was issued?" Wu's answer was: "The Chinese Communist Party has asked for a cessation of hostilities for a long time. Since it is what you have been asking for, why should it be wrong for us to issue such an order now?" Chou En-lai then turned around and bitterly attacked Wang Yun-wu, General Manager of the Commercial Press and a non-partisan, newly appointed Minister of Industry. Chou En-lai pointed to Wang and said: "You are an older man than I am, and I should not say anything against you. But since you are the first man among the non-partisan members of the P. C. C. to join the Government, I must warn you lest you become a new bureaucrat." When this kind of verbal exchange continued, Dr. Leighton Stuart excused himself and left, which was the cue for everybody else to leave, since the atmosphere was becoming too unpleasant. The members of the Democratic League, however, continued to keep in touch with Chou En-lai after leaving Sun Fo's house and advised him to be moderate and conciliatory in the Steering Committee the next day. Chou En-lai agreed, but when the Steering Committee of the P. C. C. convened, he raised the question of whether the date of November 12 for the convocation of the National Assembly could be changed. Shao Lih-tse understood his meaning and retorted, "Can the reorganization of the Government take place after the convocation of the National Assembly?" Whereupon Chou En-lai said: "But it was agreed that the list of delegates to the National Assembly will be handed in only to a reorganized government." Here was obviously another one of those numerous impasses, though Shao was willing to propose to the Generalissimo that he change the date of convocation provided that the National

Assembly meet before the reorganization of the government. Chou refused, and the meeting of the P. C. C. for the next day was called off.

In the meantime, Mo Teh-hui, a leading non-partisan from the Northeast Provinces, had a proposal to make which he thought might satisfy the Communists and lead China towards peace and unification. The next morning all the members assembled in the Bank of Communications for a meeting. I myself was late in arriving, having been engaged in a lengthy conference with General Marshall. Mo's proposal, which was passed as a resolution, was that the Changchun Railway, the trunk line in Manchuria, and the twenty-five districts along the line should come under the control of the Central Government, while the rest of Manchuria would be left to the Communists. Mo Teh-hui, as a former Minister Plenipotentiary to Moscow, thought that such a plan might satisfy the Soviet desire for security and Communist ambitions as well. Before the meeting adjourned it was decided that the resolution be reported to the three parties concerned—the Government, the Communists, and General Marshall as Chairman of the Committee of Three. Someone then hurried to Liang Shu-min, who was asked to report the resolution to Chou En-lai and ascertain whether it would be accepted by the Communists. Liang Shu-min put his hand on his bosom, which is a Chinese equivalent of "thumbs up," and said, "I can guarantee that Chou En-lai will gladly accept it." As Liang Shu-min knew the Communists well, his answer made us all feel that we were in for some agreement.

I myself reported to Sun Fo, who seemed to be pleased, but he said, "It will take two or three days for the Government to study it." I answered, "In that case, I could leave to join my family in Shanghai and await the good news there."

I arrived in Shanghai at ten o'clock that night, and at once a telephone call came for me from Nanking, saying that everything had gone wrong, and that I had to fly back the next day. I booked an air passage right away, but still managed to sleep soundly. I hope it was a case of having a good conscience. The first thing I did upon arriving, of course, was to make inquiries about what had gone wrong. I was told that when Liang Shu-min, Huang Yen-pei, and Li Huang called on Chou En-lai and showed him the resolution, tears ran down Chou's cheeks. He pointed to Liang Shu-min and said, "You are a hypocrite. Though our friendship has lasted twenty years, it is broken today." This remark was unexpected, to say the least, and the three who had called on Chou stood there speechless. Then

Huang Yen-pei, one of the three, had a happy thought; he went to the Democratic League to fetch Lo Lung-chi, who was known to be a very resourceful man. Lo proved resourceful indeed, and he pulled out one of the classical Chinese tricks known poetically as "pilfering the precious stone from the palace of the moon." His proposal was that they should go to the Government and General Marshall to say that the resolution had to be revised. By this time, I was being sought, though no one actually got hold of me. But I knew that a meeting had been held in Sun Fo's residence, a meeting at which the Government showed its satisfaction with the resolution introduced by Mo Teh-hui. The Government also knew, through its secret agents surrounding Chou En-lai's house, that Chou was stamping and weeping, and since there was no point in expressing its willingness to accept as long as Chou was so opposed to the resolution, the Government very graciously surrendered it. It would have been too compromising to its prestige if the Government started to say yes to a proposition to which Chou had said no. So that was the end of the resolution. I am giving these incidents as examples of Chinese political psychology and the way in which weighty problems were being bandied about.

But it is interesting to ask why Chou En-lai was so opposed to the plan. One explanation given to me was that if Manchuria, excepting the Changchun Railway line and the twenty-five districts along it, came under the control of the Communists, this might satisfy the Soviet Union. But at the same time the Chinese Communists would have to toe the Soviet line and restrict their activities in Manchuria, so that they would look in the eyes of the Chinese like subservient tools of the Soviet Union. If peace was achieved under this plan, there would be no further room for their expansion. Since Chou En-lai considered himself a Chinese patriot and wanted to be known as such, he could not very well subscribe to a plan that would make him and his colleagues mere tools of Russia. But this view of Chou's behavior was not accepted by everyone. One man said to me, "Chou En-lai didn't shed tears because the plan would make the Communists look like tools of the Soviet Union. That plan would have placed the Chinese Communists in a very favorable position. Nor does their stay in North Manchuria preclude any future plan for the overthrow of the government of Chiang Kai-shek. The Chinese Communists have for a long time accepted the leadership of the Kremlin, so that there is no reason why they should feel shy now of living on the Manchurian border and working clandestinely with the Soviet Union."

Another explanation was that Chou wept because Liang Shu-min, as a close friend of many years' standing, should have consulted him first, and not presented him with a fait accompli for approval or rejection. Then, Chou must have previously reported to Yenan on the reliability and impartiality of the Democratic League, but the League took a hostile attitude in the present instance and Chou was losing face with Yenan. The reasons for his weeping were many and complicated!

After all this excitement had more or less subsided and Chou En-lai's tears had dried, the Government cleverly took advantage of the confused state of affairs and pressed even harder for the names of the delegates to the National Assembly. The Government issued a notice to the effect that, "if such a list were handed in, the Government might consider changing the date of convocation of the Assembly." The Democratic League called for a meeting at once but decided to submit the names of ten members who were also members of the P. C. C. as an expression of the fact that they were not opposed to the convocation. At the same time the League sent three representatives to contact Chou En-lai, which showed that, along with other indications, it was prepared to work in close co-operation with the Communists. That move, however, precipitated a crisis and made the entire Third Group wonder if the Democratic League had become a political tool of the Communist Party. If it was an independent group, why should the three members go to Chou En-lai and ask for his instructions—since that was apparently their purpose? The indications of an uncritically pro-Communist attitude on the part of the League were later substantiated, and destroyed the League's usefulness as an independent party. Under the circumstances I had to consider whether my own party, the Democratic-Socialist Party, should stay within the League.

Let me now say a word of explanation. During my stay in Germany from 1919 to 1922, I came into contact with the members of the German Social Democratic party and heard a great deal about the activities of the Communist Party. I was then interested in the *Betriebsgesetz*. I had Karl Korsch, Professor of *Prozessrecht* at the University of Jena (now retired from politics and teaching in the United States) as my teacher. One day in 1921, Karl Korsch told me, "Within a few days a Communist uprising will break out here. Though I am the leader of the Communist Party in Jena, yet I am not for the uprising. If it starts I shall have to hide in your house." To that I answered: "I am a Chinese living here, who enjoys no extra-territoriality in Germany, as Germans used to do in China." Korsch replied, "Just because you are Chinese, it will not be suspected that I am hiding at your place." Trouble did break out just as Korsch had predicted. Halle was occupied by the German Communists and the railway station at Jena fell into their hands. The streetcars were also on strike. I waited for the appearance of Korsch, but he never came. When I met him again, later, however, I learned a great deal about the work of the Communists. Korsch told me that when the German Communists went to Moscow, they would report how the membership of the German Communist party had increased, how the subscriptions to the Communist papers had increased, and how their activities were being successfully carried on. And when the Soviet agents came to Germany, they would say that the Soviet Communist Army was ready on the border to come to the rescue of the German Communists if there was an uprising. "If your uprising took place, the Soviet army would attack, they say. But," Korsch continued, "I am tired of this kind of information and I don't believe it."

I witnessed also the coup d'état of Bela Kun in Hungary and the Council Government in Bavaria. During the same sojourn in Europe I had the opportunity of following closely the work of the Third International. Accordingly, Communist objectives and tactics had been clear to me for a long time, and I had reason to believe that the same pattern would be followed in China.

After the occupation of Manchuria by Japan, the Chinese Communists proposed the formation of a Popular Front of the different parties, encouraging the belief that they were patriots working for the good of China. So long as their demand was limited to a coalition government, I thought that it would be wrong to refuse to work wih them. But when in November, 1946, they decided to break with the National Government, I saw no possibility of my party's cooperating with them.

After the crisis with the Democratic League was over, I went to Shanghai and proposed to my party that there was no alternative but to join the National Assembly and pass the Constitutional Draft in order to lay down at least a cornerstone for the legal and peaceful development of the Chinese Republic. One section of the party members was opposed to this proposal; these members believed that a National Assembly which was boycotted by the Communists could serve no purpose. Even if the Constitution were passed, they argued, it would have no effect. The debate lasted a long time, but my resolution was finally passed in spite of the opposition.

Thus came the definite break between the Kuomintang and the Communists after a year of formal negotiation. The mediation of General Marshall and the Third Group also came to an end. The situation created a precarious position for the Third Group because, before the break, there had still been a middle-of-the-road policy, but after the Kuomintang and the Communists had come to a parting of the ways, there was no further room for that policy. Both for myself and for my party, the situation was not only embarrassing but also one which demanded that we take a definite stand. I chose the lesser of two evils and sided with the Kuomintang because it at least agreed to have the Constitution as a basis for the rule of law. On the day of the convocation of the National Assembly, Chou En-lai issued a statement which condemned the Assembly as a tool of the Kuomintang designed to strengthen the one-party rule. He said:

The one-party National Assembly, now being opened, is a denial of what the Communist Party and the Third Party Group advocated during the last stage of negotiations. It thus destroys once for all every resolution of the P. C. C., the Cease-Fire Agreement, and the Army Reorganization Agreement, and also wrecks the path of peaceful negotiations laid down by the P. C. C. At the same time it also unmasks in the most dramatic manner the fraudulent nature of the Government's "cease-fire" order of November 8.

This unilateral National Assembly is now on its way to adopting a so-called "constitution" in order to "legalize" the split and to "legalize" the selling out of the interests of the nation and the people. Should that come to pass, the Chinese people will plunge headlong into the deep abyss of human suffering. We Chinese Communists, therefore, adamantly refuse to recognise this National Assembly.

Whether it was correct or logical to say that the National Assembly was going to adopt a Constitution in order to legalize dictatorshp or to legalize the civil war, we will find out in the next chapter where we shall discuss the Constitution. But so long as there was no peace and no rule of law, it was difficult for me to take sides between the Kuomintang and the Communists. Nevertheless, in my eyes, the side which at least pretended to adopt a rule of law was preferable to the other, which was out to overthrow the government by civil war.

Now that the civil war is ended and the Communists are triumphant, what they have done can be seen in better perspective. The Communists fought "for the freedom of the people, for the interests of the peasants and workers, and for the liberation of China from feudalism and imperialism." What the Communist Party has imposed upon China is the Treaty of Alliance with the Soviet Union, the Korean War, and the stirring up of trouble in the neighboring countries of China. It has condemned all the heritage of the past, including the finest flowers of Confucianism and Buddhism, as being feudalistic. It has compelled all professors and teachers to study Marxism or to become Marxists. What freedom is left for conscience, thought, press, assembly, and association—which was what the Communists were always supposed to be fighting for?

I am more convinced than ever that I did the right thing in joining the National Assembly, or, in other words, in taking the side of Constitutionalism and Democracy. Most of the members of the Democratic League who collaborated with the Communists, like Huang Yen-pei, Chang Lan, Lo Lung-chi, Liang Shu-min, and Chang Pai-chun are either Vice-Presidents of the Government at Peking, or Ministers, or members of commissions, or members of the Political Consultative Conference. Sometimes I wonder to myself whether those erstwhile colleagues of mine of the Democratic League are contented with their present lot. I am sure they are not, for they are like birds whose wings have been clipped. It seems strange that I should be the only one among the founders of the Democratic League to stay outside of the charmed circle of Peking. I remain faithful to my convictions, and, as a free agent, I shall continue to fight for a free, independent, and democratic China until the battle is won.

CHAPTER X

The Communist-Boycotted Constitution

In the last chapter we saw how the final break of the Kuomintang and the Communist negotiations hinged on the handing in of the list of delegates to the National Assembly. To this the Communist Party could never agree, because they considered that they were the co-architects of victory, and that, accordingly, the date of the convocation of the National Assembly should have been decided by agreement with them and not unilaterally. The Kuomintang decided to fix the date because they suspected that the Communist Party did not want the question of the National Assembly and of the new constitution settled unless the conditions that they demanded were accepted. Mutual distrust and misunderstanding were so deeply rooted that an agreement on the question of the National Assembly was almost impossible. When once the date of convocation was decided a final break was bound to come, and the expectation of long-term cooperation between the Kuomintang and the Communists in the work of building a coalition government became a thing of the past.

As I mentioned before, on the day of convocation Chou En-lai issued a statement attacking the National Assembly. Theoretically speaking it is difficult to understand Chou's language, especially with regard to his charge that the adoption of a constitution would legalize the Kuomintang dictatorship. The Kuomintang Government had been a dictatorship for many years; it intended to continue as such, and it could perpetuate itself without adopting a constitution. In other words, to adopt a constitution was to submit to a legal document which would tie its hands. Therefore, I do not see any logic in Chou En-lai's statement that the new constitution was intended to mask the Kuomintang dictatorship.

Furthermore, the constitutional draft which was going to be adopted was a document agreed to by Chou En-lai as the representative of the Communist Party and by the representatives of the Kuomintang and the democratic parties. Most of the articles had been revised by Chou En-lai himself, his Communist colleagues, and the representatives of the other parties. How could the Kuomintang legalize its dictatorship on the basis of such a constitution? Chou En-lai's statement was a piece of propaganda aimed to discredit the constitutional structure in advance. As Chou is a Marxist or a Leninist, he believes that force is the most successful political expedient while legalism is only a tool of the ruling class. Because of this point of view, Chou En-lai estimated but lightly the changes in governmental structure which were to take place after the adoption of the new constitution.

I shall try to show how far Chou himself and his party colleagues had a hand in the revision of the constitutional draft. Regardless of whether the Communists call this document "minutes" or "draft," they had a hand in it. Of course they will argue that, as the Kuomintang violated the Political Consultative Conference resolutions, they were not bound by the draft. But they cannot deny that they were co-authors of this document nevertheless. This undeniable fact will come out clearly as I go on to tell the story of how the draft was made. Then will follow an explanation of the political machinery envisioned by the new constitution. These two expositions will make clear how far the Communist proposals were incorporated in it.

In Chapter VII dealing with the Political Consultative Conference, it was explained that the work of the Constitutional Draft Reviewing Committee would be based on a list of twelve subjects which was to be the foundation of the constitutional revision.

This list of twelve subjects was signed by the Kuomintang at the closing session of the Political Consultative Conference; yet, in March of the same year, when the Central Executive Committee meeting of the Kuomintang took place, the twelve items were strongly opposed. The resolutions of the Central Executive Committee of the Kuomintang were: (1) The making of a constitution should take "Plans for National Reconstruction" as its basis; (2) the National Assembly should be "visible," not "invisible"; (3) there should be no vote of confidence and the Executive Yuan should not be empowered to dissolve the Legislative Yuan—in other words, there should be no cabinet system, but the American Presidental system should be adopted instead; (4) the Control Yuan should not have the right of ratifying the appointment of the Chief Justices; (5) federalism should be discarded, that is, provinces should not have their own constitutions.

The whole tone of the Kuomintang Manifesto, however, was in favor of the work of the Political Consultative Conference. What they opposed were the five points just mentioned. It may be better to have a few quotations from this Manifesto in order to understand the mentality of the Kuomintang. Three important points of the document in question run as follows:

First. We must achieve social stability, restore peace and order, and complete the plan of National Rehabilitation in order to inaugurate the task of peaceful national reconstruction. Peace is a requisite for national reconstruction; the two are absolutely indivisible. Confronted with the extensive damage of more than eight years of war, and having encountered numerous obstacles and difficulties in national rehabilitation during the last half-year, and witnessing the plight of our compatriots in various parts of the country—the suffering awaiting relief; the homeless, repatriation; the unemployed, reemployment; the oppressed, emancipation—we fully realise that no longer should there be turmoil and strife within the country. Nor should local disorder be permitted. We can validate the party's struggle only by conforming our exertions to the needs of our country and our people.

In the past six months the Government has made great concessions in the interest of national rehabilitation. This Assembly regards such measures as correct. To bring about a favorable environment for peaceful national reconstruction, we, in a spirit of tolerance, invited representatives of the other political parties and prominent social leaders to a Political Consultative Conference before the convocation of the National Assembly. We admit that modifications in the procedure for national reconstruction, as laid down by our party, might have been made, but our consistent party spirit of placing the interests of the country and the people above everything else should be plain to all our fellow countrymen. In conformity with this spirit we will stop at nothing to bring about the speedy completion of national rehabilitation.

Second. We must convene the National Assembly as scheduled so as to return the Government to the people and to fulfill our long-cherished wish of inaugurating constitutional government.

Our party has all along advocated political democratization. It was openly declared by the Hsing Chung Hui (organised by Dr. Sun Yat-sen in 1892) as far back as fifty years ago. The revolutionary history of our party is the history of the fostering of democracy in China. Constitutional government would have been inaugurated long ago according to our original program, had Japan not launched her campaign of aggression, and had there been no military obstacles within the country.

Our determination to inaugurate constitutional government at an early date had been made amply manifest by resolutions adopted by the Kuomintang on a number of occasions, as well as by the repeated statements of the Tsungtsai (Director-General) of the Party. The Government has never slackened in preparing the way for constitutionalism, even in times of military crisis. Our earnest desire has been to return the Government to the people, but we maintain that the convocation of the National Assembly is an essential step towards that end.

Third. We wish to affirm our sincere desire to implement fully the various agreements reached at the Political Consultative Conference and our determination to uphold the "Quintuple-Power Constitution." In view of the need for peace, stability, and solidarity in the country and the urgent need of alleviating the people's sufferings, all of us should, after a careful study of the agreements reached at the Political Consultative Conference, very sincerely pledge to exert ourselves in concert with the other parties and prominent social leaders to carry out the agreements. But we maintain that the revision of the Draft Constitution must conform with Sun Yat-sen's teachings on the "Quintuple-Power Constitution."

The reason for our insistence on the "Quintuple-Power Constitution" is that the Three Principles of the People and the "Quintuple-Power Constitution" are inseparable. Without the "Quintuple-Power Constitution" the Three Principles of the People cannot be fully carried out. This political system is Dr. Sun's great and profound discovery, made as a result of his study of the European and American constitutions, of their merits and demerits, as well as of actual conditions in China, having as his object the laying of an enduring foundation for national peace and security.

A comprehensible and practical constitution is necessary to ensure a sound and firm political structure in our country. If the contents of the constitution should contravene the "Quintuple-Power Constitution," practical difficulties are certain to be encountered in its application, thereby placing the country at a disadvantage. The Kuomintang will, therefore, steadfastly uphold the "Quintuple-Power Constitution." This is indeed taking a long-range view of our national interests. We hope that the other parties and social leaders will appreciate our stand and understand our views.

For my part, after the closing session of the Political Consultative Conference, I took a trip to Shanghai and Peiping to inspect the work of my party in those areas. At the end of February, I came back to attend the meeting of the Constitutional Draft Reviewing Committee. Before the meeting started, I saw the list of twelve items in the guise of twelve threads. A constitution is like a piece of embroidery; if its threads are not woven together, we cannot tell what the constitutional document will look like. So I worked out a constitutional draft by myself, without consulting any other member. I did it as a personal project, without expecting that it would be adopted officially. When the Committee meeting started, there was an attack upon the twelve items lasting many days. The attack was headed by the advisers of the Committee who were officially appointed Kuomintang members. The Chairman, Sun Fo, saw that during the attack the representatives of the Communist Party and the Democratic League kept silent, speaking no word against the officially appointed advisers. Sun Fo felt that if things went on like this, nothing constructive could be done, and so he commented that the doctrine of Dr. Sun Yat-sen was not perfect in every respect and that the resolutions of the Political Consultative Conference were not completely wrong. After Sun Fo had thus silenced the official advisers, the work of the Constitutional Draft Reviewing Committee began. Sun Fo then went on to say, "This work of revision must have a draft as a basis. Supposing that the coming constitution has ten chapters, then the work of drafting it should be divided among so many sub-committees." I then said to Sun Fo that a constitution is like a painting or a piece of embroidery, in that it must have a central theme or an underlying principle which goes through the whole document. The different chapters should be interrelated in a way that no group of individual committees can achieve. If it were done by means of committees, there would be contradictions in the different chapters which would have to be brought into harmony and corrected. Drafting a constitution in such a way would take a much longer time. I said that I myself had a draft already made, which I had written for my own purposes. If they wanted it, I would be very glad to give it to them; otherwise, I did not mind keeping it for myself, because I had seen so many constitutional drafts done and undone. I did not mind the draft's becoming a piece of scrap paper. Sun Fo then took my draft and gave it to the Secretary-General, Lei Chen. The next morning Lei Chen had many copies of my draft printed so that it could be distributed among the members of the Committee. Thus, without being authorized to do so, I became the original author of the present constitution. The members of the Constitutional Draft Committee knew well that I was interested in constitution-making, because I had participated in such work many times and had translated into Chinese the first Soviet Constitution and the Weimar Constitution of Germany. The members of the Committee were Sun Fo, acting as Chairman, Wang Chung-hui, translator of the German civil code into English and one-time Judge of the International Court of Justice, Wu Tieh-cheng, Secretary-General of the Kuomintang, Wang Shih-chieh, Minister of Foreign Affairs, and Dr. John Wu, judge and Member of the Legislative Yuan representing the Kuomintang side. The Communist side was represented by Chou En-lai, Ching Pang-hsien and others. I myself at that time belonged to the Democratic League, and worked together with Dr. Lo Lung-chi and Chang Po-chuan. The Youth Party sent Tseng Chi and Chen Chi-tien as its representatives and stood for a cabinet system and professional representation.

I have mentioned the twelve items which constituted a basis for revising the constitutional draft. I shall summarize them once more in order to give point to the critical remarks that are to follow. (1) The voters of the whole country shall exercise the four kinds of direct popular rights—initiative, referendum, recall, and election—and the whole electorate shall constitute the national assembly in invisible form, which means that it is not situated in an office building, nor does it have sessions or terms of office for its members. (2) The legislative Yuan shall be the highest organ for lawmaking and its members shall be directly elected by the people. (3) The Control Yuan is the highest organ of investigation and supervision. Its members shall be elected by the provincial assemblies. The Control Yuan has the power to consent, to impeach, or to remind the Government of any irregularity. (4) The Judicial Yuan is the Supreme Court of Justice. The administration of justice is left to the Ministry of Justice, which is a department of the Executive Yuan. (5) The Examination Yuan is a civil service board consisting of non-party members. (6) The Executive Yuan is the highest executive organ; the President shall be responsible to the Legislative Yuan. (7) In case of a vote of no confidence, the Executive Yuan may issue emergency orders and dissolve the legislative Yuan. (8) The province is a unit of local self-government and the governors shall be elected by the people. Each province shall have its own provincial constitution. (9) The rights and duties of the people shall be in accordance with the regulations of democratic countries, where rights and freedoms are considered to be fundamental. (10) There shall be a special chapter in the constitution dealing with the procedure of elections. (11) There shall be a chapter on national policy dealing with National Defense, Economy, Culture, and so forth. (12) Amendment of the constitution shall be initiated by joint action of the Legislative Yuan and the National Assembly. The text of a given amendment shall be established by the National Assembly.

But my own draft and the subsequent emendations could not take only these twelve points as a basis; my hand was not free, because the political theories of Dr. Sun Yat-sen and the draft of May, 1936, had also to be taken into consideration.

The political theory of Dr. Sun Yat-sen is an amalgam of many elements which contradict each other, and which Dr. Sun never managed to adjust. First, he stands for the four kinds of popular rights—or a form of government based on plebiscite. (Moreover, he also wants a Legislative Yuan, but he does not tell how both the parliamentary form and the plebiscital form are to work together.) Secondly, Dr. Sun calls his system the Five-Power System; according to him the Legislative branch, the Executive branch, the Judicial branch, and the two Yuans of Control and Examination, should together constitute the government. But why should the Chief Justice of the Supreme Court have a voice in the Executive Department? What has the speaker of the Legislative Yuan to do with the government meetings? The Examination Yuan should be a commission for regulating the civil service and has little to do with meetings of the cabinet. Thirdly, according to Dr. Sun's theory of sovereignty and ability, he declares that the men in the government must have special ability. But Dr. Sun Yat-sen has no answer when the men in the government are not able, or do not have the confidence of the people.

Again, as I have indicated, I was to a considerable extent bound by the published draft of May, 1936, in which the different ideas of Dr. Sun Yat-sen were put together. First, there was a National Assembly whose members were the representatives of the people, just as members of Parliament in Britain are representatives of the people. Yet the four kinds of popular rights were granted to it, as if it were a plebiscital form of government. Secondly, a legislative Yuan whose members were elected by the National Assembly could not bring the Executive to account, so that there was no parliament provided in the whole governmental structure according to the draft of 1936. Thirdly, the power of impeachment and investigation which belongs to a parliament or congress was vested in the Control Yuan, and there was no clear-cut line of demarcation between the work of the law-making body and that of the controlling body.

Moreover, the role of Chiang Kai-shek in the government machinery was an important factor. By this time it should be clear that Chiang likes to take everything into his hands. He has been the Commander-in-Chief, he was the President of the Executive Yuan, and he also aspired to be the coming President of China after the adoption of the Constitution. He thought that a cabinet responsible to the Parliament would bind his hands too much, and there was a clique around him insisting that the American Presidential system be adopted.

These were the obstacles in the way of preparing a constitution worthy of the name. I tried my best to make China live under a truly democratic form of government, that should still be in harmony with the political doctrines of Dr. Sun Yat-sen, and also provide an important role for Chiang Kai-shek. I attempted a reconciliation between the plebiscite form and the parliamentary form and drew a line of demarcation between the Legislative Yuan and the Control Yuan. The Kuomintang members' opposition to a political structure like that of France, which would produce too many cabinet changes, had also to be taken into consideration. Lastly, the demands of the Chinese Communist Party and the Democratic League had to be satisfied. All these difficult problems had to be solved in my draft. When I began to work on it, I thought that so many difficult questions could never be solved, but still I tried, like an artist who does not care whether his painting will be sold or not.

After my draft was accepted as a basis for the new constitution, the Communist members requested that I explain the meaning of each article. There was a conference therefore every evening from eight to midnight in March and April between Chou En-lai, Tung Pih-wu and the other Communist members and the members of the Democratic League. Through these meetings a thorough understanding between the Communists and myself was established. Each morning, when the Committee's work of revising the constitutional draft began, Chou En-lai and I sometimes defended the same thesis and fought against the Kuomintang. In some cases, however, I could not agree, and told the Communists clearly that I would not take their side. My position with relation to the Kuomintang and the Communists was completely one of benevolent neutrality, and I never made any bargain with either. What I fought for was a really democratic form of government for the Chinese Republic.

A number of questions aroused hot debate in the Committee. In accordance with the five-point resolution of the Central Committee of the Kuomintang, members of the Committee for reviewing the constitutional draft began to discuss first the question of the cabinet system and of the vote of confidence. This debate lasted many days and no conclusion was reached. One morning after a long session, I felt tired and went out for a little while to get some fresh air. When I returned I did not take my seat at the round table but sat down on a back bench in a corner for a little rest. Chou En-lai then came to me and whispered in my ear, "It would be better for us to make some concessions to Sun Fo. Otherwise his position as a democrat in the Kuomintang cannot be maintained. It would be better for us to agree that the National Assembly be in a visible form, that the vote of confidence not take place, but that the responsibility of the cabinet be accounted for in another form, and that the name 'Provincial Constitution' be changed to 'Provincial Self-Government Law.' " Chou En-lai again emphasized that the concession of revising the original resolution should be made immediately. I answered, "If you think that it is the right thing to do, you can announce it yourself." Thereupon, Chou En-lai and I went back to our seats, and Chou stood up and made his announcement as he had made it to me. The leader of the Youth Party, Tseng Chi, was surprised that Chou En-lai yielded so much. He declared that his party stood for a vote of confidence, so that he would reserve the right to contest this provision when it came before the National Assembly. But in spite of Tseng's opposition, these points were settled according to Chou En-lai's announcement. The opposition within the Kuomintang was appeased, and discussions of the Committee were resumed.

After this main obstacle had been removed, the next questions were: (1) What should be the visible form of the National Assembly? (2) How can the Executive Yuan be called to account? (3) What form should a self-government law take? A long time was spent in debating all these questions.

First, the question of the National Assembly. Though Chou En-lai had agreed to a national assembly in a visible form, the Communists did not like a national assembly such as was written in the draft of May, 1936. The Communists proposed that two houses coming together should constitute a national assembly—like that of France. The Kuomintang spokesman, Wu Tieh-cheng, argued that in such an assembly the exercise of popular rights would disappear. During the debate it became clear that the reason why the Kuomintang insisted upon having a national assembly in a visible form was that, if the electorate constituted a national assembly in an invisible form, and the voters were scattered in different places so that some of them lived in the Communist areas, a boycott of the election in these areas would be difficult to prevent. If it were in a visible form, the members of the National Assembly would have to come to Nanking, where they could be controlled. At last, the Democratic League suggested a compromise—that the National Assembly have a fixed number of members who could come together to vote for the election of the President of the Republic. After the election the members were to disperse; they would have no term of office. This compromise was accepted. Next came the question of direct popular rights. I explained to the Committee that the plebiscital form of government must function in such a way that the people exercised their rights directly; in that way it would exist alongside the parliamentary form of government. On the other hand, the exercise of direct popular rights would become meaningless if these rights were vested in members of the National Assembly who were representatives of the people, like the members of a parliament. They would stand in an indirect relation to the people; how can the exercise of their powers, therefore, be called direct popular rights? In China, where there is no census and the people do not yet know how to exercise the right of election in a proper manner, how can the plebiscital form of government be applied? Yet the Kuomintang adheres so blindly to the doctrines of Sun Yat-sen that it is not easy to introduce more appropriate concepts. A compromise was reached by agreeing that after the exercise of direct popular rights had been put into practice in the districts and municipalities, and had proved workable, then the law establishing the plebiscite would be passed. This compromise had the approval of Wu Tieh-cheng, and thus the whole question was settled.

Secondly, the task of establishing a responsible cabinet system. This question was the most difficult one to settle of all the controversial points raised by the constitution. The Kuomintang members were much less opposed to the cabinet system of a parliamentary form of Government than was Dr. Sun Yat-sen himself. Most of them were afraid that if the vote of confidence existed in China, there would be too many cabinet changes. And, as mentioned earlier, some of the Kuomintang members who were intimate with Chiang Kai-shek tried to convince him that it would be better for China if the American presidential system were adopted. They meant to satisfy Chiang's ambition and refused to see that governmental responsibility is a check on corruption and incompetence. Yet, most of the Kuomintang members realized that if a president of the Republic were responsible for running the government, anything that went wrong could be charged against him, and he could be impeached. So the middle of the road policy was adopted, in the form of a responsible cabinet with no provision for the vote of confidence. As difference of opinion concerning governmental policy is bound to arise between the Cabinet and the Legislative Yuan, the American system of "reconsideration" was introduced. The Legislative Yuan is entitled to make proposals concerning governmental policy; such proposals indicate "no confidence" as it is the custom in Europe. If the cabinet does not agree, the proposals can be sent back to the Legislative Yuan for reconsideration. Thus a step is interposed before the resignation of the cabinet, for if the proposals made by the Legislative Yuan are again passed by a two-thirds vote, then the cabinet either submits or resigns. A way to prevent too many changes of cabinet has been found, and yet cabinet responsibility is not neglected. This is the essence of the 57th Article of the present Constitution, which, after much exchange of views, was put in written form by Wang Shih-chieh, the former Minister of Foreign Affairs and a constitutional jurist. This 57th Article in its draft form was originally put before the draft Committee. I would not say that it was voted upon, but Chou En-lai, after having read it, did not seem to oppose it.

Thirdly, the question of provincial self-government law. No matter what its title—provincial constitution or provincial self-government law—once there is a self-government law for each province there must be a division of governmental power between the provinces and the Central Government. What are the powers belonging to the Central Government and the provinces? These must be enumerated. Luckily the constitution of Tsao Kun, passed in 1926, contained articles on the division of powers, and most of these articles were transferred to our draft and later adopted. When the question was raised as to whether a self-government law like the constitution of the Dominion of Canada created by the British North American Act of 1867, should be passed or approved by the Legislative Yuan, the leader of the Youth Party, Tseng Chi, expressed the affirmative view. The Communist representative, Ching Pang-hsien, condemned Tseng Chi, saying, "Nonsense!" and "Ignorance!" whereupon Tseng Chi and his party colleagues walked out and absented themselves for two or three days. Then a delegation, of which I was a member, went to him and persuaded him to return in the interests of our common aim.

After each article of my draft had been passed and we were nearly at the end of the job, Ching Pang-hsien was to bring the whole text of the constitutional draft to the Communists for the approval of their Central Executive Committee. Unfortunately Ching lost his life in a plane crash. The Communist Party sent another man to be his successor. This new delegate, Li Wei-han, when he attended the meeting on the very first day, declared that the draft could only be considered as minutes recording what had been discussed, and could not be considered as a constitutional draft to which all parties had agreed. This meant, as was proved later, that if the Communists were not to take part in the National Assembly that would formally adopt the Constitution, the Kuomintang would never be able to make use of the draft by alleging that the Communists had pledged themselves to it. Wu Tieh-cheng, representing the Kuomintang, retorted to Li Wei-han that they too would reserve the right to consider the draft as minutes in the same way. At the end of April, after the final meeting of the Committee, the removal of the Government from Chungking to Nanking took place and the members of the Committee dispersed. At that time war in the Northeastern Provinces caused such tension that no one had much interest in the constitutional draft.

Since the Republic, I have seen a lot of constitution-making, and many of the resulting constitutions have been thrown into the wastepaper basket. After the dispersal of the Constitutional Draft Reviewing Committee, I fully believed that the new draft would have the same fate.

In June I tried to translate the text of the draft, as it had been passed by the Committee, into English. A copy of it was sent to General Marshall, and a reply came asking me to come down to Nanking for a talk. When I arrived, General Marshall told me that a Committee of Four, Dr. Leighton Stuart, Mr. Blandford (an official of the American Bureau of the Budget and Adviser to the Chinese Government), Professor Bates, and Mr. Mills had been appointed to study the constitutional draft. I was cross-examined for many hours. Mr. Blandford wanted to have the ideas of the Generalissimo with regard to a training corps, etc., put in the draft. I declined to do it, because such ideas do not fit in with a constitution that is to be the basis of law in a democracy.

After this cross-examination I heard nothing about the draft for a long time. The idea of waste-paper suggested itself again when I thought of the draft, but in August Wu Ting-chang, then Secretary-General of the Presidential Office, called on me and said that the draft would be adopted and presented to the coming National Assembly. This was the first hint that the Generalissimo did not consider the draft as minutes, as Wu himself had indicated at the Committee meeting.

When the definite break between the Kuomintang and the Communist Party took place, and before the National Assembly was convened, this draft was presented to the old Legislative Yuan, because it was the revised text of the draft of 1936, and therefore had to be approved before adoption. During the debate, one member raised the question, "Since this draft is so different from the draft of 1936, how can we approve it?" As Sun Fo is a very liberal-minded man, he answered: "The new draft is better than ours, so we should approve it." Sun Fo's approval contributed very much to its being passed in the National Assembly as the Constitution of the Chinese Republic. Before the convocation of the National Assembly, the Generalissimo had asked the Democratic-Socialist Party to join; I saw that my party could not cooperate with the Communist policy of overthrowing the Government by violence, and after many meetings, it passed a resolution to join the National Assembly. Before the opening session, an Agreement, the details of which will be dealt with in a later chapter, was signed by the Generalissimo and myself, in which it was stipulated that both sides, the Kuomintang and the Democratic-Socialist Party, should bear the responsibility for the passing of the constitutional draft as it was written. It was finally passed with some amendments, which however did not change substantially its original form.

I shall now give an exposition of the most important points of the Constitution. The new Constitution consists of fourteen chapters and one hundred and seventy-five articles. A list of the chapters follows:

Chapter I	General Principles
Chapter II	Rights and Duties of the People

Chapter III	The National Assembly
Chapter IV	The President
Chapter V	The Administration
Chapter VI	Legislation
Chapter VII	The Judiciary
Chapter VIII	Examination
Chapter IX	Control
Chapter X	Powers of the Central Government and Local Government
Chapter XI	The Local Government System
Chapter XII	Elections, Recall, Initiative, and Referendum
Chapter XIII	Basic National Policies
Chapter XIV	Enforcement of the Constitution

(1) *General Principles.* In the National Assembly, the first problem raised concerned the inclusion of the phrase "San Min Chu I." The Kuomintang insisted that the phrase "San Min Chu I" should be used as an adjective to qualify the word "Republic." The proposal that the orthodox teachings of one party should be set down in the Constitution for all the people and all the parties to observe raised many questions. If the phrase "San Min Chu I" were to be used as an adjective before the word "Republic," the phrase would have legal validity and, further, it would produce the impression that "San Min Chu I" were something in which everyone and every party should believe. But Dr. Sun Yat-sen himself was not quite definite about the interpretation of the "San Min Chu I," especially concerning the affinities of "San Min Chu I" and Communism. As a constitution was to be a legal document, Dr. Sun Yat-sen's book would be the first source to which the judges of the Supreme Court would refer when they interpreted the Constitution. It was better that such a political platform as "San Min Chu I" be left out of the document. It was, however, generally acknowledged that the driving force behind the movement of founding the Chinese Republic was derived from Dr. Sun Yat-sen's political theory. So the first article was devised to read "The Republic of China, founded on the Three Principles of the People, is a Democratic Republic of the people, for the people and governed by the people." Mencius had said: "The people are the foundation of the country." Another version comes from Abraham Lincoln's phrase, "government of the people, by the people, and for the people." Thus the first article was so worded

that the historical fact of having "San Min Chu I" as the driving force of the Republic was recognized; the phrase "of the people, by the people, and for the people" was considered a better way to qualify the Republic than the phrase "San Min Chu I" which might seem ambiguous when the need to interpret the constitution arose.

Another question raised in the Assembly was in regard to Article 7 which reads, "the capital of China is in Nanking." Most of the northern Chinese delegates were of the opinion that, if the Chinese capital had been in Peiping before the Mukden incident, the Northeastern Provinces would not have been lost. Six hundred members of the National Assembly introduced a motion to have the capital removed to Peiping rather than have it remain in Nanking. However, Chiang Kai-shek was more inclined towards the original provision, so the final decision was to omit that article entirely.

(2) The second chapter on the *Rights and Duties of the People* was really copied from Anglo-Saxon models. The Bill of Rights in the May Draft and in the new Constitution were nearly the same. Only, in the May draft there is a phrase at the end of each article which reads "in accordance with the law." This means that the people's rights, although considered to be fundamental, might be charged with restrictions if the Legislative Yuan passed a law concerning the exercise of such rights. But in the new Constitution this phrase was eliminated. Those who insisted upon the elimination of the phrase were the present Chief Justice of the Supreme Court in the Communist Government, Shen Chuen-ju, and the lady Minister of Justice, Shih Liang. They seem now to have forgotten these demands made in the name of human freedom and to have turned themselves into destroyers of freedom, because the recent criminal law of the counter-revolutionaries, passed by the Communist regime, was sponsored by both of them.

(3) *The National Assembly.* According to the May Draft, the National Assembly has the following powers: (1) The election of the President and Vice-President, the Presidents of the four Yuan, and the members of the Legislative and Control Yuan; (2) the recall of the President and Vice-President, the Presidents of the four Yuan and members of the Legislative and Control Yuan; (3) initiative; (4) referendum; (5) amendment of the Constitution. In this way the May Draft was supposed to agree with the ideal of Dr. Sun's plebiscital form of government, but I doubt if the exercise of popular rights as provided for in the draft of 1936 can be called plebiscital. In

Britain, where Parliament is considered a sovereign organ, it is useless to set up the plebiscital form of government as a parallel means of expressing the will of the people. In Switzerland, besides the parliamentary form of government, a plebiscital government is exercised directly by the people. The situation in China, however, is in no way comparable to either of these; the Chinese population is much greater than that of Switzerland, and about eighty per cent of the people are illiterate. And since the Chinese population is so dense, they can exercise direct popular rights only in an indirect form. This means that the people elect the members of Parliament, as they are elected under the British system, and then let these representatives exercise the direct popular rights for them. Because of the density of China's population, the May Draft provided for an indirect form of plebiscite only. The drafters of the May Constitution provided for the plebiscite in such a clumsy way that it lost its significance as an instrument for expressing the popular will. In the United States and in Great Britain, the Congress or Parliament is an assembly which makes ultimate decisions; it is a lawmaking body. It passes laws which are put into practice by the government. The work of Parliament or Congress in a certain sense is prior to the work of the executive department of the government. According to the May Draft, however, the Legislative Yuan was to be considered a department of the ruling power. Dr. Sun Yat-sen had interpreted the people's sovereign power to mean initiative, referendum, and recall, but he suggested that the ruling power belonged to the government, or rather to the five Yuan. In this we can see that it was Dr. Sun's idea to make the Legislative Yuan a part of the government, subservient to the Executive Yuan. Frankly speaking, in this way the Legislative Yuan is not a parliament, but a mere legal reference council. Further, the members of the Legislative Yuan were supposed to be elected by the National Assembly, which places them at two removes from the direct vote of the people. Another point which must be mentioned in regard to the May Draft is that the Legislative Yuan members are responsible to the National Assembly; they can be dismissed and recalled by that body. The Legislative Yuan, according to the May Draft, has no power whatsoever over the executive branches of the government.

When my draft was presented to the Political Consultative Conference, it precipitated many thorny problems. First, of course, was the question of how a plebiscite form of government, which entails the real exercise of direct popular rights, could work parallel to the Parliament? Secondly, so long as the people were ignorant, how could they exercise worthily the rights of initiative, referendum, and so forth? Thirdly, can a plebiscite function by indirect election? Fourthly, how can the Legislative Yuan, incapable of taking a final decision, be put in a position of responsibility with relation to some other body? If power is to be assigned to the National Assembly as in the May Draft, then the National Assembly is a superior parliament and the Legislative Yuan a subordinate one. It is undoubtedly true that if the members of the Legislative Yuan are to be responsible to the National Assembly, they will automatically be no longer the true representatives of the people. We were confronted with the puzzling problem of how these two forms of government, the plebiscital and the parliamentary form, could be reconciled in the new constitution. Is the Legislative Yuan one of the five branches of the ruling power of the government? If it is, how can it possibly keep a check on the executive department?

Now, Dr. Sun Yat-sen himself, as we have seen, wanted to have a plebiscital government side by side with a parliamentary one. We find that he expressed this idea only vaguely in his "Plans for National Reconstruction" and at no time entered into adequate explanation as to how these two systems were to work parallel to each other. In the May Draft, we see the hand of drafters who envisioned the plebiscite principle acting through a National Assembly that would meet every year. Not feeling sure about the exercise of the four powers, they drafted article 35, stating that, "The organization of the National Assembly and the election as well as recall of its delegates shall be determined by law." It should be apparent, however, that a plebiscital government can not take the form of a National Assembly which is indirectly elected. The primary suggestion made by the Political Consultative Conference was to let the whole electorate constitute the National Assembly. We emphasized that the plebiscital form of government could be realised only by the voters themselves and not by a National Assembly consisting merely of the representatives of the people. A National Assembly of 2000 members can scarcely be accounted the instrument of a plebiscital form of democracy. As a remedy for the ignorance of the people, we also proposed to let all the members of the district (*hsien*) councils come together to exercise the right of the four powers. In the first period of the Republic, the right of electing the President of the Republic was to be exercised in a limited way. The *hsien* council members, whose number may amount to between 40,000 and 60,000 in 2,000 *hsien,* were to exercise the right of electing the president. It is evident that such an enlarged electorate is closer to a plebiscital form of government than a National Assembly. We called this an invisible form of National Assembly. The Kuomintang flatly rejected this proposal for the reason that when the election of the President is spread throughout the country, the whole machinery can never be put under the control of the central government. Accordingly, the proposal had to be abandoned.

The question then arose as to what form of visible assembly would be the best. There were two suggestions, one from the Kuomintang and the other from the Communists. The first was based upon the May Draft, stipulating that the election of the President of the Republic is the major function of the Assembly, and that the members of that body also have the right to exercise the four powers. The proposal of electing the president thus was a feasible one, but the exercise of the other three powers by the Assembly would again be too far removed from a plebiscital form of democracy. The Communists and other parties objected to this proposal. The Communists advocated a French system of election in its place. According to the French constitution, the Senate and the Chamber of Deputies sitting together form the National Assembly. This would mean combining the Legislative and the Control Yuan into a National Assembly for the purpose of electing the President. But again the Kuomintang opposed this proposal, saying that if this form of National Assembly were adopted, the ideal of a plebiscital form of government would be impaired. There followed weary debates for many days; finally the Communists gave in, and agreed that the National Assembly should be the organ which elects the President of the Republic. This satisfied the Kuomintang, since they believed that they would be able to control the members sitting together in a visible form of National Assembly. So Article 27 of the new Constitution now reads thus: "The functions and powers of the National Assembly shall be as follows: (1) Election of the President and Vice-President. (2) Recall of the President and Vice-President. (3) Amendment of the Constitution. (4) Ratification of amendments to the Constitution proposed by the Legislative Yuan. With respect to the exercise of powers of initiative and referendum, besides what is stipulated in the preceding third and fourth sections, the National Assembly shall institute measures pertaining thereto and enforce them, after the said two powers shall have been exercised in one-half of the *hsien* and municipalities of the whole country." The four powers were inclusively stipulated, but the question of the plebiscital form remained unsolved. The Kuomintang, loyal to Dr. Sun Yat-sen's teachings, still struggled to give the National Assembly the right to exercise the powers of referendum and initiative. But all other parties questioned the advisability of these two powers being exercised by such an Assembly. They preferred to have a parliament first, to be followed at some later date by a plebiscital form of government. The final agreement to the effect that the plebiscital form shall be exercised first by the people in the *hsien* and municipal governments means that it is indefinitely postponed. With this compromise, it seemed to be generally admitted that the form of popular democracy that Dr. Sun Yat-sen advocated had been put on the shelf. The National Assembly is now an organ of the electorate, and its term of office is fixed at six years, the same as the term of the Presidency of the Republic.

The National Assembly in its present form has no right to elect the members of the Legislative Yuan, as stipulated in the May Draft. The Legislative Yuan members shall come from the people and shall not be elected or controlled by the Assembly. These two organs have separate existences. It is evident, therefore, that the Legislative Yuan can make a decision calling the Government to account, while the controlling power of the National Assembly over the Executive is limited only to the recall of the President of the Republic. As to the calling of cabinet ministers to account, the power is reserved for the Legislative Yuan.

It is definitely stipulated that the number of the members of the National Assembly shall total 2,176. The Assembly shall be constituted of delegates elected as follows: (1) Every *hsien* and municipality shall elect one delegate, but if its population exceeds 500,000, an additional delegate shall be elected for every additional 500,000. (2) There shall be 57 delegates elected from Mongolia. (3) There shall be 40 delegates elected from Tibet. (4) There shall be 17 delegates elected from the various frontier regions. (5) There shall be 65 overseas Chinese delegates. (6) There shall be 487 members representing various occupational groups. (7) There shall be 168 women delegates. (8) There shall be 17 delegates representing various racial groups.

These members or delegates are to constitute the electoral college which will elect the President and Vice-President of China. Whether the President is nominated by party conventions will depend entirely upon the growth of political conventions among the various parties in the country. The other functions of the National Assembly, such as the recall of the President and Vice-President, and amendment of the

Constitution, can be evaluated only after they have functioned for some time.

(4) *The Legislative Yuan.* The power to make laws resides in the legislature and the laws are carried out by the executive branch of the government. This is the fundamental concept of legislation in all democratic countries. Dr. Sun Yat-sen strongly believed in the principle of democracy, but this ideal was not always implemented by his proposed political structure. Dr. Sun separated the political power of the people from the ruling power of the government. To justify this idea he separated the Legislative from the Control Yuan on the one hand and from the National Assembly on the other. The people, or the voters, he maintained, should have sovereign political power. According to this theory, Dr. Sun assigns the four powers of election, initiative, referendum, and recall to the National Assembly representing the people. The National Assembly can call the government to account and appoint and dismiss the ministers. The government, to which the ruling power belongs, is divided into five branches—the Executive Yuan, the Legislative Yuan, the Judicial Yuan, the Control Yuan, and the Examination Yuan. Ranked in this way, the Legislative Yuan is only a branch of the government and not an organ for controlling the government. Although it may establish budgets, pass bills, make treaties, and so forth, it has not the power of final decision, nor has it the power to make or unmake the cabinet as has the Parliament of Great Britain.

The May 1936 draft of the Constitution provided that the members of the Legislative Yuan were to be elected by the National Assembly and not by the people. Secondly, according to article 59 of the May Draft, the members of the Legislative Yuan might be called to account by the National Assembly while the ministers of the Executive Yuan would be responsible only to the President of the Republic. Strictly speaking, the May Draft did not provide for responsible ministers. Again, article 70 provided that any bill passed by the Legislative Yuan with which the President disagreed might be referred back to that body for reconsideration. But if this bill were reconsidered and re-passed by two-thirds of the members, then the President was bound to accept it. If the case involved were a law bill, the President might send it to the National Assembly for final approval. The Legislative Yuan was obliged to give reconsideration, but it could not influence the rise and fall of the Cabinet. The most peculiar provision was that the members of the Legislative Yuan could be called to account or dismissed by the exercise of the right of recall on the part of the National Assembly. Although the May Draft indicated that the members of the Legislative Yuan should not be made responsible for their opinions outside of that body, it was evident that there was a National Assembly which would hold them responsible for them. Being in such an inferior position, the Legislative Yuan could never qualify as a parliament able to make final decisions as a sovereign body.

Of more particular interest was the electoral procedure in the Legislative Yuan. The members of the Legislative Yuan would be elected by the delegates of the National Assembly; each province might have four, six, or eight candidates, and a maximum of sixteen. The delegates in the National Assembly would be grouped according to provinces and so would nominate their provincial friends inside and outside the Assembly as candidates; in all likelihood the members of the Legislative Yuan would be duplicates of the Assembly delegates, and so their election would be twice removed from the people themselves.

We can see that the members of the Legislative Yuan elected in this way are too far separated from the voice of the voters. This was an important point of discussion in the drafting committee of the Political Consultative Conference. Thus, resolutions concerning the Legislative Yuan were expressed in point two, stipulating that the Legislative Yuan should be the highest lawmaking organ whose members would be directly elected by the people, and that its powers and functions should be similar to those prevailing in other democratic countries of the world. Point six stipulated that the President of the Executive Yuan should be appointed by the President of the Republic with the consent of the Legislative Yuan. Since the Executive Yuan was to be responsible to the Legislative Yuan, the former should request the President of the Republic to dissolve the Legislative Yuan when it passed a vote of non-confidence against the Executive Yuan. It was stipulated also that the same President of the Executive Yuan was not to be allowed to ask for dissolution on more than one occasion. The Political Consultative Conference was aiming at differentiating the Legislative Yuan from the National Assembly in order to let the Legislative Yuan derive its powers from the people, without being held accountable by the National Assembly. This gave rise to Article 62 of the present Constitution, which reads as follows: "The Legislative Yuan is the highest legislative organ of the state, and is to be composed of members elected by the people." Of course, the stipulation with regard to recalling the members by the National Assembly was also eliminated, for the members were no longer responsible to the National Assembly, which according to the May Draft would have been a super-parliament.

The question of passing a vote of confidence was hotly debated. The reason for Kuomintang opposition to the vote of confidence was that they feared it might result in too frequent changes of cabinet. Attaching great importance to the stability of the government and citing the facts of the rise and fall of the French cabinets, the Kuomintang asked the Communists and the other parties not to insist on this point. At least the minority parties agreed to the Kuomintang proposals, but to cope with future situations, they maintained that the Executive Yuan must be responsible to the Legislative Yuan with regard to occasions when the government really failed to do its duty. They found another way to call the government to account, even without a vote of confidence. This will be discussed later on.

The right to dissolve the Legislative Yuan is also of great importance in Western countries at the time of disputes between the parliament and the executive organ of the government. When a parliament passes a vote of non-confidence, it does not necessarily mean that its judgment is right and the executive wrong. When the prime minister feels convinced that the right is on his side, he may ask the King or the President to dissolve the parliament and hold a new election. In Britain this is called "the appeal to the people." Since constitutional government is just being introduced in China, and since as yet she is not well prepared to make final decisions concerning the rise and fall of cabinets, this system of dissolving parliament is clearly not suitable for her. All parties shared this view, and the proposal was completely dropped. The giving up of these two points, the vote of confidence and the dissolution of the Legislative Yuan, changed significantly the nature of the Legislative Yuan in the new constitution. The Legislative Yuan, according to the present Constitution, functions after the pattern of the United States Congress, since it cannot be dissolved by the cabinet or Executive Yuan.

The question then arose of the possibility of conflict between the Executive and the Legislative Yuan. In the United States the whole political structure of the government is built upon the basis of the theory of separation of powers. The United States version has not been fully copied in the Chinese Constitution, as the powers of the President differ in the two countries. Under the President of the Chinese Republic there is an Executive Yuan that can function successfully only with the cooperation of the Legislative Yuan. Since the vote of confidence was given up, some other way had to be found to deal with possible cabinet changes. After long discussions and debates a solution was finally found: the President of the Executive Yuan was to be appointed by the President of the Republic with the consent of the Legislative Yuan, in this way establishing a virtual vote of confidence in the first instance. Secondly, the members of the Executive Yuan were to be appointed by the President of the Republic on the recommendation of the President of the Executive Yuan. Thirdly, the President of the Executive Yuan was to be responsible to the Legislative Yuan. The precise nature of this responsibility constituted a problem, as the Communist representative wanted to specify its scope clearly while the Kuomintang members did not. At last an agreement was found, now embodied in article 57 of the Constitution, which reads as follows:

> The President of the Executive Yuan shall be responsible to the Legislative Yuan in accordance with the following conditions:
>
> (1) The Executive Yuan shall have the duty of presenting to the Legislative Yuan its administrative policies and administrative reports. Members of the Legislative Yuan during the sessions of the Yuan shall have the right to interpellate the President and the heads of the various ministries and commissions of the Executive Yuan.
>
> (2) If the Legislative Yuan dissents from any important policy of the Executive Yuan, it may by resolution ask the Executive Yuan to alter such a policy. With respect to such resolutions, the Executive Yuan, with the approval of the President of the Republic, may request the Legislative Yuan to reconsider. If, on reconsideration, two-thirds of the attending members of the Legislative Yuan uphold the original resolution, the President of the Executive Yuan shall either abide by the same or resign from office.
>
> (3) If the Executive Yuan deems a resolution passed by the Legislative Yuan on a statutory, budgetary, or treaty bill inexpedient and difficult of execution, it may, with the approval of the President of the Republic, request the Legislative Yuan to reconsider within ten days after the delivery of the said resolution to the Executive Yuan. If, on reconsideration, two-thirds of the attending members of the Legislative Yuan uphold the original resolution, the President of the Executive Yuan shall either abide by the same or resign from office.

It goes without saying that the foundation of the Executive Yuan is the confidence of the Legislative Yuan. The idea of reconsideration, no doubt, is adapted from the American Constitution, according to which a dissolution of Congress is not possible. A responsible cabinet must enjoy the confidence of the Legislative Yuan, but on the other hand, the method of reconsideration prevents frequent changes of the executive organ of the government.

According to the new Constitution the Legislative Yuan is no longer a legal reference board or a part of the ruling power of the government: it is a lawmaking body which controls the Executive Yuan and to which the Executive Yuan is responsible.

Article 71 again shows that there is no real barrier between the legislative and executive powers of government. "At the meetings of the Legislative Yuan, the President of the various Yuan concerned, as well as the heads of the various ministries and commissions concerned, may be present to voice their opinions." This is the common practice of European governments, in which the presence of ministers at sessions of the parliament is quite ordinary. In the United States the presence of ministers is not necessary because the American system is built upon the theory of separation of powers. But the Chinese cabinet system is much more akin to that of the European democracies, hence the ministers are allowed to appear before the Legislative Yuan.

Article 70 of the new constitution is equally important. "The Legislative Yuan shall not initiate any increase in the expenditures of the budget presented by the Executive Yuan." We profited on this point from the experience of the American Congress, which can propose any item of expenditure before the budget is established. Since our Executvie Yuan is patterned on the European models, we gave the budget-making power exclusively to the Minister of Finance. That is, the fiscal policy is not in the hands of the members of the Legislative Yuan, for we believed that the Legislative Yuan constituted too large a body to be able to initiate financial policies intelligently.

We must bear in mind that the quality of the members depends much upon the intellectual level of the people at large and also upon the procedure of nomination and selection of candidates by the different parties. China must exert great efforts to improve standards of education in order to produce more highly qualified representatives.

(4) *The President of the Republic and the Executive Yuan.* These must be discussed together because they both belong to the executive branch of the government. But before we enter into this discussion we must recall China's experience during the period of political tutelage.

According to the Compact Law of the tutelage period, we had a government in China that was built on two levels. The upper level constituted the National Government of the Five Yuan—the Executive, Legislative, Judicial, Control, and Examination Yuan. When the Presidents of these five Yuan met together, they constituted the National Government. In the Executive Yuan on the other hand, there were the various ministries—Interior, Foreign Affairs, Finance, Economy, National Defense, and so forth. This vast body of organizations subordinated to the Executive Yuan, forms the lower level. As can be readily seen, the two-level structure makes a system of responsible government impossible. Under the Compact Law, any policy that was proposed by the various ministers would again be referred to or discussed by the National Government, so that the ministers become subordinates who can really not be called to account for their policy. Dr. H. H. Kung complained frequently that his financial and currency policy and plans were often changed and revised by the National Government. Many other ministers faced the same difficulty, for, so long as the "two-level" political structure existed, there could be no responsible cabinet. In the resolution of the Political Consultative Conference, there is a stipulation that the President of the Republic may summon the Presidents of the five Yuan for conference, and article 44 of the new Constitution provides that: "In case of any difference of opinion arising among the different Yuan that is not covered by the Constitution, the President may summon a meeting of the Presidents of the Yuan concerned for consultation in order to settle the difference." This clause was introduced so as to resolve possible differences between the five Yuan, such as, for example, impeachment proceedings which, while they are moved by the Control Yuan, are also investigated by the Legislative Yuan—or in regard to civil service examinations, in which both the Executive and the Examination Yuan are interested. We hoped that this article might not be misconstrued as another national government constituted by the five Yuan. The important change from the status of a government of the five Yuan to that of a responsible cabinet system is a very important aspect of the new Constitution.

We come now to the Executive branch of the government as related to the President of the Republic and the President of the Executive Yuan. One may ask whether the executive branch in our new Constitution is regulated on the model of a presidential system or a cabinet system, for the articles concerned do not give a clear-cut impression of the system adopted. In a way, the Executive Yuan follows the cabinet system, because it is responsible to the Legislative Yuan.

But as the Chinese President is not without responsibility, as is the President in France, we have reason to call the government a presidential system. The question can be answered further by citing Articles 37 and 57 of the new Constitution. Article 37 stipulates that "the President shall, in accordance with the law, promulgate laws and issue mandates with the countersignature of the President of the Executive Yuan, or of both the President of the Executive Yuan and of the heads of ministries or commissions concerned."

Article 57 stipulated that the President of the Executive Yuan shall be responsible to the Legislative Yuan. And so, although the Chinese system provides for a responsible cabinet, it can rightly be said that if the President of the Republic is a forceful man he may play his part in the cabinet, and summon the President of the Executive Yuan and the ministers to a meeting such as the State Council in France. The President of the Republic has the opportunity of being a stable factor without being held entirely responsible. This solution was the result of arguments between two schools of thought. The Youth Party urged that the President of the Republic should remain aloof from any party politics, but the Kuomintang wanted to make the President an all-powerful ruler. The Drafting Committee reminded the Kuomintang members that in America the Presidential system is not so powerful as it appears, because the nomination of a secretary of a department or of an ambassador may be opposed by the Senate, the budget may be cut down by Congress, and the Chairman of the Commission of Appropriations has more power over expenses and revenues than the President himself.

The President, as provided by the new Constitution, is the head of the state, representing the Republic of China. He promulgates laws and mandates, and declares war and peace. He may declare martial law and confer honors. Within certain limits he may issue emergency decrees. Any citizen of the Republic of China, having attained the age of 40, may be elected President or Vice-President, and his term of office is six years. So far, the position of the president and his powers does not differ materially from that of the American or French President. The President of China, however, has much greater power in the selection of his cabinet ministers. The Premier or the President of the Executive Yuan does not require to be selected from among the members of the Legislative Yuan. The President's powers are also strengthened by two more functions: firstly, he may refer back any resolution passed by the Legislative Yuan, and, secondly, in the case of reconsideration, if there is no two-thirds majority of the

Legislative Yuan upholding the original resolution, the President's veto will stand. Another point must be mentioned here, and that is that no stipulation concerning collective responsibility was written into the Constitution. This omission was purposely made so as to minimize changes of cabinet. Even if one of the ministers incurs the disfavor of the Legislation Yuan, the President of the Republic may charge one and not the whole of the cabinet with this responsibility. It is expected that the omission of the vote of confidence may contribute to the stability of the executive organ of the government.

The new Constitution further stipulated that the Executive Yuan should be composed of the President, the Vice-President, the heads of the various ministries and commissions, and of ministers without portfolio. In regard to the appointment of members of the Executive Yuan, the question was asked whether the new government's first cabinet would be a purely one-party cabinet or that of a coalition government. My answer was that with regard to seats in the Legislative Yuan the Kuomintang would be in the majority, so that the Kuomintang would be in a position to form the first cabinet. But as far as the sentiment of the Chinese people was concerned, they were afraid that a Kuomintang cabinet would lead China back to one-party rule, or in other words, to dictatorship. I thought, therefore, that in all likelihood the first cabinet would be a multi-party government, in which the Kuomintang members would dominate. With regard to the selection of cabinet ministers, again a compromise was found, stipulating that while the President of the Executive Yuan was to be appointed with the agreement of the Legislative Yuan, the President of the Republic and the President of the Executive Yuan might, after due consultation, draw up the list of cabinet ministers. To avoid any more complications, we believed it to be wiser not to stipulate that the appointment of ministers must receive the consent of the Legislative Yuan.

When we consider Article 55, stipulating that the President of the Executive Yuan shall be appointed by the President of the Republic with the consent of the Legislative Yuan, and Article 57, providing that the Executive Yuan shall be responsible to the Legislative Yuan, we begin to realize that the stability of the government was of grave concern to the constitution-drafting committee. Article 58 provides that prior to the submission to the Legislative Yuan of any statutory or budgetary bill or any bill concerning the declaration of martial law, granting of a general amnesty, conclusion of peace treaties, or other important affairs, or concerning matters of common concern to the various ministries and commissions, the President and the heads of the various ministries and commissions of the Executive Yuan shall present the said bill to the Executive Yuan council for discussion and decision.

The Legislative Yuan is allowed to discuss, decide, or object to a bill on expenditure, but it is not allowed to initiate any item on this subject. Here we must mention the question of the national budget, which after all is an essential part of the executive power of the government. Dr. Sun Yat-sen ignored completely this important aspect of the government. We know that in Britain the budget is made by the Chancellor of the Exchequer, who is one of the ministers in the cabinet, so that the Treasury is on an equal footing with the other ministries. The Prime Minister concurrently has the title of First Lord of the Treasury, and may cut or increase the national expenditure. In America, until 1921, the power of budget-making was in the hands of Congress, which was able to propose items of expenditure or the increase and decrease of taxes. After the Bureau of the Budget was established, the power was transferred to the President, although Congress can still increase or decrease taxes. In China, during the tutelage period, we had a Treasury Bureau which was on a level with the five Yuan of the National Government, although the Chief Treasurer's functions were narrowly limited to the collection of estimates of expenditure from the Minister of Finance and from the various ministries. The Minister of Finance, who was in charge of collecting money, had no hand in the preparation of the budget. Up to now, the Chief Treasurer, while having nothing to do with revenue, was obliged to present a budget to the government. The new Constitution has a good remedy for this odd arrangement of giving the power of budget-making to the Chief Treasurer, who is outside of the Executive Yuan. Hereafter only the Minister of Finance is to make a budget. Statements in regard to revenues and expenditures must be submitted to the Legislative Yuan within four months after the end of the fiscal year. For the purpose of auditing, the Auditor-General is to be appointed by the President of the Republic with the consent of the Legislative Yuan, and the accounts audited must be presented to the said Yuan for final approval. However, Dr. Sun Yat-sen's government structure emphasized the Control Yuan as the supervisor of auditing. So we see that in the new Constitution the Auditor-General is part of the Control Yuan to be nominated by the President of the Republic and appointed with the consent of the Legislative Yuan. This new arrangement seems to be a good one; however, what matters most is that the audited accounts shall be sent back to the Legislative Yuan for its final approval. Thus the Legislative Yuan will have full control over the national purse, and the Executive Yuan, as the budget maker, will be responsible for every item of expenditure and revenue.

(5) *The Judicial Yuan, the Control Yuan, and the Examination Yuan.* Aside from the Legislative and the Executive power of the government, the judicial power is also of great importance. In the Constitution, the Judicial Yuan has been framed as an independent organ. According to Dr. Sun Yat-sen's principles of the political structure of the government, the Judicial Yuan is considered part of the national government. In the new Constitution, it is considered as a supreme court of justice, which is independent of the executive branch.

The functions of the Judicial Yuan during the last twenty years have been a strange mixture of the administration of justice and the normal work of a court. The new Constitution includes the administration of justice as part of the functions of the Executive Yuan together with the power of appointment of the various judges. The Judicial Yuan can function in this case purely as a supreme court.

To remove the court as far as possible from the government is to make it independent of arbitrary influence on the part of the Executive power. Even in the days of absolute monarchy, with no separation of powers, the court was allowed a certain amount of independence in China. There is the case in the Tang Dynasty, in which the wise Emperor Tai-Tsung condemned to death some students who had falsified their family's professional record. The Vice-Minister of Justice, Tai Chou, strongly protested, and advocated that they should only be exiled according to law, and the Emperor had reluctantly to agree with him. Hundred of cases can be cited to prove that the dignity of the law was maintained during the different dynasties. The independence of the court depends chiefly upon the training of judges, their irreproachable character, and their freedom from political interference.

The second point that must be brought out is that the newly created Judicial Yuan has been given the power to interpret the Constitution. The Supreme Court of Justice in the United States has done a great deal of service in the function of interpretation. In reviewing cases, the Supreme Court may declare an act of Congress wholly or partially unconstitutional. As the judges place themselves outside and above party interests, we hope that, by giving them the power to interpret the constitution, conflicts between political parties may be avoided.

The system of censorship that is now embodied in the Control Yuan has been recognised as a specific function under the rule of the Emperor for many thousands of years. The censors were allowed to admonish the rulers for misconduct and misgovernment, misconstruction of laws, and faulty trials. The Emperor could be criticized for too much drinking, hunting too often, having too many concubines, and so forth. If there were famines, floods, or other unusual natural phenomena, the Emperors would be advised by the censors to pray for divine mercy in the imperial temple. The censors also had the authority to impeach the governors of the various provinces and other local authorities. We read in our history that there were many remarkable censors who were esteemed for their straightforwardness and moral courage. In the Ming Dynasty, a eunuch, Wei Chung-hsien, became even more influential than the Emperor himself; the censors tried to impeach him many times, but they did not succeed, and some even lost their lives. This indicates that when the controlling power is not handled by the people in the form of a parliament, censorship is not efficient if the ruler is weak or tyrannical. Yet the constitutional scholars did not agree with Dr. Sun Yat-sen's ideas that a separate controlling power should be exercised. They said that if the Legislative Yuan were given the power of questioning and impeachment, there would be no point in setting up a Control Yuan. But the Kuomintang members insisted that the old system of censorship should be preserved. We have therefore included the Control Yuan in the Constitution, although its functions might be considered obsolete. As to the demarcation of powers between the Legislative and Control Yuan, it is stipulated that, while the Legislative Yuan creates the law, the function of the Control Yuan is to see that these laws are obeyed. Article 90 of the new Constitution says: "The Control Yuan is the highest organ of control to exercise the power of consent, impeachment, rectification, and auditing." Article 95 stipulates that "The Control Yuan, in the exercise of its censorial powers, may request the Executive Yuan and its ministries and commissions to present to it for perusal, orders issued by them and related documents." Article 96 says in part that the Control Yuan may, in accordance with the nature of the work of the Executive Yuan and its various committees, investigate their activities with a view to finding out whether or not they are guilty of violating the law or of neglect of duty. Article 97 goes on to say that the Control Yuan may, on the basis of examinations and resolutions of the various committees, propose measures of rectification to be sent to the Executive Yuan and its various ministries and commissions concerned, directing their attention to defects and thus bringing about improvement.

If the Control Yuan deems public functionaries of the central or local governments guilty of neglect of duty or of violating the laws, it may propose measures of rectification or institute impeachments. If the case is criminal in nature, it shall be passed on to a law court; and Article 98 says that impeachments by the Control Yuan against public functionaries of the central and local government may be instituted upon the proposal of more than one Control Yuan member and the endorsement, after due consideration, of more than nine members.

Two other powers of the Control Yuan should be emphasized. First is the power of rectification; when the control Yuan finds that the government is not working efficiently it may pass a resolution of rectification. The second power is that of impeachment. When the Control Yuan finds the central or local government guilty of neglecting the law, it may institute impeachment proceedings.

The difficulty would seem to be that so long as the Legislative Yuan may also pass bills to urge the government to improve its functioning, it may conflict with the Control Yuan. The answer to this problem is that the Legislative Yuan exercises its functions from a political point of view, while the Control Yuan directs its supervision from a legal point of view. The Control Yuan, being more independent, will probably be more fair-minded in its judgment, as it has no party affiliation. The Control Yuan, however, is no longer a censor in the full sense, as it cannot interfere with the executive power of the government so much that it might infringe the rights of the Legislative Yuan. We might well call the Legislative Yuan an ante-legal organ, and the Control Yuan a post-legal organ.

Dr. Sun Yat-sen was much impressed by the examination system which existed under the absolute monarchy in China. But whether the Examination Yuan should be considered an independent power like the Judicial or Legislative Yuan is very doubtful, because it constitutes only a branch of the civil service devoting its attention to the competitive examinations that all government officials are to take. Before the Han Dynasty, the candidates for this service were recommended by the people of the villages and districts, and were approved and selected by the government. After the Han dynasty, with the increasing power of the monarch, the selection was done without reference to popular recommendation. By the examination system, the Emperor could choose those who were best able to serve him. We remember that Tang Tai-tsung, an Emperor of the Tang Dynasty, complacently said, "All the heroes in my empire were caught in my net." The examination required of the candidates an essay on certain prescribed subjects; the system later became stereotyped and degenerated into what is known as the "eight-legged essay," confined to a narrow interpretation of the classics. It was because of this that Kang Yu-wei, after China's defeat during the war with Japan in 1894, denounced the system as a prison for the Chinese intellect. He proposed instead to establish various schools and colleges which would teach Western learning and the sciences. While the civil service examination system in China was rapidly deteriorating during the nineteenth century, Dr. Sun Yat-sen found to his surprise that in England the examination system, inspired by China, had become one of the most important factors contributing to the efficiency and stability of the British government. Upon his return, therefore, he elevated the examination power to one of the five main branches of the government. Dr. Sun Yat-sen's views on the Examination Yuan were incorporated in the May Draft, where Article 85 provided that "the Examination Yuan shall, in accordance with law, by examination and registration, determine the following qualifications:

1. For appointment as a public functionary.
2. For candidacy to public office.
3. For practice in specialised work and as technical experts.

Article 83 in the new Constitution provides that "the Examination Yuan is the highest examination organ of the state and shall attend to matters relating to examination, employment, registration and ranking, checking of records, scaling of salaries, promotion and transfer, safeguarding of tenure, commendation, compensation, the retirement pension system, etc." And Article 86 stipulates that "the following qualifications shall be determined and registered through examination by the Examination Yuan in accordance with law: (1) Qualifications for appointment as public functionaries. (2) Qualifications for practice in specialised professions and as technicians."

The minority parties attempted to prevent any privileges being given to the majority party, so Article 89 runs as follows: "The Examination members shall be independent of party affiliations and shall, in accordance with law, enjoy full independence in the exercise of their functions."

At first it was thought that the Examination Yuan, when it had bills to present to the Legislative Yuan, should do so through the

Executive Yuan, where the responsibility for political affairs is concentrated. The Kuomintang members preferred, however, that the Examination Yuan be independent in its presentation of bills, and so this was agreed to as a concession by the other parties. Accordingly, the Examination Yuan can be compared with the Civil Service Commission in the United States.

From the description of the foregoing three Yuan, it should be apparent that, while the structure of Dr. Sun Yat-sen's five-Yuan government has been incorporated into the new Constitution, the real power lies in the hands of the Executive and Legislative Yuan. Actually, the new Constitution is a compromise between Dr. Sun's five-power theory and the theory of the separation of powers that prevails in the Western countries.

(6) *The idea of Federal Government and the new position of the provinces.* Since the reign of the first Emperor in the Chin Dynasty, China has been united, and the administration of the whole country has been highly centralized. The language, customs, and basic beliefs of the people have become unified. The written language and the reading of the Confucian classics have been so widespread that one might well say that the Chinese mind has acquired a very definite stamp. After conquering the six warring states, the First Emperor abolished the feudal system and established thirty-six administrative areas throughout the country. From that time on the emperors had absolute power in appointing provincial governors and local officials. The use of this centralized power was, however, limited primarily to the collection of land taxes, the appointment of high officials, the trial of judicial cases, and the issuing of imperial decrees. Local administration was largely left to the people of the various *hsien* and villages. It was indeed a unique combination of the policy of laissez-faire with absolute political rule. Even as late as the end of the Manchu Dynasty, military men like Tseng Kuo-fan, Tso Tsung-tang and Li Huang-chang exercised a great deal of independent power in their provinces in the name of the Emperor. Since the province is a regional unit, local independence appears to be a characteristic of Chinese political institutions. This was true even after the revolution in 1911, when the provinces were ruled by military governors whom the Central Government was unable to control. It was for this reason that political leaders began to advocate that self-government on the part of the provinces which is also the basis of the American federal system. Each province, they urged, should have its own constitution and a govern-

ment which is popularly elected. Dr. Sun Yat-sen was opposed to the idea because he thought it would encourage the warlords in the various provinces to do what they pleased. The idea of provincial constitutions was thus dismissed and was not revived till after Chiang Kai-shek and the Kuomintang had seized power. What they sponsored was the Compact Law passed during the tutelage period which contained some simple provisions for the division of the central and local powers. According to this, the provinces, with their powers fairly and equally divided, might issue local by-laws not contrary to the laws of the Central Government, and every district or *hsien* had a *hsien*-government under the control of the provincial government. In other words, no real provincial autonomy was granted. After the outbreak of the Sino-Japanese war, the Central Government withdrew to the interior with fewer provinces over which to rule.

It was then that the Political Consultative Conference was held, and it began to support the view that the province should be the highest unit of self-government and that the governor of the province should be elected upon a popular basis. Each province should have its own constitution so long as it did not conflict with the national constitution, and the division of powers should be made according to the principle of fair distribution. The Kuomintang Central Executive Committee, however, did not take to the term "provincial constitution," and it was finally changed to "provincial self-government law." By and large the idea of the division of powers between the Central government and the provincial governments has been accepted by the new Constitution.

Chapter XI of that Constitution describes the lines along which the provinces and the district should be run. Real self-government is the goal. It will of course take time before self-government in the provinces and the *hsien* becomes institutionalized, and popular election of the provincial governor and of the *hsien* magistrate will not take place for some time.

I have now given an outline of the political structure according to the Constitution promulgated in 1947. Two years later, the National Government was compelled to withdraw from the mainland to the island of Formosa. Enough time has not yet elapsed to permit us to judge whether the new Constitution will work well or not, but it is well to remember that it is a document which represents the Chinese concensus in matters of government, including the compromise position of the Chinese Communists.

It was a great pity that the Chinese Communist Party boycotted this Constitution. They have no faith in the peaceful work of national reconstruction and in the continuity of the rule of law. What they aim at is the overthrow of the government by means of violence and civil war. They believe that a government which has fallen into their hands by means of violence can be maintained forever on the same basis. I hope they do not forget that many dictatorships, like the Directorate of France, the Protectorship of Cromwell, and the governments of Hitler and Mussolini lasted only a few short years. It will be so with the dictatorships of Stalin and Mao Tse-tung. Because of its lack of confidence in the rule of law, the Chinese Communist Party gave up the Constitution, with which it had already expressed its agreement. But, while a rule of violence may work surprisingly well for a short time, only a rule of law can last and contribute something substantial to the building of a purposeful society.

General Marshall, at the end of his mission, and on the day of his departure for the United States, issued a personal statement in which he made some observations on the present Constitution.

In fact, the National Assembly had adopted a democratic constitution which in all major respects is in accordance with the principles laid down by the all-party Political Consultative Conference of last January. It is unfortunate that the Communists did not see fit to participate in the Assembly since the constitution that has been adopted seems to include every major point that they wanted.

Dr. Hu Shih had this to say with regard to the Constitution:

The present draft is based on the system of representative government. Representative government is necessary in a large country like China. Personally, I do not believe that the seat of political power should be vested in an unwieldy and large body like the National Assembly, as recommended in the May Fifth Draft. The present draft gives the Legislative Yuan much greater power and makes it the equivalent of a Parliament, to which the Executive Yuan must be responsible. I think this is a great improvement over the May Fifth Draft.

Such, then, in brief is a record of my own humble contribution to the building of democracy in China. Today the Constitution is virtually scrap-paper, but as a man with an ardent faith in the final victory of democracy in China, I trust that that Constitution will in the fullness of time become the basis of a living law for the 450 millions of my countrymen.

CHAPTER XI

The Democratic-Socialists and the End of the Nationalist Regime

My association with the National Assembly in the promulgation of the new Constitution made both my own position in Chinese politics and the role of the Democratic-Socialist Party difficult. It was my wish that our group remain in the position of an opposition party for a few more years, until its membership had been enlarged and more experienced men had joined us, and we could shoulder the burden of political responsibility. Parliament would be the best school for political education. If my party were allowed to occupy seats in Parliament, then the party members would gain invaluable experience. The convention of the two-party system such as they have in Great Britain has never existed in China, and it would take a long time before the members of China's Parliament got used to such a tradition. A party government depends on so many factors—peace and law must be firmly established, public opinion must be enlightened, the party itself must have the backing of the voters, and the military force must be kept apart from politics, otherwise its approval or disapproval can make or unmake a cabinet at any moment. These are the conditions which the Generalissimo should have built up long ago, before he asked the other parties to agree to the formation of a coalition government. But the attitude of the Generalissimo has been strange. When he did not care for the idea of democracy or constitutional government, he dealt with the "outside parties" as if they were enemies or criminals, and would not even allow them to enjoy freedom of press, association, or assembly. That was his way of dealing with the Communists and with the other political parties as well. When he felt he needed a coalition, he would suddenly ask them to join his government and to take up this or that portfolio. This is like asking a boy to grow up in one day, and shoulder a man's responsibilities. I felt very embarrassed when the proposal was made to me that my party join the government, because my party was not prepared for it. When my party was carrying on propaganda work against the government in the underground period, all it could do was to enlist a few young men to do the work. But if we had been allowed a few more years to work openly, then we could have enlisted more men of experience and prestige. These men would have qualified for responsible work in the government. Unfortunately, my experience was not that happy. Only a short time before my party was considered illegal, yet all of a sudden I was asked to hand in a list of men who could take up the ministerial portfolios. As a responsible man, I felt it was too heavy a burden for my party.

After the final break with the Communists, the Generalissimo asked the other parties which were represented in the Political Consultative Conference to join the National Assembly. This request could not very well be refused, because the proposed coalition was to pave the way for constitutional democracy. But to join the National Assembly meant cooperating with the Kuomintang. Furthermore, with regard to joining the government, more questions arose: On what basis could I work with the Kuomintang and the Generalissimo? Let us think, for a moment, in terms of forming a business firm. If two men subscribe the same amount of capital, one can have as much say as the other. But if one man's investment is 90 per cent and the other's only 10 per cent, how can both have the same amount of power in the firm? This knotty question occurred to me when Chiang Kai-shek proposed that my party join the government. Between his capital holding in the Chinese Government and mine, there would be an overwhelming disproportion. He had a big party backing him up. He had an army of hundreds of divisions. He also had the police and the civil service under his control. If I went to Nanking and proposed a policy which displeased him, he could send policemen to surround my house. If I did try to please him, there would be no constitutional government and no hope of reform. So, when the question of joining the National Assembly really arose, there was an exchange of letters between the Generalissimo and myself which I think worth reproducing here:

November 20, 1946.

Dear Mr. President,

Since the Political Consultative Conference last January, I have not for a moment lost sight of the aim of peace and unity of the country and the problem of how to gather all the political parties together in the National Assembly to adopt a constitution which will be observed by all. I trust that these are also things which have been engaging your earnest attention.

Unfortunately, developments of the past few months have been contrary to what we hoped for. The friendly, consultative spirit between the Kuomintang and the Chinese Communist Party during the Political Consultative Conference disappeared with the dispute over the date for the convocation of the National Assembly. My suggestion to postpone the convocation of the National Assembly for a fortnight with the hope of reaching an agreement on outstanding issues during this extended period unfortunately failed to gain the consent of the parties concerned. As a result, the people feel there may be a complete breakdown of the Kuomintang-Communist negotiations.

Despite the issuance of the cease-fire order, it is feared that the people still cannot escape the horrors of war. Although the National Assembly is now in session, whether it can adopt a constitution which will be acceptable to all is still problematical. Moreover, members of the Political Consultative Conference seem to be divided in opinion regarding the different issues. Consequently the nation may be plunged into a catastrophe from which it would never recover.

However, I still believe that the situation is not beyond hope. It all depends on how you, Mr. President, will handle the following points.

(1) The thorough enforcement of the cease-fire order in order to prevent the spread of hostilities and to indicate the peaceful intentions of the government. (2) The early implementation of the spirit and letter of the Political Consultative Conference resolutions in order to show the Government's determination to institute constitutional democracy.

In my opinion, the following measures should be adopted immediately to enforce the cease-fire order:

First. The Executive Headquarters under the Committee of Three should continue to function so as to prevent expansion of conflicts and to preserve the possibility of re-opening peace negotiations.

Second. The Government should, with utmost tolerance, implement the agreement on army reorganization.

Third. The Government's repeatedly avowed policy of settlement of all issues by political means to remain unchanged, in order to attain real peace, to readjust public finance, and to preserve national strength.

To implement the resolutions of the Political Consultative Conference, the following steps should be carried out:

First. The Draft Constitution as revised by the Political Consultative Conference should be guaranteed by all the parties concerned that it be adopted by the National Assembly.

Second. Freedom of the person, the press, assembly, and election should be adequately guaranteed in order that real public opinion may reach the government.

Third. As the Government has decided to introduce constitutional democracy, one-party rule should be terminated as early as possible and the following measures should be taken immediately:

(1) After the promulgation of the constitution, the expenses of the Kuomintang should cease to be appropriated from the National Treasury.

(2) After the reorganization of the National Government, the State Council will be the highest policy-making body. The provincial, municipal, and *hsien* governments will be responsible for their respective administrations, and the local Kuomintang headquarters should then cease to interfere with the local governments.

(3) The participation of students in partisan and political activities creates unnecessary trouble and confusion. The Government should see to it that students refrain from any partisan activities and concentrate their efforts on the pursuit of knowledge.

(4) The purpose of Government reorganization and party cooperation is to introduce a merit system in the administration. Since the Political Consultative Conference, the chief disputing point among the various parties seems to be the division of "spoils" in the government. The most important thing, however, should be the streamlining of the whole administrative system and the selecting of officials on nothing but a merit basis. If the Kuomintang members of the Government, after its reorganization, should continue to attempt to control or check its functions, the whole organization will be paralyzed.

I have taken part in the Political Consultative Conference on the discussion of the Draft Constitution, and I am still willing to join in the task of adopting it. If the Draft Constitution can embody the resolutions of the Political Consultative Conference and the Government can announce the termination of one-party rule at an early date, enforce the cease-fire order, and implement the letter and spirit of the Political Consultative Conference's resolutions, the Chinese Democratic-Social Party will then be willing to attend the National Assembly although it deeply regrets that the National Assembly has failed to secure the attendance of each and every political party in the country. There are still people who are dubious about the actual effect of the constitution once it is adopted. I do not question such anxiety and will not refrain from discussion. I firmly believe that the success or failure of the great task of national reconstruction and the support of the people will depend on how the constitution is implemented.

Yours respectfully,

CARSUN CHANG
Chairman Committee on Organization,
Chinese Democratic-Social Party.

To this letter Chiang Kai-shek replied in the following terms:

NOVEMBER 21, 1946.

DEAR MR. CHANG,

Your letter dated November 20, 1946, was received with appreciation. Your suggestions show your dutiful regard for national affairs and are in accord with what the Government wishes to carry out.

The convocation of the National Assembly is intended to accomplish the aim and the end which Dr. Sun Yat-sen, Father of the Republic, struggled to attain throughout his life, and to realise the Government's long-cherished intention to conclude political tutelage and return the reins of government to the people. The people of the nation all understand this and I think you will agree and help to carry it out. I am very glad to learn that your esteemed party will take part in the National Assembly.

Some of the things you advise me to do in your letter have been done, and some are being done by the Government. Your advice is true and wise and fully in conformity with the Government's plan.

The Government has decided to solve the Communist problem through political means from beginning to end. The cease-fire order must be carried out thoroughly, the Executive Headquarters should continue to exist, and especially the basic agreement for military reorganization and for the integration of the Communist forces into the National Army, must be realised in order to attain the aim of nationalizing the troops. All the parties should be responsible for the adoption of the draft constitution revised and agreed upon by the Political Consultative Council. The Government has promulgated a set of measures to safeguard the freedom of the people; it will henceforth put them into effect one by one.

As for your advice regarding the conclusion of one-party rule, this party (Kuomintang) has already adopted a resolution on the matter and carried it out step by step. It will, when the Constitution is promulgated, be completed as soon as possible in accordance with your advice. Regarding the reorganization of the government and the improvement of political administration, it is necessary to gather men of ability to work together and increase administrative efficiency so as to expedite and promote the achievement of national reconstruction.

In short, the Government should do everything you mention in your letter. Further, I myself am making every effort to bring about these changes. You insist on the early realization of our constitutional government. Now, the convocation of the National Assembly is intended to secure the adoption of a constitution so as to conclude the Kuomintang rule and return the Government to the people. This is exactly what you wish to happen. It is therefore hoped that members of your esteemed party will attend the National Assembly and participate with us in the task of adopting the Constitution. This will make possible an early implementation of constitutionalism, which is your political aim.

It is sincerely hoped that members of your esteemed party and other parties and non-partisan social leaders will, in the spirit of cordial cooperation which pervaded the nation when it faced a national crisis at the beginning of the Sino-Japanese war, cooperate closely with this party to expedite the completion of the great task of national reconstruction. The future of the nation will depend on cooperation.

Yours truly,

CHIANG-KAI-SHEK

Director-General of the Kuomintang.

The purpose of my letter had been to find out if there was a common policy between us. If so, then it might be possible for me to work with Chiang Kai-shek. The central idea proposed consisted of three things: (1) The enforcement of the cease-fire order in order to prevent the spread of hostilities; (2) the early implementation of the Political Consultative Conference resolutions in order to show the Government's determination to introduce constitutional democracy; and (3) that some measures be adopted to terminate one-party rule.

The outcome of this exchange of letters was that the Generalissimo was faithful in carrying out his pledge that the Draft Constitution as revised by the Political Consultative Conferences should be passed, and it did pass in the National Assembly of 2700 members. So far he kept his word. The other points mentioned in the letter, especially the enforcement of the cease-fire order, have not been completely followed. After the passing of the new Constitution, the next step, reorganization of the Government, came in. The outside parties, like the China Youth Party and the Democratic-Socialist Party, were requested to join, so that they should also shoulder the responsibility of governing. The work of reorganization was divided into two parts: First, in March, 1947, the outside parties were asked to nominate members to the Legislative Yuan and the People's Political Council. As the Democratic League associated itself with the stand taken by the Communists, it refused to participate. The China Youth Party and my party sent members to these three organs, as had been requested by the Government in order to prove the sincerity of its wish to put an end to one-party rule. Then, in April, the talk about the reorganization of the Executive Yuan and the State Council began. This worried me very much, because participation in the Executive Yuan and in the State Council raised the following considerations: (1) Previously a coalition government that included the Communists, was expected to carry out the work of reform; what could the China Youth Party and the Democratic-Socialist Party now do by joining the Government after the Communists had left? (2) As the Generalissimo believed that he had the greatest share in the "China firm," how could the two minority parties have an equal standing with him? (3) If the Kuomintang and the minority parties signed any agreement as a common platform, this would constitute a pledge on both sides. (4) Could my party refuse to join the Government?

From the beginning I was pessimistic about this kind of coalition. If I joined the government, I would have to do better work than the Generalissimo. If I could not do anything better, then it would be preferable to remain outside the Government. But after its cooperative role in the National Assembly, it was difficult for my party to refuse to join the Government, because we had arrived at the time for the liquidation of political tutelage. The alternative was to join the Government completely, that is, to ask for an adequate number of seats in the government in order to have real power in it. If it was going to be possible to do some constructive work, I was willing to risk going along this line. After many days' deliberation, I decided that such was not the case and that I myself would not join the Government, and that my party should accept as little responsibility as possible. I was thus surprised to find recently in the House Document No. 154, part 3, of the 81st Congress, a short account of my life in which I was mentioned as a member of the State Council. My refusal to join the State Council was known to Dr. Leighton Stuart, then the American Ambassador. This mistake could have come from the editor of the document, based perhaps on inaccurate news reports.

Though I had decided that I myself would not join the Government, I did however propose to Chang Chun, then Prime Minister, that the new Government should have a platform. We discussed it in Shanghai and in Nanking for about a month, and at last the following program was decided on:

The National Government of the Chinese Republic, with a view to establishing constitutional government and promoting democracy, has, since the Political Consultative Conference, decided to reorganize the Government and to invite individuals from political parties and groups other than the Kuomintang, as well as independents, to participate. More than one year's persistent efforts have just resulted in a jointly formulated and agreed upon procedure for immediate completion of the government reorganization. Besides, a political program for the National Government after the reorganization, evolving from comprehensive and careful deliberations by all parties concerned, has just been approved respectively by the Standing Committees of the Youth Party, the Democratic-Socialist Party, and the Kuomintang; it has also been agreed upon by the independents who took part in the discussions. The embodiments of the Political Program which will be adhered to jointly by the reorganized National Government, are as follows:

One. The program of peaceful National Reconstruction shall be the guiding principle of administration for the reorganized National Government, while all participating parties and independents shall be jointly responsible for completing the interim procedure for inauguration of constitutional government.

Two. Cooperation between the various parties and groups shall be based upon the principles of "political democratization" and "nationalization of armed forces." Under this common principle no effort will be spared towards political progress and national stability.

Three. In order to promote world peace and uphold the United Nations Charter, China should pursue a foreign policy of equality and good neighborliness, towards all friendly nations without discrimination.

Four. Settlement by political means shall remain the basic principle for solution of the Chinese Communist problem. If only the Chinese Communists show willingness for peace, and the railway system can be properly restored, the Government will seek national peace and unity through political channels.

Five. The responsible Executive Yuan system shall be enforced as an experiment in accordance with the spirit of the provisions of the Constitution. The Executive Yuan shall abide by any decisions of the State Council and assume full responsibility. Equal respect should be accorded to the functions and powers of the Legislative Yuan. In presenting a bill to the Legislative Yuan, the Executive Yuan authorities shall be present to offer explanations, thereby insuring coordination between the Executive and Legislative authorities.

Six. Pending the inauguration of the constitutional government, nomination to the Presidency of the Executive Yuan shall be made by the President of the Republic with the previous concurrence of the various parties.

Seven. Provincial administrations shall be governed by principles making a clear distinction between the military and civil authorities and allowing for the adoption of appropriate measures as local conditions warrant. In matters of personnel and legislation, a thoroughgoing check-up will be made and reform instituted in order to enable the provincial governments to attain the highest degree of efficiency possible.

Eight. All laws promulgated and all institutions established to meet the needs of political tutelage shall, after reorganization of the National Government, be rescinded and abolished.

Nine. Thorough adjustments shall be made in the tax system and financial set-up, the procedure of levying taxes shall be simplified, and the categories of land-tax and additional levies shall be reduced in order to lighten the burdens of the people.

Ten. Strict guarantee shall be accorded the people's freedom of person, freedom of speech, freedom of publication, and freedom of assembly. Any illegal arrest or interference shall be strictly forbidden. Where restrictions are deemed essential for the maintenance of social order or to avert a crisis, laws governing such restrictions shall be approved by the State Council.

Eleven. Foreign loans to be contracted in the future shall all be earmarked for purposes of stabilizing and improving the people's condition and furthering production and reconstruction.

Twelve. As far as possible, there should be participation of political parties and independents in the political councils or provisional councils, municipalities and *hsien*. Local governments in the various provinces should also include representatives of various parties and independents, chosen on the principle of "selection of the able and efficient."

My intention was to accept few seats in the Government, but to ask for more compliance with the announced program. Point four was the most important one in the whole program, because I expected that within a short time negotiation for peace between the Kuomintang and the Communists would be resumed.

When my proposal regarding our future policy was placed before the Standing Committee of my party, it brought on a storm. One member said, "If we do decide to join, then we must do something. If we are not sure that something can be done, it is better for us to stay outside." Another said, "If we decide to join, we must at least show what we can do, as Kang Yu-wei did in the 'Hundred Days of Reform.' "

At last it was decided that three seats in the State Council and a position of minister without portfolio should be accepted. The ministerial positions with distinct responsibilities were to be declined. The reason for such a resolution was that so long as the Communists stayed outside, the Government could last only for a short time, and a reshuffle of the Cabinet might come at any time. Therefore, it would be fitting for my party to have one or two men in the Cabinet as a symbol of coalition. This resolution was the expression of a lukewarm attitude towards joining the Government. Besides, I was mindful of a Chinese proverb which says, "When a heavy load has been piled up, it is hard to clear it in one day." The Generalissimo was heavily weighed down by his party, his military force, and his special service men, and there was hardly any hope of changing this situation. The Stilwell episode and the experiences of General Marshall clearly taught us that, if the United States Government—which had equipped thirty nine Chinese divisions and supplied millions of dollars in goods and money—did not succeed in changing the Generalissimo's mentality, attitude, and policy, one or two ministers nominated by my party could not possibly have any influence upon him.

The resolution, however, disappointed many of my friends. Some tried to persuade me that I myself should join the Government. Mr. Phillip Fugh, adviser to Dr. Leighton Stuart, came to Shanghai and told me that the State Department had sent telegrams to find out whether I was going to join the Government. My answer to Mr. Fugh was: "If my Party asks for many seats in the Government, it means that it is greedy for position and power. If I stay outside, I can talk to the Generalissimo more freely in persuading him that the Government should adhere to its platform. What I fight for is governmental reform, not position." This is a specifically Chinese trait, one which is perhaps difficult for the State Department to understand. I thanked Mr. Fugh for his visit, but I differed with him about the policy which he had expected me to adopt.

On the other hand, some of the young party members wanted to accept more jobs in the Executive Yuan. While they did not dare to oppose the resolution openly during the debate, a letter signed by some members of the Standing Committee came to me a few days later, saying that I should withdraw the nominations for the membership of the State Council. I answered that when a resolution had been passed by the Standing Committee, I was empowered to put it into execution. It was passed at four o'clock, and at six o'clock on the same day I sent in our nominations. There was no alternative for a man like myself who took state affairs seriously.

The result was that my party began to be split wide open, and some of the party members began to malign me. Every day the Communist papers, with the assistance of my party members, published articles denouncing me. The Communists were glad to see the Democratic-Socialist Party torn by a feud. In the eyes of the left wing or the Communists, my Party was the "running dog" of the reactionaries, and it was better that it should collapse. A full-page advertisement appeared in the Shanghai English papers, the *North China Daily News,* the *China Press,* and the *Evening Post,* in which I was pictured as a man who was dictatorial and greedy for power, because I stood for participation in the Chiang Kai-shek Government.

I cared little about this advertisement since I knew my conscience was clear, and therefore no slander could hurt me. I believed that my dealings during the negotiations for the reorganization of the government had been honorable and aboveboard, so I did not mind the slander which was being directed against me. One member of the American Consulate came to me and asked, "Have you seen the advertisements in the English papers? They are damaging and you must reply. If you don't reply it will mean that what they say is true. We Americans send back reports based upon what we hear and read." My answer was, "This may be your American way of doing things, but everyone here knows that these young members of my party want to grab ministerial jobs, and because they are unable to get them, they slander me. If I reply, they will put out counter-arguments. That would mean a war of words and utter confusion. To keep silent is the best way to stop slander." The American official was confronted with a Chinese puzzle and went away. He had come to ask me to set up my defense, and, though I appreciated his good intentions I could not agree with his American way of fighting slander. I chose instead to remain supremely indifferent.

I must make it clear, however, exactly why I refused the ministerial positions. The foreign newspapers were full of talk of the "incompetence and corruption of the Chinese Government." We were in a period of inflation, and I saw clearly that acceptance of a ministry could easily involve the minister or his subordinate officials in charges of corruption, without assuring any commensurate political advantage. I decided, therefore, to accept only one or two ministries without portfolio, merely to show that the end of one-party rule had come. To do more than that was unnecessary and dangerous. That was why my party accepted only three seats on the State Council and one ministry without portfolio. The incumbents had nothing to do with the actual work of the ministry, so that they could not be involved in any cases of corruption. My duties to the party and to the country as a whole were twofold: to see to it that the political tutelage which the Kuomintang insisted upon prolonging was actually terminated, thus paving the way for constitutional government, and to see to it that my own party was kept as honest and as free as possible from any possibility of involvement in that corruption which had sounded the death knell of the Kuomintang. Many of my own party members either did not see my point of view or were unwilling to support me.

I must admit that the way I approached the problem of the reorganization of the Government was exactly opposite to that of the Communists. They considered it as a chance for seizing power. My view was that to join the Government was a heavy responsibility. The Kuomintang, during the tutelage period, had tried as much as possible to restrict the activities of the other parties, but now they suddenly decided to share the heavy responsibility of governing with us. What they expected us to do was simply beyond our capacity. I was aware of our limitations, and that was why I tried to accept as few positions of responsibility as possible. If I did not do enough to satisfy the wishes and desires of some of my friends, it was because I had sufficient sense to know that the work of government should not be taken lightly. Again, the Generalissimo is a man with whom it is difficult to work. He is alert and quick-witted. He is emotional. He never follows out a policy intelligently. He is surrounded by the C. C. Clique. Anyone who works with them is good; anyone who possesses a sense of justice and is capable of criticizing them is bad. In a political atmosphere such as this, I preferred to stay outside of the Government rather than be tarred with the same brush.

The American White Book mentions my party's role from time to time, but the American Embassy did not quite understand why I acted as I did. The situation was so delicate that I confess I did not speak quite frankly to Dr. Leighton Stuart.

Because the Generalissimo is emotional, his policy changes with his temper. When the program of the Chang Chun cabinet was decided upon, it was an agreement signed by the Kuomintang, the China Youth Party, and the Democratic-Socialist Party. Before the signing took place, I was asked to go to Nanking. Chang Kai-shek was to sign for the Kuomintang, while Tseng Chi and myself were to sign for our respective parties. When we all arrived at the official residence of the Generalissimo, Wu Tieh-cheng, the Secretary-General of the Kuomintang, suddenly expressed himself as being opposed to having the Generalissimo sign the agreement. His argument was that, as President of the Republic, he should not put his name on such a document—the implication being that the leaders of other parties were not on the same standing with the Generalissimo. But the documents and the Chinese brushes were already on the table, and, very obligingly, Chiang Kai-shek said, "Let us sign it even for the sake of having a souvenir." Thus it was that a coalition government was settled on in a friendly fashion: it could have been stillborn. Two months later I was summoned to Nanking again. The Generalissimo asked my opinion about a punitive expedition against the Communists. I said, "It all depends on what the government can do after a punitive expedition is announced. In a Western country, when a declaration of war or an order for mobilization is issued, the government can really increase its fighting power by rallying the support of the people. All our present government possesses are the army divisions in active service. I do not see that much may be expected by way of increase in its fighting power. Can the government, for instance, increase its revenue after such a declaration is made? I have my doubts. So I don't think that the term 'punitive' will do any good."

Regardless of whether the term punitive expedition or mobilization was used, it was my belief that the question of success in fighting the Communists depended on two things: (1) the quality of the civil government, and (2) the quality of its military force. If the Generalissimo could pass the test on these two points, things should go well. But it was plain that both the civil government and the fighting forces were in bad shape.

Most of Chiang Kai-shek's officers were graduates of the Whampoa Military Academy, of which the Generalissimo himself was the Director. They were trained only a few months and were then sent out on active service. Outside of familiarity with a few slogans and catchwords, they had no training in the real sense of the word. The standard of the cadets was therefore far below par. They might call themselves revolutionary military officers, but they really had no substance and simply disintegrated the moment they were exposed to temptation. During the war, these cadets were quickly promoted to command brigades, regiments, divisions, or even armies. Once at the front, they were free from civil control, which they considered in any case to be subsidiary to them. When an emergency arose, they would exploit it for the purpose of making money by smuggling. At the time of the Japanese surrender and the taking over of the Japanese properties, the commanding officers vied with each other in appropriating houses, factories, and stocks which they confiscated for their own use. This was true in Shanghai, Tientsin, Peiping, Hankow, and the other big cities. The surrender of the Japanese army accelerated the deterioration of the Chinese military officers. This was known to every Chinese after the Japanese surrender; probably the Generalissimo heard of it too, but he did nothing to prevent this wholesale pillage, which indicated that discipline among his officers, except insofar as they remained loyal to him personally, was practically non-existent. Through them the common people learned to hate the government and to lose all confidence in its integrity and honesty.

When General Wedemeyer came to China in 1947, he obtained evidence of the utter corruption of the Commanders-in-Chief in Manchuria, Tu Lih-ming and Wei Lih-huang. If General Wedemeyer could find sufficient evidence with so cursory an investigation, surely the government knew all along how bad the situation had become. It was known to the Shanghai banks that General Wei Lih-huang, after transporting troops by air-lift, continued to ask for more food. He told the government that, if it found it difficult to send food by air, he could buy it on the spot. Tons of banknotes were then airlifted to Manchuria with which to buy food. What he actually did was to confiscate food from the peasants for distribution to the soldiers, then to send the banknotes back to Shanghai as his own money to be invested in commodities, which he hoarded.

When I was in Hankow in 1949, the Hankow citizens told me that the Governor of Shantung Province, Wang Yao-wu, was one of the greatest landowners of Hankow, because he happened to be the Commander there when the Japanese surrendered. When officers became millionaires through such unscrupulous means, how could they be depended upon to fight for the cause of anti-Communism? It was asking for the impossible.

Even before the Japanese surrender, discipline in the Nationalist Army had become exceedingly lax. I can illustrate this by a case which

I knew personally. My nephew, a youngster of sixteen, volunteered as a cadet, as was very common in the war period. He joined the seventh Cadet School under the Commander-in-Chief Hu Tsung-nan. Hu was a favorite student of the Generalissimo. While an army under one of the other Commanders might consist only of 20,000 or 30,000 men, Hu's men ran to 300,000 or more. As my nephew wanted to be trained as a cadet, he was sent to Hu Tsung-nan's school. When he came back after two years, I asked him, "What have you learned?" "I carried wood," was the reply. I was surprised, and asked why it was necessary for the cadets to carry wood when board and lodging were adequately provided for by the Ministry of Defense. My nephew said, "We don't know why, but we did it because we were ordered to." My nephew told me other things. In 1942 or 1943, when the Generalissimo went to Sian and wanted to pay a visit to the seventh Cadet School, Hu Tsung-nan tried to prevent the Generalissimo's inspection. But the Generalissimo insisted, and he did visit it. At the time of his arrival all the barracks were lighted with military signal wire, and each cadet had been given a new tube of toothpaste, a cake of soap, and a new towel—but they had been told that these things were to be handed back when the Generalissimo left the school. This game of duping the Generalissimo was popular among his subordinates. They would merely put up a show, to fool Chiang, and it always worked. Chiang likes to have everything in his own hands, and never delegates his power to anybody, so that he even had to inspect a cadet school by himself. Consequently, there was no system of any kind, except that of a hoax within a hoax. It was on men of this type that the country had to depend for fighting against Communism. Is it any wonder that the attempt ended in ignominious failure?

With regard to the Generalissimo's way of running the civil government, it was of the same pattern. He believes that he is the only one to carry out Dr. Sun Yat-sen's will. He thinks that Sun's doctrine should be followed as strictly as Leninism and Stalinism are in Soviet Russia. Chiang does not realise that, while the Soviet Union imposes Leninism and Stalinism upon its people, the Conservative Party in Great Britain has never had a book called "Conservatism," or the Liberal Party a book called "Liberalism," or the Socialist Party a book called "Socialism." The Conservative, Liberal, and Socialist parties study the real situation in the political and economic field and try to find a remedy for it in their own ways. They have their party programs, which are revised from time to time. But the Generalissimo knows so little about how the Western democracies work, and runs his own government on such narrow party lines and on the basis of his personal likes and dislikes, that it is impossible for him to see things objectively. What are the departments of a government for? To look after the interests of the people. Why are there civil servants in each ministry? To run the ministry efficiently. What is a currency system for? It is the medium of economic exchange, and should be kept stable in order to avert economic hardship. But such concepts, elementary as they are, are beyond Chiang's comprehension.

What the Generalissimo did was to try to impose the party on every institution. Education to him was training the students to be Kuomintang members, not training them to be good citizens. The Examination Yuan and its training corps do not work for the improvement of the civil service but try to make young men into loyal party members. The currency system, after it was changed over from a silver-based system to that of a managed currency, had tided over China's financial difficulties during the war period; but Chiang had the idea that because China is a rural and not an industrial country, it could not suffer economic collapse even if there was super-inflation. He expounded this idea on many occasions. Even with the experience of the inflation during the war, he never believed that it could drive the country, including business people, the salaried class, and the soldiers, into ruin. I have never known a mind more unsuited to cope with the problems of the modern world. Personal power is all that Chiang understands. Under such leadership, how can there be an efficient government in China—let alone a constitutional government?

The Generalissimo would issue orders which were physically impossible to carry out. A highway, if it is to be built solidly, should take one or two years in the building, but he would give orders that it be finished within three or six months. A well-known case was the building of the railway from Kweilin to Tushan in the province of Kweichow. As the terrain is very mountainous, some engineers were against the building of such a line. But there was a certain chief engineer who wanted to gratify the vanity of the Generalissimo, and he said that it could be done. The wonder of it was that he did it. But when the railway was finished, the trains had to be pushed all along the line by two locomotives. During the evacuation of Kweilin, when the line was swamped by refugee traffic it broke down completely.

This instance is symptomatic of the way in which Chiang's government has been guided entirely by his whims and arbitrary decisions made on the spur of the moment. He sees no need for any system or organization. Under such a regime, the art of government becomes, for all practical purposes, the art of studying the infinite variety of his moods; it produces two kinds of government officials, those who have won his favor and those who have not—or, in other words, those who are always perpared to say "yes" to whatever Chiang may say, and those who believe in independent thinking, personal integrity, and personal dignity. The yes-men are those who win his favor, the flatterers and sycophants who would not utter a critical word in any gathering over which Chiang happens to preside. This was what happened when war was declared against Germany. The meeting over which the Generalissimo presided and which was attended by the ranking officials of the government, was a meeting of silence. Only the Chairman of the government, Mr. Lin Sen, dared to speak, and what he said was that the document before the meeting should be sent to his office to be signed! It is said that a house must have solid foundations before it can stand. The government of Chiang Kai-shek was built on quicksand and clay. How can it stand? Is it any wonder that it fell like a house of cards when it had to face the Communist crisis?

It is no use giving many more details about the events of the postwar period. But briefly this was what happened within the year between March, 1948, and January, 1949. The following cities fell one after another in rapid succession into the hands of the Communists:

1948	March 12	Szepingkai
1948	September 23	Tsinan
1948	October 15	Chinchow
1948	October 20	Changchun
1948	November 1	Mukden
1948	December 1	Hsuchow
1949	January 15	Tientsin
1949	January 31	Peiping

Just before the fall of Peiping, on January 31, Chiang announced his retirement; on February 5, the Government moved to Canton; on April 20, the Communists crossed the Yangtse, and a few days later Nanking and Shanghai fell. It has been truly said that if the Nationalist soldiers had had any will to resist, they could have beaten back the enemy with bamboo sticks while they crossed the mighty Yangtse River. Yet in America, distinguished members of Congress are still arguing to this day that Chiang Kai-shek was sold down the river because America did not give the Nationalists enough military assistance. To think that thirty-nine American-equipped and trained divisions could be annihilated in so short a time! Surely American equipment was not made of tissue paper! I went to the Vice-Minister of the Ministry of Defense and the Deputy Chief of Staff and asked for an explanation. They answered that all the defeats could be reduced to a formula. When the Communists took the initiative and started to fight, the Government troops were sent to defend the point attacked. Having no will to fight, they kept within the city. After a few days' fighting, they sent telegrams asking for reinforcements. The Government could not do otherwise than answer in the affirmative. When the commander of the army of reinforcement received the order to go, he offered the excuse that he must wait till his supplies of food and ammunition were brought up to the proper level. It would be many days, therefore, before the reinforcements got under way. By the time they arrived at their destination, the army defending the city had already been beaten by the Communists, and so the army that had been sent in by way of reinforcement simply joined in the surrender. That was how it accomplished its mission of reinforcement!

It is interesting to know how a tank squadron or an armored division of the Nationalist Army could be annihilated by the Communist forces. When a tank unit was defending the city of Hsuchow, the Communist forces dug a long trench to encircle it and hamper its mobility. Every night the Communists sent thousands of men to dig an arc of trench in order to make the area in which the tank brigade could move still smaller. The last arc was dug so that the tank unit would be cut off from all communications, and then its food supply would have to be airlifted. When the area became so small that the tanks were crowded in one place, they had no alternative but to surrender. That a tank unit could be immobilized and made useless merely by the use of the spade may appear strange to a Western strategist, but that was what happened in the battle of Hsuchow. What further comment is necessary?

In September, 1948, I was on a lecture tour to Wuchang, Hankow, Chungking, and Chengtu, but I was very much worried over the situation. I saw clearly that the National Government of Chiang Kai-shek would not last much longer and that everything would go to pot. The idea came to me that I should tell the Government, freely and honestly, what was in my mind. I gave up part of my lecture tour and hurried back to Shanghai. After many days of deliberation, of drafting and revising, I submitted a letter to the Standing Committee of my party urging Chiang's retirement, in the hope that a new situation could be created with another leader to take his place. Under this new leadership, I thought that China might perhaps escape falling into the Communists' hands. I was glad to find in the American White Book that Dr. Leighton Stuart had the same idea, which he expressed in his report to the State Department. On October 23, Dr. Stuart suggested a number of possible alternatives in the following way:

(a) Will we continue to recognise and support the Nationalist Government should they be forced to move elsewhere in China because of continuing military reverses?

(b) Would we advise the retirement of the Generalissimo in favor of Li Tsung-jen or some other National political leader with better prospects of forming a republican non-Communist government, and of more effectively prosecuting the war against the Communist rebels?

(c) Would we approve the retirement of the Generalissimo in favor of some Chinese leader who could bring an end to the civil war on the best possible terms for the Nationalist forces and the non-Communist political parties?

(d) In the latter course would we recognise and support a Coalition Government resulting from termination of hostilities and involving cooperation with the Communists for a united China? Or,

(e) Would we give de facto recognition to such governments, the while withholding any E.C.A. or other support?

It is, to say the least, unusual that an Ambassador should prefer to see the liquidation of a government to which he was accredited and to whose Chief of State he had presented his credentials. But that was the only alternative open to Dr. Stuart. In order to save China from disintegrating so rapidly, the only way out was to recommend to his own government that a new leader in the person of Li Tsung-jen or some other national political figure take the place of Chiang Kai-shek. My own letter to Chiang Kai-shek was written at the end of October and delivered on November 8. This was what I said:

Since the end of World War II, many governments have fallen. It happened to Churchill and General de Gaulle, both of whom won the war for Great Britain and France. Your present position is different from that of Churchill and de Gaulle, because you have been elected President of the Republic by the National Assembly. As far as I can see, the present condition of the army, the Government, and the Party is so rotten that it needs a complete overhauling. It is like a room in which the things have been shut away from sunshine and ventilation for a long time. Everything in this room is buried in dust, and is dirty, mildewed, decayed, and rotten. Such a room is bound to be stifling and malodorous. A thorough sweeping is required, and the windows need to be opened. My advice is that it will be better for you, as the President of the Republic, to go abroad. You should delegate your power to someone else who should have the full power to do the housecleaning work for you. While you are abroad you will make a number of friends in the anti-Communist camp, and then you can wait for another chance.

When this letter was handed in, the Secretary-General Wu Ting-chang asked, "Does Mr. Chang know what the consequences will be for him?" My friend Chi Yih-chao, a member of the State Council, answered, "Mr. Chang is ready to be arrested and the Headquarters of the Democratic-Socialist Party to be closed down." I waited for a long time to hear that the Generalissimo had read my letter. Chang Chun, one of his closest friends, explained to him that Mr. Chang's letter represented not only his private opinion, but was based on the information which he had gathered from different sides. The Generalissimo did not order me arrested. But in January, 1949, after his New Year's message was issued, an invitation to dinner was sent to me. The party consisted of about a dozen people: the Generalissimo, Chang Chun, Wu Tieh-cheng, Wang Shih-chieh, Chang Shih-chung, Shao Lih-tse, and some others. The guests invited were Tso Shun-sen, then Minister of Agriculture representing the China Youth Party, Chiang Yun-tien from my party, and myself. At the table a debate took place as to whether the Government's policy towards the Communists should be one of war or of negotiating for peace. Shao Lih-tse and Chang Shih-chung were for peace negotiations, while Wang Shih-chieh, astute and adept in studying Chiang's moods, showed bad temper and said that since the men at the table were not determined for war, we were already defeated. Tso Shun-sen and Chiang Yun-tien gave the advice that the Generalissimo should go abroad. The situation had become critical, and the opinions at the table were naturally divided. I said, at the end of the dinner, that when a crisis arose it was natural that there should be two camps—one standing for war to the bitter end, and another for peace. But we had to ask ourselves: Why is there a party for peace? It is because the army has been consistently defeated. The proposal that we negotiate for peace would not have been made if the army had been victorious. It is futile to denounce either one party or the other. "As a leader," I said finally, "Chiang Kai-shek should look at both points of view and make the best of the situation." The Generalissimo then asked me the question, "Are you still of the opinion you expressed in your letter of November?" I answered "Yes." This dinner was perhaps meant as a farewell party to all those who had been invited. On January 21, the Generalissimo announced his retirement and left Nanking for his native town of Feng-Hua.

Thus concluded one chapter of Chinese history—that of the Kuomintang's political tutelage and Chiang Kai-shek's domination.

CHAPTER XII

America's China Policy at the End of World War II

Since the end of the last century, United States policy in China has been characterized as the "Open Door Policy." It has aimed at maintaining equality of opportunity for commerce for all countries in China. It has meant also the safeguarding of China's territorial and administrative integrity. This policy was put to the test by the Twenty-One Demands presented by Japan in 1915, at the Versailles Conference in 1919, and by the Nine-Power Treaty at the Washington Conference in 1922. The principle of territorial and administrative integrity was greatly compromised when the Japanese army occupied Manchuria in September of 1931. It is perhaps fair to say that the independence of a nation could not be maintained over a long period only by the guarantee of other powers. So long as China was unable to protect herself, the guarantee of other powers was next to being worthless. That became evident in 1931.

The strong resistance offered Japan by China from 1937 was followed by the attack on Pearl Harbor in 1941, and the United States came to China's rescue. From this time on, through the Lease-Lend Bill, the appointment of General Stilwell as the American Commander on the Far-East front, and the signing of the Atlantic Charter, Sino-American cooperation grew so intimate that China hoped she would be strengthened to the status of a great power among the family of nations. But the expectation that China would become a united, independent and prosperous nation on the side of the free world was very short-lived. Three years after the Japanese surrender, China had become a Communist power. Communist China and the Soviet Union signed a Treaty of Alliance, Friendship, and Mutual Assistance early in 1950, and China suddenly announced Marxism-Leninism-Stalinism as the official doctrine of the Chinese Government. Towards the end of the year, Communist China sent troops to fight in Korea in defiance of the United Nations' resolution. What, then, is the reason that China, within so short a period, went over from the Democratic camp to the Communist bloc? This is a big question, which will be studied for a long time to come. Again, was there ever a chance that China might be kept on the side of the free world? My answer is that there was a chance which was unhappily missed by the United States and the Chinese Government. Let us, however, first consider American policy during the war and the post-war periods. It went through four stages: (1) the Yalta Conference, (2) General Marshall's mission of mediation, (3) General Wedemeyer's suggestion of putting Manchuria under a United Nations Trusteeship, and (4) the China Aid Bill in 1948.

(1) *The Yalta Conference.* As a price for the Soviet Union's entry into the Far Eastern war, the Soviet Union was promised the following rights at this Conference:

(A) The status quo in Outer Mongolia (the Mongolian Peoples' Republic) shall be preserved.

(B) The former rights of Russia, violated by the treacherous attack of Japan in 1904, shall be restored, viz:

  (a) The Southern part of Sakhalin as well as all the islands adjacent to it, shall be returned to the Soviet Union.

  (b) The commercial port of Dairen shall be internationalized, the preeminent interests of the Soviet Union in this port being safeguarded and the lease of Port Arthur as a naval base of the U. S. S. R. restored.

  (c) The Chinese Eastern Railroad and the South Manchurian Railroad, which provide an outlet to Dairen, shall be jointly operated by the establishment of a joint Soviet-Chinese company, it being understood that the preeminent interests of the Soviet Union shall be safeguarded and that China shall retain full sovereignty in Manchuria.

(C) The Kurile Islands shall be handed over to the Soviet Union.

The premise upon which these privileges were granted the Soviet Union was that China, having been saved by Russia's entry into the Far Eastern war, had to pay a price. That, to say the least, is a new and unorthodox view of international relations. By the same token, France, Belgium, Holland, and even Britain should be asked to pay a similar price, but we have not heard the faintest suggestion on that score. However that may be, let us pursue the subject a little further.

According to the State Department's White Paper on China, Mr. Harry L. Hopkins, in his conversation with Marshal Stalin, said

1. Stalin repeated all of his statements made at Yalta that he wanted a unified and stable China, and China to control all of Manchuria as part of a united China. He stated categorically that he had no territorial claims against China and mentioned specifically Manchuria and Sinkiang and that in all areas his troops were centered to fight the Japanese he would respect Chinese sovereignty.

2. The Marshal stated that he would welcome representatives of the Generalissimo to be with his troops entering Manchuria in order to facilitate the organization in Manchuria of Chinese administration.

3. He agreed with America's open door policy and went out of his way to indicate that the U. S. was the only power with the resources to aid China economically after the war. He observed that for many years to come Russia would have all it could to do to provide for the internal economy of the Soviet Union.

4. He agreed that there should be a trusteeship for Korea under the United States, China, Great Britain, and the Soviet Union.

If we keep this record of conversation in mind, it is apparent that many things which were promised at the time were never carried out. Why was the idea of trusteeship changed into a divided Korea with the 38th parallel as the dividing line? Why was the "open door," which Stalin guaranteed, shelved in spite of Mr. W. Averell Harriman's protest? Again, why was Stalin's promise, that the Generalissimo's representatives could go with the Soviet troops entering Manchuria, not put into practice? And why was the organization of Chinese administration in Manchuria not facilitated?

(2) *General Marshall's Mission of Mediation.* From the time of Harry Hopkins' conversation with Stalin till the appointment of General Marshall as the Special Representative of President Truman to China in December, 1945, the situation in Manchuria did not develop as Stalin had promised. It seems that there was a sudden change of attitude on the Soviet side. Bitter as the pill was, China observed both in letter and spirit the Sino-Soviet Treaty of Friendship and Alliance signed in August. Russia, on her side, however, did nothing to redeem the solemn promises made by Stalin, but, on the contrary, gave every encouragement and facility to the Chinese Communists to penetrate into Manchuria. When they succeeded in doing that, it became clear that the Marshall mission and the Political Consultative Conference

were doomed to fail. There was no further need, from the point of view of the Chinese Communists, for any mediation. The occupation of Changchun by the Chinese Communist army on April 18, 1946, shows the real intention of the red conspiracy in Manchuria. It was their aim first to occupy all of Manchuria, and then, with this stronghold firmly in their hands, they would proceed to conquer the rest of China.

General Wedemeyer, in his report made in November, 1945, to the State Department, said:

> He [the Generalissimo] will be unable to occupy Manchuria for many years unless satisfactory agreements are reached with Russia and the Chinese Communists.
>
> Russia is in effect creating favorable conditions for the realization of Chinese Communist and possibly their own plans in North China and Manchuria. These activities are violations of the recent Sino-Russian Treaty and related agreements.

If General Wedemeyer's valuable report had really been appreciated, I think that the United States Government would have seen clearly that Manchuria was the pivotal point in the mediation work of General Marshall. Why was it, then, that General Marshall did not attach the same importance to the situation in Manchuria as to the Cease-Fire Order and the Political Consultative Conference? There are two aspects of the Manchurian situation which we should bear in mind.

After the Yalta Agreement and the Sino-Soviet Treaty, it was clear that Soviet Russia was back in the position of Tsarist Russia prior to 1904. Why was the United States willing to give Soviet Russia the freedom to exploit Manchuria which it vigorously denied to Japan in the forty years from 1904–1945? It seemed that the United States was willing to recognise the geographical propinquity of Soviet Russia to China, and particularly her special interest in that part to which her possessions were adjacent. It took Japan all of her diplomatic skill and duplicity to negotiate the Lansing-Ishii agreement, but even so, it was denounced so heartily that Japan made no headway, in a legal sense, in the conquest of Manchuria. And now this huge territory of half a million square miles, with all its rich resources, was handed to Soviet Russia on a silver platter, thanks to the generosity of the United States! China was too weak in the post-war period to negotiate with Soviet Russia with any hope of success. She looked towards America for moral and material support, and that was the support she received!

Why was there no insistence that Stalin's suggestion to allow Chinese Nationalist representatives to go into Manchuria be carried out? Why was the idea of an Allied Commission to look after the interests of all allied powers for a peaceful Far East, not put into practice? Why was the infiltration of the Chinese Communist Army not checked, as well as the expansion of its capacity for fighting? The United States was expecting too much from China if she left these questions to be solved by the Generalissimo himself. Manchuria and Korea have been the most thorny problems since the Sino-Japanese War in 1894, the Russo-Japanese War in 1904 to 1905, and the Japanese occupation in 1931, and yet the American Government would pay no more attention to them as of 1945.

As the State Department allowed the situation to remain in a fluid state, it was natural that Soviet Russia should step in to exploit a golden opportunity. If General Marshall, in addition to working for the Cease-Fire order and the Political Consultative Conference, had also paid attention to the Manchuria question, the situation would have been vastly different. If Manchuria had not been given to the Chinese Communists as a base for overthrowing the Chinese Government, the mediation work might have yielded substantial results.

But to come back to General Wedemeyer's report. He said that Generalissimo Chiang would be unable to occupy Manchuria for many years unless satisfactory agreements were reached with Soviet Russia and the Chinese Communists. That such was the case was clear not only to General Wedemeyer but also to us Chinese. Under the circumstances, it seems unusual that the American Government gave no instructions to General Marshall, in his efforts at mediation, to try and establish a coalition government—if that was what he and his government wanted—locally in Manchuria itself in the first place, so as to forestall the complete Communist infiltration which seemed imminent. It is true that Chiang was anxious to reestablish Chinese sovereignty over all of Manchuria; no Chinese leader could have wanted anything less. But I am sure that he or any other person would have enough sense of reality to understand that, if full sovereignty was difficult of achievement, it would have been the better part of wisdom to create a regime which was not going to be out and out Communist and over which he could still exercise a measure of control. If General Marshall, under the instructions of the State Department, had spoken frankly and openly with Chiang along those lines, I feel confident that the advice would have been accepted. But instead of that,

Wedemeyer's report was ignored, practically speaking. It was pigeonholed and its recommendations left unheeded, and, eventually, the result was the complete domination of Manchuria by the Chinese Communists, which led finally to the present unhappy situation in Korea. I remember that in March and April of 1946 I myself proposed more than once to the members of the Democratic League that we should advocate the establishment of a provincial coalition government in Manchuria so that we could devote our time to the other problems of peace and unification in China. The obstacle was precisely as we predicted: the Generalissimo was adamant on the full recovery of Manchuria as an integral part of China. But General Marshall was in a strategic position. Backed by the strength of his government, his words would have carried weight which none of us presumed to have, and Chiang would have given in if there were enough persuasion. The battle of Changchun could thus have been avoided. The problem of Manchuria might then have been considered solved, however unsatisfactory the solution might have appeared to Chiang and to his followers. This would have established a basis for genuine Sino-American cooperation. The loss of this opportunity I still consider to be the basic reason for the failure of the Marshall mission.

(3) *General Wedemeyer's idea of Trusteeship over Manchuria.* General Wedemeyer first suggested the idea of Trusteeship over Manchuria to the State Department in November, 1945. This idea was likewise ignored. In 1947 he was sent again to China as the Special Representative of President Truman. General Wedemeyer's recommendations with regard to China after his tour of study were so important that I think it is best to quote them at some length:

It is recommended:

That the United States Government provide as early as practicable, moral, advisory, and material support to China in order to contribute to the early establishment of peace in the world in consonance with the enunciated principles of the United Nations, and concomitantly to protect United States strategic interests against militant forces which now threaten them.

That the United States policies and actions suggested in this report be thoroughly integrated by appropriate government agencies with other international commitments. It is recognised that any foreign assistance extended must avoid jeopardizing the American economy.

China

That China be advised that the United States is favorably disposed to continue aid designed to protect China's territorial integrity and to facilitate her recovery, under agreements to be negotiated by representatives of the two governments, with the following stipulations:

That China inform the United Nations promptly of her request to the United States for increased material and advisory assistance.

That China request the United Nations to take immediate action to bring about a cessation of hostilities in Manchuria and request that Manchuria be placed under a Five-Power Guardianship or, failing that, under a Trusteeship in accordance with the United Nations Charter.

That China make effective use of her own resources in a program for economic reconstruction and initiate sound fiscal policies leading to reduction of budgetary deficits.

That China give continuing evidence that the urgently required political and military reforms are being implemented.

That China accept American advisers as responsible representatives of the United States Government in specified military and economic fields to assist China in utilizing United States aid in the manner in which it is intended.

Apart from the other points in the shelved recommendations, what I want to discuss is the idea of Trusteeship over Manchuria. General Wedemeyer based his recommendations on the following arguments:

The situation in Manchuria has deteriorated to such a degree that prompt action is necessary to prevent that area from becoming a Soviet satellite. The Chinese Communists may soon gain military control of Manchuria and announce the establishment of a Government. Outer Mongolia, already a Soviet satellite, may then recognize Manchuria and conclude a "mutual support agreement" with a de facto Manchurian Government of the Chinese Communists. In that event, the Soviet Union might accomplish a mutual support agreement with Communist-dominated Manchuria, because of her current similar agreement with Outer Mongolia. This would create a difficult situation for China, the United States, and the United Nations. Ultimately it could lead to a Communist-dominated China.

The United Nations might take immediate action to bring about cessation of hostilities in Manchuria as a prelude to the establishment of a Guardianship or Trusteeship. The Guardianship might consist of China, Soviet Russia, the United States, Great Britain, and France. This should be attempted promptly and could be initiated only by China. Should one of the Nations refuse to participate in Manchurian

Guardianship, China might then request the General Assembly of the United Nations to establish a Trusteeship under the provisions of the Charter.

Initially China might interpret Guardianship or Trusteeship as an infringement upon her sovereignty. But the urgency of the matter should encourage a realistic view of the situation. If these steps are not taken by China, Manchuria may be drawn into the Soviet orbit, despite United States aid, and lost, perhaps permanently, to China.

It is interesting to note that the American White Book made the following comment on the Wedemeyer recommendations:

Among the recommendations of the Report, however, was one requiring immediate action by the United Nations to place Manchuria under a Guardianship of Five-Powers, including the Soviet Union, or a United Nations Trusteeship. It was the conviction of the President and the Secretary of State that any such recommendation, if made public at that time, would be highly offensive to Chinese susceptibilities as an infringement of Chinese sovereignty, and representing the Chinese Government as incapable of governing Chinese territory. It was also believed that it would no doubt be rejected by the Chinese Government as it would in a sense represent at least a partial alienation of Chinese territory to a group of powers including the Soviet Union. In any event, they believed that to place upon the United Nations responsibility for action to implement such a recommendation might well seriously endanger the future of that organization, which at that time was already confronted with other grave and pressing problems.

As far as I understand the situation, I think General Wedemeyer's suggestion would have had a good chance of success if it had been taken up promptly at the time when it was made, which was in 1945. The autumn of 1947 was much too late, because it was two years after the end of World War II, during which period Soviet Russia and the Chinese Communists had already made Manchuria their stronghold. Also, if it had been made at Yalta, in combination with the concessions offered Russia by President Roosevelt, Stalin would have had to swallow it. In such a combination, Soviet Russia would have regained in Manchuria her status prior to 1904, but at the same time Chinese territorial and administrative rights would have been protected under such a Trusteeship. That this was not done was a great error on the part of the United States.

The American fear that China would feel offended, was not a correct estimate of the Chinese mind. The lease of Port Arthur as a naval base to Soviet Russia and the joint management of the Changchun Railway was obviously a greater infringement of China's sovereignty. If she could be advised by America to make these concessions to Soviet Russia, how could America say that she would refuse a Trusteeship which was temporary, since the trust territory would later be returned to China? What was given to Soviet Russia by the Yalta Agreement afforded China no other protection than the Sino-Soviet Treaty. If the concessions had been made in combination with a plan for trusteeship, China would thereby have been protected from further violation by an international guarantee. She would have been in a much more favorable position, and could not feel that she would be any worse off. Indeed no other situation could have given greater offense to China than the Yalta concessions.

How such a plan of trusteeship in Manchuria would really be carried out depended on the policy and determination of the United States. If the State Department was really determined to keep China's independence and sovereignty intact, I think that, before or after General Marshall's mission, the United States Government should have taken a strong attitude in separating the Nationalist Army from the Communist Army in North China and in Manchuria. Such a step could not have offended Soviet Russia because it would have been carried out according to Stalin's statement about "United States leadership in the Far East," and certainly it would have facilitated greatly General Marshall's work of mediation. Also the step would not have cost any American lives: all that was needed were a few hundred soldiers holding a town or a railway line merely as a token and a symbol. The fact was that the United States Army was so popular at the conclusion of the war in China that not even the Communists would have dared fight against it. It all goes to show how heavily the world has to pay because of a few miscalculations. I am positive that Manchuria could have been saved and that the whole situation in Asia would have been today totally different if the United States Government had thought a little more carefully in those days.

Let me touch again upon the story of how a parallel case was handled, that is, how the Greek Communists were restrained by the British. When the Greek Communists began to make trouble in Athens in 1945, General Scobie said:

> I am determined so far as lies within my power to make a success of the tasks assigned to me by my Government. I am convinced that in many parts of the country there is no freedom of speech, no freedom of the press, and that terrorism and victimization still exist. I

stand firm behind the present constitutional government until the Greek state can be established with a legally armed force and free elections can be held. I will protect you and your Government against any attempt at a coup d'état or act of violence which is unconstitutional.

Reginald Leeper, British Ambassador to Greece from 1934 to 1946, told us that, in order to make General Scobie's warning more effective, the following statement was issued from Ten Downing Street:

> The Prime Minister wishes it to be known that General Scobie's message to the Greek people stressing the need for unity and emphasizing our full support of the present Greek Government, was made with the knowledge and entire approval of His Majesty's Government.

This meant that British policy towards the Greek civil war was backed up by force and determination.

In 1948, the Soviet delegates made four charges against Great Britain with regard to the presence of British troops in Greece:

> (1) There was prevailing in Greece a very tense situation, which might have very unhappy consequences, not only for the Greek population, but also for peace and security.
>
> (2) The presence in Greece of British troops was not necessitated by circumstances, because there was no need to protect communications as is the case in defeated countries.
>
> (3) The presence of British troops in Greece had become a means of pressure on the political situation in the country.
>
> (4) These circumstances had resulted very often in support for reactionary elements in the country against democratic ones.

But Mr. Ernest Bevin, then Foreign Secretary, made a vigorous reply to these charges. He said:

> It had been arranged that British Administrators and troops with Marshall's agreement, should go to Greece and help revive the country, turn the Germans out, and seek to get order and civil government in operation. We went. The process of revival had been interrupted by the Communists seeking to obtain a minority government to control the country. We believe that Democracy must come from the bottom and not from the top. We do not want these forces there. But the Greek Government have stated over and over again: "We must get settled government, we must get the elections, and you, the British, must help us to do it."

Using the same logic and argument in the case of China, the American Government could very well have replied to the Russians that the American soldiers had come to China in order to turn the Japanese out. Marshal Stalin had agreed to the United States leadership in the Far East. Unless China got a settled government and a democratic one, the United States had not done its job. It was as simple as all that.

Nay, it could have been even simpler. Upon the surrender of the Japanese, the United States did not have to be as outspoken as General Scobie or Churchill. If the United States had just said, "The civil war in China must be stopped. United States troops will keep communications open. In certain designated areas the United States will offer its good offices to keep the Kuomintang and the Communist armies apart,"—then the fighting would have been stopped immediately. General Marshall's work of mediation would then have had a more solid foundation on which to build.

The trouble with the United States policy was that it was full of good intentions, but those intentions were never backed up with any determination. American policy in China has been one of vacillation between action and inaction, between humanitarianism and strategic realism. This view is widely held in China and is confirmed by an American expert on Chinese affairs whom we have cited before, Mr. John K. Fairbank.

> The result has been, I think, to encourage in our traditional China policy a disconcerting split between humanitarian ideals and strategic realism. At [times] we have been almost preternaturally concerned about the fate of "China," meaning some cause or fraction which we supported there with admirable righteousness. Yet we pass moral judgment more readily than we take action. Sometimes we are irresponsible. Our policy has oscillated between involvement and abstention, action and inaction.

If we accept the terms of Mr. Fairbank's analysis of American policy towards China, we may say that from 1937 to Pearl Harbor was the period of abstention; with Pearl Harbor began the period of involvement. After the Japanese surrender, because of America's sympathy for the underdog—in this case the Communist Party and the Democratic Parties—the period of abstention changed to one of activity again. Of course, the corruption and incompetence of the Nationalists were so manifest that they gave the Americans no encouragement to help China. Even so, something could have been done to forestall the tragic developments which later took place. It is inevitable that the question arises, "Why did the United States not back up General Marshall by applying a little military force to stop the civil war, rather than depend only on the good faith of the Kuomintang and the Communists?" And again, "If the State Department had to rush the question of concessions in Manchuria at the Yalta Conference because of military necessity, why was a door not left open to combine it with the idea of trusteeship at a later time?" Even if we admit that General Wedemeyer's suggestion of Trusteeship over Manchuria was made too late, the idea of stopping the civil war in August, 1947 could have been applied to the region inside the Great Wall. Before the occupation of Szepingkai on March 12, 1948, by the Communist Army, the whole of China proper could have been saved if a committee like the Balkan Commission had been appointed to deal with China. It is a misfortune that General Wedemeyer's suggestion was not applied to China even in a limited and partial way. There would have been at the present day a completely different situation in China if the matter had not been handled in an "all or nothing" way.

(4) *The China Aid Bill.* At the end of January, 1948, after I had finished my series of lectures on the new Constitution of China at the University of Washington in Seattle, I flew to Washington, D. C. to attend the Senate Foreign Relations Committee's hearings. What struck me most was General Marshall's pronouncement, "The United States cannot underwrite the Chinese Government militarily and economically." This meant that the United States would not assume any responsibility for the Chinese civil war and would not pour money down a rathole. I do not blame him for this attitude, because every nation should be responsible for her own peace and order.

This "Hands Off" policy was more explicitly stated in a message from Marshall, then Secretary of State, to the American Embassy in China in October, 1948:

There is general agreement with your assumption that the United States' purposes in the Far East would as in the past be best served by the existence of political stability in China under a friendly government, and American policy and its implementation have been consistently directed towards that goal. However, underlying our recent relations with China have been the fundamental considerations that the United States must not become directly involved in the Chinese Civil War and that the United States must not assume responsibility for underwriting the Chinese Government militarily and economically. Direct armed intervention in the internal affairs of China runs counter to traditional American policy towards China and would be contrary to the clearly expressed intent of Congress, which indicated that American aid to China under the $125,000,000 grants did not involve the use of United States combat troops nor United States personnel in command of Chinese troops. Public statements in Congress by leaders of the Senate Foreign Relations Committee, which initiated Section 404(b) of the China Aid Act, indicated that aid to China under the $125,000,000 grants must be completely clear of the implication of the United States, underwriting the military campaign of the Chinese Government, since any such implication would be impossible over so vast an area.

Our China Aid Program was designed to give the Chinese Government a breathing spell to initiate those vital steps necessary to provide the framework within which the base for economic recovery might be laid and which are essential for its survival. It was clear that, in the main, the solution of China's problems was largely [a task] for the Chinese themselves and the aid was intended to give the Chinese Government further opportunity to take measures for self-help.

The general basic considerations governing our approach to the China problem were set forth in my statement before the Senate Foreign Relations and House Foreign Affairs Committees' executive sessions, a copy of which was forwarded to you. The United States Government must be exceedingly careful that it does not become committed to a policy involving the absorption of its resources to an unpredictable extent, as would be the case if the obligations are assumed of a direct responsibility for the conduct of the civil war in China or for the Chinese economy or both. To achieve the objective of reducing the Chinese Communists to a completely negligible factor in China in the immediate future, it would be necessary for the United States virtually to take over the Chinese Government and administer its economic, military, and governmental affairs. Strong Chinese sensibilities regarding infringement of China's sovereignty, the intense feeling of nationalism among all Chinese, and the unavailability of qualified American personnel in the large numbers required, argue strongly against attempting such a solution. It would be impossible to estimate the final cost of a course of action of this magnitude. It certainly would be a continuing operation for a long time to come. It would involve the United States government in a continuing commitment from which it would practically be impossible to withdraw, and it would very probably involve grave consequences to this nation by making China an arena of international conflict. Present developments make it unlikely that any amount of United States military or economic aid could make the present Chinese government capable of re-establishing and then maintaining its control throughout China. There is little evidence that the fundamental weaknesses of the Chinese Government can be basically corrected by foreign aid. These considerations were set forth in my statement in February, and they are certainly no less true under present circumstances.

In November, 1948, the Generalissimo found that the military situation of the Nationalist Government had so deteriorated that he could not help sending a telegram to President Truman asking for a speeding up of, and an increase in, military aid, which can be summarised as follows:

The general deterioration of the military situation in China may be attributed to a number of factors. But the most fundamental is the non-observance by the Soviet Government of the Sino-Soviet Treaty of Friendship and Alliance which, as your Excellency will doubtless recall, the Chinese Government signed as a result of the well-intentioned advice of the United States Government. I need hardly point out that, but for persistent Soviet aid, the Chinese Communists would not have been able to occupy Manchuria and develop into such a menace.

As a co-defender of Democracy against the onrush and infiltration of Communism throughout the world, I would appeal to you for speedy and increased military assistance and for a firm statement of American policy in support of the cause for which my Government is fighting. Such a statement would serve to bolster up the morale of the armed forces and . . . would strengthen the Government's position in the momentous battle now unfolding in North and Central China.

My government would be most happy to receive from you as soon as possible a high-ranking military officer who will work out in consultation with my Government a concrete scheme of military assistance, including the participation of American military advisers in the direction of operations.

President Truman's reply was cold, as could have been expected. He could do nothing beyond the China Aid Act of 1948. His answer to Chiang Kai-shek was:

Your attention may have been called to my public statement on March 11, 1948, in which I stated that the United States maintained friendly relations with the Chinese Government and was trying to assist the recognised Government of China to maintain peace. I also stated that I did not desire Communists in the Chinese Government.

Secretary Marshall stated publicly on March 10, 1948, that the Communists were now in open rebellion against the Chinese Government and that the inclusion of the Communists in the Government was a matter for the Chinese Government to decide, not for the United States Government to dictate. I believe that these statements and the action of my Government in extending assistance to the Chinese Government under the China Aid Act of 1948 have made the position of the United States Government clear.

CHAPTER XIII

The Communist Regime—Government Structure and Policy

On Chiang Kai-shek's retirement Vice-President Li Tsung-jen succeeded him as the acting President of the Chinese Republic. The situation created by this change of leadership was a ticklish one, as this was the most critical moment in the history of the Kuomintang since the days of the Northern Expedition.

The first major event after Li's accession to power was the opening of peace negotiations with the Communists. The opinion of the Government was by no means unanimous on the issues of peace or war. The Prime Minister and some of the Cabinet ministers had already moved to Canton, but a number of ministers still remained with Li Tsung-jen in Nanking. The President was able to muster an unofficial delegation to fly to Peiping in order to make the necessary arrangements for the reception of an official peace mission.

According to my information, there was also considerable divergence of opinion in the Communist camp. Some thought that with victory just around the corner there was no point in any peace talks. The spokesman of this group was Tung Pih-wu, now one of the Vice-Premiers. Others said that it was advisable to announce peace conditions in order to show publicly the Communist desire for peace. One way or another, the following eight points constituted the terms on which the Communists were willing to talk peace:

1. Strict punishments of war criminals.
2. Abolition of the Constitution.
3. Abolition of the Kuomintang legal system.
4. Reorganization of the Nationalist troops on "democratic principles."
5. Confiscation of "bureaucratic" capital.
6. Reform of the land system.
7. Abolition of treasonous treaties.

8. Convocation of a Political Consultative Conference without the participation of reactionary elements, the establishment of a democratic coalition government, and the taking over of all the authority of the reactionary Kuomintang government and all its branches.

The concluding provision of these terms—the taking over of all the authority of the reactionary Kuomintang government—shows the determination of the Communists to extirpate the Kuomintang government completely. Naturally there was little hope of any successful negotiation on such conditions.

Li Tsung-jen tried to convince the American Government of the wisdom of lending support to China in order to bolster the morale of the Nationalist army. On March 24, the Acting President presented a draft formula to the Executive Yuan with a list of official peace delegates who were to proceed to Peiping. When the Communists were asked to explain their eight points, they promised to make some concessions, but these did not change the substance of their demands. On April 12, the Nationalist delegates were presented with an ultimatum, setting the same day as the deadline for the acceptance of the Communist conditions. Though it was postponed till the 20th, the Communist army actually crossed the Yangtse River and occupied the capital city of Nanking four days later. The rout continued, and Hankow and Shanghai were occupied on May 16 and May 25 respectively.

Although the Nationalist army south of the Yangtse still amounted to 500,000 men, desertions and disagreements prevented any real resistance in the battles of Hengyang and Canton. In the latter city the Generalissimo wanted the armies to form a protective screen, but the local commanders, who knew the terrain much better, advised a stand on the plateau north of Kuangtung. Such internal dissension meant that no effective defense would be offered against the Communist advance south of the Yangtse.

How rapidly the government forces disintegrated was described in the magazine *Free China* in its January 16, 1950 issue, published in Formosa, a magazine of which Mr. Lei Cheng, a Kuomintang member, is the chief editor. He said:

From the fall of Tsinan in September, 1948, to the time of writing stretches a period of fifteen months. In that time the Government army of 3,000,000 men has completely disintegrated and on the Chinese mainland about 1,000,000 square miles, including most of the big cities and lines of communication, have come under Communist control. How has this been possible? It was made possible because of strategical mistakes and disagreements of the high command. There were also mistakes and incompetence on the political side. These political mistakes created dissatisfaction. . . . This dissatisfaction in turn accelerated the military collapse. There was disharmony between people and government, within the government between officers and soldiers, and between the commanders. After the battles of Hsuchow and Pengpu, this condition became more and more serious and widespread. The commanders knew only self-interest, and the soldiers lost all will to fight. The people were unwilling to support the army, and this disintegration rapidly set in within the army. Desertions occurred everywhere. Except for a stiffening of resistance by the Nationalist army against the Communist forces in Shanghai, the provinces along the Yangtse Valley, the Southeastern coastal provinces, the high plateau of the Northwest and the stronghold of Southwest China were all lost through internal disharmony. Today we are at the climax of this Chinese tragedy.

This is the confession of an enlightened Kuomintang member. And how truly it describes the end of Kuomintang rule. But with the Communists now in complete control of the mainland, let us turn our attention to the structure of their new government.

In May, 1948, Mao Tse-tung already realized that a Communist victory was in sight. In order to rally all fellow-travellers to his cause he issued an appeal to the so-called democratic parties and to leaders in the various professions. The aim of this appeal was to call a new Political Consultative Conference in order to bring a democratic coalition government into being. Most of the people who were prepared to work with the Communists replied expressing their approval.

No limit as to the nature of this government was set until Li Chisen left Hongkong for North China toward the end of 1948. Very few people knew his mission. He went to Harbin to discuss there the convocation of the new Political Consultative Conference. Before long it became known that only those parties, associations, and non-partisan leaders who openly opposed American imperialism, reactionary Kuomintang rule, feudalism, and bureacratic capitalism, would be admitted as members, and that all reactionary parties or members who worked with the Nanking Government would be ipso facto debarred. The new Political Consultative Conference would meet in 1949, the exact date to be fixed later, and would consider two points: (a) a common program and (b) the establishment of the government of the People's Republic.

An agreement was reached on November 25. Soon after came the victory of the Communist forces in Northern China and in the Hsuchow-Pengpu area. Then, in the first half of 1949, Peiping, Tientsin, Hankow, Nanking, and Taiyuan fell one after another to the Communists. Before the Communist conquest of the provinces was complete, a committee for the convocation of the Political Consultative Conference met to decide the list of its members, its procedure, and the drafting of a "common program and an organic law of the government." The formal announcement was then made that the conference was to meet on September 17. The membership was decided as follows:

1. Representatives of the fourteen political parties or groups	165
2. Representatives of the nine regional areas	116
3. Representatives of Army Headquarters and the five field armies	71
4. Representatives from sixteen public bodies	235
5. Representatives specially invited by the Communist Government	75
	662

The first session began on September 21 and ended on October 30. Three important documents—the Organic Law of the Peoples' Political Consultative Conference, the Organic Law of the People's Government, and the Common Program of the Peoples' Political Consultative Conference—were passed in the plenary session. Moreover, the capital of the Peoples' Republic was fixed at Peking, the Nationalist name Peiping reverting to the older form. The Peoples' Republic would adopt the universally prevalent Gregorian calendar. The marching song of the volunteers was adopted as the national anthem.

On the last day, Mao Tse-tung was elected Chairman of the Peoples' Government with six Vice-Chairmen—Chu-Teh, Commander-in-Chief of the Communist Army, Madame Sun Yat-sen, Liu Shao-chi, the theoretician of the Chinese Communist Party, Li Chi-sen, Chairman of the Revolutionary Committee of the Kuomintang, Chang Lan, Chairman of the Democratic League, and Kao Kan, Chairman of the Government of the Northeastern Provinces.

The main work of the Political Consultative Conference lay in the adoption of the three documents mentioned above, in the election of the Chairman, the six Vice-Chairmen, the fifty-four members of the

State Council, and the one hundred eighty members of the National Standing Committee of the Political Consultative Conference. There is, however, no mention in the records of the Conference of any discussion of the three documents. What I did find included was the assurances given by Mao Tse-tung and the various army commanders, and confessions of their past errors by the Kuomintang members.

Among other things, Mao Tse-tung said:

This Political Consultative Conference of the Chinese people is convoked on an entirely new basis. It is qualified to represent the people of the whole country [Mao was well aware that all the members were appointed and not elected by the people] and it has the confidence and support of the people.

After outlining the main work of the Political Consultative Conference he went on:

The people of China have been great in this modern age, courageous and hardworking. But China remains backward. Her backwardness is the result of oppression and exploitation by foreign imperialisms and reactionary governments. For more than a century our ancestors fought bravely against the foreign and internal oppressors and never faltered. Among them is Dr. Sun Yat-sen, the pioneer of the Chinese revolution. Our ancestors have asked us to carry out their will. This we have done. Through the war of liberation and the revolution of the people against internal and external foes we announced the establishment of the Chinese People's Republic. Our nation will be a member of the great family of peace-loving and free nations. She will work hard, and bravely create her own civilization and happiness, and promote the peace and freedom of the world. Our nation will stand no further insult; it is now solidly on its own feet. Our revolution has gained sympathy and applause from the great majority of other peoples in the entire world.

Then he went on to say that China must work together with the Soviet Union:

The Peoples' democratic dictatorship is the best weapon to insure the fruits of victory of the popular revolution and to fight against the intrigue of domestic and external enemies working for the restoration of the old regime. We must use this carefully. Internationally we must work together with those nations or peoples who are peace-loving, especially the Soviet Union and the peoples' democratic countries, so that China during her fight to insure the fruits of victory and against the intrigues of the restoration party will not be isolated. By holding fast to the peoples' democratic dictatorship and by being united with international friends, victory will be ours forever.

Following Mao Tse-tung, Liu Shao-chi, representing the Political Bureau of the Chinese Communist Party, gave assurances to the so-called fellow-traveller parties that his party stood for a united front, and would carry out faithfully any resolution which was passed by the Political Consultative Conference.

Further, Liu pointed out that the common program of the Political Consultative Conference was for the Communist Party a minimum program. The maximum program, which was Socialism or Communism, was not mentioned. When that stage was reached, Liu said, the Chinese Communist Party would be glad to have the collaboration of the other parties. This meant that those parties who had worked with the Communists would not be dropped in the future.

The Peoples' Political Consultative Conference wanted to show that the Chinese Communist Party had the support of the other political parties. Most of these parties or groups were dissenters from the Kuomintang, except the Democratic League and the Chih Kung Tang consisting of overseas Chinese. Some of these groups had no program, nor had they any history. They were organized in order to win seats in the Peoples' Political Consultative Conference. They were:

The Revolutionary Committee of the Kuomintang.
The Democratic League.
The Democratic National Reconstruction Association.
The Association for Promoting Democracy.
The Peasants' and Workers' Democratic Party.
The Chih Kung Tang.
The September 3 Society.
The Taiwan Democratic Self-Government League.

The other groups—the National Salvation Association and the Democratic Promotion Society of the Kuomintang—were dissolved following the advice of Mao Tse-tung. Most of the groups had previously been anti-Communist. Li Chi-sen, Chairman of the Revolutionary Committee, was Governor of Kuangtung Province and Director of the Generalissimo's Headquarters in Kuangsi during the war. Chen Ming-chu, a co-worker of Li Chi-sen, had been Commander of the 19th Army, Commander of the Nanking Garrison, and Minister of Communications under the Nationalist Government.

Li Chi-sen's and Chen Ming-chu's collaboration with the Chinese Communists can be traced back to their activities in founding the Peoples' Government in Fukien, which declared its independence from the Government of Nanking in 1934-35. Each headed a group; one was the revolutionary committee of the Kuomintang and the other the association of the followers of the Three Principles of the People. The other groups—the Association for Promoting Democracy and the September 3 Society—were also off-shoots of the Kuomintang. Most of these groups had left the Kuomintang because of their dissatisfaction with Chiang Kai-shek. The Democratic League, including Chang Lan and Lo Lung-chi, were believers in democracy, but through continued persecution by Chiang Kai-shek they were forced to join the Communists. I tried to get interested in the speeches of the leaders before the Conference. In Chang Lan's speech I cannot find anything but compliments to Mao Tse-tung's wise leadership. Lo Lung-chi's speech had nothing to do with the work of the Political Consultative Conference and vigorously denounced T. F. Tsiang, the Nationalist Representative in the UN Security Council. Lo Lung-chi also posed now as being against American imperialism, though since his student days he had been pro-American and had worked with General Marshall during his mission in China from 1946 on. I must say that the so-called democratic parties working under the Communist regime showed a surprising lack of independent thinking.

What interested me most were the speeches of the representatives of the Liberation Armies. Ho Lung, the Commander-in-Chief of the First Liberation Army, gave the assurance that he would carry out his mission in the provinces of Northwestern China, and that he would work with the other armies to liberate Southwestern China. Liu Paichen, the Commander-in-Chief of the Second Liberation Army, said: "The Liberation army is an anti-imperialistic, anti-feudalistic, anti-bureaucratic-capitalistic army, which, under the leadership of the working class, is united with the masses of the people. This army has gone through the hardships of twenty-two years of fighting. When this army has fulfilled its mission of defeating the enemy, it will, under the leadership of the peoples' government, obey its laws and orders and pledge itself to fulfill the requirements of the military authorities and finish the job of liberation."

What disgusted me most were the speeches of the defectionists who, having served under Chiang Kai-shek as provincial governors and commanders, now turned away from him and joined the Communist camp. These were Chang Shih-chung, Governor of Sinkiang,

Shao Lih-tse, Governor of Kansu and Secretary-General of the Political Consultative Conference, Cheng Chien, Governor of Chekiang and Minister of the Interior, and Chen Min-jen, hero of the battle of Szepingkai under the Nationalist Government. All these men strongly denounced Chiang Kai-shek and his war policy, as if they were in no way responsible for any action of the government under which they had served. Compared with them the Communist leaders were actually milder and more moderate in tone. Besides, what they spoke carried conviction, since they were at least sincere.

The Kuomintang members who joined the Communists after their victory were real opportunists, utterly devoid of principle or character. Their words were meant as confessions, as repentance, and represented an attempt to curry favor with the new masters. They had nothing to do with the work of the Political Consultative Conference. The three important documents which were passed by the Conference were not in the least affected by these speeches. They were written by committees behind closed doors, so that what opinions were expressed during the debate were not disclosed.

Let us now examine these documents. First, the one concerning the structure of the Central Government based on the organic law of the Peoples' Central Government. The first five articles of this law are as follows:

Article 1. The Peoples' Republic of China is a State of the Peoples' democratic dictatorship under the leadership of the working class, based on the alliance of workers and peasants and uniting all democratic classes and the various nationalities within the country.

Article 2. The Government of the Peoples' Republic of China is a government of the peoples' congress system based on the principle of democratic centralism.

Article 3. Prior to the convocation of the All-China Peoples' Congress by universal franchise, the plenary session of the Chinese Peoples' Political Consultative Conference shall perform the functions and exercise the powers of the All-China Peoples' Congress, enact the organic law of the Central Government of the Peoples' Republic of China, elect the members of the State Council, and vest it with the authority to exercise state power.

Article 4. The State Council represents the Peoples' Republic of China in international relations and assumes the leadership of the state apparatus at home.

Article 5. The State Council shall set up: The Council of Political Affairs as the highest executive body for administration, The

Peoples' Revolutionary Military Council as the supreme military command of the state, the Peoples' Supreme Court and the Peoples' Procurator-General's office as the highest judicial and prosecuting bodies of the country.

According to these five articles the hierarchy of the governmental structure consists of:

1. The Peoples' Political Consultative Conference which elects the members of the State Council.
2. The Peoples' State Council which sets up the council of political affairs.
3. The Council of Political Affairs consists of a Premier, a number of Vice-Premiers and a number of Council members appointed by the State Council.
4. The Council of Political Affairs shall set up the committees of (a) political and legal affairs, (b) financial and economic affairs, (c) cultural and educational affairs, (d) popular supervision.
5. The Council of Political Affairs shall also set up ministries, commissions, academies, bureaus and banks, 30 units in all.
6. All the ministries, commissions, bureaus, and banks shall come under the direction of five committees.

(A) Committee of Political and Legal Affairs	(1. Ministry of the Interior (2. Ministry of Public Security (3. Ministry of Justice (4. Commission of Legislative Reference (5. Commission of the Nationalities' Affairs.
(B) Committee of Financial and Economic Affairs	(1. Ministry of Finance (2. Ministry of Trade (3. Ministry of Heavy Industry (4. Ministry of Fuel Industry (5. Ministry of Textile Industry (6. Ministry of Food Industry (7. Ministry of Light Industry (8. Ministry of Railways (9. Ministry of Posts, Telegraphs, and Telephones (10. Ministry of Communications

(B) Committee of Financial and Economic Affairs (Cont'd)	(11. Ministry of Agriculture (12. Ministry of Forestry and (Land Reclamation (13. Ministry of Water Works (14. Ministry of Labor (15. The Peoples' Bank (16. Customs Administration.
(C) Committee of Cultural and Educational Affairs	(1. Ministry of Cultural Affairs (2. Ministry of Education (3. Ministry of Public Health (4. Academy of Science (5. Press Bureau (6. Publications Bureau.
(D) Committee of Peoples' Supervision	Responsible for supervising the execution of official functions by government institutions and of public functions.

The structure of the Chinese Communist Government is nothing more than another version of the government of the Soviet Union. The name "Democratic Dictatorship" has a close affinity with the Russian "Proletarian Dictatorship."

Article 2, stating that this is a government of the peoples' congress system based on the principle of democratic centralism, means that under the present system there is no parliament which can call the cabinet to account, and that there is no responsible cabinet which can be dismissed by the parliament. Neither under the present system is there any separation of powers, according to which each of the three branches, the legislative branch, the executive branch, and the judicial branch, exercises its functions. Since the Chinese system is a copy of the Russian system, instead of separating the powers it tries to do the very opposite by combining the three powers in one organ, as in the Supreme Soviet of the U. S. S. R. According to the Russian Soviet system all power is concentrated in one organ, the Supreme Soviet—or rather the Praesidium of the Supreme Soviet. The basis of the structure is a broad one because the Soviet is elected by the citizens of the U. S. S. R. on the basis of one deputy for every 300,000 of the population. The next step is that the Supreme Soviet elects the Praesidium of the Soviet. This Praesidium can interpret laws and issue decrees, appoint and relieve Peoples' Commissars of the U. S. S. R., and ratify international treaties. The Supreme Soviet, which is supposed to be the parliament, thus surrenders its power to forty-two members. This is like the Chinese way of making wine out of rice, according to which, after the first distillation, the essence is condensed again and yet a third time, until the most concentrated essence is formed. By the process of narrowing and condensing, power comes to reside in the hands of a few. This is the Soviet system: in China it is re-baptized with a new name, a Government of the Peoples' Congress system, which, through one election after another, gives all the power of the congress to a few—"the Praesidium." This is why the system is called democratic centralism, which means in practice monopoly of political power by a few. There is no cabinet in Soviet Russia which can dismiss ministers, and there is no general election in Soviet Russia which can put another party into power. The whole system negates the effect of its own popular basis by the process of contraction. Regardless of whatever beautiful name may be applied to this system, the divorce of the parliament from the broad basis of the people is complete in Russia. Now the system has been completely transplanted to China, as this comparison will readily show:

The Peoples' Republic of China.	*The U. S. S. R.*
1. The Chinese Peoples' Political Consultative Conference.	1. The Supreme Soviet of the U. S. S R.
2. The Peoples' State Council, consisting of a Chairman, six Vice-Chairmen and fifty-six Council Members. It shall have a Secretary-General elected by the Council.	2. The Praesidium of the Supreme Soviet of the U. S. S. R., consisting of a President, sixteen Vice-Presidents, a Secretary, and twenty-four Members.
3. The Premier and Vice-Premiers and members of the Council of Political affairs are appointed and removed by the State Council.	3. The council of Peoples' Commissars of the U. S. S. R. is appointed and relieved by the Praesidium of the Supreme Soviet.
4. Within the Council of Political Affairs there are more than thirty ministries, commissions, boards, academies, and banks.	4. In the Council of the Peoples' Commissars of the U. S. S. R. there are All-union Peoples' Commissariats consisting of twenty-four units, and the Union Republican Commissariats consisting of seventeen units.

The Peoples' Republic of China.	*The U. S. S. R.*
5. The more than thirty units come under the direction of four committees: (1) Committee of Political and Legal affairs, (2) Committee of Finance and Economic affairs, (3) Committee of Cultural and Educational affairs, (4) Committee of Peoples' Supervision.	5. In the Council of Peoples' Commissariats, there are six Vice-Premiers, each charged with the Chairmanship of a committee of coordination embracing all ministries interested in the same group of affairs.

The Peoples' Political Consultative Conference in Communist China was a temporary organ, the delegates being appointed by the Chinese Communist Party and other parties. It was not elected directly by the citizens. But it has played the role of a constituent assembly and passed three fundamental documents: the Organic Law of the Peoples' Consultative Conference, the Common Program of the Peoples' Consultative Conference, and the Organic Law of the Central People's Government. After a few years I presume that these organic laws will be combined into a constitution. Finally the Political Consultative Conference will be turned into a People's Congress, which is the counterpart of the Supreme Soviet of the U. S. S. R.

Let us also compare the powers of the Praesidium of the Supreme Soviet in Russia with the powers of the Chinese State Council.

The State Council of China	*The Praesidium of the Supreme Soviet of the U. S. S. R.*
1. Enacting and interpreting the laws of the state, promulgating decrees and supervising their execution.	1. Interpreting laws of the U. S. S. R.; issuing of decrees.
2. Determining the administrative policies of the state.	2.
3. Annulling or revising any decisions and orders of the Council of Political affairs which do not conform to the laws and decrees of the state.	3. Annulling decisions and orders of the Council of Peoples' Commissars of the Union Republics where they do not conform to law.

The State Council of China	*The Praesidium of the Supreme Soviet of the U. S. S. R.*
4. Ratifying, abrogating, or revising treaties and agreements concluded by the Peoples' Republic of China with foreign countries.	4. Ratifying international treaties.
5. Dealing with questions of war and peace.	5.
6. Approving or revising the state budget and financial statement.	6.
7. Promulgating acts of general amnesty and pardon.	7. Exercising the rights of pardon.
8. Instituting and awarding orders, medals and titles of honor of the state.	8. Awarding decorations and conferring titles of honor of the U. S. S. R.
9. Appointing or removing government personnel.	9. Relieving of their posts and appointing Peoples' Commissars of the U. S. S. R. Appointing and removing the higher commands of the armed forces of the U. S. S. R.

In the Soviet Union, the multi-party system is not allowed to exist. Stalin said on November 24, 1936, "There is no question of any freedom for political parties in the Soviet Union apart from the Communist Party." As there is no other party aside from the Communists, in each constituency there is only one candidate. The result of this one-party system is that there is no opposition party, no vote of confidence, and no responsible ministers.

This kind of dictatorship has very much inspired the Chinese Communists, especially those who drafted the Organic Law of the Peoples' Central Government. The present Vice-Premier, Tung Pih-wu, presented the bill of Peoples' Central Government to the Political Consultative Conference with the following explanation:

The underlying spirit of the organization of the Government is the principle of democratic centralism. Its concrete expression is that the Government should be based on the Peoples' Congress and the

Peoples' Government in the different grades. The Peoples' Congress in the different grades is elected by the people according to universal franchise. The Peoples' Government in the different grades is elected by the Peoples' Congress. In the intervals between sessions of the Peoples' Congress, the Peoples' Government exercises the political power of the different grades. The highest organ of state authority is the all-China Peoples' Congress.

During the adjournment of the Peoples' Congress the Central Government of the People is the highest organ to exercise the state authority.

Tung Pih-wu goes on to explain why the principle of democratic centralism is sound:

The principle of democratic centralism is contrary to the theory of separation of powers under the old type of democracy. Under the democracy of the old type, there is a parliamentary system. This system allows one part of the bourgeois class to be in power and another part to be in opposition, that is, the opposition party. Though the minority can talk a great deal in the parliament, the party in power holds the political power tightly and carries out a program likely to further their own interests. This is the politics of exploitation and maneuvering, division of spoils and playing tricks. The judiciary is also supposed to be independent, but in reality it also exists merely to serve the interests of the ruling class. We gave up this kind of political institution. We prefer a political system which combines discussion and execution in one hand. This is the system of Peoples' Congress in which all power is centralized.

These words show the extent to which the minds of the Chinese Communists have come under the influence of Stalinist ideology.

In this connection I shall say a few words about local government in Communist China. The different provinces and cities which the Communists have conquered have been placed under military control so as to establish revolutionary order and suppress counter-revolutionary activities. Following the example of the Political Consultative Conference in Peking, a local all-Circles Representative Conference will gradually assume the functions and powers of the local Peoples' Congress elected by universal franchise. According to Article 15 of the Common Programme of the Political Consultative Conference, it is stipulated:

The organs of state power at all levels shall practice democratic centralism. The main principle shall be: the Peoples' Congresses shall be responsible and accountable to the people; the Peoples' Government shall be responsible and accountable to the Peoples' Congress.

As the working class and the peasants can be organized only by the Communist party and not by the democratic parties, they are quite sure that the majority of the people will be on their side. Yet the Chinese Communists will not leave everything in a locality in the hands of the local populace. The following provision is made in Article 15:

The appointment of the Peoples' Government of each level shall be ratified by the Peoples' Government of the higher level; the Peoples' Government of the lower level shall obey the Peoples' Government of the higher level and all local Peoples' Governments throughout the country shall obey the Central Government of the People.

Such a provision is of course contrary to the fundamental principle of self-government, because it is recognized in all democracies that a local government should have the power to run its own business, including the election of its own officers.

It is interesting to note the remarks of Liu Shao-chi, a right-hand man of Mao Tse-tung, in a speech made on February 28, 1951, on the occasion of the Third Peoples' Congress of the Municipality of Peking.

Besides reaffirming the system of the Peoples' Congress as the foundation of Chinese political institutions and advancing the thesis that the system of the Peoples' Congress is a hundred times more democratic than the system of parliamentary government under democracy of the old type, Liu Shao-chi described for us the actual working of the Peoples' Congress in Peking. He said: "Eighty-three per cent of the Representatives of the Peoples' Congress are elected by the people; seventeen per cent are invited after agreement with the various circles; three per cent are nominated by the Government. All the representatives are not elected in the same way. Some of them are elected by the voters' assemblies, which make use of the factories, industrial enterprises, and colleges as units. The representatives of the peasants in suburbs, of business men, industrialists, youth, and women, and the regional representatives, are elected by the electors' assemblies, which exercise the right of voting for the people at large."

Liu Shao-chi also told us that voting in the colleges and factories took place by secret ballot, because the students could write, and that voting in the electors' assemblies took place by a show of hands. Liu Shao-chi tries to explain why the method of the show of hands was adopted. He said: "The slogan of universal franchise on an equal and direct basis and by a secret ballot had its meaning in terms of overthrowing the dictatorship of Chiang Kai-shek. As we are now living under the new democracy, the application of universal franchise under the present circumstances is not the right thing, because most of the people belonging to the working class are illiterate, do not know how to vote, and are not enthusiastic in casting their votes. Under such circumstances they demand that a census of voters should be taken, that the constituencies should be marked out in which a unit of so many people is entitled to elect one representative and that the voting should be by secret ballot. This kind of demand, according to our experience in many areas, is a matter of formalism. This kind of voting gives the people a lot of difficulties and does not mean that the people will be able to choose someone who can represent them better. Under the democracy of the old type, formalism is preferred, under cover of which the bourgeois class can maneuver to keep the political power for themselves. We, as believers in the new democracy, do not care about the formalities, but demand only that the working class can have those elected who can really represent their will." Liu Shao-chi thinks the voting method now applied in Peking is more practical. Universal franchise on an equal and direct basis and by secret ballot should be postponed until the population can write and get used to elections.

Liu Shao-chi also declared that the Peoples' Congress in the big cities should have three sessions annually; in the medium-sized and small cities, four sessions; in a province, one session; in a district, two sessions. The Peoples' Congress in villages should meet as often as it is stipulated in the laws. In Liu Shao-chi's words, we recognize the tactics of the Chinese Communist politicians. They first use the slogans of universal franchise and secret ballot for the sake of overthrowing an enemy. When they themselves are in power, they warn that progress can only be made slowly.

Now I come to the actual working of the Communist regime. I shall only give articles from Chapters III, IV, V, and VII of the Common Program, in which the fundamental policy of the present regime is described.

(A) *The Military System.*

Article 20. The Peoples' Republic of China shall build up a unified army, the Peoples' Liberation Army and Peoples' Public Security forces, which shall be under the Command of the Peoples' Revolutionary Military Council of the Central Government of the people; it shall institute unification of command, system, formation, and discipline.

Article 21. The Peoples' Liberation Army and the Peoples' Public Security forces shall, in accordance with the spirit of unity between the officers and the rank and file and between the army and the people, set up a system of political commissariat work and shall educate the commanders and rank and file of these forces in a revolutionary and patriotic spirit.

Article 22. The Peoples' Republic of China shall strengthen its modernized army and shall establish an air force and a navy in order to consolidate national defense.

(B) *Economic Policy.*

Article 26. The basic principle for the economic construction of the Peoples' Republic of China is to develop production and bring about a prosperous economy through the policies of taking into account both public and private interests, of benefiting both labor and capital, of mutual aid between the city and the countryside, and circulation of goods between China and abroad. The state shall coordinate and regulate state-owned economy, cooperative economy, the individual economy of peasants and handicraftsmen, private capitalist economy and state capitalist economy, in their spheres of operation, supplies of raw materials, marketing, labor conditions, technical equipment, policies of public and general finance, etc. In this way all components of the social economy can, under the leadership of the state-owned economy, carry out division and coordination of labor and play their respective parts in promoting the development of the social economy as a whole.

Article 27. Agrarian reform is the necessary condition for the development of the nation's productive power and for its industrialization. In all areas where agrarian reform has been carried out, the ownership of the land acquired by the peasants shall be protected. In areas where agrarian reform has not been carried out, the peasant masses must be set in motion to establish peasant organizations, and to put into effect the policy of "land to the tiller" through such measures as the elimination of local bandits and despots, the reduction of rent and interest, and the distribution of land.

Article 28. The state-owned economy is of a socialist nature. All enterprises relating to the most vital parts of the economy of the country and exercising a dominating influence over the peoples' livelihood, shall be under the unified operation of the state.

Article 29. The Cooperative economy is of a semi-socialist nature and is an important component of the peoples' economy as a whole. The Peoples' Government shall foster its development and accord it preferential treatment.

Article 30. The Peoples' Government shall encourage the active operation of all economic enterprises beneficial to the national welfare and to the peoples' livelihood, and shall assist in their development.

(C) *Cultural and Educational Policy.*

Article 41. The culture and education of the Peoples' Republic of China shall be New Democratic: National, Scientific, and Popular. The main tasks of the Peoples' Government in cultural and educational work shall be the raising of the cultural level of the people, the training of personnel for national construction work, the eradicating of feudal, comprador, and fascist ideology, and the developing of the ideology of service to the people.

Article 44. The application of a scientific-historical viewpoint to the study and interpretation of history, economics, politics, culture, and international affairs shall be promoted.

(D) *Foreign Policy.*

Article 54. The principle of the foreign policy of the Peoples' Republic of China is protection of the independence, freedom, integrity of territory and sovereignty of the country, upholding of lasting international peace and friendly cooperation between the peoples of all countries, and opposition to the imperialist policy of aggression and war.

After reviewing the common program and selecting articles of special significance to the Peoples' Republic of China, I have the feeling that the Chinese Communist Party tried hard to avoid many of the mistakes of Lenin: confiscation of industries, the nationalization of land, and then the return to the New Economic Policy. The "Common Program" is full of common sense and was drafted with a balanced mind. Though I am neither a believer in Communism nor a fellow-traveller of the Chinese Communist Party, I can endorse the policies expressed in Chapters III to VII insofar as the official language is concerned. I suppose most of the articles are cast in language which will not offend anybody, as it is a document which must be agreed to by the different parties and the coalition government. However, it is not what is written that is important, but what has actually been put into practice. Let us illustrate.

(1) Marxism-Leninism-Stalinism. In the three fundamental documents this term is never mentioned once. We know that Marxism-Leninism-Stalinism is the Bible of present-day China. A professor is dismissed if he does not conform to these beliefs. Anyone who tries to refute Marxism-Leninism-Stalinism is persecuted. That is what I find in the university curriculum published by the Committee of Higher Education of North China. The following books are prescribed for university students:

1. Selected Works of Marx
2. Selected Works of Lenin
3. F. Engels, *Origin of the Family, Private Property, and the State*
4. K. Marx, *The Class Struggle in France*
5. " " *Eighteenth Brumaire of Louis Bonaparte*
6. " " *The Civil War in France*
7. V. I. Lenin, *What the Friends of the People Are*
8. " " " *The State and Revolution*
9. " " " *Imperialism*
10. " " " *History of the C.P.S.U.*
11. " " " *Anarchism or Socialism*
12. " " " *Marxism and the National Question*
13. " " " *Dialectical and Historical Materialism*
14. " " " *Communist Manisfesto*

(2) Peoples' Public Security Forces. This term appears only twice, in Articles 20 and 21. It is not clear whether the fellow-travellers, by the inclusion of this term, have agreed to the transplanting of the Russian G. P. U. or M. K. V. D. system to China. Is it clear to the fellow-travellers that the inclusion of this term means that there will be hundreds of thousands of "public security cells" all over China for every thirty to fifty families? And again, thousands of civilian cells are organized which watch *every* member of *every* family. No one can leave his town without a travel permit; without a permit no ticket can be sold; anyone who does not register himself will be considered a reactionary and sent to the concentration camp.

(3) In Article 54 we find the expression "The foreign policy of the Peoples' Republic of China is the upholding of lasting international peace and friendly cooperation between the peoples of all countries, and opposition to the imperialist policy of aggression and war." Does this language tell us that China's foreign policy is to be that of a satellite of the Soviet Union, and anti-American, and that China is to participate in the Korean war against the UN forces?

(4) In Article 27 we find that the policy of "Land to the Tiller" is to be put into effect. Let us grant that the land of the big landlords can justly be taken away without any compensation. State action, then, should be restricted to the confiscation of land. But the Chinese Communists, going much further, consider the landlord class as criminals, and compel them to parade in the streets carrying self-denunciatory placards. They are ordered to pay for grain twice the amount they can collect from rents. Hundreds of cases have occurred in which those unable to pay have committed suicide. We are told that these landlords are summoned to appear before the Class-Struggle Society and are subjected to torture. To the question of land ownership there is attached a moral judgment according to which a landlord is a bad man and a criminal.

Wherever I turn, I see a denial of the rights of the people, which are being mercilessly trampled upon. The Communist regime in China is purely and simply a dictatorship of the Russian type.

CHAPTER XIV

The Communists' Foreign Policy

At the end of 1948, when the Chinese Communist forces were victorious in the Hsuchow-Pengpu area and when the establishment of a Communist government was already in sight, a great deal of speculation went on among the fellow-travellers who came to me to exchange views on the subject with regard to its probable foreign policy. Most of them believed that even if the Chinese Communists were pro-Soviet, they would not disregard completely the friendship of the Western democracies. What China needed was industrialization; for that she needed machinery and capital which could come only from America or Britain and hardly at all from Soviet Russia. These fellow-travellers felt that in their collaboration with a Communist regime their hands would be greatly strengthened if they could have American backing.

Their disappointment, however, came soon enough. I remember reading at the end of 1949 an article contributed by Mao Tse-tung on the occasion of the twenty-eighth anniversary of the foundation of the Chinese Communist Party, and entitled "On the Peoples Democratic Dictatorship"—an article in which he outlined his pro-Soviet policy:

> Twenty-four years have elapsed since Sun Yat-sen's death, and, under the leadership of the Chinese Communist Party, Chinese revolutionary theory and practice have made tremendous strides fundamentally altering the face of China. The Chinese people have by now accumulated vital and basic experience along the following two lines:
>
> (1) Internally the people must be awakened. This means welding the working class, the peasantry, the petty bourgeoisie, and the national bourgeoisie into a united front under the leadership of the working class, and from this, proceeding to the creation of a state under "Peoples' Democratic Dictatorship," a state led by the working class and based on the alliance of workers and peasants.
>
> (2) Externally we must unite in a common struggle with the peoples of all countries and with those nations which treat us as equals. This

means allying ourselves with the Soviet Union, with every new democratic country, and with the proletariat and broad masses in all other countries. This means forming an international united front. This means turning to one side. That is right. The forty-nine years' experience of Dr. Sun Yat-sen and the twenty-eight years of the Chinese Communist Party have convinced us that, in order to attain victory and consolidate it, we must turn to one side. In the light of these experiences the Chinese people must fall in either on the side of Imperialism or of Socialism. There can be no other alternative. It is impossible to sit on the fence; there is no third road. We oppose Chiang Kai-shek's reactionary clique, which inclines to the side of Imperialism. We also oppose illusions about a third road. Not only in China but throughout the world without exception, one either inclines towards Imperialism or towards Socialism. Neutrality is merely a camouflage; a third road does not exist.

There could be nothing more explicit on Mao Tse-tung's foreign policy of alliance with the Soviet Union. It is so clear and definite that it exploded any dreams of cooperation with the Western democracies on the part of the fellow-travellers. In December, 1949, Mao Tse-tung went to Moscow. Almost three months later the Sino-Soviet Treaty of Friendship, Alliance, and Mutual Assistance was announced. The negotiation of the six articles of the treaty surely did not require such a long time. There was a supplementary agreement on the Changchun railway, Port Arthur, and Dairen, but that could not have provoked any lengthy discussion either. Why then did Mao Tse-tung remain so long in Moscow and why was it necessary for Chou En-lai later to join him there? Most probably certain other subjects were on the agenda, subjects too secret and delicate for public mention. Did they, for example, talk, among other things, about China's participation in the Korean war and the support to be given to the Communists elsewhere in Asia? Did they discuss the expansion of the Chinese armed forces, the strengthening of Chinese defenses, or the building of strategic railways? Only the inclusion of such complicated questions could have justified Mao's lengthy stay in Moscow.

When the Treaty was published, I assumed it to be an ordinary treaty on the lines of the alliance between Germany and Austria or the Anglo-Japanese Alliance of earlier days. As a matter of common sense I took it for granted that the Chinese Communists, even when flushed with recent victory, would be fully aware of China's exhaustion after so many years of external and internal strife. It was surely clear to everyone that China needed, above all, a period of rest, rehabilitation, reconstruction, and most important of all, of industrialization. It was in the interests of the Communist Party that they should give China and the Chinese people a breathing space. Even when the North Korean invasion started, I still believed that Mao Tse-tung would have enough sense to avoid becoming involved in it. Yet, soon after the invasion, the best available army of the Chinese Communists were moved from Kuangtung to the Manchurian border. When the United Nations' forces approached the Yalu River, this army was thrown in to challenge them. It was then I realised that Mao Tse-tung's stay in Moscow must have been devoted to intriguing with Stalin for the development of Communist aggression in Asia.

But the question remains perplexing. So long as China is unable to feed her own population, remains industrially backward, and is in need of large sums of money for irrigation schemes, hydro-electric works, and other related enterprises, why should she concern herself with questions of world revolution, with a Korean war, and with adventures in Indo-China and elsewhere? Lenin, after having been successful in the Russian revolution, thought it advisable to sign the Treaty of Brest-Litovsk and to concentrate on the defense of Russia against the Generals Koltchak and Deniken, but certainly not to fight a war outside of Russia. If Mao Tse-tung were a faithful follower of Lenin, he would have done likewise. Chinese intervention in Korea refutes any claim that the Sino-Soviet Treaty was signed for common defense and reveals it in its true colors as an agreement for carrying on world revolution. The treaties signed by the Nationalists and Molotov in 1945 and by Chou En-lai and Vishinsky in 1950 bear the same title, but their motives are poles apart. The 1945 treaty was directed against Japan, with which country the contracting parties were then at war. The first article in the 1950 treaty stipulates that both parties undertake jointly to adopt all necessary measures at their disposal for the purpose of preventing the resumption of aggression and the violation of peace on the part of Japan or any other state which may collaborate with Japan directly or indirectly in acts of aggression. In plain words, this treaty regards the United States as the potential enemy if she makes use of Japan as a military base in any war. Having signed this treaty, China is bound to fight on the side of Russia. A further purpose of the Treaty is that China pledged herself to side with Russia in demanding that the peace treaty with Japan be concluded with all the allies and not in a bilateral form as proposed by John Foster Dulles. What is not clear to me is how this treaty can be applied to Korea. Japan is not in the Korean war. Even the United States was not involved directly or indirectly in the conflict before June, 1950. There is no obvious obligation for China to participate in the war.

A careful search of the articles of the treaty leaves only two potential loopholes for Chinese entry into the war, namely, the second paragraph of the first article and the fourth article. The first passage seems to be concerned with united action on the part of China and Russia in their dealings with the United Nations. The fourth article envisages "consultation on all important international problems affecting the common interests of China and the Soviet Union." The wording is rather vague, but it is quite possible that the Russians, making use of its very vagueness, persuaded China to become involved in the Korean war.

In this connection, an article by Chou En-lai in *Pravda* of February 14, 1951, is very enlightening. He said: "Not only have clauses of the Chinese-Soviet Treaty of Friendship, Alliance, and Mutual Assistance in the past year exerted a tremendous influence on the real cause of the struggle against aggression in the East for the maintenance of peace in the Far East and throughout the world, but in the future they will exert still greater influence." It is now quite clear that Soviet Russia, working on these two clauses, persuaded China to assume the burden of sending armies to Korea. This united action of China and Russia in the invasion of South Korea is to be interpreted as "co-operation in all international actions aimed at insuring peace and security throughout the world." *The Peoples' Daily News* (the organ of the Chinese Communist Party) also said on one occasion, "the great alliance of the two countries is a fraternal alliance directed against imperialists and serving the cause of the defense of universal peace."

A representative of the Nationalist regime in Formosa, in commenting on the 1950 Treaty, underlined the following eight motives behind the Treaty:

(1) *Cancellation of the 1945 Treaty.* The signing of the new treaty coincided with a Russian declaration that the old treaty was abolished. This procedure put Mao Tse-tung's government in a legitimate position to contract a new treaty with a foreign country. Superficially, the wording of the Treaty seems to favor China, but in actual fact it gave the Soviet Union a firmer control over China's sovereignty.

(2) *America is now the potential enemy.* Though the treaty was signed ostensibly to prevent any revival of Japanese imperialism or the resumption of Japanese aggression, it was really designed to brand America and make her the objective of all the joint measures adopted

by the signatories. This put China under an obligation to fight on the Soviet side, and no choice of action is left to her in the event of a third World War.

(3) *Preparing for the coming war.* The stipulation in the second paragraph of the first article—the contracting parties declare their readiness to participate in a spirit of sincere cooperation in all international actions aimed at insuring peace and security throughout the world—means that they are ready to create trouble in different places and instigate another world war.

(4) *Intrigue in Japan.* The second article puts China and the Soviet Union under an obligation to stand together for a general peace treaty with Japan. If they can succeed in restraining American influence and in giving more support to the Japanese Communist Party, then the Soviet Union will have a stronghold in Japan and the whole of the Far East will become a Communist bloc.

(5) *Political Control over China.* The third article stipulates that each contracting party undertakes not to conclude any alliance against the other and not to take part in any coalition or any actions or measures against the other. This article is identical with article IV in the 1946 treaty, with the additional words "in any actions or measures." These additional words are aimed at establishing a stricter control over Mao Tse-tung. The obligation of mutual consultation stipulated in the fourth article is a trap for the Chinese Communist government.

(6) *Cultural infiltration.* The fifth article deals with the development and consolidation of cultural ties between China and the Soviet Union. This, however, is one-way traffic in that China is to learn from the Soviet Union. The article has been implemented in various ways. One thousand scholarships have been awarded to Chinese university students for education in seventeen Russian universities. In 1949, no fewer than 3756 books were donated to China by the Russian V. O. K. S. Fifty-seven Russian lectures were delivered last year and were attended by 70,000 Chinese. In addition, a Sino-Soviet friendship rally was held which was attended by about half a million Chinese. The Sino-Soviet Friendship Society is an organ of the greatest importance for cultural infiltration, as all the Russian advisers in China are invited in the name of that society.

(7) *Economic exploitation.* The fifth article also mentions that each party undertakes to develop and consolidate economic ties between

the two countries and to carry out all necessary economic cooperation. By virtue of this clause, U. S. $300,000,000 has been promised to China for five years, from which sum China can draw one-fifth for the purchase of machines and materials from the Soviet Union. Three Sino-Soviet companies have been set up, one for petroleum, one for non-ferrous metals, and a third to deal with civil aviation. Moreover, a barter agreement was signed in 1950.

(8) *Violation of Chinese territorial sovereignty.* The terms of the agreement on the Changchun Railway, Port Arthur, and Dairen stipulated that the administration of this railway would revert to China on the signing of a peace treaty with Japan. This peace treaty must, however, be drafted as a general treaty to be signed by all the allies. If a peace treaty is signed, as it has been signed, along the lines suggested by John Foster Dulles, will this promise of transfer still hold good?

In the fourth paragraph of the fourth article, it is stipulated: "In the event of either of the contracting parties becoming the victim of aggression on the part of Japan, or any state that may collaborate with Japan, and, as a result thereof, become involved in hostilities, China and the Soviet Union may, on the proposal of the Peoples' Republic of China, and with the agreement of the government of the U. S. S. R., jointly use the naval base of Port Arthur for the purpose of conducting jointly military operations against the aggressor."

Thus, even after the transfer of Port Arthur to China, the Soviet Union retains the right to use Port Arthur as a naval base in a war against Japan or the U.S.A.

Another quotation from Mao Tse-tung's article on the "Peoples' Democratic Dictatorship" is relevant and revealing: "It is said that 'it is possible to be victorious even without international assistance.' This is a mistaken idea. In an era in which imperialism still exists, it is impossible for a genuine people's revolution in any country to win its own victory without many different kinds of help from the internationally revolutionary forces. Even should the victory be won, it could not be consolidated without international help. This was true of the victory and consolidation of the October Revolution, as Stalin told us long ago. This was also the case in overthrowing the three imperialistic countries during the Second World War and in establishing the new democratic countries. This is also true of the present and future of the Peoples' Republic of China. Let us consider this. If the Soviet Union did not exist, if there had been no victory over Fascism in the Second World War, if Japanese imperialism had not been defeated, if the various New Democratic countries had not arisen, if the oppressed nations of the East had not begun to fight, if there were no struggle inside the United States, Great Britain, France, Germany, Italy, Japan and other capitalist countries between the populace and the reactionaries who rule over them, and if this were not the sum-total of all the developments, well then, the reactionary forces bearing down upon us would certainly be immeasurably greater than at present. Could we be victorious under such circumstances? Obviously not. Furthermore, it would be impossible to consolidate the victory were it attained."

Thus Mao Tse-tung comes to the conclusion that he can have friends only in the anti-imperialist camp—all outside this camp are, by inference, enemies. "Internationally we belong to the side of the anti-Imperialist front, headed by the Soviet Union," he said. "We can only turn to this side for genuine and friendly assistance, not to the side of the Imperialist front." The implication that those outside the Communist bloc are enemies is not openly expressed, but is clear from Mao's attitude and policy towards the U. S. A. and Britain.

Many of us feel that it must have been most difficult for the Communist regime in China to make the decision to intervene in the Korean war. But was this decision reached by the Chinese government acting independently, or was it made at the request of the Soviet Union? There was a vast crop of rumors at the time the decision was made. The version which seems to me most credible is one which involves four stages: (1) Molotov's trip to China, (2) long and anxious discussion among the Communist leaders in China, (3) Chou En-lai's visit to Moscow, and (4) the final decision in Peking.

In August, 1950, the North Korean army was fully in retreat when the UN forces made a successful landing at Inchon. Seoul was captured and the allied forces were way beyond the 38th Parallel. The situation must have given rise to grave concern among the Chinese leaders, and when Pyongyang fell, Mao Tse-tung must have spent some sleepless nights. At this critical moment, Molotov arrived in Peking by plane, with instructions from Stalin that China should send troops into Korea. According to a high-ranking Communist, the following conversation took place between Molotov and Mao Tse-tung: Molotov told Mao, "In 1949 Stalin was not in favor of crossing the Yangtse Valley immediately. Since you were convinced that the morale of the Communist army was high and that the Kuomintang was deteriorating so rapidly that a victory was easy, you advanced and won. Though your crossing was successful and China became united under Communist rule, nevertheless it was a great surprise to the U.S.A. The coming world war would on that account break out five years earlier than it should. As you are responsible for the leadership of affairs in Asia, I hope that you will accept the message which Marshal Stalin offers to you. The North Korean army is now being defeated, but as Asian affairs are under your control, the Peoples' Republic of China should participate in the Korean war in order to drive off the American army and prevent the total collapse of North Korea. This message from Marshal Stalin is the reason for my trip to China."

These words must have caused Mao considerable concern. He was fully aware that China was not in a position to fight a prolonged war. Though the morale of the Chinese army was high, the army was not equipped, by modern standards, with the requisite weapons. In particular the air force and the navy were lamentably weak as compared with those of the enemy. Russian backing was essential, and for this an adequate price would have to be paid. Before even consulting his party leaders, Mao gave a secret promise to Molotov who then left Peking. Soon after, Mao called a meeting of the leading party men, ostensibly in order to arrive at a decision. At this meeting most of the old Communists, such as Tung Pih-Wu, expressed the view that, since the power of the Communists in China was not yet consolidated, it was not the moment to embark on military adventures in other countries. It would be much better to give secret help to North Korea without open participation. Perhaps a strip of land around the district of Antung might even be ceded to North Korea to become its capital. North Korean Communists could be trained there and sent back to carry on the war in the form of guerilla activities on a long-term basis. This opinion was understood and appreciated by the fellow-travellers present, but unfortunately, Mao Tse-tung was no longer in a position to make any free choice, because he was surrounded by Russian advisers and the so-called internationalist school of the Communist Party, in which men like Jen Pih-shih (now dead), Kao Kan, Chairman of the Northeastern Government, Chou En-lai, Li Lih-san, and Li Fuchun were opposed to Tung Pih-wu's policy. They held that the opinion of the old guard was antiquated and differed too much from modern revolutionary theory, and they advanced numerous arguments to refute it. Finally the decision was made to participate in the Korean war on condition that the Soviet Union would give China adequate military support.

To carry out this decision, Chou En-lai went to Moscow on October 5 to consult with Stalin and negotiate for the supply of arms and the strengthening of the Chinese Communist air and naval forces. Stalin was reported to have said that if China sent men to the front, the Soviet Union would give every kind of support. The dockyards in Vladivostock and Dairen would build warships for China. Several hundreds of new aircraft and anti-aircraft guns would be sent to China. The Soviet Union would also help China in the defense of the important cities of Peking, Mukden, Tientsin, Shanghai, Hankow, Canton, Sian, Taiyuan, Hsuchow and Nanking if and when they were attacked. The Soviet Union also promised that the fifty divisions of the Russian army in which more than 200,000 Japanese prisoners-of-war are included, would be transferred from Chita and Vladivostok to Kiamohssu as reinforcement for the Chinese Communists. In the event of the American army's crossing the Yalu River, the Soviet Union would enter the war.

On the other hand, the Chinese Government would be responsible for sending to Russia all kinds of minerals and metals, such as iron, wolfram, tin, antimony, zinc and mercury. China would also supply food in the form of soya beans and tea to the greatest extent possible. She would purchase in Southeast Asia and in the Pacific Islands rubber and metals for transportation to Russia. The Soviet Union would ask Czechoslovakia, Eastern Germany, Poland, and Roumania to send arms, chemical equipment, and gasoline to China. The Soviet Union would also buy strategic materials from Europe for Communist China and the Chinese gold reserve should be earmarked for such procurement.

After these successful negotiations, Chou En-lai returned to China on October 16 and reported to Mao Tse-tung. On the basis of this report Mao expressed the following views: "Peace is something to fight for. Peace will not come by sitting idle. America will not fight against China. Since she is a capitalist country, she will be forever the enemy of Socialism. Victory or defeat depends very much on manpower. In this regard, China is in a better position than America. The best policy is for China to fight outside Chinese territory. The second best is to fight along the coast and the Yangtse River. The worst is to withdraw into the interior." Mao Tse-tung's policy is to send Chinese volunteers to Korea in the first place. According to his calculations, with these alone there is a possibility of driving the American army out of Korea, even if under those circumstances the third world war should break out somewhat earlier than expected. Another remark reportedly made by Mao is illuminating: "Though the Americans will not be defeated very soon, within five to ten years the capitalist countries of the world will collapse." At another conference he was asked for his view on the coming world war and he answered, "We Communists are standing for peace and avoidance of war, but if war is inevitable, we are not afraid of it."

Once the decision to intervene was made, Mao Tse-tung invited Lo Lung-chi and other fellow-travellers to his house for a discussion. When a declaration involving resistance to America and aid to North Korea was brought in, Mao was asked to sign his name. He replied that since it was well known that he was pro-Soviet, it was pointless for him to sign. And then, as an ironic comment on what American help to China in the past has meant the gathering asked Lo Lung-chi, a returned American student, to sign it. There was no alternative for Lo but to put his signature on the document.

Admittedly, there is no way of verifying the account given above of these important events. It does, however, in my opinion, contain a great deal of truth. Firstly, China's participation in the Korean war was not initiated by China alone, but was resolved upon at the instigation of Soviet Russia. Secondly, some Russian emissary, Molotov or someone else, must have come to Peking to apply pressure for Chinese intervention in Korea. Thirdly, a military agreement for the supplying of arms to China by Russia must have been negotiated and signed. Fourthly, Tung Pih-wu would be the most likely person to oppose a policy of intervention, because he always professes to be a *Chinese* Communist, while such men as Chou En-lai, as diplomats, play the tune called by Stalin. Fifthly, the story of the signing of the fellow-travellers was told by Lo Lung-chi himself. These five points are reasonably authentic, and that is why I feel that the story is not far from the truth. The effect of Chinese intervention in Korea, the withdrawal of the UN forces south of the 38th Parallel, and the appearance of a Chinese Communist delegate at the United Nations, are events well known to everybody and need not be discussed. But an important point that has escaped attention is the reason for the refusal of the Chinese Communist mission to the UN to accept a "cease-fire" agreement in Korea. The price demanded by the Communists was as follows: (1) withdrawal of the United Nations Army from Korea, (2) withdrawal of the American Fleet from Formosa, and (3) admission of Communist China to the UN. If the United States or the United Nations had accepted these conditions, it would have constituted a major victory for the Communists. But why did the Communists refuse a cease-fire and insist on a conference first? This kind of extremist policy is not inherently Chinese; it is typically a Russian maneuver. Men like Chou En-lai and Tung Pih-wu secretly favored an immediate truce, but, surrounded as they were by Russian "advisers," they had to consult the Kremlin. Although America was then willing to admit China to the UN, the Chinese Communists, clinging to their ideology, preferred to gamble on heavy American losses in men and materiel in a prolonged Korean war rather than to choose the path of peace and loyal membership of the UN. Certainly a high proportion of leading Communists and fellow-travellers were profoundly disappointed with this procedure of boycotting the UN. If these conditions had been accepted by the United Nations, the Chinese Communists regime and Soviet Russia would have succeeded in establishing themselves as by far the strongest force in the Far East, and the way would have been clear for further expansion in Southeast Asia. Quite naturally, they would have been hailed as the conquerors of the American army by the Communists in Indo-China, Malaya, and India.

It may be asked whether Communist China, if admitted to the United Nations, would have carried out faithfully the World Charter and would have cooperated with all other members to further the aims of international peace and prosperity. There is unfortunately no doubt about what Chinese policy would have been. In the first place, the Nationalist delegation would be evicted. Then, safely ensconced as one of the great powers, Communist China would have made full use of the veto to block every constructive move of the UN. She would have pressed for the banning of the atom bomb and would have denounced the violations of the Potsdam and Yalta Declarations by the remilitarization of Germany and Japan. There is no clearer case of wishful thinking than the idea that Communist China could act independently of the USSR. After all, if China had been able to enter the UN as a result of the Korean war, she would owe this to Soviet support, and the result would have been a tightening of the bonds between them and not the reverse. So much for the idea that Mao Tse-tung might become a Chinese Tito. Such a situation could arise only if and when the Communist satellites felt that too much restraint was being placed on them by the Kremlin. The situations in China and Yugoslavia are totally different. Stalin is astute enough to know that the kind of control he exerts over Eastern Europe would not operate in China, and so he leaves ample liberty of action to Mao Tse-tung in the field of Chinese domestic politics. Mao regards it as a great honor that China has now become the ally of the Soviet Union.

At the time of the signature of the Treaty in Moscow, we find Chou En-lai using the words "fraternal friendship" and "permanent cooperation." Clearly, China is quite satisfied with the position of a younger brother. Mao Tse-tung and Chou En-lai do not at any time seem to have freedom of action for China in mind in their dealings with Soviet Russia; what they are interested in is world revolution. Chou En-lai has said expressly, "The Imperialistic bloc, with the U.S.A. as its leader, has applied all kinds of means to break the friendship of China and the Soviet Union, but this shameless attempt has proved to be a total failure." If such is the mentality of Mao Tse-tung and Chou En-lai, where are the grounds for hoping that they will become Chinese Titos? A realistic view of the Chinese situation is to see in the cooperation of 700,000,000 Chinese and Russians an invincible power so long as the two countries stand together. If any further doubt exists, the words of a Chinese Communist pamphlet should clear it up. This pamphlet, entitled "How to learn about the Sino-Soviet Friendship," makes abundantly clear the Communist standpoint on matters of basic importance, as shown in these few excerpts:

1. *Clear understanding of the Class-concept.* Internationalism is a part of the idea of the class struggle. The spirit of internationalism is the concrete expression of the idea of the proletariat class. It is the standpoint from which the proletariat may know and handle the questions of international relations and of nationalism. International relations are no more than the continuation of the class-struggle in domestic politics. Diplomatic policy and domestic policy are necessarily identical. The state is a tool for the preservation of class interests. So long as the state represents the interests of the bourgeois class, its foreign policy will serve the interests of the bourgeois class also. On the contrary, if the state represents the interests of the working class, then its foreign policy will be to work with the U. S. S. R. and the new democratic countries, to unite with the oppressed peoples, and to fight against the imperialist aggressors.

2. *On making a distinction between friends and foes.* The world is divided into two camps—the aggressors' camp with American imperialism as its leader, which includes the reactionaries of the different countries, and the anti-Imperialist and peace-loving camp with the U. S. S. R. as its leader, which includes the new Democratic countries, the proletariat class, and the democratic force of the people and the oppressed nationalities. After the end of the anti-Fascist war, the American-British imperialism is undoubtedly preparing for a new war and threatening world peace. The whole world must unite under the leadership of the U. S. S. R. in order to fight against the imperialists.

3. *Where should China stand?* Should China side with the Imperialists or with the peace-loving camp? There is no doubt that China should side with the peace-loving camp, because imperialism, especially the American form of imperialism, is the deadly enemy of the Chinese people, while the U. S. S. R., the New Democratic countries, the democratic force of the working people, and the oppressed peoples are the real friends of the Chinese people. The revolution of China is a part of the world revolution. As the interests of the Chinese are identical with those of the people throughout the world, they must stay on the same side.

4. *There is no third road.* Neutrality is a disguise. The line of demarcation between these two camps is so clear and the fight between them so fierce, that if you do not fight against the intrigues of the Imperialist camp, you commit the crime of siding with Imperialism. The Imperialists will be very glad if we strike a third road, because by pointing to our example they can compel their people to become their cannon-fodder. On the contrary, if everyone fights against their aggression and exploitation, then the Imperialists will find themselves isolated and will be defeated.

5. *The relations between China and the U. S. S. R.* (a) The U. S. S. R. is a socialist state, in which no exploitation, no oppression, no class-distinction, exists. The people in this country can live, work, and learn freely. The U. S. S. R. will not and does not like aggression on the part of other countries. (b) The goal of the U. S. S. R. is world revolution. Again, it defeated the fascist countries, Germany, Italy, and Japan, and annihilated the Kwantung army of Japan, thereby reducing the loss of American lives in the Second World War. Now the U. S. S. R. is the stronghold of world peace. Because of the growing power of the U. S. S. R., the reactionaries in the different countries dare not start a new war.

6. *The relationship between the U. S. S. R. and China.* In the first place, after the October Revolution, the U. S. S. R. was the first country which declared itself in favor of the abolition of China's unequal treaties. Secondly, the U. S. S. R. worked with Dr. Sun Yat-sen in the Northern Expedition. Thirdly, after Chiang Kai-shek's betrayal, though there was a break in diplomatic relations between China and the U. S. S. R., the U. S. S. R. was still giving assistance to the Chinese peoples' revolutionary struggle. Fourthly, the U. S. S. R. gave assistance to China at the beginning of the Chinese resistance against Japan. After the German invasion, there was no direct help coming to China, but owing to the existence of the powerful U. S. S. R., the Kwantung Army was confined to Manchuria. Fifthly, during the three

years of the war of liberation, the U. S. S. R. also gave a great deal of assistance to the Chinese army of liberation.

7. *Why real assistance could be obtained only from the Soviet side.* The Imperialists depend on robbery and exploitation, and are therefore the deadly enemy of the Chinese people. Their assistance to the Kuomintang reactionaries and the Marshall aid is designed to make the Kuomintang, the United Kingdom, France, and other European countries into slaves, bodyguards, and satellites of American imperialism. The Atlantic Pact and the White Paper of the United States are the best proofs of this. To get real aid from the Imperialist side is impossible; only the U. S. S. R. is the real friend of the Chinese people. She is the Socialistic state which gives aid to the revolutionary movements of the weak nationalities. She is consistent in her policy of giving aid to the oppressed peoples. Real aid must be obtained from the U. S. S. R.

8. *Preservation of peace and prevention of war.* Peace in the world is endangered. The reactionaries in the different countries, having American Imperialism as their leader, are positively making war preparations, producing more munitions, building up military alliances, reviving the remaining fascist forces in Germany and Japan, and refusing to enter into peace talks with the U. S. S. R. These war-instigating activities are serious threats to World peace.

These extracts from the pamphlet lead inevitably to the conclusion that the foreign policy of the Communist regime in China is world revolution under the leadership of the U. S. S. R., while the interests of China as an independent country are submerged or non-existent. American imperialism or aggression is the target against which the whole Communist effort is being directed. The intervention in Korea is thus regarded as a peace-loving and anti-imperialist step, while the UN expedition is aggressive and imperialistic.

Such, then, is the real policy of the Communist regime in Peking. I do not see how the Western democratic countries can discuss with the Communist regime a possible truce in Korea, the admission of Red China into the United Nations, the settlement of the claim on Formosa, and a general peace settlement in the Far East. I want to make it clear that the leading members of the Chinese Communist regime are not diplomats, and not responsible ministers of Chinese foreign policy; they are revolutionaries, fanatics, and reckless followers of Stalin. It will be a great mistake if the Western Democracies take the Red ministers and delegates as men who can look after the interests of China and who wish to talk reasonably. From the dealings of the Chinese Communists with the different countries we learn their real attitude. While the British have wanted to establish diplomatic relations ever since January 6, 1950, this desire has not to this day been reciprocated. The recognition of Ho Chi-minh's regime in Indo-China was given by Communist China after three days of correspondence. Communist China tries to close most of the American and British Consulates in China, but they made a request to send a committee of investigation to Malaya. The anti-democratic policy is called peace-loving. What Communist China is doing can only be understood in the sense that China should be sacrificed for the cause of world-revolution under the leadership of Stalin, and not governed for its own sake as an independent nation or for the sake of its 450 million people.

CHAPTER XV

India and Communist China

The foreign policy of the new India has been very much a subject of discussion, especially as regards her relations with Communist China.

The Communists in India and the members of other leftist parties in the country are of course unhappy about her position in the British Commonwealth. But Nehru feels that, for the present, at any rate, membership in the Commonwealth is an asset rather than a liability, since international friction and rivalry are as intense as they are. India's foreign policy should therefore be a relatively simple matter in that all she would need to do, seemingly, would be to follow the lead of Downing Street and remain on the side of the Western democracies. That, however, is precisely what Nehru has not done. He has chosen to evolve his own policy of impartiality and of remaining aloof from what he calls the two major power blocs. India, under Nehru's leadership, wishes to maintain her freedom of action, and has not hesitated to declare herself now on the side of Soviet Russia and now on the side of the United States.

Perhaps the most unusual step that India has taken is her recognition of Communist China on the ground that the existence of this new regime in China is a fact and a reality which is beyond the power of anyone to deny. But India has gone even further. She has not only exchanged diplomatic and consular representatives with the Red regime in China, but has also come out openly for its admission into the councils of the United Nations, as well as for the inclusion of Taiwan (Formosa) within its territorial limits. On both of these points it would seem that India has forsaken her position of aloofness and adopted a pro-Communist stand. The question is whether such a stand is justified.

Let us illustrate India's policy towards China by quoting the words of her ambassador in Peking, of Mr. Nehru himself, and of India's representative at the UN.

Sardar Pannikkar, the Indian ambassador to Peking, gave a speech before the Press Association in New Delhi on October 28, 1951. His defence of the regime to which he is accredited, is perhaps quite natural, but he also made a number of observations on Communist rule in China which strike me, a Chinese, as superficial and wide of the mark. On the nature of the present government in Peking, this is what Mr. Pannikkar said: "While Communists undoubtedly had the leadership of the government and the various parties in the coalition, the Communists were bound by a common program evolved after months of discussion between leaders of the various groups. The Communists strictly adhered to that program and had agreed not to give effect to all the Communist doctrines in China till certain conditions had been satisfied." Pannikkar also said that the new Central Government has never claimed to be a Communist Government—that, in fact, it objects to being called a Communist Government.

It is all very well to say that there is a common program which was decided upon after discussion by the various groups. But the fact remains that it is neither "common" nor a program "strictly adhered to." It was from beginning to end a Communist arrangement to which the other parties had perforce to agree. And one must be very bold to say that the program has been strictly observed by the Communists. Is Marxism-Leninism-Stalinism, for instance, which is now taught and must be taught by all Chinese professors and others who live on the mainland, mentioned in the so-called common program? Was any representative of the so-called democratic groups, besides Mao Tse-tung and Chou En-lai, present at the Moscow Conference table when the Sino-Soviet treaty of 1950 was signed? If the other parties were not consulted when so important a decision was made, by what right can the program be called a "common program"?

Sardar Pannikkar has stayed in Peking long enough to know that the members of the various groups are actually being fed by the Communists. How much rice is allowed for each of them is decided upon and rationed out by the Communists. The question as to whether the meals of a member should be classified under the category of "a small kitchen," "a middle kitchen," or "a common kitchen," is decided by the Communists. The funds required to maintain the different parties are also supplied by the Communists. If the decision over the means of subsistence of a party member or a party organization is in the hands of the Communists, this naturally places the other parties in an inferior position, with no other alternative than to obey implicitly the orders of the Government. It is the Chinese

Communist party which makes all the decisions. The signing of the Sino-Soviet treaty of 1950 and the intervention of the Chinese Army in Korea are the work of the Communists, and the other parties were merely induced to chime in. That is their *raison d'être* in the Communists' scheme. Mr. Pannikkar may say that the regime objects to being termed a Communist government, but as far as I know, it neither raises any objection nor pretends to be anything else. It is a Communist totalitarianism of the purest water.

Sardar Pannikkar next discussed the question of the right of private property, and this was what he said:

> In the intervening period, private property in land and in capitalist industry as well as in other spheres, would continue, and would to a certain extent even be encouraged. Furthermore, except for those who were actively working against the present Chinese Government under the orders of the Taiwan dissidents and the landlords who opposed land-reform schemes, everyone in the composite Chinese society would flourish under the conditions laid down in the common program.

These words of Pannikkar make it seem as if the right of property in land and in industry is protected under the Communist regime, except in the case of the counter-revolutionaries who are working for Formosa and of the landlords who are opposing land reform. But is there any real protection for the right of property under the present regime?

If there is any legal protection for the right of property, there must be (1) a code of laws—the laws of mobile and immobile property and the laws of inheritance; (2) a system of judicial procedure to which one can appeal in cases concerning property rights; and (3) principles of decency in dealing with the citizen in regard to his house, land, and the duty of paying taxes. So far as I know, after the abolition of the Nationalist Civil Code by the Communist Government, there was no new code created to take its place. There is also no court system except that of the so-called people's court, which is an ad hoc arrangement designed merely for the purpose of condemning the "reactionaries" and landlords.

Up to the present time, the owners of industries are still running their factories. This is because what they produce is necessary for the nation's economy or is exported in order to get foreign exchange. Also the landlords of ten *mou* or one hundred *mou* (a *mou* is one-sixth of an acre) must give up what is considered to be in excess of the amount of property one should hold. Nevertheless, this sounds as if the right of property in land and in capitalist industry is still allowed to exist. But everyone in China knows that property as such has become a thing of little certainty. The reason is that the Communist Party, whether through Government orders or by means of instigated mass meetings, can always force the owners of factories or of land to make contributions whenever it feels the need—for instance, when the Communist Army was marching southward, or when it became an expeditionary army in Korea. The Korean adventure has given rise to numerous requests for contributions to buy airplanes, tanks, and guns. These are not called taxes, but the amounts and frequency of these payments are so controlled that very little, if anything, is left to the property owners after the payments are made. Any refusal to pay is of course followed by the most serious consequences. A person can on that account be branded a reactionary and immediately thrown into prison. Under these circumstances it is difficult to believe that there is still any right of property left in Communist China.

On the question of land reform, Sardar Pannikkar had this to say: "Land was redistributed to peasant families on the basis of three-fifths of an acre for each member of the family. Landlords were given the same consideration, but their surplus land and property was confiscated. The same principle applied to farm property. To counteract possible ill effects of such fragmentation, the Chinese had evolved a system of cooperative farming through labor brigades."

I should like to point out to Sardar Pannikkar that the story of land allotment on the basis of three-fifths of an acre to each member of the family is simply not true. The re-distribution of land under Communist auspices has had no uniform basis throughout the whole of China. It depends upon the density of population in each district. In some places each member of the family is given two to three *mou,* or about half an acre. In some places each person is given one *mou,* or one-sixth of an acre. In the province of Kuangtung, each one was given seven-tenths to eight-tenths of a *mou.* This kind of re-distribution is rightly called fragmentation by Pannikkar himself. Is a person who gets only one to two *mou,* or less, always able to meet his needs with the produce from his land? Obviously not. With re-distribution of land on so a gigantic scale, accompanied by the loss of millions of lives of people of the landlord class, one should expect that each peasant family's means of subsistence would be assured. For, so far as we know, the landlords as a class have been liquidated. Their property has been taken away from them, sanctions reaching as far as the death sentence have been imposed on them, or, as in many authenticated cases, they simply committed suicide. Millions of lives have been sacrificed in this way, but the poor peasants, who were supposed to be given land and property, are not any better off than they were. The so-called re-distribution of land has not solved the problem of poverty among the peasants. In fact, after carefully studying the situation, experts have come to the conclusion that even this kind of small holding of one to two *mou* will be abolished after a few years, when the next step will be taken in the adoption of the Russian collective farm system. There will then be no more land-owners, and each member of the collective farm will simply be a slave of the Communist Government. Land reform in China, as carried out by the Communist regime, is not giving enough land to the peasants: it is the first step towards land serfdom, a thing which China has never known in her long history of 5000 years!

On the question of China's position in the family of nations, Pannikkar told us that China's political approach was conditioned by the fact that for one hundred years she had been subjected to humiliation at the hands of foreigners. Therefore, the first thing the Chinese Communist Government tried to do was to organize the country's military strength, in the conviction that "unless we have the necessary military strength, we shall continue to be treated as a second-class power and be humiliated again."

If it is the objective of the Communist Government to make China a first-class power, this is quite a legitimate ambition. But it is an ambition which can only be realised through China's own efforts, not by her becoming a satellite of the U. S. S. R. The policy of attaining the position of a great power should be carried out by starting extensive scientific studies, industrial development projects, and genuine agricultural reform. In other words, China should spend money for scientific research, irrigation, steel works, automobile and airplane manufacture, and other similar projects. Before the heavy industries are ready and weapons can be manufactured by China herself, she will not have the necessary military strength. If she begins by depending on the U. S. S. R. for getting modern weapons, she will always be militarily dependent on Russia. If Communist China is really striving for the position of a first-rate power, she should save money for home investment rather than squander it upon military adventures in Korea and elsewhere.

Sardar Pannikkar also told us that Chinese foreign policy through the ages has been concerned with Korea, Japan, Formosa, Indo-China, and Tibet. He said that, regarding these matters, the present Chinese Communist Government is following the same policy as did Chiang Kai-shek, or the Chinese Emperors in the past. This comparison with the past is superficially correct, but the historical facts have been badly twisted. In the time of the Chinese Emperors, this kind of expansionist policy was carried out by China's own efforts, not by dependence on a foreign power. So long as it is done by depending on the U. S. S. R., it has not even China's own good in view, but something else, which, in this case, is the spreading of world-revolution. It makes all the difference in the world whether China's expansionist policy is being carried out on her own initiative or whether it is done at the behest of the Comintern as a part of its program of world-revolution. The resemblance, if there is any, is all on the surface: essentially the two are completely different.

There is no doubt that Sardar Pannikkar's attitude is deliberately in favor of Communist China. Whether he was talking merely as a diplomat, in order to win the friendship of Communist China, or whether he was speaking from conviction, as a man who believes that the Communist regime is for the good of China, is of course another question. However that may be, India and Communist China, thanks to Mr. Pannikkar's efforts, today enjoy the best of relations, which may some day be put to a test through the liberation of Tibet. The fact that Pannikkar's recommendations have influenced India's foreign policy is fully attested by the Indian Government's attitude towards the Korean War and the Japanese Peace Treaty.

In this regard, one must go further, and study Nehru's attitude towards Communist China. The Indian Government was the first after the U. S. S. R. to recognize the Communist Government of China. In the Korean war, Nehru advised strongly that the UN Army should not cross the 38th Parallel. Furthermore, Nehru advocated that Communist China be admitted into the UN. With regard to the Japanese Peace Treaty, he demanded that Formosa, as promised in the Cairo Declaration, be given to Communist China. Nehru tried his best to make Communist China a full-fledged member of the community of nations.

Now, what is the motive behind Nehru's policy toward China? Is it merely that he wants to win China's good will, or does he expect, by his policy of support for China, to free her from bondage to the U. S. S. R.? Or is it because, as a new Asiatic nation, China will be able to cooperate with India? Or does Nehru hope that a middle-of-the-road group, including India and China, can be formed, to become a powerful buffer between the two contending blocs of the Anglo-Saxon countries and the Soviet Union?

I believe that the overall question is difficult to determine for the reason that it is predominately a psychological one, and therefore very elusive. In Nehru's interview with Norman Cousins, published in the *Saturday Review of Literature,* he said: "China thinks for itself. China is closely allied to Russia in many ways, but in the final analysis it decides for itself what it has to do and what it has not to do." Thinking for itself is a creative function and a big task for every nation. The Asiatic nations for a long time have, in a sense, been without the power for independent thinking. In the field of science, we Asians have had to follow the teachings of a Newton or an Einstein. In the field of economics and finance, we have had to adopt the European or American currency or banking system. When the European countries changed from the gold standard to a managed currency, we followed them here too. At the present time, in the field of political institutions, we either have to adopt the parliamentary or cabinet system, or follow the Soviet pattern. It will take a long time before we in Asia can again think independently. Communist China has now abandoned the lead of the Western countries in the field of science, economics, finance, and political institutions, and has openly espoused the Marxist-Leninist-Stalinist creed. That, to my mind, is a clear indication that Communist China is doing exactly the opposite of what Nehru wishes to see. After the Sino-Soviet Treaty of 1950, I do not see that there is much room left for independent thinking in China. In the same talk with Norman Cousins, Nehru also said:

> I don't know about the next few years, but I should have thought that the last few years proved conclusively that the present Chinese Government came into power with the largest possible backing of the Chinese people. At the present moment that more or less continues. In fact, they came into power with the greatest of ease and only because they had that large backing. Otherwise it would have been almost impossible for them to do it.

Let me, as a Chinese, speak frankly. The establishment of the Communist regime in China is due more to the unpopularity of Chiang Kai-shek rather than to the popularity of the Communists. Between these two contentions there is a wide difference; one cannot reason that a negative force will produce positive results. Chiang Kai-shek had tight control over his party and over all the channels of information, so that what the world hears of Chinese affairs comes largely from official Nationalist sources. The real opinion of the people has been suppressed since 1924; Chiang Kai-shek's way of ruling was to shut people's mouths. But the newspapers, news agencies, and the broadcasting stations of the Yenan Communists were carried on underground. They were beyond the reach of Chiang Kai-shek. The people listened, and learning the truth, they began to hate Chiang and his corrupt and selfish henchmen. The people did not want to support Communism, but when it came to the choice of two evils—a party known to be grasping, inefficient, incompetent, and corrupt, and another whose disposition was as yet unknown—there was no question as to which they would choose. That was the one and only reason why the people renounced their support of the Chiang government and rallied to the Communists, even though a wise man might have predicted that the Communists would prove to be equally unworthy of their support. It has been said that Chiang Kai-shek was the best friend of Mao Tse-tung. The remark may be sardonic, but that it is true no one can deny.

So the Communists won: but what have they done with their victory? It is all too evident that, in their turn, they are becoming more unpopular every day. What with mass executions to the tune of millions of people, which the Communists themselves have found it useless to deny, with the heavy burden of taxation, with extorted confessions, with controlled broadcasting and newspapers, a totalitarian government has been established which has no contact with anything approaching genuine public opinion. What is happening in China today is a repetition of what has happened in Soviet Russia. When, in a so-called election, 99 per cent of the votes are cast for Stalin, it is a joke to speak of popular government. But let us review further Nehru's remarks on China and the Communists.

In the same talk Nehru said: "Surely the United Nations cannot claim two things at the same time. One is to ignore a country within its councils and at the same time try to impose its will on that country that has been ignored." With this argument Nehru tries to have communist China accepted as a member of the United Nations.

It is quite correct to say that when the UN ignores a country within its councils it should not seek to impose its will on this country. But to what extent is the will of the UN being imposed on the U. S. S. R.? Russia is now within the UN Council. She is a member of the Security Council, but—thanks, in great part, to the veto power which she makes use of so irresponsibly, it is difficult to see that the UN is in any manner imposing its will on her. There is no question that exactly the same situation would arise the moment that Communist China became a member of the UN.

Nehru has made another proposal, that Formosa, in accordance with the Cairo Declaration, be given to Communist China. It is on record that the U. S. A., Great Britain, and China made a declaration in Cairo that all the Chinese territories stolen by Japan should be returned. But between 1943 and 1951 a great change has taken place in China. China is now split in two; there is a Communist China on the mainland, and there is an anti-Communist China on the island of Formosa. So long as the Government on the mainland is a dictatorship under the Marxist-Leninist-Stalinist program, and is led by the Chinese Communist party, no anti-Communist Chinese likes to see Formosa, the last stronghold of free China, come under Communist rule. This attitude represents genuine public opinion, not only of the Chinese in Formosa, but also of the 30 millions of overseas Chinese, and numberless Chinese living on the mainland. If Nehru really desires to remain aloof from the two power blocs, why does he make such a proposal which is so clearly in favor of Communist China? Though the Chinese in Formosa, but also of the 10 millions of overseas Chinese, whether on the mainland or outside of it, are hoping that some day a democratic China will be restored. Why should Nehru, merely for the sake of expediency, make a proposal which is counter to the wishes of millions of anti-Communist Chinese? I can assure him that such a policy will have a deleterious effect upon future relations between India and China.

Again, Nehru is vitally interested in obtaining a cease-fire in the Korean war, after which, he thinks, a settlement of the general situation in the Far East would follow. I should like to point out that so long as China is ruled by a dictatorial form of government, led by the Chinese Communist Party, there will be no peace in the Far East. Firstly, even if the war in Korea can be stopped, the Chinese Communists will start trouble somewhere else; and secondly, the life of the Chinese on the mainland is now even worse than that of the Indians under British rule. If Gandhi and Nehru have deservedly won universal praise in overthrowing British rule in India, how can millions of Chinese experiencing the terror of mass executions be expected to remain silent and indifferent?

Since first meeting Jawaharlal Nehru in a Chungking bomb-shelter, I have always considered him a great leader and statesman fighting for India's freedom and independence. He will make a greater contribution toward Asian freedom if he can lead the continent along the path of peace, not of world conquest; of democracy, not of dictatorship; of freedom and love, not of violence and mass executions; of broadmindedness, not of bigotry; of spiritual independence, not of mental slavishness. The way to reconstruct Asia is to give individuals more freedom and independence, not to make them mere tools and ciphers. In the past we have had enough of absolutism and tyranny; it is right that men like Nehru should assume leadership and fight against it. But the least he should do for the benefit of India and Asia is to let Communist China know in no uncertain terms that its policy of violence and war, applied to the sphere of national or international politics, will not pay any dividend. Otherwise, there is danger that it may be extended from China, Korea, and Indo-China to other areas also, including perhaps India herself. India is the close neighbor of Communist China. Nehru does not think that the next war will take place on the Indian-Chinese border, but through subversive activities or infiltration, the Communists can overthrow any government without recourse to open war. It is far wiser, it seems to me, for India to try in all possible ways to oppose the claims of Communist China than to give her encouragement with regard to her aspirations toward possession of Formosa and a seat in the United Nations.

As a friend of India, I consider her new-born freedom and independence as the greatest asset of modern Asia. That is why I feel I must tell the people of India to be wary of the traps which the Communists may be setting for them. Their first objective is to drive a wedge in the British Commonwealth, in order to split India from the rest of the members. This is the initial step, designed to bring India nearer to the Communist bloc and farther away from the democracies. If the Communists succeed in this policy of "divide and rule," they will have made another great gain ranking with the conquest of China.

Before I conclude this discussion of India's attitude toward Communist China, let me consider some of the statements made by Sir Benegal N. Rau before the United Nations. On one occasion Sir Benegal said:

> The main objectives of New China's foreign policy seem to be the same as those of the Kuomintang and in some respects even of the Manchus before them. They are: (1) recovery of China's complete sovereignty over areas regarded as historically part of China—namely, Manchuria, Tibet, and Taiwan (Formosa). (2) The exclusion of foreign influence potentially hostile to China from areas considered

vital to her security in Korea and Indo-China. (3) Recognition of China's position as a great power in the Far East. These were also the objectives of Chiang Kai-shek's government. In regard to the recovery of Manchuria, Formosa, and Tibet, the Kuomintang was even more insistent than the new regime. So far as Tibet is concerned, the Kuomintang went to the extent of protesting to the Government of India about Tibet being marked on the map as Tibet.

The attitude of the Kuomintang and indeed even of the Manchu rulers was not different in respect to Korea and Indo-China. It should not be forgotten that even in the time of her greatest weakness, China fought a war with Japan rather than allow Korea to pass unchallenged under Japanese domination. China has never been able to forget her attack on Manchuria and the Chinese mainland.

The Kuomintang government had looked forward to an independent Korea within the orbit of Chinese influence. So far as Indo-China was concerned, the Kuomintang appears to have looked upon Tonkin as an integral part of Chinese territory, which had been violently wrested from China.

The recognition of China as a great power has been as much a point of honor with the Kuomintang as with New China.

It would seem that in none of these matters is New China following a new policy under external inspiration. Whether expansionist or defensive, wrong or right, it is the old policy of China inherited by the new regime from its predecessors.

It is very evident from this that Sir Benegal is trying to cultivate friendship with Communist China. He has made a very clever defense of the foreign policy of Communist China, which is, according to Sir Benegal, a mere continuation of what the Communists' predecessors did. But did these predecessors believe in the theory of world revolution or dictatorship? Did they say what Mao Tse-tung said: "If the Soviet Union did not exist, could we be victorious?" If the policy of Communist China towards Korea, Indo-China, and Tibet were merely the traditional expansionist policy, then the situation would be simple. But unfortunately something more is involved.

Everybody knows that Chinese intervention in the Korean war was begun after consultation with Soviet Russia, as is testified by Chou En-lai's article on the anniversary of the signing of the Sino-Soviet Treaty of 1950. The Kuomintang Government was at least sensible enough to know that putting the Chinese house in order should come first, and not starting a war in Korea or in Indo-China. As a Chinese, I have never heard anything about the Kuomintang's "looking forward to an independent Korea within the orbit of Chinese influence." When China conceded joint management of the Changchun Railway, and joint use of Port Arthur to Russia, it meant that she gave up her sovereignty in order to gain Russian participation in the war against Japan. How, then, was she to look forward to an independent Korea in her own orbit of influence? As to "looking upon Tonkin as an integral part of Chinese territory," Sir Benegal may point as evidence to the Kuomintang army's being sent to Indo-China at the time of the Japanese surrender. At that moment, China might have had the idea of making Indo-China independent, but this does *not* mean that she looked upon Tongkin as an integral part of Chinese territory. Even granting that the Kuomintang Government tried to follow an expansionist policy in Korea and Indo-China, it could not have hoped for the cooperation of Soviet Russia, aiming to create trouble for the sake of world revolution. This working together with Soviet Russia makes all the difference in the world to China's domestic and foreign policies. How can Sir Benegal leave this point out? Even if the policies of the Kuomintang and Communist China are on the surface somewhat similar, there is a great deal of difference between them nevertheless, if only because in the one case these policies were carried out by the Kuomintang itself, while in the other, they reflect the joint activity of Communist China and the Soviet Union. That the question as to whether the Soviet Union would come into the war if Manchuria were bombed played so important a part in the discussions of the Congressional committee investigating General MacArthur's dismissal, shows the absurdity of Rau's theory that China is following her own policy without external inspiration.

As regards the nature of the Chinese Communist Government, it is in the last analysis a question of whether or not China is a satellite of Soviet Russia. Sir Benegal said:

> No Cominform direction of Chinese policy has been attempted, or appears likely to be attempted. The independence of Chinese Communism being a fact beyond question, and asserted and emphasized as such by the Chinese leaders, there would appear to be no temptation for Russia to exercise any authority or control. Sino-Soviet relations, though very close, are contractual, strengthened by an ideological similarity and a feeling that in joint action lies strength for both.

I am astonished that Sir Benegal can use the phrase, "independence of Chinese Communism." Communism in China is imported from the Soviet Union. The tactics of class struggle, dictatorship, confiscation of land, and the "united front" came from the Kremlin. The chapter on the formation of the Chinese Communist Party has given, I hope, enough proofs that one of the two entities is a teacher and the other a disciple. China's ideological and political situation is like that of the pious Moslem who must read his Koran and make his pilgrimage to Mecca. This being the case, whether China is a satellite or a co-worker is a quibble. In the matter of the interpretation of Marxism and Leninism, of the experience of world revolution, and of the collection of information by the Cominform, since China is not an equal of the Soviet Union it stands to reason that she must follow the lead of the Kremlin. As Mr. John Foster Dulles has said, "By the test of conception, birth, nurture, and obedience, the Mao Tse-tung regime is a creature of the Moscow Politburo. . . . We should treat the Mao Tse-tung regime for what it is—a puppet regime." But it is not of great importance to distinguish whether Sino-Soviet relations should be called contractual, as Sir Benegal calls them, or those of a puppet state with its ruler, as Mr. Dulles avers. So long as the Soviet Union and Communist China are tied together by an identical outlook, there is a natural hierarchy of command and obedience maintained.

CHAPTER XVI

What to Do with Communist China

The fundamental question in the Far East today is what do with Communist China. There are two aspects to the problem: first, how to bring about and strengthen the internal forces for democracy in China; secondly, what the other countries can do to help in setting up this democratic government.

I am firmly convinced that 90 per cent of the Chinese population will be glad to see China a democratic country and would much prefer to have nothing to do with revolution and conquest. They would like to maintain their valuable old traditions and beliefs, and evolve gradually towards a democratic, scientific, and industrial order. The Communist slogan of "Down with Feudalism" is only a pretext under which the Communists are wiping out the tradition of Chinese humanistic ideals and imposing upon China the formula of Stalinist orthodoxy. This Marxist-Leninist-Stalinist way of life is a complete denial of the individual and of individualism. It may very well fit into the pattern of life characteristic of Russia, with its history of tyranny and absolutism, but it will never be effective among a people who have lived in an atmosphere of laissez-faire for thousands of years. I have heard often that the control of the Communist regime over China is completely effective: no doubt the Communist army is an efficient one, the Chinese Communists have a well-disciplined party and police force, they watch over the movements of every family and every individual, and the life of every person is being regimented and brought under strict control. But, although there is no reliable way in which we can find out how the people feel under this new regime, as a Chinese, knowing the long history of China and the characteristics of my own people, I think that they cannot be happy under the new dispensation, and sooner or later, in a manner which may not even be predictable, they will rise against the new oppression. There is one predominant truth of overwhelming importance in this sad story of China which must be emphasized over and over again, and that is, that the Chinese people went over to the Communists for the simple reason that they could not stand the government of Chiang Kai-shek any longer, that they were repeatedly duped, cheated, and oppressed by the shameless political debauchery, dishonesty, and corruption of the government until they were willing to take any chance and submit to any change because they thought that no change could be any worse than the conditions under which they were living. They have now learned to their regret that there is indeed no difference between the devil and the deep sea.

What the historian Grote said about the Greek usurpers—that they employed the machinery of fraud whereby the people were to be cheated into temporary submission, as a prelude to using the machinery of force whereby such submission was to be perpetuated against the people's consent—can very well be applied to explain the success of the Chinese Communist Party from 1946 to 1949.

The Chinese people now realize that the policy of the Chinese Communists can only lead them to disaster. Communist control over China is only maintained by means of bayonets. Their hold on the country is effected through the secret police; it is not rooted in the hearts of the people. Their government is a house built of bamboo and mud, and can very easily be pulled down. It is a tree whose roots are exposed to rain and wind, and which can be shaken and uprooted. There is no reason to think that the control of the Chinese Communists over China can be effective for any length of time. Once it is shaken it will soften and weaken. The political psychology of the Chinese has been explained by the old sage Mencius: "Ke and Sui lost the Empire because they lost the people, and they lost the people because they lost their hearts. There is only one way to hold the Empire—hold the people. There is only one way to hold their hearts—that is to get for them what they like and not to impose on them what they dislike." This political philosophy is true now as it was true 2000 years ago; it is true of China as it must be true of other peoples in other parts of the world. It means that behind a government there must be a sincere popular will. Let us look at the present situation in China. Is the Chinese intervention in the Korean war what the Chinese people want? Is the Sino-Soviet military alliance what the Chinese people like? Can mass executions make the present regime popular? Nothing that the Chinese Communists are doing has promoted the welfare of the people; they simply perform what Stalin commands. Can such a government last? No, it cannot last.

Under these circumstances I have a few observations to make which I hope will be helpful in eventually restoring China to the free world.

1. *China's Independence should be restored.* Since the establishment of the Chinese Communist regime in Peking, China's position in the world is that of a close ally of the Soviet Union. With China in the Communist bloc, one feels that a stable factor in the Far East has been lost, just as the disappearance of the Austro-Hungarian Empire created a vacuum and reduced Central Europe to a congeries of fragmentary states. The establishment of a Communist China must create a feeling of insecurity in neighboring countries. A strong Communist China is a threat to Korea, Japan, and the Philippine Islands to the east. On the western side she can threaten India, Pakistan, and the states bordering on India. From the south and the west she can reach Indo-China, Thailand, Burma, and the Malay Peninsula. So long as China is a member of the Communist bloc, these neighboring countries will never feel safe. This has been abundantly demonstrated by the lesson of Chinese intervention in Korea and Indo-China.

Conversely, if China remains on friendly terms with the democratic countries and maintains her peaceful traditions, she should prove an asset not only to the security of these neighboring countries but to that of the entire world. I think that anybody wih a proper understanding of the world situation must realise that China is that important. And yet how callously and with what insouciance did the leading powers regard the Chinese problem—as if China deserves nothing more than casual attention! I am afraid it takes a non-Westerner, without that traditional European or Anglo-Saxon indifference towards things non-Western, to adopt anything like a proper approach to the Chinese situation. Mr. Charles H. Malik, the Lebanese delegate to the UN, has expressed some views which are well worth considering. In his article "The Challenge of Communism," he said:

> Europe is weak and exposed. The Middle East is weak and exposed. Asia and the Far East are weak and exposed. There is really nothing to prevent Communism from walking into these various places from without except the goodness of its heart. Consequently, the balance of power at these points must be redressed if there is going to be honest, peaceful co-existence.
>
> Consider, for example, the situation in the Far East. It is not clear whether the present Communist China can strike out on an independent path. Entirely apart from ideology, if Communist China must follow the Soviet Union in sheer combination of power, the peaceful

balance of the world will be disturbed. These two giants taken together will in time constitute a most formidable combination of strength, the like of which the world has never known before. Even if the Communists were angels—which I doubt, or at least they are not any more so than the rest of us—the rest of the world . . . will gradually fall into their hands. Therefore, the real problem of war and peace today, so far as the Far East is concerned, is the problem of the independence of China. He works for peace today who works for the independence of China.

2. *The two governments, one Communist on the mainland and the other Nationalist in Formosa, must for the moment remain as they are.* After the establishment of the Communist regime in Peking, it looked as if a united China, duly accepted by the world, would soon be achieved. Recognition was given to Peking by many countries, and recognition was soon followed by exchanges of diplomatic representatives. These countries also expressed the opinion that Communist China should be admitted to the United Nations and to the Security Council. It was also agreed that Formosa should be considered a part of Communist China and included in the Japanese Peace Treaty. All these issues arise logically enough when a revolutionary government has established itself. But is it necessary that all these questions should be settled now? And *can* these questions be settled at the present moment? If the Communist regime observed the rules of international law and aimed at living peacefully with all the countries in the world, these questions might have been settled long ago. But after Chinese intervention in the Korean war, it became obvious that Communist China was working for world revolution and considered Russia her only friend and the other countries her enemies. It is abundantly clear that she has chosen to be the advance guard of the Comintern. Would it not be better, therefore, for the countries outside the Communist bloc to leave these questions in abeyance—the question of recognition, of China's seat in the UN, of her claim to Formosa, and of her right to negotiate a peace treaty with Japan? If the countries outside the Communist bloc try to bring China into the UN or to the enjoyment of the rights which otherwise should belong to her, the world as a whole will not benefit thereby, while Communist China will be all the more consolidated in her international status. This will lead her to think that, by cooperating slavishly with the Soviet Union, she can get anything she wants and that there is no need to live amicably with other countries. Formosa, in particular, is the last stronghold of non-Communist China, from which the 450 million Chinese people hope

that their freedom and independence will be regained in the future. Including the surrender of Formosa to Peking in the Japanese treaty or in any other international agreement can be done only at the instance of the Western democracies themselves and will arouse the deep resentment of non-Communist China. Formosa may be weak and insignificant in its material aspects, but nevertheless it is immensely significant as a symbol of a free China, and a free China is one of the most valuable assets of a free and peaceful world.

3. *The illusion that Communist China can cooperate with the Western democracies must be given up.* There is much speculation as to whether Communist China, if she is given a seat in the United Nations, will be brought back into the fold of the family of nations. Others go even further and claim that Communist China can be detached from the Soviet Union, and that Mao Tse-tung can eventually become a Tito. All these are illusions which it is best to disabuse ourselves of.

As I mentioned in previous chapters, the historical ties between the Chinese Communists and the Soviet Union are so deep-rooted that they cannot be broken. Most members of the Central Committee of the Party are Russian-trained; most of them never want to know anything said or done in the democratic countries. All that they know and read comes from the works of Marx, Lenin, or Stalin, or from the Tass Agency. Anything opposed to these sources of information is considered capitalistic rubbish. The vision of the Chinese Communists is so restricted by ideological blinders that they cannot see the facts of life except from the Soviet point of view. The Party, as a branch of the Comintern, is carefully watched over by the latter. Any resolution passed by the Central Committee, any change in the personnel of the Party and the Government, have to be reported to the Comintern. The Chinese Communists are firmly convinced not only that the Russians will never let them down, but that they are their only friends in time of need. It is therefore less than likely that they will ever give up Russia's friendship. In China now, there are more than 10,000 Russian advisers in the army, navy, and air force organizations, and in the railways, telegraphic services, and public works. If there is the slightest indication of disaffection, the Kremlin will be able to find it out before it is translated into fact or deed. In other words, Mao Tse-tung and Chou En-lai are insects in a spider's web; the more they struggle to free themselves, the more entangled they become. Anyone who proclaims the hypothesis that Mao Tse-tung can become a Tito has no true understanding of the situation and does immeasurable harm to the cause of democracy.

4. *A united policy on the part of the British Commonwealth and the United States towards Free China will relieve the Communist threat in Asia.* Since the Korean war began the British Commonwealth is the only one of the major powers which has sent a comparatively large force to the aid of the U. S. A. in Korea. But as the war proceeds, we find that there is a great divergence of opinion between the two powers with regard to China and the Korean war. It appears that Britain has sought a reconciliation with Communist China. She wanted the UN forces to halt at the 38th Parallel and did not favor MacArthur's methods of conducting the war. She also supported the cease-fire negotiations. It was even rumored that it was Britain who brought forward the proposal that Formosa be given over to Peking. There is also bickering over the Hongkong trade and the export of rubber to Communist China. But I hope that Britain realises that so long as there is a Communist China, the British Commonwealth will live under a perpetual threat, especially with regard to its interests in Hongkong, India, Pakistan, the Malay Peninsula, and other bordering states. Will appeasement of Communist China have any good effect on the relations between China and the British Commonwealth? I do not think so. Britain, in the eyes of the Communists, is an enemy as important as the U. S. A. The fact that negotiations for the exchange of diplomatic representatives have been dragging on from early 1950 till now and that Britain is labelled an enemy when a ban is placed on rubber exports to China, surely proves that a conciliatory policy will never change the attitude of Communist China towards Britain. My belief is that, in dealing with Communists, the American policy of meeting force with force has a better chance of success. Non-recognition of the Chinese Communist regime, assistance to Formosa, and the exclusion of Communist China from the negotiations for the Japanese Peace Treaty, are the correct antidote to Mao Tse-tung's policy of "leaning to one side." It is to be hoped that Britain will adopt a firmer policy towards China. Otherwise the Soviet Union will once again attempt to divide the two Western democracies and create confusion within the democratic camp. The American line of action will in the end bring peace and security to the Far East and to Southeast Asia. Britain's policy cannot make even Hongkong immune from Communist attack. If the two democracies can work together wholeheartedly, the countries of the Far East and Southeast Asia will also be

encouraged and united and will look to them for leadership in the fight against Communism.

5. *The new Asian nations face a special problem.* Most of the Asian nations—India, Burma, Indo-China and Indonesia—were colonies under British, French, or Dutch rule. Though now they are independent or about to be so, the memory of colonial government has not disappeared. The Comintern makes use of this mentality and incites the Asians to battle against colonialism. These people, though freedom and independence have been or are being won for them, still bear animosity towards their former masters. They are now trying a policy of aloofness from the two blocs; what they really aim at is to keep the Anglo-American democracies at arms' length, in order not to arouse the antagonism of the Soviet Union. But will this policy really strengthen their position? Will this policy not give the Soviet Union the chance to divide them? The experience of China in the last three decades provides a valuable lesson. Sun Yat-sen and Mao Tse-tung tried the same policy, and the result is dictatorship internally and a Russian alliance externally. Is that what the new Asian nations hope to gain after their liberation?

The Asian nations have had enough of absolutism and oppression. What they should fight for now is constitutional guarantee of the rule of law, the right of criticism in parliament and in local self-government, economic progress, and a raising of the common people's standard of living. What benefit can they derive from world revolution, from a Communist monopoly of power, and from creating social disruption everywhere? What they can expect benefits from is order, not disorder; real democracy, not dictatorship; cooperation among all the people in the land, not class struggle. They should be free to develop their own traditions and not have Marxism-Leninism-Stalinism imposed upon them. If freedom is their ideal, how can they side with Russia and not with the Western democracies? If these new Asian nations go on flirting with the Soviet Union and with Communist China, the fate which befell Poland, Czechoslovakia, Roumania, and Bulgaria will be theirs too.

6. *The shape of the coming war is already determined by the two opposing camps.* The North Atlantic Treaty Pact Powers are lined up against the Communist bloc in Europe, while in Asia the nucleus of military force on the Communist side is the Sino-Soviet alliance together with its Communist followers in Korea, Japan, India, Pakistan, Indo-China, the Philippines, and the Malay Peninsula.

This coming war will not be fought like the First World War, which started in different places at different times, and which could be settled peacemeal. Nor will it be like the Second World War in which America could stay out at first and then joined in after Pearl Harbor. It is quite certain that all the protagonists in the coming war will plunge in at the same time all over the world. The degree of preparedness of the democracies and the Communists is a complicated subject beyond the scope of this book, but the military situation of Asia can be briefly described. The lesson of the Japanese role in the Second World War cannot serve as a guide for the coming war. Japan, as an insular empire, divided her strategy between her navy and her army; while the army was busy in China, including Manchuria, the navy was in the South Seas on transport and patrol duty around Indo-China, the Philippines, the Malay Peninsula, and the Dutch Indies. Her forces were so scattered that she had to defend herself in China, watch the Russians on the Manchurian frontier, and later fight naval and air battles against the U. S. A. It took about two years for American arms to mount a full-scale counter-offensive. As Japan's natural resources were very limited, time favored the Americans, who grew ever stronger and could come back to retake what they had lost.

The Asian enemies of the U. S. A. in the coming war are the Soviet Union and Communist China in a joint partnership. Naval warfare is likely to be restricted on the Communist side to submarine warfare and the Communist air effort is likely to be mainly defensive. The first thing their vast armies will do is to rush into Southeast Asia, because they can move freely on the whole continent of Asia by land routes. They are even now building strategic railways connecting Soviet Russia with China. While in 1938 and 1939 Russia was sending arms and munitions to China, my brother Chang Kia-ngau, then Minister of Communications, came to the conclusion that a railway line should be built connecting Russian Central Asia and the Chinese Lung-hai line. As Dr. Sun Fo was then paying a visit to Moscow, my brother asked him to sound out Stalin about building this line. When the proposal was made, Stalin took a rule from his pocket and measured on a military map the distance from Lanchow, the capital of the province of Kansu, to Novosibirsk. Stalin said that the work of construction would take many years, so that the railroad would be of no use for the war then being waged between China and Japan. The idea of connecting the Lung-hai railway to Novosibirsk was then abandoned, but it was revived after the signature of the Sino-Soviet alliance of 1950. The construction of a railway to link up Central Asia and China means solving a problem of troop transport for the coming war. Other blueprints exist for more railways to be built in the interior rather than on the coast.

The solid bloc of Russian and Chinese power will certainly exert strong influence in all the neighboring countries on the borders of Russia and China—Korea, Indo-China, Burma, Thailand, India, Pakistan, and the Malay Peninsula. Some of these countries, like India and Burma, try to maintain friendly relations with Communist China and Russia in order to avoid provoking the ill-will of the Communist bloc. It is very unlikely, however, that their policy of aloofness will save them from being overrun when the Communist bloc is determined to take them. Soviet Russia and Communist China will be able to take the initiative both in Western Europe, and in Asia, thus producing a kind of see-saw warfare. The Soviet Union will send weapons and instructors to China to train a modern army. Since Japan was an island, it was possible, by the use of overwhelming naval power, to cut her off from her occupied territories, but in the event of another war, Russia and China can overrun vast territories by land routes alone if the appropriate preparations are made. How long it will take for these Asian countries to be liberated once they are lost is beyond our ability to predict.

But I believe that there are ways of bringing about a change in Asia before this war breaks out. The Western powers must show their determination to detach China militarily from Soviet Russia, support must be given to Formosa and the guerilla bands on the mainland of China, and the British Commonwealth and the United States must lead the Asian countries in united action against Communism. These measures will restrict the scope of the coming disaster, give a feeling of security to Southeast Asia, and perhaps stimulate the Chinese people to free themselves from their present slavery. There is a Chinese proverb which says that the one who bends the flue and removes the fuel, is not considered deserving, while he who scorches his head and smashes his forehead is an honored guest. In other words, the great merit of devising the means of guarding against danger is not appreciated, while the work of one who actually comes to the rescue in an emergency is alone recognized. It is to be hoped that this will not be true in the coming war.

It is perhaps appropriate to say a few words concerning a cease-fire in Korea and its wider implications. This may mean stalemate or a return to the status quo ante in Korea. It is doubtful whether negotiations for a real cease-fire will be successful, because the Communists wish to keep the U. S. A. fully committed in Korea and thus divert her attention from Formosa, which in Communist eyes is of far greater importance. The Nationalists on Formosa are the deadly enemies of the Communists and a perpetual thorn in their flesh, for the Communists never know when a landing on the coast may announce the return of the Nationalists to the mainland. Even if negotiations for a cease-fire in Korea come to a successful end, it can mean only a temporary truce and not any permanent peace in the Far East, for the American government has declared that Formosa shall not fall into the hands of the Communists and that it will not recognise the Peking regime because it is only a satellite of the Russian government. These words of Dean Rusk must have aroused greater resentment in Peking than the sending of the UN army to Korea. The cease-fire in Korea, which is a matter of first-rate importance for the UN, can only smooth out a ripple on the surface of the water. The real trouble lies much deeper.

These suggestions will not assure a complete settlement of the whole question of Communism and Democracy in China; they may, however, create an attitude of fairplay in examining the claims of both sides. The final decision depends on both the national and international struggle. Nationally, the leaders in Formosa, and more especially the Chinese democratic forces outside of Formosa, must unite to put the government on a really democratic basis, which will strongly counteract the influence of the Chinese Communist regime. In the final estimate of the Chinese situation, we must always bear in mind that it was the denial of freedom and democracy, followed by all manner of corruption and incompetence that precipitated the present crisis. This feudalism and absolutism can and must be uprooted by the liberal forces which are not under the immediate control of the Nationalist Government in Formosa. On the international side, the Soviet Union is backing up the present regime in Peking which it will not under any circumstances abandon. To combat this, the Western democracies should, in their own interest, give as much sympathy and assistance as possible to non-Communist China. The least the Western democracies can do is not to kill the seeds of anti-Communism, which are their greatest potential assets, and not to encourage Communism, which is their greatest enemy.

CHAPTER XVII

Conclusion

It will be a case of tragic misunderstanding if people are led to believe that Communism in China has much in common with the Socialist movement in Europe. Chinese Communism is a product that developed much too late to have any affinity with the socialism which existed in nineteenth-century Europe.

The socialist movement which began with Robert Owen (1771–1858), Henri de Saint-Simon (1760–1825), Charles Fourier (1772–1837), Louis Blanc (1811–1882), Karl Marx (1818–1883), and Friedrich Engels (1820-1895), and culminated in the British Labor Government, has been largely motivated by humanitarian ideals; in other words, it is the expression, in a different form, of the ideals of the French Revolution—liberty, equality, and fraternity. The founders of the movement were inspired by the belief that class distinctions and unequal distribution of wealth should be abolished, and that the right to vote should be given to every citizen, rich and poor alike. Before Lenin came to power in Soviet Russia, the European socialists, in spite of the influence of Marxist ideology, were forming trade unions for collective bargaining, pressing for factory-code legislation to ameliorate conditions of labor, starting cooperatives for collective buying and distribution of commodities, agitating for workmen's insurance against accident and old age, and for extension of the suffrage to the working class in order to place democratic government on a really egalitarian basis.

When the Second International, composed of Socialist parties, was organized in 1889, it rejected the doctrine of a universal proletarian uprising, and declared that control by the laboring classes over industry must be the result of long and assiduous effort by proletarian organizations in both the political and economic fields and of the gradual conquest of local and national legislative assemblies.

The Socialist or Communist movement in China knows nothing about Robert Owen, Saint-Simon, Louis Blanc, etc., because these thinkers were condemned by Karl Marx as Utopian Socialists. But in Europe, in spite of this view, even the Marxists themselves had to apply the same method of the gradual peaceful conquest of local and national assemblies in Great Britian, France, Germany, and other countries.

In China, when Communism or Socialism was introduced, the main objective of the Chinese Communist Party, in contrast to that of the European Socialist parties, was from the very beginning a proletariat uprising and the conquest of political power by overthrowing the existing government. To achieve their ends, the Chinese Communists paid no attention to the interests of the working class which they were supposed to represent. Factory-code legislation was a feature of their party program, but it was something for which they never agitated because there were too few factories and too few workmen to make the subject interesting in political terms. Universal suffrage was also a subject written into their party program, but they had no interest in this question either, as Liu Shao-chi admitted. The Chinese Communists from the very start adopted the policy of overthrowing the government by violent means, that is, by military force. The term "reactionary," which was first applied to the warlords of the Northern Military Party, was applied also to Chiang Kai-shek after their break with him, though he had been considered their friend only a few months before. Since they did not have Chiang's military power, they withdrew to the mountainous areas and engaged in guerilla warfare. They organized their party on lines of the strictist discipline, because they depended upon it for their very existence, and they differed basically from the European Socialist parties which had been allowed to carry on their propaganda openly, as legally recognized parties. The principal concerns of the Chinese Communists are party discipline, military power, spying, and infiltration. They believe implicitly in Marxism-Leninism-Stalinism. Marxism is the categorical imperative; that it is a real remedy for the ills of Chinese political, economic and cultural life is beyond discussion as far as they are concerned. Because they are interested in fighting against the "reactionaries," "exploiters," and "imperialists," they must obey a commander-in-chief who will enforce discipline. They do not much care about freedom of discussion because they do not consider it a necessary feature of personal freedom but merely a means to action. Those who dare to differ with the policy of the party after discussion is over are either killed or purged. Before their conquest of power, the Communists never hesitated to use every means to win sympathy from outsiders, as for example, by agitating for war against Japan or for the popular front. These were only temporary measures, however; in the last analysis their policy is to turn China into a dictatorship under which they can secure the monopoly of political power. The only analogy to the phase of Communist domination in the long history of China is a fourteen-year period during the Chin Dynasty. In 207 B.C., under Chin Shih-huang, the first Emperor of the Chin Dynasty, there took place what was called "The Burning of the Books," which, along with other measures, was the first practical application of the principles of totalitarian dictatorship in China. After defeating his rivals, the Emperor converted China into a universal empire. His ministers believed that feudalism was a good system to provide support for the Imperial House, and suggested that the Emperor revive it. But the Prime Minister, Li Ssu, held a different view, which he developed in the following memorandum to the Emperor:

Formerly the feudal lords fought against each other and invited travelling scholars [the Chinese version of the Greek Sophists] to be their advisers. Now the whole Empire has been united. Laws and commands emanate from a single source. The common people in their family life should busy themselves with agriculture and industry. The scholars should learn more about laws, commands, and prohibitions. Nevertheless, nowadays, the scholars do not take the present as their teacher, but devote themselves to the past, in order to defame the present regime and to spread doubt and uncertainty among the common people. The Prime Minister, Li Ssu, not fearing his death, would like to make the following suggestions. In the past, when the Empire was divided and disturbed, no one could unite it. The princes ruled simultaneously. The scholars in their discussions speak of the ancient times as models and decry the present. In the cloak of their Utopian language they stir up confusion about the reality of actual conditions. They proclaim the excellence of their own doctrines which they study privately in order to oppose what Your Majesty has established. Since the Emperor has united the empire, there should be a clear distinction between white and black and a single authority should rule everywhere. But those who devote themselves to private studies teach the people in their own way; as soon as they know that new edicts are issued, they discuss them in accordance with their own doctrines. While at the court they conceal their resentment, they initiate discussions among small groups of people in their houses. In the name of the Emperor they vaunt themselves as advisers, but they try to show that they have their own originality. They lead the people in spreading calumnies. This being the case, unless measures are taken against them, the prestige of the sovereign will be lowered, the associations among the people will grow in power and in number. It is necessary to prevent this. Your Minister proposes that the histories of the feudal states, with the exception of Chin, shall all be burned. All men in the Empire who possess copies of the Shu-King, the Shih-King and the works of the Hundred Schools, must take these books to the Magistrates to be burned. Those who dare to discuss and comment on the Shu-King and the works of the Hundred Schools, shall be put to death and their bodies exposed in the marketplace. Those who praise the ancient times and decry the present shall be exterminated together with all the members of their families. Officials who condone breaches of this law shall receive the same punishment. Thirty days after the publication of this decree, all who have not given up their books for burning will be branded and sent to do forced labor on the work of building city walls. The books which shall be allowed to be kept are only those which treat of medicine, divination, agriculture, and arboriculture. Those who wish to study laws and commands should take the governing officials as their masters.

This memorandum as drafted by Li Ssu was approved and became a decree. We find in it a number of affinities with modern dictatorships. Is not Li Ssu's emphasis on the present and on the realities of existing conditions an expression of the same mentality as the modern attitude of realism, Realpolitik, or the "scientific" outlook of the Communists? Is not Li Ssu's advocacy of a united Empire and a single authority the same as the Soviet insistence on centralism and dictatorship? Is not Li Ssu's abhorrence of the private doctrines of the scholars, and his demand that the scholar should study laws and commands with only the officials as his masters, similar to the Communists' adherence to their version of Marxism and their faith in its infallibility? To prohibit criticism of the present and the adoption of the past as a model means the destruction of tradition: the burning of books in the possession of the people, except those which are kept by the doctors—is this not precisely what was done by Stalin and Hitler? Li Ssu urged that there should be no freedom of conscience, no freedom of thought, no freedom of the press. The sentence, "unless measures are taken against them, the prestige of the sovereign will be lowered, and the associations of the people will grow in power and in number," clearly shows that freedom of association and assembly was not to be countenanced. This decree is the foundation of official Chinese despotism and absolute monarchy which lasted from 221 B.C. till the abdication of the Manchu Emperor in 1911, when the Chinese Republic was established—a period of over 2000 years.

From that time on, contact with the outside world became increasingly close. Kang Yu-wei and Liang Chi-chao were the pioneers of emancipation. Their work was later taken up by Hu Shih, Chen Tu-hsiu, and a host of younger intellectual leaders who established a new literary and philosophic outlook. It was Sun Yat-sen who introduced a new political order. What these men tried to promote was a rule of law founded on a constitution, a republican form of government, a parliament, local self-government, the fundamental rights of the individual, and a scientific view of society. Just when this great movement of emancipation was being crowned with success, along came the Chinese Communists, who in the name of democratic centralism, the people, the mass, the peasants, the working class, have established a new dictatorship in which power is monopolized by the Communist Party. In other words, they are bringing the Chinese back to the old despotism. Behind the slogans "People's Democracy," "Land to the Tiller," and "Welfare of the Working Class," they are actually subjugating China by a policy of deliberate oppression, torture, and inhumanity. In the light of history there is no doubt that the Chinese Communist Party is retrogressive rather than progressive.

Having discussed the development of the present political situation in China, let me now answer, with reference to Chinese political philosophy, the following two basic questions: (1) Why has no democratic government developed in China? and (2) Are the historical roots in China strong enough to support the restoration of a democracy when Chinese Communist domination is no more?

There is no doubt that democracy, freedom, and constitutionalism are concepts that have been introduced in China as a result of her contact with the West. No doubt there is a gap between China's tradition of absolute monarchy and modern democratic constitutional government, in the same way as there is a gap between the Roman Empire and the political system of the Middle Ages, or between the feudal loyalties of the Middle Ages and the Nationalism of the Renaissance. There is no doubt also that such a change is bound to produce chaos and disorder, but the problem is whether this disorder and chaos is only a temporary phenomenon or whether China will exhaust herself before this new form of government can be placed on a firm foundation.

Some Chinese scholars believe that a democratic form of government is entirely a product of European civilization, and, accordingly, can never be applied to a Chinese background; others believe that China's traditional form of government was essentially as democratic as that of the West although it expressed itself in a somewhat different form. Again, there is a third school of thought which holds that the historical roots of Chinese democracy, when crossbred and nourished with modern democratic concepts, can establish a stable and working democracy in China—using the term democracy in its political connotation with reference to governmental organization.

Some European writers have referred to the Orient as a non-political area because the Orient has so far failed to establish a theory of the state, or a theory of the relationship between the state and the individual. Professor Lord, for instance, adopts this view in his book, *The Principles of Politics*. Janet, in his *Histoire de la science politique,* also says, "The Orient in general, and India in particular, does not have the concept of the state."

Closely connected with this idea of the non-political Oriental society is Hegel's belief, expressed in his *Philosophy of History,* that the Orient has never been concerned with the importance of the individual. "The consciousness of freedom first arose among the Greeks, and therefore they were free; but they and the Romans likewise knew only that some are free. . . . The German nation, under the influence of Christianity, was the first to attain the consciousness that man is free, and that it is the freedom of the spirit that constitutes its essence. The Orientals, on the other hand, have not attained the knowledge that spirit—or man as such—is free, and because of this they do not know that they are free. They only know that one person is free, namely, the Emperor."

The views of Lord, Janet, and Hegel seem to be that the Orient thus far has recognised neither the rights of the individual, nor the broader ideal of human freedom, nor, indeed, the entity of the state itself. I believe that this view is based upon a misunderstanding. Although the Orient does not use the term freedom, it certainly is familiar with the concept of freedom. When Williams says of the Chinese in his book *The Middle Kingdom* that "Liberty is unknown among the people; there is not even a word for it in their language," I should like to remind him of what Confucius says: "From the Emperor down the root of everything is in the cultivation of the person." Confucius further says: "An army can be deprived of its commander, but the common people cannot be deprived of its own will." What is this will? If a people is conscious of its own power, what is this consciousness but the sense of liberty? When people are conscious of the need for considering the needs and feelings of others, there exists an awareness of the rights and integrity of man. Although under the institution of absolute monarchy there did not exist an organ or a law that protected human rights and freedoms, although there was no constitution based upon the dignity of the individual, the idea of protecting the people from the tyranny of a despot goes far back in the history of China. Before the birth of Christ, the Chinese sang a song that was already ancient: "It was the lesson of our great ancestor: the people should be cherished; they should not be downtrodden; the people are the root of the country; if the root is firm, the country is tranquil. When I look throughout the Empire of simple men and women, anyone may surpass me." Mencius, faithful follower of Confucius, wrote, "The people are the most important element in a nation; the spirits of the land and the grain come next; and the Emperor is the least important of them all." And he continues, "People turn toward a benevolent ruler as water flows downward, and as wild beasts fly to the wilderness."

I could give hundreds of such quotations to substantiate my view that the concept of popular will is familiar to Chinese philosophy. But it is true that the Chinese have not given to governmental institutions the same importance as they have assumed in Western thought. The functions of a government have been confined to the collection of taxes, the exercise of judicial power, and the maintenance of military power—the belief being that a government should interfere as little as possible with the life of the people. About this policy of noninterference, Mr. Herbert C. Giles has truly said, "Everyone who has lived in China and has kept his eyes open, must have noticed what a large measure of personal freedom is enjoyed by even the meanest of subjects of the Son of Heaven. Any Chinaman may travel all over China without asking anyone's leave to start, and without having to report himself, or be reported by his innkeeper at any place at which he may choose to stop. He requires no passport. He may set up any legitimate business at any place. He is not even obliged to be educated or to follow any particular calling. He is not obliged to serve as a soldier or a sailor. There are no sumptuary laws, not even any municipal laws. Outside of the penal code, which has been pronounced by Western lawyers to be a very ably constructed instrument of government, there is nothing at all in the way of law, civil law being altogether absent as a state institution. Even the penal code is not too rigidly enforced. So long as a man keeps clear of secret societies and remains a decent and respectable member of his family and of his clan, he has little to fear from his officials."

If it be accepted, then, that we have, in theory as well as in practice, a well-defined democratic tradition in China, the question may well be asked, Why did not China follow through with the establishment of a democratic, constitutional government?

There are, I think, very good reasons for this. First of all, in Europe, during the transitional period that transformed European society from a feudal to a democratic one, there existed an aristocracy that held the balance between the king and the people. The existence of the aristocracy made a legal system possible, and prepared the basis for the smooth evolutionary transition from feudalism to democracy. The same is true in the case of Japan, where the Meiji reform had the sponsorship of the aristocratic class in replacing feudalism with a constitutional government. The English bicameral parliament, in which the aristocracy exercises certain functions and shares in the government, provides historical testimony of the role of this class in the development of democratic institutions in Britain; an early document of this role is the Magna Carta itself. In China, as has been pointed out previously, the situation is different. When feudalism was abolished at the time of Chin Shih-huang, there was no group to fill the void left between the people and the Emperor, and an absolute monarchy was established which made it exceedingly difficult for China to develop formal democratic institutions in her evolution from a feudal to a modern state. When an aristocratic class exists, this class can claim its rights and establish conventions according to which the power of the king is more and more narrowly delimited; and when the idea of rights for the aristocracy has been established, it is only a step further to guaranteeing the rights of the people at large. In China after the period of the Warring Kingdoms, the Chin Dynasty succeeded in establishing a highly centralized government, destroying completely the aristocratic class that had existed previous to that time. After the abolition of the aristocracy, the people who were interested in working for the government could do so only by passing a civil service examination; in other words, the people were levelled into one class. While the levelling process meant the abolition of privileges for a certain class of people, it did not mean the development of legally guaranteed rights for the people at large, such as the claims of the aristocracy helped to establish in Europe. In this respect one may say that the premature abolition of an aristocratic class in China was a misfortune, for it made the evolution towards a constitutional government most difficult.

The second reason for China's failure to develop indigenous democratic institutions hinges on the power of the emperor within the framework of an absolute monarchy. With the disappearance of the aristocracy, the emperor constituted the sole political power in the country, seen from a structural institutional point of view. The only genuine power granted to the people was the right of revolution, which could be staged in protest against the sovereign. The right of revolution, or the right to change the existing government, as later advocated by Locke and Jefferson, was recognized in Chinese history before the beginning of the Chin Dynasty. While within this system there existed no real sense of the emperor's responsibility to the people, there did exist the idea of the Mandate of Heaven that must be returned to the people in the form of the right of rebellion if the emperor abused his powers to such an extent that the people were no longer able to carry the burden. This Mandate of Heaven, this sense of responsibility, while not limited by law or based upon constitutional concepts, yet controlled the emperor's behavior and held his prerogatives within certain prescribed limits. We see, therefore, that Chinese democracy had nothing to do with class distinctions, human rights, or property rights, but was founded upon a sentiment which has come down through the ages and which can best be expressed in the Confucian saying, "the people should be cherished; they should not be downtrodden." Functional democracy in China rests upon the institution of local self-government, and has ultimate theoretical reference to the principle of man's privilege to act when discontented—or, in other words, the right of rebellion.

But in comparing the Chinese system of government with that of the Western world, it must be pointed out that while the West bases its principles of government upon a code of law, China bases its principles of government upon a code of ethics. This is a fundamental difference, and one of great importance. The Chinese political thinker approaches political questions purely from a moral or ethical point of view, and not, as is common in the West, from the Machiavellian point of view which regards the state and the individual as two separate entities under the control of different principles. When government is built upon a legal and institutional foundation, then it can be discussed, and therefore placed under the control of a parliament, whose functions, in turn, can be regulated by settled convention. But as long as government is based upon the will of the emperor and his statesmen, then the question of whether the regime in power is a good or bad one can only be decided by the emperor or by the people at large. There can be no doubt that the right of rebellion is better exercised within a parliamentary system, by the passing of bills, than by physical revolution after the sufferings of the people have accumulated over a long period of time to a point past enduring.

Another question that must be asked centers round the absence of a parliament or a representative form of government within the pattern of Chinese history. It is usually supposed that during China's feudalistic period, there was a kind of council similar to the Witenagemot, the Anglo-Saxon national council, which assisted the emperor in ruling the country. For the purposes of our inquiry into the absence of a parliamentary system in China, we may draw an analogy with France, where the council gradually disappeared so that by the time of the French Revolution there were no traces left of any such institution. Continuity of a parliamentary system has existed only in Britain, and later in the United States, but not in other countries of the Western world.

Probably the most important power of the government is the control of the purse. When the power of levying taxes is in the hands of the representatives of the people or of the aristocracy, then there is a way to control the tax powers of the government, but the only way the Chinese people were able to protest against the heavy burden of taxation was, again, by rebellion. In other words, the absence of a parliament or a representative form of government of any kind in China can again be explained by the absence of an aristocratic class.

The way in which the people as such have been looked upon in the history of Chinese political thought is also important. The idea of "considering the people as ignorant" has served as the basis of political philosophy in China. Although the principle, "the people shall be nourished; they shall not be downtrodden," served as the foundation of governmental policy, the people were never considered masters of their own country; they were regarded as masses confined within their own ignorance. The words of Confucius, "the people can be told to act in conformity, but they cannot be told why, as they are not fit to know," are often quoted, but they appear to be a contradiction of his emphasis on the spreading of education, which will be discussed later. Throughout Chinese history there was no popular education that went beyond the civil service system, which separated the intelligentsia from the masses of the people. The benefits of the civil service system could be conferred only on the saving few, even though it was open in theory to everybody, so that the people as such could assume no intelligent leadership. Apart from the higher officials who were taken into government service through the examination system, the lesser gentry were relegated in each village and district to the function of looking after the irrigation system, grain system, grain storage, road building, and institutions of charity. The idea of controlling the government by a council, or a parliament, occurred to no one, since the people at large were considered to be too ignorant to share such a responsibility.

In connection with this point, we must not forget that the idea of individualism or of individual rights was never considered to be a fundamental principle in the social organization of the country, because the individual was primarily considered as a member of a family, a clan, or a district rather than as an entity sufficient unto itself. The emphasis that was placed on family relationships might be regarded as a strong retarding influence in the development of the conscientiousness of the individual. But economic factors have also contributed to this slow development. China was traditionally divided into five classes of people: the intelligentsia at the top, followed by the farmers, the artisans, the merchants, and lastly the soldiers. The fact that the farmers or peasants were considered the second-highest class is symptomatic of the fact that China until today had never developed its potential natural resources, so that the only profession left to the masses was farming and the farmer's function was regarded as vital. Moreover, the land was parcelled into such small pieces that there never existed a landlord class as in European society. This may be the reason why the general standard of living, or the general standard of education, was never raised among the people; and so long as the standard of living was not raised, so long as the idea of individual rights was not introduced into the country, the people naturally could not be expected to take an enlightened point of view in matters concerning the government.

When we look, therefore, at the development of democracy or of democratic thought in China, we must keep in mind that the abolition of feudalism at an early period gave rise to an absolute monarchy, while the aristocracy became extinct. We must also keep in mind that, although the people had the right of revolution, they were kept in such ignorance that an enlightened public opinion could not develop. We must remember, again, that the Chinese took a moral point of view with regard to the science of government, and this made it difficult indeed to establish a system of public law.

In China, a codified system of criminal and civil law existed in very early times. The whole field of public law, however, according to which the state sets a limit to its own functions, powers, and activities, was never considered a very important part of jurisprudence. In the same way, constitutional law, dealing with the auto-limitations of the state itself, was considered unimportant. What was the reason for so limited a legal viewpoint? In an absolute monarchy, the state, the land, and all its people were regarded as the private property of the monarch, a concept which made impossible the idea of public law under which the concept of auto-limitations of the state arises. Of course, the idea of the state and its resources as "private property of the monarch" might well be interpreted as meaning property under civil law. But it was actually the public property of a body politic.

The codification of law began very early in China, although there was always a school of thought that was opposed to such codification in the belief that the primary aim of Chinese law was to promote virtue or morality, which made legal interpretation unnecessary. In Tso's "Commentary on the Spring and Autumn Annals," written as early as 400 B.C., we find the following: "In our country what need is there for any code? When once the people know the grounds for contention, they will cast propriety away. . . . They will all be contending about a matter as small as the point of an awl or a knife. Disorderly litigations will multiply, and bribery will walk abroad. Tsin [the name of a feudal country] will go to ruin, it is to be feared, in the age succeeding yours. I have heard the saying that 'When a state is about to perish, there will be many new codes.' " This conversation about the advantages or disadvantages of the codification of law took place before Confucius, though the advice it gives was actually not followed by later dynasties; since millions of people were living together in China, inevitably civil or public offences occurred which had to be judged on some basis of codified law. We find, therefore, that from the Han Dynasty to the Manchu Dynasty, there were always some codes of law in force. But law was never separated from the concept of virtue or morality. Confucius once said: "I can try a lawsuit as well as other men, but surely the great thing is to achieve that there be no lawsuit." Too many lawsuits were considered to be a bad sign for the government in power; since the people were ignorant, it was believed that more laws would produce more litigation and crime—though it is doubtful, of course, whether there would be less need for legal codes and sanctions even if the people were better educated.

In Europe, from the beginnings of Roman law down to the modern constitutional period, the interpretation of law was in professional hands which kept the law in an institutionalized form to be observed both by the government and the people. In China, law was made to fit man, rather than man to fit the law, so that the legal profession was placed in a secondary role. Actually, legal study was never pursued with any seriousness except perhaps in the Tang Dynasty, when we find that the Academy for Higher Learning created a separate department for the study of law. Before it was enacted, law in China was not discussed by a popular representative body, so the people who were expected to abide by the law were kept in ignorance of its purpose and intention. Law was manipulated by those who were in power. It was precisely because law was considered a tool to be manipulated by those who were in power that it was regarded as inferior to morality. As long as law was a tool in the hands of the ruler, it could not be considered the primary means of regulating the life of the individual or of society.

The question remains of whether or not the historical roots in China are good and strong enough to permit the establishment of a genuine democracy. I believe that within Chinese history one does find the roots of democracy, and it should be the task of the Chinese leaders today to find a way of crossbreeding these historical roots of Chinese democracy with the new democratic concepts of the West. In spite of the system of absolute monarchy of which Chin Shih-huang laid the foundation, the underlying principle of government was that taught by the Confucian school. Confucius himself said, "When a country is densely populated, the most important thing is to make the people wealthy; and when a people is wealthy, the most important thing is to give the people education." The master continued, "The most important thing for the government is to give the people sufficient food and to inspire sufficient trust in the ruler." Mencius was even more conscious of the significance of the material standard of living for the people. "When the grain and fish and turtles are more than can be eaten, and there is more wood than can be used, such a condition enables the people to nourish their living and bury their dead, without ill feeling against anybody. This condition, in which the people nourish their living and bury their dead without any feelings of animosity, is the first step in royal government. Let mulberry trees be planted about the homesteads with their five *mou*, and persons of fifty years can be clothed in silk. In keeping fowls, pigs, dogs, and swine, let not their times of breeding be neglected, and persons of seventy years can eat flesh. Let there not be taken away the time that is proper for the cultivation of the farm with its hundred *mou,* and the family of several mouths that is supported by it shall not suffer hunger. Let careful attention be given to education in schools. It never has been that the ruler of a state, when such results are seen—persons of seventy wearing silk and eating flesh, and black-haired people suffering from neither hunger nor cold—did not attain to royal dignity." The material standard of living and the intellectual standard of the people are the things that are dominant in the minds of the two sages, and we can safely say that in these principles we have the foundation of a modern democratic state.

Even socialistic ideas are not lacking in the history of Chinese political thought. Confucius said, "To centralise wealth is to disperse the people; to distribute wealth is to gather the people together." Again, "A ruler of a country should be concerned more about fair distribution of wealth than about lack of wealth. He should also be more concerned about insecurity than about poverty. When there is fair distribution there will be no poverty; when there is harmony there will be no complaint of shortage; when there is content and peace there will be no rebellion."

These ideas of Confucius, Mencius, and others, are in perfect agreement with the modern theory that democracy can flourish only on a basis of material and spiritual well-being. The people must be well-clothed, well-fed, and well-educated before their interest can be directed toward the public welfare. The guarantee of an adequate living standard brings peace among men, not only in the economic field, but also in the political field. And when the people's intellectual standard and material living standard have been raised and made secure, they will know how to choose intelligently the representatives of their central, provincial, and local governments. Leaders of the government will be chosen who have the support of public opinion in carrying out their policies. Modern democratic government is, after all, the product of the trials and errors of many centuries. When we consider that the British parliamentary system has existed for many hundreds of years, and that America has lived under a democratic constitutional government for more than one hundred and fifty years, we must admit that China has a long struggle ahead of her. The size of her territory is in itself a formidable obstacle. But we Chinese are fortunate not only in having sound democratic concepts but also in having an unusually homogeneous culture which has produced a unified outlook upon life. There exists, in the truest sense of the word, a Chinese way of life developed by a common language and a community of ideas and values. With proper economic development and popular education, not only could a stable and democratic government be achieved in China, but it could become a reality within a reasonably short period.

Let us discuss, at this point, the basic concepts of Chinese philosophy in relation to Western rationalism, even though the subject is far from the burning issues of Chinese politics.

That the revival of philosophical and scientific thought in Europe, as expressed in terms of Rationalism, Natural Rights, and Natural Law, was inspired to a great extent by the study of the Chinese Classics, has been pointed out by Adolph Reichwein in his book *China and Europe*. Other writers have shared the same opinion. L. D. Thomas, formerly senator from Utah, tracing the source of the political thought of Thomas Jefferson, the leading American champion of the principle of Natural Rights, made this interesting observation:

> The writings of Mencius to whom I have already referred a few times, and of other classic Chinese social and political thinkers, found their way into Europe through translations as early as the thirteenth century. The merits and defects of the fundamental philosophical thought of the Far East were well aired, especially at the Vatican, because of the great controversy between the Jesuits and the Franciscans in China. Jefferson may therefore have had some knowledge of Eastern thought, though there is no proof of this.

Supported by the research of Reichwein, I venture to say that the ideas of Reason and Natural Law (the Pure Reason and Practical Reason of Kant) which spread so rapidly in the seventeenth and eighteenth centuries are closely related to the Chinese terms Li and Tao, which form the two fundamental concepts of Chinese philosophy. These terms are equivalent to the starting points of the philosophical systems of Descartes, Leibnitz, and Kant. When Reason finds philosophical and scientific truths, they are called Natural Law. The fundamental freedom of the individual is hypostatized under the name of Natural Rights. No doubt these philosophical and scientific concepts are formulated in the European way, but their sources of inspiration do seem to be Chinese. The entire question offers a wide and fruitful field for inquiry, and I am sure that later researchers will find much that is common between Chinese thought and European Rationalism.

What I want to emphasize here is that Rationalism, which is the hallmark of the Period of Enlightenment in Europe, gave rise to the new philosophy and science, and also to democratic theory. The question may of course be raised as to why the traditional philosophy of Confucius has given China an absolute monarchy, while, when it was transported to Europe, it gave a new impetus to the development of democratic government. My answer is simple: The philosophy of Confucius is based upon the theory that human nature is intrinsically good and that every human being has a natural personal dignity. But Confucius worked for the unification of China under a king or an emperor because he was disgusted with the wars of the feudal lords and the aristocratic families. For this reason, he has been accused by unthinking modernists in China of being the protagonist of absolute monarchy. Men like Hu Shih, for instance, think, that the "House of Confucius" should be pulled down. But in Europe, during the seventeenth and eighteenth centuries, when Confucian ideas were popular, they were responsible for the rise of the new intellectual movement which culminated in the spread of popular government and the Industrial Revolution. At the basis of these movements were the new concepts of the rights of man and the dignity of the human individual which constitute the central thought of the Confucian system. But the environment was different, and it was this difference which accounted for the divergences in the development of the basically similar concepts. The important thing to remember is that democratic ideas are an integral part of the Confucian system of thinking, and if they helped to promote democracy as we now understand it in Europe and America, there is every reason to believe that, given a different atmosphere, the same development will take place in China too.

Let me quote here a few sayings of Confucius and Mencius which are surprisingly close to the sayings of Thomas Jefferson, a man who more than anyone else believed in the theory of human reason and human rights and laid the political and philosophical foundation of the United States.

When Mencius was asked, "May a minister put his sovereign to death?" he answered, "He who outrages the benevolence proper to his nature is called a robber; he who outrages righteousness is called a ruffian; the robber and the ruffian we call mere fellows. I have heard of the cutting off of the fellow Chou, but I have not heard of putting a sovereign to death in his case." In other words, when the ruler behaved like a ruffian or a robber, he could no longer be considered a sovereign, and he forfeited his right of office. Now, in a letter to Madison in 1787, this is what Jefferson wrote: "A little rebellion now and then is medicine for the sound health of government." And the right of revolution was justified by the Declaration of Independence, which says that governments are instituted amongst men, deriving their just powers from the consent of the governed, and that whenever any form of government becomes destructive of these ends, it is the right of the people to alter or to abolish it, and constitute a new government. I think everyone will agree that Mencius said the same thing two thousand years before Jefferson was born.

It can be said that religious tolerance is natural to the Chinese, and in China freedom of conscience has prevailed because, according to Confucius, what is beyond our earthly life is something which is beyond the knowledge of the human mind, so that Confucius himself seldom discusses it. That is the reason why, in China, where Confucianism is the dominant belief, Buddhism, Mohammedanism, Christianity, and other religions were introduced and tolerated. In the United States, this freedom of conscience has been very much emphasized. One may join a given church and then transfer one's allegiance to another. Jefferson said: "A Church is a voluntary society of men, joining themselves together of their own accord, in order to perform the public worshipping of God in such a manner as they judge acceptable to Him and effectual to the salvation of their souls. It is voluntary, because no man is by nature bound to any church. The hope of salvation is the cause of his entering into it. If he find anything wrong in it, he should be free to go out as he was to come in." This idea also, if I may say so, is in the best Chinese tradition.

Confucius also emphasized the necessity for education. As it is said in the *Li Ki*, "The jade uncut will not form a vessel for use: and if men do not learn, they do not know the way in which they should go. On this account the ancient kings, when establishing states and governing the people, made instruction and schools a primary object; as it is said of Yueh, 'Thy thoughts from first to last should be fixed on learning.'" The school system in olden days took the following shape: "According to the system of ancient teaching, for families of a hamlet there was the village school; for a neighborhood there was the *hsiang;* for the larger districts there was the *hsu;* and in the capitals there was the college."

In the same way, Jefferson gave much thought to the part education was to play in the democratic state. He himself placed the founding of the University of Virginia side by side with the writing of the Declaration of Independence as one of his two great accomplishments. Jefferson said in his Notes on Virginia: "The bill proposes to lay off every County into small districts of five or six miles square, called hundreds, and in each of them to establish a school for teaching reading, writing, and arithmetic. The tutor to be supported by the hundred, and every person in it entitled to send their children gratis, and as much longer as they please, paying for it. These schools to be under a visitor who is annually to choose the boy of best genius in the school, of those whose parents are too poor to give them further education, and to send him forward to one of the grammar schools, of which twenty are proposed to be erected in different parts of the country for teaching Greek, Latin, geography, and the higher branches of numerical arithmetic."

It was Jefferson's idea to educate every person in the state at public expense, and to select the best minds for advanced training. The state was to assume responsibility for the education of all of its citizens.

Again, the fundamental principle of a democracy is to make the people play their role in government. So, as we have seen, Mencius said: "The people are the most important element in a nation; the spirits of the land and grain come next; and the sovereign is the least important of all." Mencius is also of the opinion that public opinion is something to which the government should pay heed. "Those [ministers] whom you advanced yesterday are gone today, and you do not know it." The King said, "How shall I know that they have not ability, and so avoid employing them at all?" The reply was, "The ruler of a state advances to office men of talents and virtue only as a matter of necessity. Since he will thereby cause the low to overstep the honorable, and strangers to overstep his relatives, may he do so but with caution? When all those about you say, 'This is a man of talents and worth,' you must not believe it. When your great officers all say, 'This is a man of talents and virtue,' neither may you for that believe it. When all the people say 'This is a man of talents and virtue,' then examine into the case, and when you find that the man is such, employ him. When all those about you say 'This man won't do,' do not listen to them. When all your great officers say, 'This man won't do,' do not listen to them. When the people all say, 'This man won't do,' then examine into the case, and when you find that the man will not do, send him away."

When Mencius says "all the people," he means the opinion of the majority of the people. How this is related to public opinion is evident. The reason why so much importance was attached to public opinion and yet no parliament arose in China is difficult to trace. But who will deny that public opinion is one of the basic ideas in the political philosophy of Mencius?

There are other similarities between Jefferson's philosophy and traditional Chinese thought. Take, for instance, Jefferson's view of the nature of human beings. Jefferson expressed the idea that "the moral sense is as much a part of our constitution as that of feeling, seeing, or hearing, which a wise Creator must have seen to be necessary in an animal destined to live in society." Again, he says, "I sincerely believe in the general existence of a moral instinct. I think it is the brightest gem with which the human character is studded, and want of it is more degrading than the most hideous of bodily deformities." Compare these words of Jefferson with what was said by Mencius: "From this case we may perceive that the feeling of love is inherent in man, that the feeling of shame is inherent in man, and that the feeling of modesty is inherent in man, and that the feeling of approving and disapproving is inherent in man.

"The feeling of love is the principle of benevolence. The feeling of shame is the principle of righteousness. The feeling of modesty is the principle of propriety. The feeling of approving and disapproving is the principle of knowledge.

"Men have these four principles just as they have their four limbs. When men, having these four principles, yet say of themselves that they cannot develop them, they play the thief with themselves, and he who says of his prince that he cannot develop them, plays the thief with his prince."

Traditional Chinese philosophy estimates highly the worth and dignity of man. It emphasises the will-power of man, but the exercise of this will-power was limited to the upper classes because of the illiteracy of the people. The Chinese Confucianists did not stress the idea of individualism, but it cannot be denied that human dignity and human worth are the foundations of their philosophy. Wherein lies the dignity of man? Confucius answered: "Riches and honors are what men desire. If they can be obtained in the proper way they should be held. Poverty and meanness are what men dislike. If they cannot be avoided in a proper way, they should not be avoided." This idea of free and moral personality is the same as Jefferson's, who said, "Under the law of nature, all men are born free, everyone comes into the world with a right to his own person, which includes the liberty of moving and using it at his own will. This is what is called personal liberty and is given him by the Author of nature, because it is necessary for his own sustenance."

The highest ideal which Confucius had in his mind was world government, which he called Grand Union or Grand Harmony. This ideal has been advocated by Kang Yu-wei and Dr. Sun Yat-sen, although, one being a conservative and the other a revolutionary, they differed in their interpretation and argued with each other for a long time. This theory of Grand Union appears in a chapter in the book *Li Ki*: "When the Grand Course was pursued, a public and common spirit ruled all under the sky; they chose men of talents, virtue, and ability; their words were sincere, and what they cultivated was harmony. Thus men did not love their own parents only, nor treat as children only their own sons. A competent provision was secured for the aged till their death, employment for the able-bodied, and the means of growing up for the young. They showed kindness and compassion to widows, orphans, childless men, and those who were disabled by disease, so that they were all sufficiently maintained. Males had their proper work and females had their homes. They accumulated articles of value, disliking that they should be thrown away but not wishing to keep them for their own gratification. They labored with their strength, disliking that it should not be exerted, but exerting it only with a view to their own advantage. In this way selfish schemings were repressed and could not develop. Robbers, filchers, and rebellious traitors did not show themselves, and hence the outer doors remained open and were not shut. This was the period of what we call the Grand Union."

Here one finds the idea of democracy, social security, socialised wealth, and also world government, under which the national sovereignty of each country is held in check. Such an ideal of world government is what the United Nations Organization is trying to establish.

If Jefferson, with what I conceive to be Chinese influences, laid the philosophical foundation for the government of the United States, then why should not the traditional philosophy of China be revived to strengthen modern democracy in that country? If its philosophy, transplanted to Europe and the United States, gave rise to the new philosophy, science, and democracy of the West, could it not be equally effective in laying a foundation for Chinese democracy under the proper circumstances, and after being re-fertilized by modern concepts and ideals?

I feel confident that we do indeed have in China the moral basis on which to erect a genuine and permanent democratic government after the downfall of the Communist regime.

Index